AVIATION SUPPLIES & ACADEMICS, INC.
NEWCASTLE, WASHINGTON

Brittany D. Hagen
Sarah K. Anderson
Leslie M. Martin
Paul R. Snyder

AVIATION
HIGH SCHOOL

Teach Science, Technology, Engineering, and Math through an exciting introduction to the aviation industry

FACILITATOR GUIDE

Aviation High School Facilitator Guide: Teach Science, Technology, Engineering, and Math through an exciting introduction to the aviation industry
by Brittany D. Hagen, Sarah K. Anderson, Leslie M. Martin, and Paul R. Snyder

AVIATION SUPPLIES & ACADEMICS, INC.
7005 132nd Place SE
Newcastle, Washington 98059
asa@asa2fly.com | 425-235-1500 | asa2fly.com

Copyright © 2021 Aviation Supplies & Academics, Inc.

Resources for instructors using this facilitator guide in their classrooms are available at:
www.asa2fly.com/instructor/avhsfg

All Rights Reserved. No part of this publication may be reproduced, stored in a retrieval system, or transmitted in any form or by any means, electronic, mechanical, photocopy, recording, or otherwise, without the prior written permission of the copyright holder. While every precaution has been taken in the preparation of this book, the publisher and Brittany D. Hagen, Sarah K. Anderson, Leslie M. Martin, and Paul R. Snyder assume no responsibility for damages resulting from the use of the information contained herein.

None of the material in this book supersedes any operational documents or procedures issued by the Federal Aviation Administration, aircraft and avionics manufacturers, flight schools, or the operators of aircraft.

ASA-AVHS-FG
ISBN 978-1-61954-937-1

Additional formats available:
eBook PDF   ISBN 978-1-61954-940-1
eBook EPUB   ISBN 978-1-61954-938-8
eBundle   ISBN 978-1-61954-941-8 (print + eBook PDF download code)

Printed in the United States of America
2025 2024 2023 2022 2021   9 8 7 6 5 4 3 2 1

Cover images—Top: iStock.com/yongyuan. Bottom row (left to right): iStock.com/Jetlinerimages; iStock.com/Jetlinerimages; Pixabay; iStock.com/Dushlik; Mr. teerapon tiuekhom/Shutterstock.com.

Charts and other excerpts from the Piper Archer III PA-28-181 Pilot's Operating Handbook, reports VB-1563 and VB-2749, are courtesy Piper Aircraft, Inc., and are for illustrative purposes only.

Library of Congress Cataloging-in-Publication Data:
Names: Anderson, Sarah K. (Sarah Katherine), author. | Martin, Leslie M., author. | Snyder, Paul R., author. | Hagen, Brittany D. (Brittany Dawn), author.
Title: Aviation high school facilitator guide : teach science, technology, engineering and math through an exciting introduction to the aviation industry / by Sarah K. Anderson, Leslie M. Martin, Paul R. Snyder, Dr., Brittany D. Hagen.
Description: Newcastle, Washington : Aviation Supplies & Academics, Inc., [2021]
Identifiers: LCCN 2019054235 | ISBN 9781619549371 (trade paperback) | ISBN 9781619549388 (ebook) | ISBN 9781619549401 (pdf) | ISBN 9781619549418 (eBundle)
Subjects: LCSH: Aeronautics—Study and teaching (Secondary)—United States—Guidebooks. | Airplanes—Piloting—Study and teaching (Secondary)—United States—Guidebooks. | LCGFT: Guidebooks.
Classification: LCC TL560.1 .A735 2021 | DDC 629.130071/273—dc23
LC record available at https://lccn.loc.gov/2019054235

CONTENTS

About the Authors   viii
To the Facilitator   1
How This Guide is Organized   2
    Chapter Introduction   2
    Lessons   3
    Assessments   4
    Aircraft References   4
    Demonstrating Concepts with Flight Simulation and/or Small Unmanned Aircraft Systems (sUAS)   5
    The Design Process   5
    Inquiry Questions   6
    Online Instructor Resources   6
    Incorporating Current Events   7
Educational Standards Cross-Reference Guide   8

CHAPTER 1: AVIATION TRAINING REQUIREMENTS   11

Introduction   11
Lesson 1: Pilot Certificates and Ratings   13
Lesson 2: Training Programs   15
Lesson 3: Aviation Medicals   17
Lesson 4: Aviation Organizations   19
Lesson 5: Review: Aviation Training Requirements   20
Lesson 6: Chapter 1 Exam   22
Answer Keys   25

CHAPTER 2: AIRCRAFT BASICS   31

Introduction   31
Lesson 1: Parts of an Airplane   33
Lesson 2: Aircraft Flight Instruments   36
Lesson 3: Fundamental Maneuvers   39
Lesson 3a: Flight Simulation—Fly the Maneuvers   40
Lesson 4: Normal Takeoffs and Landings   41
Lesson 4a: Flight Simulation—Normal Takeoffs and Landings   43
Lesson 5: Traffic Patterns   45
Lesson 6: Helicopter Basics   49
Lesson 7: Review: Aircraft Basics   51
Lesson 8: Chapter 2 Exam   53
Answer Keys   58

CHAPTER 3: AIRPORT OPERATIONS   63

Introduction   63
Lesson 1: Introduction to Airports   66
Lesson 2: Airports   67
Lesson 3: Marking and Signage   68
Lesson 4: Airport Lighting   71
Lesson 5: Guest Speaker—Operations   74
Lessons 6 & 7: Airport Design Project—Introductory and Work Days   75
Lesson 8: Airport Design Project—Presentations   77
Lesson 9: Airport Operations Review Study Guide   81
Lesson 10: Review: Airport Operations   82
Lesson 11: Chapter 3 Exam   83
Answer Keys   87

CHAPTER 4: WEIGHT & BALANCE and PERFORMANCE   95

Introduction   95
Lesson 1: Weight and Balance Introduction   99
Lesson 2: Weight and Balance Computation   102
Lesson 3: Current Event   107
Lesson 4: Performance Introduction   110
Lesson 5: Enroute, Climb, and Descent Performance Charts   119
Lesson 6: Range, Endurance, and Glide Charts   128
Lesson 7: Guest Speaker: Aviation Professional   135
Lessons 8 & 9: Review: Weight & Balance and Performance   137
Lesson 10: Chapter 4 Exam   138
Answer Keys   141

CHAPTER 5: COMMUNICATION   147

Introduction   147
Lesson 1: Air Traffic Control History   149
Lesson 2: Effective Communication   151
Lesson 3: Air Traffic Control Jobs   153
Lesson 4: Air Traffic Control Field Trip   155
Lesson 5: Radio Transmissions   157
Lesson 6: Air Traffic Control Simulation   161
Lesson 7: Current Events in Air Traffic Control   164
Lessons 8, 9, & 10: Air Traffic Management Group Research Project   165
Lesson 11: Review: Communication   167
Lesson 12: Chapter 5 Exam   168
Answer Keys   172

CHAPTER 6: PEOPLE, EVENTS, and TRENDS in AVIATION   175

Introduction   175
Lesson 1: Aviation Pioneers   177
Lesson 2: Aviation History—World War I through the Golden Age   179
Lesson 3: Aviation History—World War II, the Cold War, and the Jet Age to Today   183
Lesson 4: Famous People in Aviation—Introduction   185
Lesson 5: Famous People in Aviation—FakeBook   187
Lessons 6 & 7: Famous People in Aviation—Research Paper Workshop   189
Lessons 8, 9, & 10: Hot Air Balloons   192
Lesson 11: Review: People, Events, and Trends in Aviation   194
Lesson 12: Chapter 6 Exam   196
Answer Keys   198

CHAPTER 7: AVIATION CAREERS   199

Introduction   199
Lesson 1: Career Article and Introduction   201
Lesson 2: Career Investigation/Education & Training (Day 1)   203
Lesson 3: Career Investigation/Education & Training (Day 2)   205
Lesson 4: Career Investigation/Education & Training (Day 3)   207
Lesson 5: Current Events   209
Lesson 6: University, Community College, and Training Options   211
Lessons 7 & 8: Scholarship Applications   213
Lesson 9: Guest Speaker   215

CHAPTER 8: AERODYNAMICS of FLIGHT   217

Introduction   217
Lesson 1: Forces of Flight   219
Lesson 2: Introduction to Airfoils   221
Lesson 3: Lift—Newton and Bernoulli   223
Lesson 4: Drag and Design   225
Lesson 5: Stalls and Spins   229
Lesson 6: Review—Aerodynamics of Flight   231
Lesson 7: Chapter 8 Exam   232
Answer Keys   237

CHAPTER 9: AIRCRAFT SYSTEMS   243

Introduction   243
Lesson 1: Introduction to Aircraft Systems   245
Lesson 2: Engine   246
Lesson 3: Fuel Systems   248
Lesson 4: Flight Instruments Review   254
Lesson 5: Vacuum and Electrical Systems   256
Lesson 6: Review: Aircraft Systems   261
Lesson 7: Chapter 9 Exam   264
Answer Keys   270

CHAPTER 10: FLIGHT MANEUVERS   273

Introduction   273
Lesson 1: Fundamental Maneuvers: Straight-and-Level Flight, Climbs, Descents, Turns   275
Lesson 2: Normal Takeoffs and Normal Landings   278
Lesson 3: Short-Field Takeoff and Landing   280
Lesson 4: Soft-Field Takeoff and Landing   282
Lesson 5: Stalls: Power-On and Power-Off   284
Lesson 6: Steep Turns   286
Lesson 7: Flight by Reference to Instruments   288
Answer Keys   290

CHAPTER 11: AIRSPACE   291

Introduction   291
Lesson 1: Introduction to Airspace: Controlled vs. Uncontrolled   293
Lesson 2: Class C, D, and E Airspace   295
Lesson 3: Uncontrolled Airspace: Class G   297
Lesson 4: Special Use and Other Airspace   299

Lesson 5: Review: Airspace   302
Lesson 6: Chapter 11 Exam   303
Answer Keys   310

CHAPTER 12: WEATHER   317

Introduction   317
Lesson 1: Weather Theory (Day 1)   320
Lesson 2: Weather Theory (Day 2)   322
Lesson 3: Weather Products: METAR   325
Lesson 4: Weather Products: TAF   329
Lesson 5: Weather Products: AIRMETs and SIGMETs   332
Lesson 6: Weather-Related Decision Making   337
Lesson 7: Review: Weather   339
Lesson 8: Chapter 12 Exam   340
Answer Keys   346

CHAPTER 13: AEROMEDICAL FACTORS   349

Introduction   349
Lesson 1: IMSAFE Checklist   351
Lesson 2: Hypoxia and Hyperventilation   354
Lesson 3: Other Aeromedical Factors   356
Lesson 4: Visual Illusions   357
Lesson 5: Night Flight   359
Lesson 6: Review: Aeromedical Factors   361
Lesson 7: Chapter 13 Exam   363
Answer Keys   366

CHAPTER 14: NAVIGATION and CROSS-COUNTRY FLIGHT PLANNING   369

Introduction   369
Lesson 1: E6B Introduction   372
Lesson 2: Considerations for Planning a Cross-Country   374
Lesson 3: Introduction to Navigation and Using Pilotage   377
Lesson 4: Dead Reckoning   379
Lesson 5: Radio Navigation   381
Lesson 6: Cross-Country Planning   385
Lesson 7: Cross-Country Scenario   389
Answer Keys   393

Notes   395

ABOUT THE AUTHORS

Sarah K. Anderson

Sarah K. Anderson is a Senior Lecturer in Education at the University of Glasgow in Scotland. Sarah has a PhD in Teacher Education with a cognate in Educational Leadership from the University of North Dakota, USA, in addition to a master's degree in special education and an undergraduate degree in teaching secondary level social sciences. Sarah is a Fulbright Scholar to Norway (2011–2012). From 2012–2020, Sarah worked at Mayville State University in the role of associate professor and accreditation coordinator. As a teacher educator, she has instructed graduate and undergraduate pedagogical courses at the secondary level, taught courses in special education, advised capstone portfolios, and supervised clinical experiences. Her research interests include teacher appraisal for continual improvement, progress monitoring for response to intervention, high-impact practices, and effective instructional strategies.

Brittany D. Hagen

Brittany D. Hagen, PhD, is an Associate Professor of Education and CAEP accreditation coordinator at Mayville State University. She earned her Bachelor of Science in Education at Mayville State University, majoring in Elementary Education with a minor in Educational Technology. Dr. Hagen earned a Master of Science in Elementary Education and a Doctorate of Philosophy in Teaching and Learning, both from the University of North Dakota. Dr. Hagen teaches courses on education methods, educational technology, and educational assessment. Additionally, she has developed both online and classroom curriculums for a variety of age groups, including teach-the-teacher programs and assessment data modules. Her research has focused on teacher preparation programs, reading curriculum, effective delivery and assessments, instructional design and techniques, as well as how adults can engage with children to further their educational goals.

Leslie M. Martin

Leslie Martin is an Associate Professor for the John D. Odegard School of Aerospace Sciences at the University of North Dakota in Grand Forks, North Dakota. She holds a Bachelor of Science in Aeronautics Commercial Aviation and a Master of Science in Education. Professor Martin teaches a wide variety of courses from Private Pilot to Certified Instrument Flight Instructor ground school and is a flight instructor and check pilot for UND Flight Operations. She also works part-time at the Grand Forks Public School District teaching a high school course titled Aviation Technology I to high school sophomores, juniors, and seniors. Professor Martin's research interests include Automatic Dependent Surveillance–Broadcast, weather technology in the cockpit, and unmanned aircraft systems (UAS).

Paul R. Snyder

Paul Snyder is the Director of the Unmanned Aircraft Systems (UAS) Program and Associate Professor in the Aviation Department at the John D. Odegard School of Aerospace Sciences at the University of North Dakota (UND). Paul Snyder has recently taught Safety Management Systems (SMS), introduction and advanced UAS operations courses, and advanced flight instructor courses. Professor Snyder continues to be active in UAS research, UAS education, and UAS flight operations as the Director of the UND UAS Program, a Boeing Insitu OEM Certified ScanEagle UAS pilot, and Part 107 Remote Pilot Operator.

Mr. Snyder has more than 15 years' experience as a Chief Flight Instructor as well as a FAA Designated Pilot conducting FAA practical tests in single and multi-engine aircraft for Pilot and Flight Instructor certificates and associated ratings. Professor Snyder holds a degree in Aeronautical Studies and Master of Science in Educational Leadership.

TO THE FACILITATOR

"The fascination of flight can't be expressed with words. But it really lies beyond the capabilities of human endeavor. Once you've experienced it, you'll never be able to forget it."[1]
—Friedrich Oblessor, 127 victories WWII

ALONG WITH Aviation Supplies & Academics, Inc. (ASA), we have created this *Facilitator Guide* and corresponding interactive *Student Notebook* to address a growing need for solid instruction, inquiry, and development of future-ready competencies in aviation at the high school level. The aviation industry continues to experience a shortage of professionals, and our goal with this curriculum is to help develop interest prior to collegiate training. We know facilitators of a high school introduction to aviation course may come from a variety of backgrounds; you may be an aerospace mechanic, engineer, private pilot, military personnel, airline pilot, or high school career and technical education teacher. Whatever background you bring to teaching, the goal of helping students experience the fascination of flight and a career in the aviation industry remains the same.

We hope you find the *Aviation High School Facilitator Guide* and *Student Notebook* two effective tools for introducing students to aviation. This guide provides you with curriculum for fourteen essential topics divided into chapters to engage the next generation of the aviation workforce. It has been backward-designed; that is, goals were set before choosing instructional methods and forms of assessment. We know that the industry offers great career opportunities. Through these lessons, students are provided with an understanding of the science of flight, the history of aviation, and possible career paths within the industry. *Aviation High School* also covers physics, the relationships of weight and balance, principles of navigation and flight control, ground and airport operations and services, and Federal Aviation Administration (FAA) regulations. The curriculum is intended to be used in a high school setting (grade levels 9–12), and is aligned to Next Generation Science Standards, Common Core State Standards for Math and Language Arts, and North Dakota Aviation Standards.

We also encourage you to check out the supplemental online Instructor Resources and other materials available from Aviation Supplies & Academics, Inc., at **www.asa2fly.com/instructor/avhsfg**. There you will find a variety of information and resources to support your use of the *Aviation High School Facilitator Guide* and *Student Notebook* in your classroom. If you have any comments or questions, please contact us.

Sincerely,

Leslie Martin, M.S.
Associate Professor of Aviation
Aviation High School Teacher

Dr. Brittany D. Hagen, Ph.D.
Assistant Professor of Education

Dr. Sarah K. Anderson, Ph.D.
Senior Lecturer

Paul Snyder, M.S.
Associate Professor of Aviation

HOW THIS GUIDE IS ORGANIZED

Your *Aviation High School* complete lesson plans are student-oriented, straightforward, and designed to be easy to follow. Each lesson is planned for a standard, 50-minute lesson time or could be combined to accommodate block scheduling.

Following is an explanation of how each chapter and lesson is organized and the educational tools and activities they include to help you fully utilize this guide and the accompanying student notebook in your classroom.

CHAPTER INTRODUCTION

Each chapter begins with an introductory section that includes information applicable across the entire chapter.

- **Standards and Objectives**—The applicable education standards for students who successfully complete activities in each chapter are indicated. These include lesson-aligned high school standards for North Dakota aviation, as authors are affiliated with the University of North Dakota and Mayville State University in North Dakota; Common Core State Standards (CCSS) for Math and Reading and Writing in Technical Subjects; and Next Generation Science Standards (NGSS). From these, lesson-specific measurable objectives can be specified by the facilitator.

- **Essential Questions**—These are questions you want students to be able to answer that point to the big ideas of a subject. A question can be considered essential when it helps students make sense of important but complicated ideas, knowledge, and know-how. A question is essential when it:
  - causes genuine and relevant inquiry into the big ideas and core content;
  - provokes deep thought, lively discussion, sustained inquiry, and new understanding as well as more questions;
  - requires students to consider alternatives, weigh evidence, support their ideas, and justify their answers;
  - stimulates vital, ongoing rethinking of big ideas, assumptions, and prior lessons;
  - sparks meaningful connections with prior learning and personal experiences; and/or
  - naturally recurs, creating opportunities for transfer to other situations and subjects

- **Lesson Outline**—The lessons included in the chapter are listed in order with the lesson numbers, titles, and corresponding *Student Notebook* activities for each.

LESSONS

Each lesson is separated into the following sections:

- **Purpose**—The purpose statement answers for the facilitator and students, "Why do I need to know/do this?" Simply put, when students understand the purpose of a lesson, they learn more. From the purpose statement, the facilitator's expectations can be well communicated in the form of learning goals, and there is clear intent of what the class will be doing and what students should be learning.

- **Accommodations for Students with Learning Needs**—This is included in every lesson as a reminder to the facilitator to plan for and accommodate the needs of learners, particularly those with identified disabilities. Lessons may be changed to accommodate your students with learning differences by referring to their personalized learning plan, Individualized Education Program (IEP), and/or 504 plans and working with special education and support staff in your school. A resource list of school accommodation and modification ideas for students who receive special education services from the PACER Center is linked in each lesson for convenient access (**https://www.pacer.org/parent/php/PHP-c267.pdf**).

- **Preparation**—This section notes materials that should be ready and accessible before the beginning of each class period and should be previewed before each lesson. Following are some of the resources needed throughout the course:
    - *Aviation High School Student Notebook*
    - FAA *Pilot's Handbook of Aeronautical Knowledge* (FAA-H-8083-25)
    - FAR/AIM (Federal Aviation Regulations/Aeronautical Information Manual) or **eCFR.gov**
    - FAA *Instrument Flying Handbook* (FAA-H-8083-15)
    - FAA *Airplane Flying Handbook* (FAA-H-8083-3)
    - FAA *Helicopter Flying Handbook* (FAA-H-8083-21)
    - *Chart Supplements U.S.*
    - Piper Archer (PA-28-181) Pilot's Operating Handbook (POH)
    - Current VFR Sectional Chart for your local area (laminated)
    - CP-1 Sectional Plotter
    - E6-B Flight Computer

- **Directions:**
    - **Introductory Activity**—This is also known as a hook, anticipatory set, or previewing strategy that is designed to grab the student's attention. It re-engages students in the topic being studied, builds excitement to learn, and puts students in a receptive frame of mind for the lesson.
    - **Steps**—The step-by-step set of instructions for carrying out the lesson. You may want to discuss the plan with students before they begin the lesson so they know what to expect. Embedded in the steps of the lessons are common elements.
        - *Multiple instruction strategies:* The type of instruction in each lesson is varied because transfer and retention are enhanced when multiple strategies are used to learn something; these include direct, indirect, independent, experiential, and interactive teaching methods.

- *Active processing:* The learner actively engages in cognitive processing for learning to occur, acting on instructional inputs to generate, reorganize, self-explain, or otherwise go beyond the presentation of material.
- *Formative assessment:* Assessment is conducted by the facilitator to monitor student learning, address problems immediately, and provide ongoing feedback that can be used by students to improve their learning; these checks for understanding are typically not graded.
  › **Concluding Activity**—Closure strategies are done in a few minutes at the end of the lesson to help students organize their learning, to reinforce major points, to check on student learning, or to clarify any confusion. It brings the lesson to an end and helps students to make sense of what they just learned. Often this step can serve as a formative or summative assessment method.
- **Facilitator Information**—This includes content-specific information such as examples of images, completed graphic organizers, or exam questions that are helpful to the facilitator to prepare for the lesson and to reference during the lesson.

ASSESSMENTS

Assessment should provide evidence for the facilitator that students have learned and that they have met the objectives of a lesson or chapter. Activities included in each lesson can serve as measures of progress as well as assessment for you and your students. You will see various activities that can serve as informal (formative) and formal (summative) assessments for you to determine if students have met the learning goals. Formative assessment measures if the students are meeting the objectives *during* the lesson. These are often called checks for understanding. Summative assessment measures if the students have met the intended objectives *at the end* of the lesson. Formative and summative assessment methods can be interchangeable. For example, an ungraded quiz used as a formative assessment might also be used as a summative assessment at the end of a lesson or unit. Work that is formatively checked during lessons might be summatively assessed in a portfolio. Some examples of assessments include:

- rubrics
- exams
- checklists
- quizzes
- papers
- quick writes
- demonstrations of skills
- presentations
- graphic organizers
- inquiry projects
- simulations
- research projects
- informal observations of students working
- interviews
- real-life applications of skills (e.g., flight planning, scholarship and certificate applications)

AIRCRAFT REFERENCES

In this guide, lessons are structured to reference small general aviation aircraft, specifically the Piper Cherokee Archer (PA 28-181) and Cessna 172. If the facilitator is more familiar with a different type of aircraft, the authors suggest adding in personal examples or switching references to an aircraft that makes sense given resources and access to particular types of aircraft.

DEMONSTRATING CONCEPTS WITH FLIGHT SIMULATION AND/OR SMALL UNMANNED AIRCRAFT SYSTEMS (sUAS)

The authors recommend that key concepts of aeronautical knowledge and flight be demonstrated, if possible, using flight simulation and/or commercially available small unmanned aircraft systems (sUAS). Lesson plans can be implemented without flight simulation or a sUAS. However, simulation and sUAS utilization is encouraged as a way to engage and motivate students. Any lesson can be enhanced using simulation and sUAS at the facilitator's discretion. For example, in Chapter 8: Aerodynamics of Flight, the forces of thrust, lift, drag, and weight are learned. During or after a lesson, simulation or sUAS could be used to increase active processing and reinforce concepts taught through explicit instruction (e.g., interactive lecture).

We recommend the use of a basic aviation training device (BATD) or the following flight simulation equipment and sUAS options due to ease of use and cost.

1. Flight simulation equipment could include:
   - Computer
   - Flight simulation software (e.g., X-plane, RealFlight Simulator, Zephyr)
   - Control yoke or joystick
   - Rudder pedals
   - Throttle quadrant
2. Small Unmanned Aircraft Systems (sUAS) available with educational discounts:
   - Parrot Mambo (**edu.parrot.com**)
   - DJI (**store.dji.com/education**)

The authors have identified locations within lessons where a simulator or sUAS activity is either included or would be appropriate, designated with the icon shown on the right.

THE DESIGN PROCESS

The engineering design process is a series of steps that engineers follow when they are trying to solve a problem and design a solution for something; it is a methodical approach to problem solving. In this guide, projects are included that utilize this process according to the following steps:

1. **Imagine** solutions to the problem.
2. **Plan** steps you will take.
3. **Create**—follow your plan and test your design.
4. **Improve**—learn from mistakes and try again.
5. **Present**—share your design.

The authors encourage you to explore opportunities that naturally occur in the classroom to adapt lessons in this guide into design activities.

INQUIRY QUESTIONS

This curriculum is grounded on a set of inquiry questions that define the important essential skills, core concepts, and supportive content; they are also intended to engage students' genuine curiosity. The questions are an invitation to think and take action—not to simply recall, summarize, or detail facts—and they are integrated across all the topics/lessons included in this introduction to aviation. Inquiry questions should be posted in the classroom and included in written course outlines so that students can immediately see that they will have to think through answers.

1. How does this aviation topic facilitate social, economic, scientific, and/or cultural exchange/change?
2. What larger concept, issue, or problem underlies this topic in aviation?
3. What do you notice about how things work in this aviation topic?
4. What are some things we could not do without understanding this topic in aviation?
5. If we changed one thing about how this works, what do we think would happen?
6. How do small changes in aviation affect the larger system?
7. What is the impact of this part of aviation on society?
8. How does this part (e.g., ATC, airports, UAS, flight training, etc.) of the aviation industry affect the other parts?
9. What mistakes have been made in aviation? What did we learn from them? What changes were made?
10. What are current issues in aviation? What caused them? What is a viable solution? What would be consequences of the solution?
11. Can you suggest a different way of doing this in aviation?
12. What conclusions about this topic can be made?
13. What patterns can you see across topics in aviation?
14. What reasons might there be for these patterns?
15. How do you think technology might change how we do this in the future?
16. How will automation and/or autonomous operations change how this is accomplished in the future?

ONLINE INSTRUCTOR RESOURCES

A dedicated website was established to provide you with additional resources to support your classes where the *Aviation High School Facilitator Guide* and *Aviation High School Student Notebook* are in use. Throughout the *Facilitator Guide*, the icon shown on the right appears next to lesson content for which additional outside resources and suggestions are provided in the online Instructor Resources. Direct links to resources referenced in the *Facilitator Guide*, such as videos and articles, are also included for your convenience.

Aviation High School Instructor Resources are available at **www.asa2fly.com/instructor/avhsfg**. To request login information, email **resource@asa2fly.com**.

INCORPORATING CURRENT EVENTS

The facilitator is encouraged to make real-life connections often by bringing current aviation events into the classroom. Recent happenings in the industry may better serve to introduce a lesson than what is included in this guide. The authors encourage you to take advantage of recent news about important people, events, issues, and developments in aviation to encourage students to explore and learn more about aviation.

Many of the chapters conclude with an activity focused on a current event article. The facilitator should select an article that ties into concepts that will be taught in the next chapter as a preview and introduction to upcoming areas of study. Specific articles are suggested in some lessons, but others are open-ended to allow facilitators or students to select current event topics that are the most recent, relevant, and local. Many of the articles suggested for incorporating current events are available on Newsela, aligned with standards and with built-in assessments, but they can also be found on other media outlets through an internet search of the title.

In addition to the current events activities incorporated into the lessons, the *Aviation High School* online Instructor Resources (**www.asa2fly.com/instructor/avhsfg**) provide the facilitator with flexible lesson plans and expanded student activities that can be used for a variety of topics and as frequently as desired. These online resources include a current events lesson plan, anchor standards, assignment description, response form, rubric, student log to record major themes in aviation, guide to annotated text markings, narrative summary frame, and extension activities.

Articles can be from a major news magazine, newspaper, radio/TV segment, or professional organization. Examples of professional organizations that may be good sources for articles and which have current events or issue briefs for reference include American Association of Airport Executives (AAAE), Aircraft Owners and Pilots Association (AOPA), Women in Aviation International (WAI), The Ninety-Nines Inc., University Aviation Association (UAA), National Air Traffic Controllers Association (NATCA), Civil Air Patrol (CAP), Association for Unmanned Vehicle Systems International (AUVSI), and Experimental Aircraft Association (EAA).

EDUCATIONAL STANDARDS CROSS-REFERENCE GUIDE

For more details about how each lesson aligns with specific educational standards and objectives, see the list in the Introduction at the beginning of each chapter.

	English Language Arts / Literacy Key Ideas and Details, Craft and Structure, Integration of Knowledge and Ideas, Range of Reading and level of text complexity.	**Library and Technology** Information and Inquiry, Media and Technology Literacy, Personal Learning and Growth, Responsible Use of Information and Technology
Chapter 1 Aviation Training Requirements	X	X
Chapter 2 Aircraft Basics	X	X
Chapter 3 Airport Operations	X	X
Chapter 4 Weight & Balance and Performance	X	X
Chapter 5 Communications	X	X
Chapter 6 People, Events, and Trends in Aviation	X	X
Chapter 7 Aviation Careers	X	X
Chapter 8 Aerodynamics of Flight	X	X
Chapter 9 Aircraft Systems	X	
Chapter 10 Flight Maneuvers	X	
Chapter 11 Airspace	X	X
Chapter 12 Weather	X	X
Chapter 13 Aeromedical Factors	X	X
Chapter 14 Navigation and Cross Country Flight Planning	X	X

Mathematics Modeling, Number and Quantity, Algebra, Functions, Geometry, Statistics and Probability	Science Concepts and Processes of Science, Scientific Inquiry, Physical, Principles of earth and space, Technology and Society, Personal Health, People in Science, Science and Society	Social Studies Visual Representations, Research processes, History, Global persons, events, figures and movements	Career and Technical Education
	X	X	X
		X	X
		X	X
X	X	X	X
	X		X
	X	X	X
		X	X
X	X		X
	X		X
	X		
		X	X
X	X	X	X
	X		X
X	X	X	X

Educational Standards Cross-Reference Guide

CHAPTER 1
AVIATION TRAINING REQUIREMENTS

Introduction

STANDARDS & OBJECTIVES

North Dakota Aviation Content Standards (Grades 10–12)
- **3.2.5**—Categorize the pilot qualifications needed for each class of airspace.
- **4.2.1**—Describe flight training processes.
- **4.2.3**—Identify the mission of aviation organizations.
- **4.2.4**—Determine FAA Pilot certificate requirements.
- **4.3.2**—Discuss the IMSAFE checklist.
- **4.3.3**—Describe the medical qualifications requirements for pilots.
- **4.4.3**—Discuss pathways to an aviation career.

Language Arts—CCSS.ELA-LITERACY.CCRA
- **L.1**—Demonstrate command of the conventions of standard English grammar and usage when writing or speaking.
- **L.2**—Demonstrate command of the conventions of standard English capitalization, punctuation, and spelling when writing.
- **R.1**—Read closely to determine what the text says explicitly and to make logical inferences from it; cite specific textual evidence when writing or speaking to support conclusions drawn from the text.
- **SL.1**—Prepare for and participate effectively in a range of conversations and collaborations with diverse partners, building on others' ideas and expressing their own clearly and persuasively.
- **SL.2**—Integrate and evaluate information presented in diverse media and formats, including visually, quantitatively, and orally.
- **SL.4**—Present information, findings, and supporting evidence such that listeners can follow the line of reasoning and the organization, development, and style are appropriate to task, purpose, and audience.
- **W.4**—Produce clear and coherent writing in which the development, organization, and style are appropriate to task, purpose, and audience.
- **W.7**—Conduct short as well as more sustained research projects based on focused questions, demonstrating understanding of the subject under investigation.

- **W.8**—Gather relevant information from multiple print and digital sources, assess the credibility and accuracy of each source, and integrate the information while avoiding plagiarism.
- **W.9**—Draw evidence from literary or informational texts to support analysis, reflection, and presearch.

ESSENTIAL QUESTIONS

- What are the requirements for pilot certification?
- What medical requirements are there for pilots?
- What are the specifications of the IMSAFE checklist?
- What is the purpose of aviation organizations and the services they provide?

LESSONS

Lesson	Topic	Student Notebook Activities
Lesson 1	Pilot Certificates and Ratings	1. Quote Review 2. Types of Pilot Certificates and Ratings 3. Student versus Private Pilot Questions
Lesson 2	Training Programs	1. Top 10 Biggest Flight School Scams Recording List 2. Flight Training Worksheet 3. Final Thoughts Reflection
Lesson 3	Aviation Medicals	1. IMSAFE Checklist 2. Inquiry Question 3. Aviation Medicals Graphic Organizer 4. Aviation Medicals Comprehension Questions
Lesson 4	Aviation Organizations	1. List of Aviation Organizations 2. Professional Aviation Organization Research 3. Persuasive Argument Exercise
Lesson 5	Review: Aviation Training Requirements	1. Note-Taking Graphic Organizer
Lesson 6	Chapter 1 Exam	1. Writing Prompt

CHAPTER 1 AVIATION TRAINING REQUIREMENTS

LESSON 1
PILOT CERTIFICATES AND RATINGS

PURPOSE
The purpose of this lesson is to compare and contrast the types of aviation certifications.

ACCOMMODATIONS FOR LEARNING DIFFERENCES
It is important that lessons accommodate the needs of every learner. These lessons may be modified to accommodate your students with learning differences by referring to **www.pacer.org/parent/php/PHP-c267.pdf**.

PREPARATION
- Prepared slides for interactive lecture
- FAR/AIM or **eCFR.gov**

DIRECTIONS

Introductory Activity: Display the two quotes found below on the board and/or have students reference Activity 1 (Quote Review) in their Student Notebooks. Have students think for one minute silently about their own motivations for studying aviation and then share out loud with a partner. Discuss student thoughts about their own motivations for studying aviation as a whole class.

> Charles Lindbergh: "Science, freedom, beauty, adventure: what more could you ask of life?"[1]

> Wilbur Wright: "More than anything else the sensation is one of perfect peace mingled with an excitement that strains every nerve to the utmost, if you can conceive of such a combination."[2]

Step 1: Divide the class into two or three groups. Have students hypothesize which pilot certificates listed in the Student Notebook in Activity 2 (Types of Pilot Certificates and Ratings) require least to most training in rank order. Students must provide their reasons for the placements and explain to the other groups why they ranked each as they did. After each group shares their rankings, the class must come to a consensus ranking. The facilitator will not share the correct ranking until the end of the lesson.

Step 2: Conduct an interactive lecture that presents important regulatory information from the Federal Aviation Regulations, focusing on 14 CFR §§61.89, 61.93, 61.95, 61.103, 61.109, and 61.113. The lecture must answer each of the questions for students found in Activity 3 (Student versus Private Pilot Questions) in the Student Notebook. Students will complete the Activity pages along with the lecture. (An answer key is provided at the end of the chapter.)

Concluding Activity: After the questions have been answered through the interactive lecture, have students revisit their hypothesis to confirm or deny the original class rankings. Students should state their conclusions using proper support (i.e., grounds) from the FAR/AIM.

LESSON 2
TRAINING PROGRAMS

PURPOSE
The purpose of this lesson is to locate and evaluate options for manned aircraft flight training.

ACCOMMODATIONS FOR LEARNING DIFFERENCES
It is important that lessons accommodate the needs of every learner. These lessons may be modified to accommodate your students with learning differences by referring to **www.pacer.org/parent/php/PHP-c267.pdf**.

PREPARATION
- FAR/AIM or **eCFR.gov**
- Computers/devices and internet access for students

DIRECTIONS

Introductory Activity: Finding a trustworthy and honest flight school can be a challenge for any student pilot or potential aviator. As you watch the video "Top 10 Flight School Scams,"[3] assign students to record the biggest flight school scams and pitfalls in their Student Notebooks under Activity 1 (Top 10 Biggest Flight School Scams Recording List). Discuss how each of these scams might impact the question, "What patterns can you see across flight school training issues?"

Step 1: Lead a whole class brainstorming session to list flight training centers around the area (up to 300 miles away). Assist students by listing a few airports and then as they catch on, they should give names of other large airports in the region. Write all of the training options on the board.

Define "fixed base operator (FBO)" and discuss the various services that various FBOs offer. You may find an FBO's website to display in class to illustrate some of the typical programs and services offered.

Model researching and recording key information about a training center. Students will follow along, filling in the correct information in their Student Notebooks in the Example 1 table under Activity 2 (Flight Training Worksheet).

Example 1	
Name of Business	
Location	
What types of aircraft do they have?	
How much do they charge for ground instruction (CFI rate)?	
How much do they charge per hour for flight instruction?	

Step 2: Assign students to research two of the flight training centers to find out each center's flight training costs, type of flight training conducted, and types of aircraft used. Students will record their findings in the Example 2 and Example 3 tables under Activity 2 (Flight Training Worksheet) in their Student Notebooks.

Note: This can be a hard task, as many websites are not up to date or are hard to navigate. As the facilitator, assist students in locating required information. AOPA Flight School Finder is a good resource.

Concluding Activity: Students will share out loud with a partner which training facility they would select and why. A place to record their final thoughts can be found in the Activity 3 (Final Thoughts Reflection) in the Student Notebook.

I would choose _____ *[enter flight training center name]* because:

1. _____
2. _____
3. _____

Be sure all students walk away with an understanding of what flight training entails.

CHAPTER 1 AVIATION TRAINING REQUIREMENTS

LESSON 3
AVIATION MEDICALS

PURPOSE
The purpose of this lesson is to comprehend aviation medical requirements and the differences in medical certificates.

ACCOMMODATIONS FOR LEARNING DIFFERENCES
It is important that lessons accommodate the needs of every learner. These lessons may be modified to accommodate your students with learning differences by referring to www.pacer.org/parent/php/PHP-c267.pdf.

PREPARATION
- FAR/AIM or **eCFR.gov**
- Screen and projection for visual display and video

DIRECTIONS
Note: This lesson may take two class sessions to complete and review.
Introductory Activity: Watch the introduction video "Airman Medical Certification: Understanding Airman Medical Standards," produced by the Aircraft Owners and Pilots Association (AOPA).[4] Pose the following questions to the students:

- "How are pilots different than other people?"
- "Why is a medical so important?"

Have students turn and talk to a classmate near them and then share out answers with the whole class.

Step 1: Using visual aids, present the IMSAFE mnemonic to students. Using an interactive lecture, reveal each area of fitness to fly, one area at a time. Model answering the questions about yourself. Have students evaluate their own readiness to fly at the current time given the checklist. Students should fill in the Activity 1 (IMSAFE Checklist) table in their Student Notebooks as the information is presented and as they self-evaluate.

Flight Fitness | The "I'm Safe" Checklist

I	Illness	Do I have an illness or any symptoms of an illness?
M	Medication	Have I been taking prescription or over-the-counter drugs?
S	Stress	Am I under psychological pressure from the job? Am I worried about financial matters, health problems, or family discord?
A	Alcohol	Have I been drinking within eight hours? Within 24 hours?
F	Fatigue	Am I tired and/or not adequately rested?
E	Emotion	Am I in control of my emotions?

Step 2: Ask pairs of students to discuss with each other the answer to the inquiry question: "How could the requirement of medicals affect the aviation industry both positively and negatively?"

Next have each group share out ideas and record answers on the board and/or in their Student Notebooks under Activity 2 (Inquiry Question). Provide feedback on responses that correlate with FAR/AIM regulations.

Step 3: Students will use FAR regulations in 14 CFR §61.23 to complete Activity 3 (Aviation Medical Graphic Organizer) and answer the questions in Activity 4 (Aviation Medicals Comprehension Questions) in their Student Notebooks to compare and contrast the classes of medical standards and answer key comprehension questions. (An answer key is provided at the end of the chapter.) Monitor student learning as they work in pairs to complete the graphic organizer. Question students to check for understanding and clarify any misconceptions or incorrect answers about the privileges and limitations of the different classes of licenses.

Step 4: Have students self-correct by leading them through the correct answers.

Concluding Activity: Lead a whole class discussion about the differences observed among the classes of licenses and why these differences exist.

FACILITATOR INFORMATION
Aviation Medicals Comprehension Questions

(An answer key is provided at the end of the chapter.)

1. What are the privileges of a First-Class Airman Medical Certificate?
2. What are the privileges of a Second-Class Airman Medical Certificate?
3. What are the privileges of a Third-Class Airman Medical Certificate?
4. Where would you go to receive an Aviation Medical?
5. What would be a reason why your aviation medical would be revoked?
6. What is an aviation medical certificate?
7. Who must hold an aviation medical certificate?
8. What medical conditions does the FAA consider disqualifying?
9. What are the minimum and maximum ages for obtaining a medical certificate?
10. Can I get my student pilot certificate at the same time I take my initial flight physical?
11. Am I prohibited from exercising the privileges of my pilot certificate during medical deficiency?
12. Is a pilot required to report to the FAA that he or she has undergone LASIK or other laser eye surgery to correct vision?
13. Can I appeal if my application for medical certification is denied?
14. How can I contact the FAA about my medical certificate?
15. I lost my medical certificate; how can I obtain a copy?

LESSON 4

AVIATION ORGANIZATIONS

PURPOSE

The purpose of this lesson is to explain the role of aviation organizations within the industry.

ACCOMMODATIONS FOR LEARNING DIFFERENCES

It is important that lessons accommodate the needs of every learner. These lessons may be modified to accommodate your students with learning differences by referring to www.pacer.org/parent/php/PHP-c267.pdf.

PREPARATION

- Computers/devices and internet access for student research
- Note cards

DIRECTIONS

Introductory Activity: Ask the students to write the names of any aviation organizations that they are aware of under Activity 1 (List of Aviation Organizations) in their Student Notebooks. Have students share with the class the organizations that they listed. The facilitator should then list additional organizations that were not shared by the students. Examples of professional organizations include: American Association of Airport Executives (AAAE), Aircraft Owners and Pilots Association (AOPA), Women in Aviation International (WAI), The Ninety-Nines Inc., University Aviation Association (UAA), National Air Traffic Controllers Association (NATCA), Civil Air Patrol (CAP), Association for Unmanned Vehicle Systems International (AUVSI), and Experimental Aircraft Association (EAA).

Step 1: Divide the class into small groups and assign them to research a professional aviation organization. They need to answer the following questions and record their answers in the Student Notebook under Activity 2 (Professional Aviation Organization Research):

1. What is the impact of this aviation organization on the industry?
2. What are three reasons why you would join this organization?
3. How much does it cost to join this organization?
4. What are the requirements to join this organization?

Step 2: The groups will share the information with the rest of the class through Activity 3 (Persuasive Argument Exercise) described in the Student Notebook.

Concluding Activity: Students will complete an exit ticket on a note card answering the question, "If you could pick only one organization to join, which one would it be and why?" The note cards should be collected by the facilitator at the door as students leave the classroom and analyzed for accuracy.

LESSON 5

REVIEW: AVIATION TRAINING REQUIREMENTS

PURPOSE

The purpose of this lesson is to reinforce essential information about aviation training and medicals.

ACCOMMODATIONS FOR LEARNING DIFFERENCES

It is important that lessons accommodate the needs of every learner. These lessons may be modified to accommodate your students with learning differences by referring to **www.pacer.org/parent/php/PHP-c267.pdf**.

PREPARATION

- Game instructions (ready to read aloud or display visually to class)
- Printed, cut, and shuffled set of "Will the Winners Lose" scoring cards
- Review questions based on the content students learned in this chapter (ready to read out loud or display on PowerPoint)

DIRECTIONS

Introductory Activity: Re-engage the students on the topic of aviation by sharing a relevant occurrence about aviation training or medicals close to the date of the review and Chapter 1 Exam from the website This Day in Aviation (**www.thisdayinaviation.com**). Display relevant pictures as you share the story. Have students turn and talk with a partner about what impact this historical event had on aviation training and/or medical requirements.

Step 1: Introduce the review game "Will the Winners Lose?" and explain the directions to students by reading or displaying the game instructions, found below in Step 2. Introduce the stack of scoring cards to students, found below under "Facilitator Information." Put the stack of prepared scoring cards face down on a desk.

Step 2: Take the review questions you prepared prior to class and display them on a PowerPoint or simply be ready to read them off your printed text. Split students into two teams. Have one student from each team come to the front of the classroom. Ask one of the questions; the first student to answer gets to pick a "scoring card." The scoring cards can increase or decrease the amount of points the team has. For example, if the team has 0 (zero) points and the selected card reads "Earn 50 points," the team will then have a total of 50 points. If the card reads, "Double your present score," the team doubles its score of 0, for a total of 0 points. If the card reads, "Deduct 50 points from your score," the team subtracts 50 from 0, for a score of −50. If the student answers incorrectly, the first student on another team to raise his or her hand earns the right to "steal" the question. Again, a correct answer earns that student the opportunity to choose a scoring card.

Of course, the scoring card could carry a negative message, so answering a question correctly is no guarantee that a team will earn points; as a matter of fact, the team could lose points. A team could conceivably answer all the questions correctly and lose the game.

Concluding Activity: End the activity with a quiz that includes ten of the questions you anticipate students will struggle with that were posed in the game. Students can take notes on the questions that are causing them confusion using the Note-Taking Graphic Organizer found in Activity 1 in their Student Notebooks.

FACILITATOR INFORMATION

"Will the Winners Lose" Scoring Cards

Print two sets of the following "Will the Winners Lose" scoring cards, and cut out and shuffle the cards in advance of the game.

Earn 100 points	Lose a turn	Take 50 points from the other team
Earn 70 points	Double your total points	Take an extra turn
Earn 500 bonus points	Deduct 50 points from your score	Halve your points

Alternative Idea: You might post the scoring cards in random order on a bulletin board or chalkboard. Post the cards *with the blank side facing students and the scoring instructions hidden from view*.

A Couple More Twists:

- You might have each student track the score for each team. Students track the team scores on their own. At the end of the game, each student who correctly calculated each team's final score would earn 50 bonus points for his or her team.
- You might introduce another rule. Since no team member knows whether the scoring card he or she selects will earn or lose points, you might allow students the option of *not* selecting a card when they answer correctly. If the student thinks the next card in the stack might carry a negative scoring instruction, he or she is free to pass and earn (or lose) no points for the team. Students only learn whether that was a good move or not if the next student to choose a card reveals the scoring instruction on the card.

CHAPTER 1 AVIATION TRAINING REQUIREMENTS

LESSON 6
CHAPTER 1 EXAM

PURPOSE
The purpose of this lesson is to summatively assess student knowledge of aviation training and medical requirements.

ACCOMMODATIONS FOR LEARNING DIFFERENCES
It is important that lessons accommodate the needs of every learner. These lessons may be modified to accommodate your students with learning differences by referring to www.pacer.org/parent/php/PHP-c267.pdf.

PREPARATION
- Exam copies
- Newsela teacher account with article assigned to class: "The once regal 747 will soon be reduced to transporting only cargo," by *Los Angeles Times*, adapted by Newsela staff.[5] The online article is available at a variety of reading levels.
- Computer/device access per student or paper copies of the Newsela article and questions.

DIRECTIONS
Introductory Activity: Display a picture of an aviation medical certificate such as the one shown here. If you as the facilitator are certified, show students your own certificate. Have students explain to a partner why training and certificates are required at various preparation levels for pilots.

Step 1: Create an exam using the questions found in the test bank under Facilitator Information below. (An answer key is provided at the end of the chapter.) Write the exam and include directions and points totals. As you share the exam with students, clear up or re-explain any points from the review activity that students struggled with. Ask for questions on review information. Review the directions for completing the exam and expectations for what to do when the exam is finished.

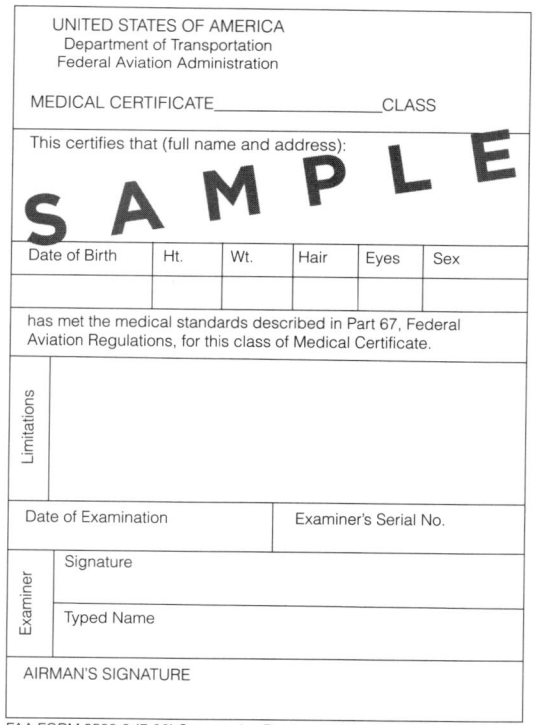

▶ Aviation medical certificate.

Step 2: When students have turned in the exam, make available to them the article "The once-regal 747 will soon be reduced to transporting only cargo," by the *Los Angeles Times* on Newsela.[6] Have students independently read the article, annotate it with interactive text markings, and then write a short, one-paragraph response to the prompt, "Explain why the Boeing 747 has run into problems recently and what it means about the aircraft," in the Student Notebook (Activity 1: Writing Prompt). Students must use at least two details from the article to support their responses.

Concluding Activity: No formal summary activity. Students will work independently to finish the exam at different times and begin reading the article as an independent introductory activity to Chapter 2 on aircraft basics.

FACILITATOR INFORMATION
Chapter 1 Exam: Aviation Training Requirements

(This exam is available in the online Instructor Resources in a format ready for use in the classroom. An answer key is provided at the end of the chapter.)

1. When can a student pilot log time as pilot-in-command?
    a. All of the time they are flying the aircraft
    b. Only the time when they are flying solo

2. The FARs define a cross-country as _____ for a student pilot.
    a. 15 NM
    b. 25 NM
    c. 50 NM

3. The FARs define a cross-country as _____ for a private pilot.
    a. 15 NM
    b. 25 NM
    c. 50 NM

4. Can a student pilot fly to Canada?
    a. Yes
    b. No

5. Can a private pilot fly to Canada?
    a. Yes
    b. No

6. Can a student pilot fly with passengers?
    a. Yes
    b. No

7. Can a private pilot fly with passengers?
   a. Yes
   b. No

8. Why would a pilot train to obtain an instrument rating?
   a. So the pilot can carry passengers in the aircraft
   b. So the pilot can get paid to fly
   c. So the pilot can fly into the clouds

9. How many flight hours do the Federal Aviation Regulations require for you to obtain a private pilot's license?
   a. 20
   b. 40
   c. 60
   d. 80

10. What class of medical certificate does an airline transport pilot (ATP) need?
    a. First
    b. Second
    c. Third

11. How long does the medical in the previous question last for an ATP who is under the age of 40?
    a. 12 calendar months
    b. 24 calendar months
    c. 60 calendar months

12. Any doctor can give you an Aviation Medical Exam to receive your aviation medical.
    a. True
    b. False

13. You are a private pilot at the age of 17 and possess a first class medical that was issued on April 20, 2017. For the purpose of a private pilot, when does your medical certificate expire?
    a. April 30, 2018
    b. April 30, 2019
    c. April 30, 2020
    d. April 30, 2022

ANSWER KEYS

CHAPTER 1

LESSON 1, Activity 3
Student versus Private Pilot Questions (Student Notebook)

1. A student pilot is someone who is learning how to become a private pilot. This is very similar to getting a car driver's permit compared to a full driver's license.
2. No.
3. During the day: 3 SM. At night: 5 SM.
4. No.
5. No.
6. No, it is greater than 25 NM, which means it's a cross-country. A student pilot needs a cross-country endorsement to go on a flight greater than 25 NM.
7. A flight instructor must give the student pilot an endorsement to go on this flight.
8. 17 years old
9. An oral exam and a flight exam
10. Total flight time required to become a private pilot: 40 hours (Reference §61.109)
    a. an authorized instructor
        i. cross-country
        ii. night training
        iii. sole reference to instruments
    b. solo flight
        i. cross-country
11. No, you would be operating as a commercial pilot.
12. Carry passengers; fly internationally; go on cross-country flights; fly as pilot-in-command of a flight for charitable, nonprofit, or community events.
13. Aeronautical knowledge areas are listed under 14 CFR §61.105 and flight proficiency items are under 14 CFR §61.107.
    §61.105 Aeronautical knowledge.
    (a) General. A person who is applying for a private pilot certificate must receive and log ground training from an authorized instructor or complete a home-study course on the aeronautical knowledge areas of paragraph (b) of this section that apply to the aircraft category and class rating sought.

(b) Aeronautical knowledge areas.

    (1) Applicable Federal Aviation Regulations of this chapter that relate to private pilot privileges, limitations, and flight operations;

    (2) Accident reporting requirements of the National Transportation Safety Board;

    (3) Use of the applicable portions of the "Aeronautical Information Manual" and FAA advisory circulars;

    (4) Use of aeronautical charts for VFR navigation using pilotage, dead reckoning, and navigation systems;

    (5) Radio communication procedures;

    (6) Recognition of critical weather situations from the ground and in flight, windshear avoidance, and the procurement and use of aeronautical weather reports and forecasts;

    (7) Safe and efficient operation of aircraft, including collision avoidance, and recognition and avoidance of wake turbulence;

    (8) Effects of density altitude on takeoff and climb performance;

    (9) Weight and balance computations;

    (10) Principles of aerodynamics, powerplants, and aircraft systems;

    (11) Stall awareness, spin entry, spins, and spin recovery techniques for the airplane and glider category ratings;

    (12) Aeronautical decision making and judgment; and

    (13) Preflight action that includes -

        (i) How to obtain information on runway lengths at airports of intended use, data on takeoff and landing distances, weather reports and forecasts, and fuel requirements; and

        (ii) How to plan for alternatives if the planned flight cannot be completed or delays are encountered.

§61.107 Flight proficiency.

(a) General. A person who applies for a private pilot certificate must receive and log ground and flight training from an authorized instructor on the areas of operation of this section that apply to the aircraft category and class rating sought.

(b) Areas of operation.

    (1) For an airplane category rating with a single-engine class rating:

        (i) Preflight preparation;

        (ii) Preflight procedures;

        (iii) Airport and seaplane base operations;

        (iv) Takeoffs, landings, and go-arounds;

        (v) Performance maneuvers;

        (vi) Ground reference maneuvers;

        (vii) Navigation;

        (viii) Slow flight and stalls;

        (ix) Basic instrument maneuvers;

        (x) Emergency operations;

        (xi) Night operations, except as provided in § 61.110 of this part; and

        (xii) Postflight procedures.

14. **§61.109 Aeronautical experience.**

    (a) *For an airplane single-engine rating.* Except as provided in paragraph (k) of this section, a person who applies for a private pilot certificate with an airplane category and single-engine class rating must log at least 40 hours of flight time that includes at least 20 hours of flight training from an authorized instructor and 10 hours of solo flight training in the areas of operation listed in §61.107(b)(1) of this part, and the training must include at least—

    (1) 3 hours of cross-country flight training in a single-engine airplane;

    (2) Except as provided in §61.110 of this part, 3 hours of night flight training in a single-engine airplane that includes—

    (i) One cross-country flight of over 100 nautical miles total distance; and

    (ii) 10 takeoffs and 10 landings to a full stop (with each landing involving a flight in the traffic pattern) at an airport.

    (3) 3 hours of flight training in a single-engine airplane on the control and maneuvering of an airplane solely by reference to instruments, including straight and level flight, constant airspeed climbs and descents, turns to a heading, recovery from unusual flight attitudes, radio communications, and the use of navigation systems/facilities and radar services appropriate to instrument flight;

    (4) 3 hours of flight training with an authorized instructor in a single-engine airplane in preparation for the practical test, which must have been performed within the preceding 2 calendar months from the month of the test; and

    (5) 10 hours of solo flight time in a single-engine airplane, consisting of at least—

    (i) 5 hours of solo cross-country time;

    (ii) One solo cross country flight of 150 nautical miles total distance, with full-stop landings at three points, and one segment of the flight consisting of a straight-line distance of more than 50 nautical miles between the takeoff and landing locations; and

    (iii) Three takeoffs and three landings to a full stop (with each landing involving a flight in the traffic pattern) at an airport with an operating control tower.

15. Fixed-base operators at various airports; flight schools; and flight training academies

16. Although it depends on the location, aircraft rental can range from $100–$300 per hour for most single-engine training aircraft. The price range will be impacted by such factors as age of aircraft, complexity of aircraft, technology available, and if fuel is included in the price.

17. Although it depends on the location, flight instructor rates will range from $30 per hour for independent flight instructors to up to $100 per hour, depending on aircraft type and type of instruction provided.

LESSON 3, Activity 4

Aviation Medicals Comprehension Questions (Student Notebook)

1. Generally, a first-class medical certificate is designed for the airline transport pilot. Further explanation can be found at 14 CFR §61.23(a)(1).

2. Generally, a second-class medical certificate is designated for the commercial pilot. Further explanation can be found in 14 CFR §61.23(a)(2).

3. Generally, a third-class medical certificate is designated for the student, recreational, and private pilot. Further explanation and exceptions can be found in 14 CFR §61.23.

4. A medical certificate is obtained by passing a physical examination administered by a doctor who is an FAA-authorized AME. There are approximately 6,000 FAA-authorized AMEs in the nation. To find an AME near you, go to the FAA's AME locator at **www.faa.gov/pilots/amelocator/**. Further guidance on how to obtain a medical certificate can be obtained on FAA's Medical Certification webpage.

5. Examples include events such as if you have a heart attack, have a stroke, or get arrested for driving under the influence of alcohol. A summary of medical standards can be found on the FAA's website.

6. Under 14 CFR Part 1, the FAA defines a medical certificate as "acceptable evidence of physical fitness on a form prescribed by the Administrator." The primary goal of the airman medical certification program is to protect not only those who would exercise the privileges of a pilot certificate but also air travelers and the general public. A person who meets FAA airmen medical standards, based on a medical examination and an evaluation of medical history, is entitled to a medical certificate without restriction or limitation other than the prescribed limitation as to its duration. Individuals required to hold a medical certificate must have it in their personal possession at all times when exercising the privileges for which they are licensed.

7. Most pilots must have a valid medical certificate to exercise the privileges of their airman certificates. Glider and free balloon pilots are not required to hold a medical certificate. Sport pilots may hold either a medical certificate or a valid state driver's license. Regardless of whether a medical certificate or driver's license is required, 14 CFR §61.53 requires every pilot not to act as a crewmember if they know, or have reason to know, of any medical condition that would make them unable to operate the aircraft in a safe manner.

8. A summary of medical standards and disqualifying medical conditions can be found on the "Medical Certification" section of the FAA website, **www.faa.gov**.

   The FAA medical standards, 14 CFR Part 67, specify fifteen medical conditions that are considered disqualifying by "history or clinical diagnosis." Regardless of when one of these conditions was diagnosed and treated, an airman may not be issued a medical certificate except through a process called a "Special Issuance Authorization," as explained in 14 CFR §67.401. A special issuance is a discretionary issuance by the FAA Federal Air Surgeon and requires satisfactory completion of special testing determined by the FAA to demonstrate that an airman is safe to fly for the duration of the medical certificate issued.

   Unless otherwise directed by the FAA, the Examiner must deny or defer if the applicant has a history of: (1) Diabetes mellitus requiring hypoglycemic medication; (2) Angina pectoris; (3) Coronary heart disease that has been treated or, if untreated, that has been symptomatic or clinically significant; (4) Myocardial infarction; (5) Cardiac valve replacement; (6) Permanent cardiac pacemaker; (7) Heart replacement; (8) Psychosis; (9) Bipolar disorder; (10) Personality disorder that is severe enough to have repeatedly manifested itself by overt acts; (11) Substance dependence; (12) Substance abuse; (13) Epilepsy; (14) Disturbance of consciousness and without satisfactory explanation of cause, and (15) Transient loss of control of nervous system function(s) without satisfactory explanation of cause.

However, this list includes only the mandatory disqualifying conditions. There are many other medical conditions that fall into the General Medical Condition section of the regulations that are considered by the FAA to be disqualifying even though they are not stated in the regulations. Conditions such as cancer, kidney stones, neurologic and neuromuscular conditions including Parkinson's disease and multiple sclerosis, certain blood disorders, and other conditions that may progress over time require review by the FAA before a medical certificate may be issued. The important thing to remember is that with very few exceptions, all disqualifying medical conditions may be considered for special issuance. If you can present satisfactory medical documentation to the FAA that your condition is stable, the chances are good that you will be able to qualify for an Authorization.

9. There are no minimum or maximum ages for obtaining a medical certificate. Any applicant who is able to pass the exam may be issued a medical certificate. However, since 16 years is the minimum age for a student pilot certificate, people under 16 are unlikely to have practical use for an airman medical certificate.

10. No. Effective April 1, 2016, Aviation Medical Examiners (AMEs) are not authorized to issue combination Airman Medical and Student Pilot certificates to applicants.

11. Yes. You are prohibited from acting as pilot-in-command or as a required pilot flight crewmember during any medical deficiency that would be disqualifying or may interfere with the safe operation of an aircraft. For more information, see 14 CFR §61.53.

12. Yes, but you need to let your AME know that you had the surgery.

13. Yes. 14 CFR §67.409 sets forth the appeal process within the FAA for applicants who are denied medical certification. Within 30 days after the date of the denial, you may apply for reconsideration to the FAA Federal Air Surgeon.

14. You can call or write:

    Aerospace Medical Certification Division, AAM-300
    Federal Aviation Administration
    Civil Aerospace Medical Institute
    P.O. Box 25082
    Oklahoma City, OK 73125
    (405) 954-4821

    You can also contact the Regional Flight Surgeons' offices

15. You should submit AC Form 8060-56 (PDF) to:

    Federal Aviation Administration
    Aerospace Medical Certification Division, AAM-331
    ATTN: Duplicate Desk
    PO Box 26200
    Oklahoma City, Oklahoma 73125

    You must include a check or money order for $2.00 made payable to the FAA. The Aerospace Medical Certification Division can fax you a record of your certificate that is valid for no more than 60 days, which should be enough time to receive your replacement certificate. To receive this fax and order a duplicate certificate, call (405) 954-4821 and select option 3 to reach the duplicate certificate desk.

LESSON 6
Chapter 1 Exam

1. (b) Only the time when they are flying solo
2. (b) 25 NM
3. (c) 50 NM
4. (b) No
5. (a) Yes
6. (b) No
7. (a) Yes
8. (c) So the pilot can fly into the clouds
9. (b) 40
10. (a) First
11. (a) 12 calendar months
12. (b) False
13. (d) April 30, 2022

CHAPTER 2
AIRCRAFT BASICS

Introduction

STANDARDS & OBJECTIVES

North Dakota Aviation Content Standards (Grades 10–12)
- **A.1.1.1**—Identify the parts of an airplane.
- **A.1.1.1**—Develop a basic understanding of the parts of a helicopter.
- **1.1.2**—Compare and contrast categories and classes of aircraft.
- **1.2.1**—Identify the seven basic/standard instruments.
- **1.2.2**—Describe the operation/limitations of the pitot-static system.
- **1.2.3**—Describe the operation/limitations of the gyroscopic system.
- **1.2.4**—Describe the operation/limitations of the magnetic system.
- **A.3.1.1**—Understand traffic patterns in order to maneuver around an airport to conduct a normal landing.
- **NA**—Describe and perform fundamental flight maneuvers performed by an aircraft.
- **NA**—Introduce students to the procedures of normal takeoffs and landings.

Note: Standards beginning with "A" indicate the objectives align with but do not exactly match the identified ND Aviation Standards. Lines marked "NA" do not align with specific aviation standards but identify important standards essential for progression of student learning.

Language Arts—CCSS.ELA-LITERACY.CCRA
- **L.1**—Demonstrate command of the conventions of standard English grammar and usage when writing or speaking.
- **L.2**—Demonstrate command of the conventions of standard English capitalization, punctuation, and spelling when writing.
- **SL.2**—Integrate and evaluate information presented in diverse media and formats, including visually, quantitatively, and orally.
- **SL.4**—Present information, findings, and supporting evidence such that listeners can follow the line of reasoning and the organization, development, and style are appropriate to task, purpose, and audience.
- **W.7**—Conduct short as well as more sustained research projects based on focused questions, demonstrating understanding of the subject under investigation.
- **W.8**—Gather relevant information from multiple print and digital sources, assess the credibility and accuracy of each source, and integrate the information while avoiding plagiarism.

- **W.9**—Draw evidence from literary or informational texts to support analysis, reflection, and research.

ESSENTIAL QUESTIONS

- Why are various types of aircraft designed differently?
- Why does a pilot need to know the parts of an airplane?
- What are the primary flight controls in an airplane, and what does each of the controls do?
- Does this change if we are talking about a Piper Cherokee Archer (PA 28-181) versus a Boeing 737?

LESSONS

Lesson	Topic	Student Notebook Activities
Lesson 1	Parts of an Airplane	1. Parts of an Airplane Pre-Test 2. Note-Taking Organizer for Parts of an Airplane 3. Parts of an Airplane Post-Lesson Test
Lesson 2	Aircraft Flight Instruments	1. Aircraft Flight Instruments—Round Dial Cockpit 2. Aircraft Flight Instruments—Glass Cockpit
Lesson 3	Fundamental Maneuvers	1. Inquiry Research Project • *Inquiry Chart (I-Chart)* • *Fundamentals of Flight Inquiry Questions*
Lesson 3a	Flight Simulation: Fly the Maneuvers (2–3 days) (See Chapter 10, Lesson 1)	
Lesson 4	Normal Takeoffs and Landings	1. Pre-Lesson Question 2. Normal Landings Outline 3. Post-Lesson Question
Lesson 4a	Flight Simulation—Normal Takeoffs and Landings (See Chapter 10, Lesson 2)	
Lesson 5	Traffic Patterns	1. Traffic Patterns Outline
Lesson 6	Helicopter Basics	1. Helicopter Questions
Lesson 7	Review: Aircraft Basics	1. Chapter Review Notes
Lesson 8	Chapter 2 Exam	1. Current Event Article • *Article Response* • *Response Rubric*

LESSON 1
PARTS OF AN AIRPLANE

PURPOSE
The purpose of this lesson is to identify parts of an airplane.

ACCOMMODATIONS FOR LEARNING DIFFERENCES
It is important that lessons accommodate the needs of every learner. These lessons may be modified to accommodate your students with learning differences by referring to www.pacer.org/parent/php/PHP-c267.pdf.

PREPARATION
- *Pilot's Handbook of Aeronautical Knowledge* (PHAK) (FAA-H-8083-25)
- Prepared "I Have, Who Has" review game

DIRECTIONS
Introductory Activity: Write several of the vocabulary words from this chapter (introduced in Step 2 below) on the board and ask students how familiar they are with each or any of the terms (fuselage, wing, ailerons, empennage, powerplant, etc.). Display the *Pilot's Handbook of Aeronautical Knowledge* and explain to students the importance of using this book as a reference for familiarizing themselves with the components of an aircraft.

Step 1: Have students complete Activity 1 (Parts of an Airplane Pre-Test) found in their Student Notebooks. This test will not be graded but will be used by students to self-assess what they know about the parts of an airplane. Reference the *Pilot's Handbook of Aeronautical Knowledge*, Chapter 3: Aircraft Construction, for the answers to the test questions, or see the answer key provided at the end of the chapter.

Step 2: Create a presentation (with text, pictures, and/or video) to share the major components of an airplane. Include the following parts/terms:

Airframe
- Fuselage
- Empennage
  › Pitch control
    - Stabilizer
    - Elevator vs. stabilator
- Powerplant
- Wings
  › Roll control
    - Ailerons
  › Flaps
- Undercarriage
  › Landing gear

Cockpit
- Flight instruments
  - Round dial vs. glass cockpit
- Flight controls
- Engine instruments
- Power controls
- Electrical controls
- Avionics

Step 3: Students can record information from the presentation in their Student Notebooks under Activity 2 (Note-Taking Organizer for Parts of an Airplane).

Step 4: If time allows, have students create and play an "I Have, Who has?" game. See the directions and game template in the Facilitator Information section below the concluding activity.

Concluding Activity: Have students complete Activity 3 (Parts of an Airplane Post-Lesson Test) in the Student Notebook, which contains the same questions as the Pre-Test. (An answer key is provided at the end of the chapter.) Have students share what they learned during today's lesson.

FACILITATOR INFORMATION
"I Have, Who Has?" Game Directions

As students match up the answers on their cards with questions on other students' cards, they get valuable practice with vocabulary and listening skills.

First choose a list of words. Then begin filling in the blanks on the "I Have, Who Has" card templates with these words.

Hand out a card to each student. Some students may need to have two cards depending upon how many in a set. It is important to use all the cards in a set.

Choose a student to go first, and have the student read his or her card aloud.

The student who has the card with the word then reads that answer aloud: "I have _____." This student will then read the question at the bottom of their card: "Who has _____?" Then the student with the card that answers the question responds. Every card in the set is connected to a card before it and a card after it. To keep the game moving at a quick pace, all students need to pay attention to every question that's asked.

Play continues in this fashion until all of the cards have been played. The game will end with the same student who started play.

Here is an example:

- First card—"I have the first card, who has the main body of an aircraft?"
- Second card—"I have fuselage, who has the compartment for the pilot?"
- Third card—"I have cockpit, who has the part of the plane used for steering?"
- Cards continue in that pattern.
- Last card—"I have _____. Who has the first card?"

Game Card Template

I have the first card. Who has _____?	I have _____. Who has _____?
I have _____. Who has _____?	I have _____. Who has _____?
I have _____. Who has _____?	I have _____. Who has _____?
I have _____. Who has _____?	I have _____. Who has _____?
I have _____. Who has _____?	I have _____. Who has the first card?

CHAPTER 2 AIRCRAFT BASICS

LESSON 2

AIRCRAFT FLIGHT INSTRUMENTS

PURPOSE

The purpose of this lesson is to identify and explain the pitot-static system and associated instruments, the vacuum system and related instruments, gyroscopic instruments, and the magnetic compass.

ACCOMMODATIONS FOR LEARNING DIFFERENCES

It is important that lessons accommodate the needs of every learner. These lessons may be modified to accommodate your students with learning differences by referring to www.pacer.org/parent/php/PHP-c267.pdf.

PREPARATION

- Whiteboard
- Picture examples of pitot tube, static port, and gyroscope
- *Pilot's Handbook of Aeronautical Knowledge* (FAA-H-8083-25)

DIRECTIONS

Introductory Activity: Write the words "pitot tube," "static," and "gyroscope" on the board. Ask students to think to themselves about the definition of the words. Then, students can pair up and share their ideas with each other before sharing with the class. Allow time for student responses and discussions, and write ideas on the board, if applicable. Define these terms for students. (*Answers:* Pitot tube: A part of the pitot-static system. It is a tube or a mast where dynamic or ram air enters the system. Static: Either in reference to the static port or static pressure. Static pressure is stationary or non-moving air. The static port is a part of the pitot-static system either on the pitot static mast or a separate port on the side of the aircraft where static air enters the system. Gyroscope: A moving disc or object. A gyroscope is found in each of the three gyroscopic flight instruments—heading indicator, attitude indicator, and turn coordinator.)

Step 1: Locate and print one picture for each of the three words written on the board at the onset of the lesson: pitot tube, static port, gyroscope. Have students work together as a class to match the picture with the correct word. Allow time for discussion and clear up students' misconceptions.

Step 2: In their Student Notebooks, have students reference the picture of the flight instruments in a round dial cockpit configuration. Ask the students, "What are each of these flight instruments?" (*Answers:* airspeed indicator, attitude indicator, altimeter, turn coordinator, heading indicator, vertical speed indicator, and magnetic compass. See labels under Facilitator Information below.) Have students label these flight instruments in Activity 1 (Aircraft Flight Instruments—Round Dial Cockpit) in their Student Notebooks. Ask the students, "What do each of these instruments tell us? Where are they located in the cockpit? Why should I look at them?" (*Answers:* Reference *Pilot's Handbook of Aeronautical Knowledge*, Chapter 8. An answer key is also provided at the end of the chapter.) Students can record 1–2 facts about each instrument next to the pictures of the instruments in their Student Notebooks.

Step 3: Review with students that the flight instruments are divided into two groups: pitot-static and gyroscopic. Ask, "What are the pitot-static instruments?" (*Answer:* airspeed indicator, altimeter, and vertical speed indicator.) "What are the gyroscopic instruments?" (*Answer:* attitude indicator, heading indicator, and turn coordinator.) If students are interested in learning more about how these instruments work, they can reference the *Pilot's Handbook of Aeronautical Knowledge*, Chapter 8. This topic will also be studied in more depth later in this textbook in Chapter 9: Aircraft Systems.

Concluding Activity: Now that students have learned about the flight instruments, have them label the flight instruments on the glass cockpit primary flight display found in Activity 2 (Aircraft Flight Instruments—Glass Cockpit) in their Student Notebooks.

Note: The turn coordinator is the only instrument that is split into two separate instruments on the glass flight display. Students may have difficulty labeling this instrument. Provide support as necessary.

FACILITATOR INFORMATION
Aircraft Flight Instruments—Round Dial Cockpit

A. Airspeed indicator
B. Attitude indicator
C. Altimeter
D. Turn coordinator
E. Heading indicator
F. Vertical speed indicator
G. Magnetic compass

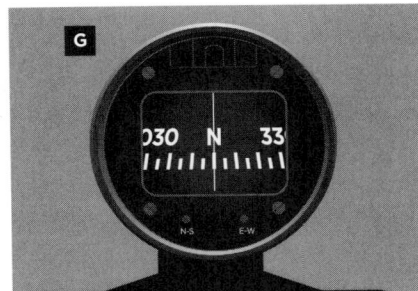

(FAA-H-8083-15B, FAA-H-8083-25B)

Aircraft Flight Instruments—Glass Cockpit

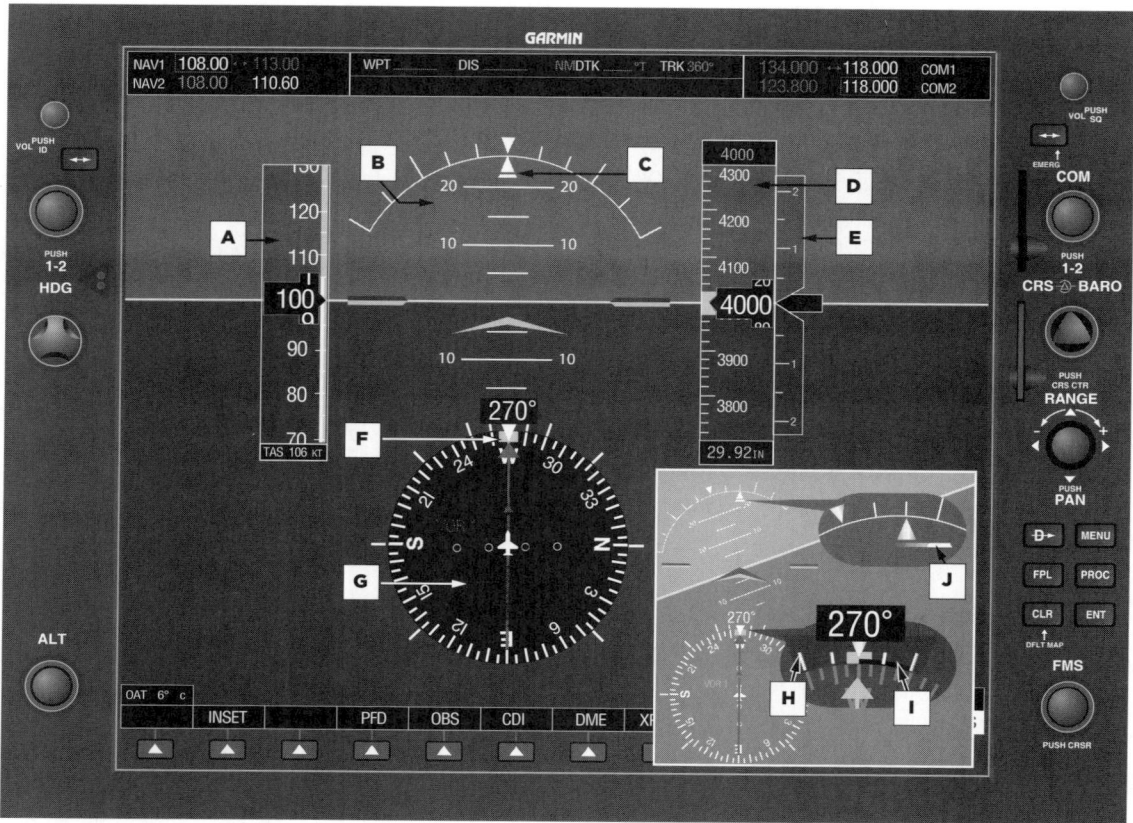

(FAA-H-8083-25B)

- **A.** Airspeed indicator
- **B.** Attitude indicator
- **C.** Slip skid indicator
- **D.** Altimeter
- **E.** Vertical speed indicator (VSI)
- **F.** Turn indicator
- **G.** Horizontal situation indicator
- **H.** Turn rate indicator tick marks
- **I.** Turn rate trend vector
- **J.** Slip/skid indicator

CHAPTER 2   AIRCRAFT BASICS

LESSON 3

FUNDAMENTAL MANEUVERS

PURPOSE
The purpose of this lesson is to apply knowledge of the flight instruments used to conduct the four fundamental flight maneuvers. These maneuvers are used every day by pilots flying in every kind of weather and every aircraft.

ACCOMMODATIONS FOR LEARNING DIFFERENCES
It is important that lessons accommodate the needs of every learner. These lessons may be modified to accommodate your students with learning differences by referring to **https://www.pacer.org/parent/php/PHP-c267.pdf**.

PREPARATION
- *Airplane Flying Handbook* (AFH) (FAA-H-8083-3)
- Flight simulation software (if planning to use Lesson 3a extension)

DIRECTIONS
Introductory Activity: Pair up students and have them brainstorm the four fundamental maneuvers with their partner (straight-and-level flight, turns, climbs, and descents). Use the following prompt, "What are the four fundamental maneuvers used when operating an aircraft?" Have students share their ideas with the class.

Step 1: Today's lesson is dedicated to learning more about the fundamentals of flight. Students will work in pairs to complete an inquiry research project using the graphic organizer found in Activity 1 (Inquiry Research Project) in their Student Notebooks. Of the Fundamentals of Flight Inquiry Questions listed below (and provided in the Student Notebook), students can select four questions or groups of questions that they would like to learn more about. As outlined in the Inquiry Chart graphic organizer, pairs of students must find at least three different sources to answer the inquiry questions. (Reference Chapter 3 in the *Airplane Flying Handbook* to answer the following questions.)

Fundamentals of Flight Inquiry Questions:
1. What are the four fundamental maneuvers?
2. How should the pilot hold the controls?
3. What is meant by "feeling the airplane"?
4. What is attitude flying?
5. How much time should be spent looking inside versus looking outside the airplane?

6. What do the aircraft's flight instruments tell us?
    a. Airspeed indicator
    b. Attitude indicator
    c. Altimeter
    d. Vertical speed indicator
    e. Heading indicator
    f. Turn coordinator
    g. Magnetic compass
7. Straight-and-Level Flight:
    a. What instruments will tell us that the aircraft is level at 3,000 feet, on a heading of 350 degrees and at 110 knots?
    b. By looking outside, what are some ways in which the pilot can tell if the aircraft is straight and level?
8. Level Turns:
    a. What instruments will tell us that the aircraft is level at 3,000 feet, turning from 350 to 090 degrees heading, at 110 knots?
    b. By looking outside while in flight, what are some ways in which we can tell if the aircraft is in a level turn?
    c. How does a constant airspeed impact the turn radius and rate?
    d. How does a constant angle of bank impact the turn radius and turn rate?
9. Climb:
    a. What instruments will tell us that the aircraft is climbing from 3,000 to 4,000 feet, on a heading of 350 degrees and at 110 knots?
    b. By looking outside, what are some ways in which we can tell if the aircraft is in a climb?
10. Descent:
    a. What instruments will tell us that the aircraft is descending from 4,000 to 3,000 feet, on a heading of 350 degrees and at 110 knots?
    b. By looking outside, what are some ways in which we can tell if the aircraft is in a descent?

Step 2: Students will use the remainder of the class period to complete their research.

Step 3: Lesson 3a Extension—If you have an available flight simulator, refer to Chapter 10, Lesson 1, to learn more about the flight maneuvers and for a simulation that can be used in conjunction with this lesson.

Concluding Activity: Students will submit their inquiry charts and the facilitator will select several ideas to discuss as a whole group, highlighting information aligned to lesson objectives and state standards.

CHAPTER 2 AIRCRAFT BASICS

LESSON 4
NORMAL TAKEOFFS AND LANDINGS

PURPOSE
The purpose of this lesson is to introduce students to the procedures of normal takeoffs and landings. These general rules can be applied for any aircraft.

ACCOMMODATIONS FOR LEARNING DIFFERENCES
It is important that lessons accommodate the needs of every learner. These lessons may be modified to accommodate your students with learning differences by referring to www.pacer.org/parent/php/PHP-c267.pdf.

PREPARATION
- *Airplane Flying Handbook* (AFH) (FAA-H-8083-3)
- Aircraft Pilot's Operating Handbook (POH)
- Sheets of paper to create paper airplanes
- Flight simulation software (if planning to use Lesson 4a extension)

DIRECTIONS
Introductory Activity: Pose the following questions to students: How do you perform a normal takeoff in a small general aviation aircraft such as a Cessna 172 or Piper Cherokee Archer? Allow time for students to respond to this prompt in their Student Notebooks in Activity 1 (Pre-Lesson Question), as this question will be revisited at the end of the lesson. (*Answer:* Apply full power, a little left rudder to maintain the centerline, and ease back on the yoke! It is that easy. The aircraft wants to fly, and it will actually take off by itself given enough runway.)

Discuss with students the important fact that even though a normal takeoff takes very few steps, it is important to learn how to do it. Pilots need to know specific takeoff information because there are times when they need to perform a short-field or soft-field takeoff and need to know the difference.

Step 1: Have small groups of students create a paper airplane. There should also be enough room in your classroom for a small runway for practicing takeoffs and landings. On the top of students' airplanes, have them draw the following instruments, all needed for takeoffs: control yoke, rudder pedals, and airspeed indicator. Have students do some research on takeoffs in Chapter 5 of the *Airplane Flying Handbook* to see how to use these instruments when conducting a normal takeoff.

Step 2: Once students have drawn the instruments on their aircrafts and researched them, lead a discussion on how to perform a normal takeoff. Reference an actual aircraft POH to find the lift-off or rotation speeds. The following is an excerpt from a Piper Cherokee Archer (PA-28-181) POH on normal takeoff procedures.

```
4.5i Takeoff Checklist
    TAKEOFF
    NORMAL TECHNIQUE

    Flaps ............................................... Up
    Trim ................................................ SET
    Brakes ..................................... APPLY & HOLD
    THROTTLE .................................. FULL POWER
    Brakes ........................................... RELEASE
    Rotation Airspeed ............................. 60 KIAS
                    SMOOTHLY ROTATE TO CLIMB ATTITUDE

    See Flaps Up Takeoff ground roll and Flaps Up Takeoff Performance
    charts in Section 5 for ground roll/takeoff distances and applicable gross
    weigh vs rotation speed information. The rotation airspeed shown is
    applicable for the airplane at maximum gross weight.
        When the available runway length is well in excess of that required and
    obstacle clearance is no factor, a rolling takeoff technique (no brakes prior
    to application of power) may be used.
```

▶ Normal takeoff checklist from Piper Archer Pilot's Operating Handbook. *(From the Piper Archer III PA-28-181 POH. For example only; do not use for flight planning.)*

Search the internet to find short videos to show the class demonstrating how to conduct takeoffs in a small airplane, such as a Cessna 172.

Step 3: Have students apply what they learned about takeoffs from their reading and the videos. Using their airplanes and corresponding instruments, ask them to verbally describe how to complete a takeoff. Have several groups of students model how to complete a takeoff using their paper airplane and instruments. Observe students' application of takeoff knowledge and recognize when they are applying the concepts correctly and clear up misconceptions as necessary. Use these follow-up questions to lead a discussion:

- How does wind impact the takeoff? (*Answer:* A tailwind will increase the takeoff distance as it is pushing the aircraft. A headwind will shorten the takeoff distance because there will be an increase of airflow over the wings creating lift.)
- How does a crosswind (side wind) affect the takeoff? (*Answer:* A crosswind will cause the aircraft to be pushed sideways. The pilot needs to crab or turn slightly into the wind.)
- For takeoff, should the pilot take off into the wind or with the wind? (*Answer:* Take off into the wind.)
- Why should the aircraft take off into the wind? (*Answer:* Air is needed to create lift; therefore, a takeoff is conducted into the wind to create this flow of air over the wing.)

(Note: Runway numbers will be discussed in further detail in Chapter 3).

Step 4: With students still in small groups, have them use their paper airplanes to simulate a normal landing. Students should use the airplanes they created in Step 1, which have the instruments needed for landing (control yoke, rudder pedal, airspeed indicator) drawn on top. Be sure they include labels showing the names of their controls and flight instruments while referring to the *Airplane Flying Handbook* (Chapter 3: Basic Flight Maneuvers).

They should also reference the AFH for how to conduct a normal landing. While reading in the AFH, students can complete Activity 2 (Normal Landings Outline) found in their Student Notebooks to further apply their knowledge of approaches and landings.

Step 5: Once students have drawn the instruments needed for landing on their aircraft and researched how the instruments are used during landing, lead a discussion on how to perform a normal landing. Reference an actual aircraft POH to find the approach and landing speeds. An excerpt from a Piper Archer (PA-28-181) POH on normal landing procedures is provided on the next page.

Search the internet to find short videos to show the class demonstrating how to conduct landings in a small airplane, such as a Cessna 172.

Step 6: Using their airplanes, ask students to verbally describe how to complete a normal landing. Have several groups of students model how to complete a landing using their paper airplane making sure to be specific as to what their controls are doing and what their flight instruments look like. Observe students' application of landing knowledge and recognize when they are applying the concepts correctly and clear up misconceptions as necessary. Use these follow-up questions to lead a discussion:

- How does wind impact the landing? (*Answer:* A tailwind will increase the ground speed of an aircraft; therefore, an aircraft is likely to take up more runway when landing with a tailwind. A headwind results in a slower ground speed and greater aircraft control on approach. Note that the aircraft ground speed is different than the aircraft's indicated airspeed.)
- How does a crosswind (side wind) impact the landing? (*Answer:* Same impact as takeoff, the pilot needs to crab into the wind.)
- For landing, does the pilot land into the wind or with the wind? Why? (*Answer:* Into the wind. The reason is that landing into the wind results in a slower ground speed and more aircraft control. The airplane will take up less runway when landing into the wind.)

Concluding Activity: To close the lesson, ask students to complete the Post-Lesson Question (Activity 3) in their Student Notebooks to once again answer the question: "How do you perform a normal takeoff in a small general aviation aircraft such as a Cessna 172 or Piper Archer?" Allow time for students' responses, and have them compare how their answer to that question changed from the beginning of the lesson to the end of the lesson.

Lesson 4a: Chapter 10, Lesson 2, is a simulation that can be used in conjunction with this lesson.

> Normal landing procedures from Piper Archer Pilot's Operating Handbook. *(From the Piper Archer III PA-28-181 POH. For example only; do not use for flight planning.)*

NORMAL PROCEDURES   **PA-28-181, ARCHER III**

4.5m Approach and Landing Checklist

APPROACH AND LANDING

NOTE

The HSI will auto slew during CDI transitions to LOC, LOC BC, LDA, or SDF approaches if an approach is activated in the G1000 system. The pilot should always double check the inbound course pointer prior to initiating VHF NAV approach.

COM/NAV Radios and Avionics	CHECK & SET
Altimeter/Standby Altimeter	SET
Seat Backs	ERECT
Seat Belts, Harnesses	FASTEN/ADJUSTED
Armrests	STOWED
FUEL PUMP	ON
FUEL Selector	PROPER TANK
FLAPS	SET (102 KIAS max.)
ALTERNATE AIR	AS REQUIRED
MIXTURE	FULL RICH
AIR COND Switch (if installed)	OFF
Landing Light	AS REQUIRED
PARK BRAKE	Verify OFF
Toe Brakes	DEPRESS TO CHECK
Autopilot	DISCONNET
	(Above 200 FT AGL)

4.5m Approach and Landing Checklist (continued)

APPROACH AND LANDING (continued)

Initial Approach Speed	75 KIAS
Final Approach Speed (Flaps 40°)	66 KIAS
Touchdown	MAIN WHEELS
	(Above 200 FT AGL)
Braking	AS REQUIRED

NOTE

TAS aural alerts will be muted when GPS altitude is lower than ~400 FT AGL.

Check to ensure the fuel selector is on the proper (normally fullest) tank and that the seat back are erect, with the seats adjusted and locked in position. The seat belts and shoulder harness should be fastened and adjusted and the inertia reel checked.

The mixture control should be kept in full RICH position to ensure maximum acceleration if it should be necessary to open the throttle again. Alternate air should be closed unless there is an indication of induction system icing, since the use of alternate air causes a reduction in power which may be critical in case of a go-around. Full throttle operation with alternate air open can cause detonation.

The amount of flap used during landings and the speed of the aircraft at contact with the runway should be varied according to the landing surface and conditions of wind and airplane loading. It is generally good practice to contact the ground at the minimum possible safe speed consistent with existing conditions.

Normally, the best technique for short and slow landings is to use full flap and enough power to maintain the desired airspeed and approach flight path. Reduce the speed during the flareout and contact the ground close to the stalling speed. After ground contact hold the nose wheel off as long as possible. As the airplane slows down, gently lower the nose and apply the brakes. Braking is most effective when flaps are raised and back pressure is applied to the control wheel, putting most of the aircraft weight on the main wheels. In high wind conditions, particularly in strong crosswinds, it may be desirable to approach the ground at higher than normal speeds with partial or no flaps.

CHAPTER 2 AIRCRAFT BASICS

LESSON 5
TRAFFIC PATTERNS

PURPOSE
The purpose of this lesson is to understand traffic patterns in order to maneuver around an airport to conduct a normal landing.

ACCOMMODATIONS FOR LEARNING DIFFERENCES
It is important that lessons accommodate the needs of every learner. These lessons may be modified to accommodate your students with learning differences by referring to www.pacer.org/parent/php/PHP-c267.pdf.

PREPARATION
- *Airplane Flying Handbook* (FAA-H-8083-3)

DIRECTIONS

Introductory Activity: Display the picture of the runway (shown here) to all students. Give them the following scenario: "You just took off of runway 18; how do you maneuver back around to land on runway 18?" (*Answer:* It is a right-hand pattern, meaning all right turns in the traffic pattern.) Select 2–3 students to share their "traffic pattern" with the class. Discuss why their traffic patterns would or wouldn't work.

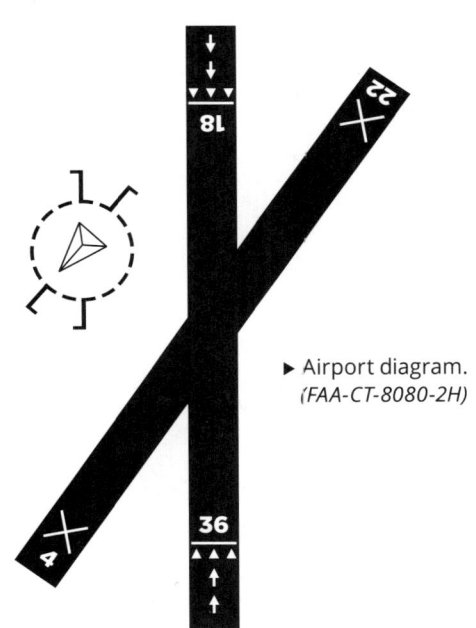

▶ Airport diagram. *(FAA-CT-8080-2H)*

Step 1: Pose the following question for students: "What is a traffic pattern?" Have them reference the *Airplane Flying Handbook* to research each part of a traffic pattern (standard versus non-standard, altitudes to fly them at, what each leg of the traffic pattern is called, what the pilot is doing on each of the legs). Lead a discussion with students about traffic patterns and have them take notes in their Student Notebooks under Activity 1 (Traffic Patterns Outline) (separated into parts as referenced below).

Step 2: To apply their knowledge, show students where to find information about specific airport traffic patterns in the *Chart Supplements*, available online from FAA Aeronautical Information Services.

Find an example to work through with students before expecting them to try it on their own. Students can record information in Part 1 of their Traffic Patterns Outline (Activity 1). For the following three examples, airport information from the *Chart Supplements* is provided below for reference.

- Reference Alexandria, MN (KAXN), using the *Chart Supplements* search available online through FAA Aeronautical Information Services. There are no notes about traffic pattern altitude, so the altitude is standard 800–1,000 feet above field elevation. Field elevation is 1,425, so 800 feet above would be 2,225 feet. It also does not state that the patterns are right traffic, so they are all standard left-hand traffic patterns.

- Now reference Albert Lea Municipal Airport (KAEL) in Minnesota. What is the traffic pattern altitude? In the example shown below, look for TPA under the initial header. This indicates a Traffic Pattern Altitude that should be used. In this case, it is published as 2,001 feet MSL (or 740 feet above ground level). Their patterns are all left hand (standard), as well. (A right-hand traffic pattern would be indicated in the runway headers; for example, "RWY 17 Rgt tfc" would indicate right traffic when landing on runway 17.)

- Grand Forks Air Force Base (KRDR) in North Dakota is a good example of an airport with both published traffic pattern altitudes (TPAs) and non-standard traffic patterns. TPA is under remarks: "Heavy, large and high performance acft: overhead 2500 (1589), rectangular 2000 (1089), lgt acft and helicopters 1500 (587)." Runway 17 is non-standard right-hand turns.

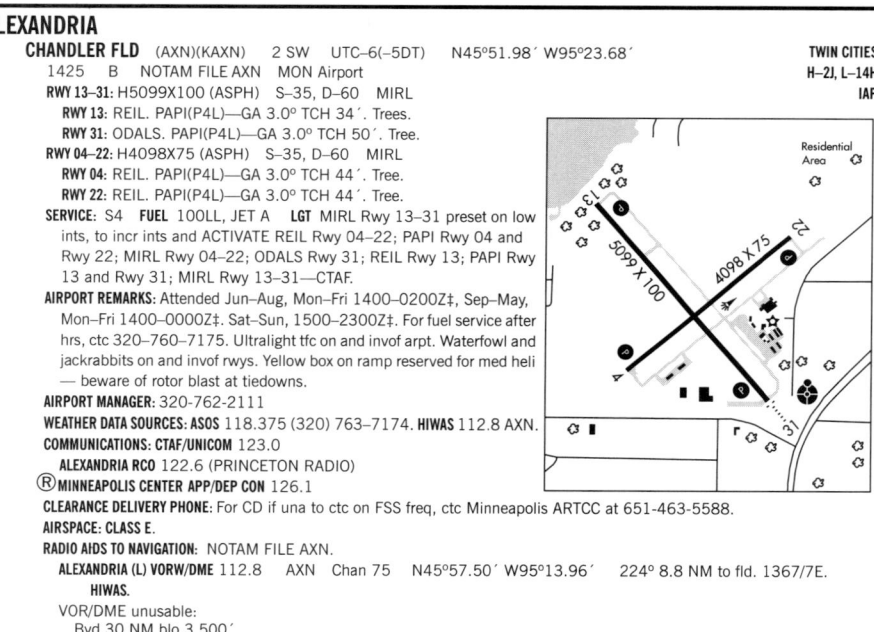

▶ Alexandria (KAXN) airport information from *Chart Supplements U.S. (FAA)*

ALBERT LEA MUNI (AEL)(KAEL) 3 N UTC–6(–5DT) N43°40.88′ W93°22.09′   **OMAHA**
1261 B TPA—2001(740) NOTAM FILE AEL   H–5D, L–12J
  RWY 17–35: H5000X100 (ASPH) S–19, D–29 MIRL   IAP
    RWY 17: ODALS. REIL. PAPI(P4L)—GA 3.0° TCH 30′.
    RWY 35: REIL. PAPI(P4L)—GA 3.0° TCH 30′. Tree.
  RWY 05–23: H2898X75 (ASPH)
    RWY 05: Trees.
  SERVICE: S2 **FUEL** 100LL, JET A, MOGAS **LGT** ACTIVATE ODALS Rwy 17; REIL Rwy 17 and Rwy 35; PAPI Rwy 17 and Rwy 35; MIRL Rwy 17–35—CTAF. MIRL Rwy 17–35 preset to low SS–SR, to incr ints—CTAF.
  AIRPORT REMARKS: Attended Apr–Oct Mon–Fri 1400–0200Z‡. Attended Nov–Mar Mon–Fri 1400–2300Z‡, Sat–Sun 1400–2300Z‡. For svc after hrs call 507–826–3451. 100LL and MOGAS fuel avbl 24 hr with credit card. Arr/Dep bldg access code: 1215. Gliders and helicopters use turf parallel to Rwy 17–35 on east side and approach area to Rwy 23. TV tower 9.5 NM southeast. Multiple transitional obstructions Rwy 05 and Rwy 35. Numerous primary sfc obstns all rwys.
  AIRPORT MANAGER: 507-373-0608
  WEATHER DATA SOURCES: AWOS–3 109.8 AEL (507) 377–1583.
  COMMUNICATIONS: CTAF/UNICOM 123.0
    RCO 122.05 (PRINCETON RADIO)
  ® **ROCHESTER APP/DEP CON** 119.8 (1100–0500Z‡)
  ® **MINNEAPOLIS CENTER APP/DEP CON** 135.35 (0500–1100Z‡)
  CLEARANCE DELIVERY PHONE: For CD ctc Rochester Apch at 507-424-8111.
  RADIO AIDS TO NAVIGATION: NOTAM FILE AEL.
    (T) **VORW/DME** 109.8   AEL   Chan 35   N43°40.90′ W93°22.25′   at fld. 1252/1E. **AWOS–3** VOR/DME unmonitored.

▶ Albert Lea Municipal Airport (KAEL) information from *Chart Supplements U.S. (FAA)*

GRAND FORKS AFB (RDR)(KRDR) AF 13 W UTC–6(–5DT) N47°57.68′ W97°24.05′   **TWIN CITIES**
911 B TPA—See Remarks NOTAM FILE GFK Not insp.   H–2I, L–14G
  RWY 17–35: H12351X150 (ASPH) PCN 125R/B/W/T HIRL   DIAP, AD
    RWY 17: ALSF1. PAPI(P4L)—GA 2.6° TCH 50′. Rgt tfc.
    RWY 35: ALSF1. PAPI(P4L)—GA 2.6° TCH 50′.
  SERVICE: S4 **FUEL** 115, JET B+ **OX** 2 **MILITARY—JASU** (A/M32A–86) (AM32–95) **FUEL** J8 **FLUID** SP PRESAIR **OIL** Avbl in package product only, hand transfer rqr. O–133–148 **TRAN ALERT** Opr 1300–0100Z‡ Mon–Fri, 1400–2200Z‡ Sat and Sun. No nml ops will take place on Fed. hol.
  MILITARY REMARKS: Opr H24 from 1200Z‡ Mon thru 0530Z‡ Sat; Sat and Sun 1200–0530Z‡; clsd hol. See FLIP AP/1 Supplementary Arpt Info. After hrs req must have approval of ARW/CV. **RSTD** All inbound passenger/cargo acft must ctc Comd Post no later than 30 min prior to ldg. Acft with dangerous materials ctc PTD 30 min prior to ETA. PPR all tran acft, ctc AM OPS DSN 362–4409, C701–747–4409, fax extension 4217. All acr ops except civ acrs are subject to restrictions and potential delays during BASH Phase II, Sep thru Nov, Apr thru Jun and other times as determined by the current Bird Watch condition (BWC). BWC MODERATE procedures are in effect during the Phase II BASH windows (1 hr prior to 1 hr after sunrise and 1 hr prior to 1 hr after sunset.) Arpt acft ctc twr or afld OPS for the current BWC and the ARW/CV thru command post (Nordic Cntl 311.0). Tran a rcrews inbd who RON ctc Warrior Inn DSN 362–7200 prior to arr. Ltd classified storage for tran aircrews. **CAUTION** Uncontrolled vehicle tfc on twy and ramps. UAV ops within 11 DME half circle RDR R–180 thru RDR R–360 west of Grand Forks AFB, sfc to FL 180. UAV ops in entire Class D airspace. **TFC PAT** TPA—Heavy, large and high performance acft: overhead 2500 (1589), rectangular 2000 (1089), lgt acft and helicopters 1500 (587). VFR overhead and rectangular tfc pat rgt hand Rwy 17. **MISC** First/last 1,100′ of Rwy 17–35 is concrete. Middle 10,150′ of Rwy 17–35 is asphalt. Acft with VHF radio equipment only may ctc AM OPS thru ATC. Rwy cond code and FICON not rpt. Ltd hangar space. All acft with Distinguished Visitors on board ctc Comd Post 60 NM prior ldg. Wx svc avbl H24. DSN 362–4396, C701–747–4395. AN/FMQ–19 Automated Observing Sys in use; augmented by human obsn when nec. Ctc 15 OWS Scott AFB DSN 576–9755, C 618–256–9755 dur wx flt closure or evac. Bldg obstn may impact prevailing vis 010°–220°.
  AIRPORT MANAGER: 701-747-4409
  COMMUNICATIONS: SFA D–ATIS 273.45 (data link enabled) **PTD** 372.2
    RCO 122.2   122.6   255.4 (GRAND FORKS RADIO)
  ® **GRAND FORKS APP/DEP CON** 118.1 318.1 (Opr 24hrs from 1200Z‡ Mon thru 0530Z‡ Sat; Sat and Sun 1200–0530Z‡; clsd hol). Other times ctc.
  ® **MINNEAPOLIS CENTER APP/DEP CON** 132.15
    RED RIVER TOWER 124.9   349.0 (Opr 24hrs from 1200Z‡ Mon thru 0530Z‡ Sat; Sat and Sun 1200–0530Z‡; clsd hol)
    GND CON 119.15   275.8 **CLNC DEL** 119.15   360.7
    COMD POST 311.0   321.0 **PMSV METRO** 343.5 WX support unavbl Mon–Fri 0500–1300Z‡, and Sat, Sun, and hol.
  AIRSPACE: CLASS D svc 1200Z‡–0530Z‡ Sat, Sat and Sun 1200–0530Z‡, clsd hol; other times CLASS G.
  RADIO AIDS TO NAVIGATION: NOTAM FILE GFK.
    RED RIVER (H) TACAN   Chan 111   RDR (116.4)   N47°57.42′ W97°24.36′   at fld. 904/6E.
      No NOTAM MP: 1200–1500Z‡ Mon, Wed, Fri
    (H) **VORW/DME** 114.3   GFK   Chan 90   N47°57.29′ W97°11.12′   264° 8.7 NM to fld. 840/9E.
    ILS 111.3   I-AVA   Rwy 17.   Class IE.
    ILS 109.9   I-RDR   Rwy 35.   Class IE.   No NOTAM MP: 1000–1400Z‡ Mon, Tue.

▶ Grand Forks Air Force Base (KRDR) information from *Chart Supplements U.S. (FAA)*

Step 3: Select local airports and have the students look up the runway layouts and traffic patterns in the *Chart Supplements*. Have students work in small groups to locate a runway example online, as modeled by the facilitator. Give them time to research and be able to explain the traffic pattern altitude and direction and label each leg. Students can record this information in Part 2 of their Traffic Patterns Outline. The facilitator should take note of students' understandings and misconceptions to use in a later class discussion. Reference Chapter 7 in the *Airplane Flying Handbook*, which is available online.

Step 4: Lead students through Part 3 of the Traffic Patterns Outline guided notes found in the Student Notebook. Along with sharing facts, you can prepare pictures or video files to review information related to approaches and landings. Consider searching online for videos that demonstrate airport traffic patterns and share them with the class.

Concluding Activity: Have each student share one thing they learned about traffic patterns from today's lesson. Close the lesson by asking students to consider this question: How would this traffic pattern change if flying a F-18 (or any fighter jet) rather than a Piper Archer or Cessna 172? (*Answer:* The traffic pattern is the same, only a lot bigger!)

LESSON 6
HELICOPTER BASICS

PURPOSE
The purpose of this lesson is to provide the student with a basic understanding of the parts of a helicopter.

ACCOMMODATIONS FOR LEARNING DIFFERENCES
It is important that lessons accommodate the needs of every learner. These lessons may be modified to accommodate your students with learning differences by referring to www.pacer.org/parent/php/PHP-c267.pdf.

PREPARATION
- Dice
- Presentation
- *Helicopter Flying Handbook* (FAA-H-8083-21)

DIRECTIONS

Introductory Activity: Have students brainstorm different ways that helicopters are utilized. Write the students' ideas on the whiteboard. Potential answers include: military, emergency medical services, search and rescue, construction, agricultural, news gathering, law enforcement, firefighting, tours, air taxi, tree harvesting, offshore oil rig transport, cherry drying, etc. Ask students why there are so many different potential missions for helicopters. (*Answer:* They are very maneuverable and are able to get into tight spaces.)

Step 1: Search online to find videos that showcase different types of helicopter missions. Show the videos to students in class. Ask students to share what they find most interesting about the videos.

Step 2: Create and share a presentation (referencing the *Helicopter Flying Handbook*, Chapter 1) that showcases the following information with accompanying pictures:

- Helicopter controls
  › Throttle
  › Collective
  › Cyclic
  › Anti-torque pedals
- Maneuvering
  › Hovering
- Airframe
  › Truss type
- Rotor blades
  › Main rotor
  › Tail boom and tail rotor
- Systems
  › Powerplant
  › Fuel system
  › Landing gear
  › Transmission

Step 3: Take time to discuss the different systems and parts of a helicopter. Answer questions as they arise.

Step 4: Ask students to turn to their Student Notebooks where the following six cubing questions from the lesson are displayed in Activity 1 (Helicopter Questions).

1. List one way in which a helicopter is like a fixed-wing aircraft such as a Cessna 172 or Piper Archer.
   (*Answer:* Lots of different answers are acceptable: both create lift, both transport people and things, both have engines, both have control surfaces, etc.)

2. List one way in which a helicopter is different than a fixed-wing aircraft such as a Cessna 172 or Piper Archer.
   (*Answers:* Lots of different answers are acceptable: one has wings and the other does not; in an airplane, lift is created by the wings and thrust is created by the propeller, while in a helicopter, lift and thrust are created by the rotors; a helicopter has a collective to control rotor blades while an airplane has a fixed-speed prop; etc.)

3. What does the collective do? (Also, have students point to which control it is in the cockpit of a helicopter.)
   (*Answer:* The collective changes the pitch of the main rotor blades and controls manifold pressure or torque.)

4. What does the throttle do? (Also have the students point to which control it is in the cockpit of a helicopter.)
   (*Answer:* The throttle controls the engine and main rotor RPM.)

5. What does the cyclic do? (Also have the students point to which control it is in the cockpit of a helicopter.)
   (*Answer:* The cyclic changes the pitch of each blade individually.)

6. If I have a private pilot airplane pilot's license, can I fly a helicopter? Why or Why not?
   (*Answer:* No, you are only able to fly an airplane; a helicopter is in a different category.)

Divide students into groups of four. Give each group one die. Each student rolls the die and answers the question with the corresponding number. If a number is rolled more than once, the student may elaborate on the previous response or roll again. Responses may also be written.

Concluding Activity: Select 2–3 students to summarize today's lesson.

LESSON 7
REVIEW: AIRCRAFT BASICS

PURPOSE

The purpose of this lesson is to review the information that will be on the end-of-chapter aircraft basics assessment.

ACCOMMODATIONS FOR LEARNING DIFFERENCES

It is important that lessons accommodate the needs of every learner. These lessons may be modified to accommodate your students with learning differences by referring to www.pacer.org/parent/php/PHP-c267.pdf.

PREPARATION

- Sticky notes or note cards and tape
- List of review questions (found below)

DIRECTIONS

Introductory Activity: Ask how many students have played the game "Headbands." Allow any students who know how to play to describe the game to their peers. Basically, the game requires players to place a term, concept, or question on their foreheads, either in the form of a headband or a sticky note. Players are not allowed to view the card on their own foreheads. Students walk around the classroom giving clues or answers to help students guess what term, concept, or question is written on their heads. For example, if a student has "Altimeter" written on their sticky note, their classmates would give them clues, such as "It is an instrument that measures altitude" or "Keep an eye on this instrument when you're flying low," to help the student guess the term and review the concept. (Simply search the internet for how to play the game if you need more clarification.)

Step 1: The ultimate goal of the game is for students to review the information that will be on the end-of-chapter assessment. Sticky notes can contain terms, concepts, or questions. Use the following list of terms, questions, and concepts to create sticky notes for each student (students could also help create these).

1. What are the four fundamental maneuvers?
2. Describe one of the following flight instruments and state what information each one provides the pilot: altimeter, attitude indicator, airspeed indicator, vertical speed indicator, heading indicator, and turn coordinator.
3. What information does the magnetic compass provide the pilot?
4. What does it mean that an altimeter is a pressure sensitive altimeter?
5. What instruments tell you that the aircraft is in level flight on a heading of 270 degrees, at 3,000 feet and 110 knots?

6. What instruments tell you that the aircraft is in a climbing turn from a heading of 240 to 060, from 2,000 to 4,000 feet at 80 knots?
7. You are in a standard rate turn and notice that your attitude indicator shows that you are in a 20-degree bank. When should you start your roll out if turning left from 180 to 090?
8. You are in a descent from 3,500 to 2,500 feet at a rate of 600 feet per minute. When should you start your level off?
9. By looking outside, how can you tell if you are descending?
10. By looking outside, how can you tell if you are turning?
11. When entering a turn, you may have to add back pressure. Why?
12. To get the proper feel of the aircraft and to prevent over-controlling, how should you hold the control yoke?
13. Why would the pilot use trim?
14. What is the powerplant?
15. Give two different examples of undercarriages?
16. What do the ailerons do?
17. List or explain the parts of the tail surface (stabilizer, rudder, elevator).
18. Give an example of a common training aircraft.
19. Describe how to conduct a normal takeoff.
20. What are the legs of a traffic pattern called?
21. What should the pilot be doing on each of the legs?
22. Describe how to conduct a normal landing.

Concluding Activity: Have students come up to the board and write one thing they learned about in the Aircraft Basics chapter that they will remember for the exam and beyond. Students may record notes in their Student Notebooks under Activity 1 (Chapter Review Notes).

LESSON 8
CHAPTER 2 EXAM

PURPOSE

The purpose of this lesson is to assess students' knowledge of aircraft basics.

ACCOMMODATIONS FOR LEARNING DIFFERENCES

It is important that lessons accommodate the needs of every learner. These lessons may be modified to accommodate your students with learning differences by referring to www.pacer.org/parent/php/PHP-c267.pdf.

PREPARATION

- Test bank questions (listed below)
- Computers/devices and internet access for students
- Current event article relating to Chapter 3 (Airport Operations)

DIRECTIONS

Step 1: Create an exam using the question bank below and make enough copies for the students in your class. Pass out exams and review directions, highlighting questions that may challenge students.

Step 2: Remind students where they should hand in their exam once it is complete. Allow time and provide a quiet space for students to complete the exam.

Step 3: When students finish the exam and are waiting for others to finish, provide them with a current event article you selected relating to the upcoming Chapter 3 topic, Airport Operations. The article can be from any major news outlet (newspaper, magazine, radio/TV segment) or professional organization, such as one of those listed in Chapter 1, Lesson 4. After carefully reading the article, students will complete the article response under Activity 1 (Current Event Article) in their Student Notebooks. They will summarize the main point of the article in their own words and then write a reflective response that addresses at least two of the inquiry questions listed in the Student Notebook. Student responses will be graded using the provided rubric.

Concluding Activity: Review correct exam answers with students once everyone has completed the exam. (An answer key is provided at the end of the chapter.) Students can share general findings from their preview of the Chapter 3 current events.

FACILITATOR INFORMATION
Chapter 2 Exam: Aircraft Basics

(This exam is available in the online Instructor Resources in a format ready for use in the classroom. An answer key is provided at the end of the chapter.)

Read each question carefully. There is only one correct answer for each question.

1. What are the four fundamental flight maneuvers? (4 points)

2. What instruments would give you the indications that the aircraft is in a 30-degree banking turn, level at 5,000 feet and 95 knots?
    a. Turn coordinator, attitude indicator, vertical speed indicator
    b. Turn coordinator, altimeter, airspeed indicator
    c. Attitude indicator, altimeter, airspeed indicator
    d. Attitude indicator, heading indicator, vertical speed indicator

3. You are in a descent from 5,000 to 3,000 feet at a rate of 400 feet per minute. When should you start your level off?
    a. 3,400 feet
    b. 3,200 feet
    c. 3,040 feet
    d. 3,020 feet

4. You are in a right turn and notice that the aircraft's attitude indicator shows that it is in a 30-degree bank. When should you start your roll out if turning right from North (0) to 090?
    a. 075
    b. 087
    c. 090
    d. 105

5. By looking outside, how can you tell if you are climbing?
    a. Nose of the aircraft is below the horizon.
    b. Nose of the aircraft is above the horizon.
    c. Wings are angled.
    d. You have to look inside to see if you are climbing.

6. By looking outside, how can you tell if you are in a turn to the left?
    a. The nose of the aircraft is below the horizon.
    b. The nose of the aircraft is above the horizon.
    c. The left wing is below the horizon and the right wing is above the horizon.
    d. The right wing is below the horizon and the left wing is above the horizon.

7. What component of lift causes the aircraft to turn?

   a. Vertical component of lift

   b. Horizontal component of lift

   c. Total lift

8. Pilots use trim to help _____ control pressures.

   a. Relieve

   b. Increase

For questions 9–15 (2 points per question):
(a) write the name of the flight instrument below the picture *and*
(b) describe what information it gives the pilot.

9. (a)_____

   (b)_____

10. (a)_____

    (b)_____

11. (a)_____

    (b)_____

12. (a)_____

    (b)_____

 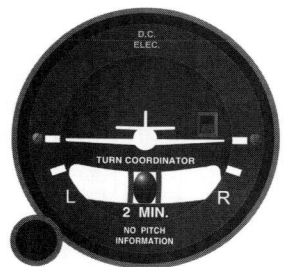

13. (a)_____   14. (a)_____
    (b)_____   (b)_____

15. (a)_____
    (b)_____

(Images from FAA-H-8083-15B and FAA-H-8083-25B)

16. Match each option in the left column with the corresponding airspeed indicator marking in the right column.

Indication	Airspeed indicator marking
Caution range	a. White arc:_____
Normal operating speeds	b. Green arc:_____
Never exceed speed	c. Yellow arc:_____
Flap operating speeds	d. Red line:_____

17. Reference the airplane pictured on the next page to identify the labeled components.

A. _____   F. _____
B. _____   G. _____
C. _____   H. _____
D. _____   I. _____
E. _____   J. _____

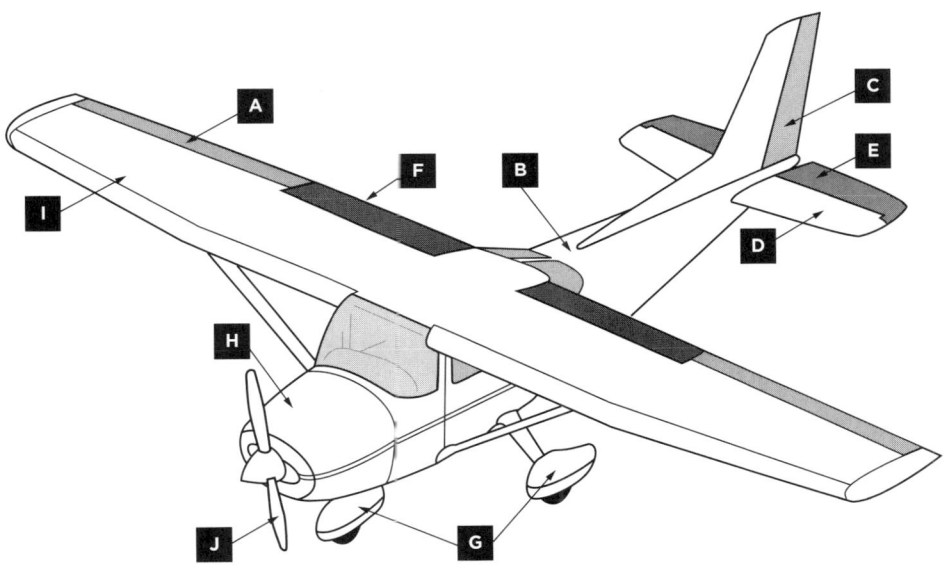

18. Reference the helicopter photos below to identify the labeled components.

   A. _____
   B. _____
   C. _____

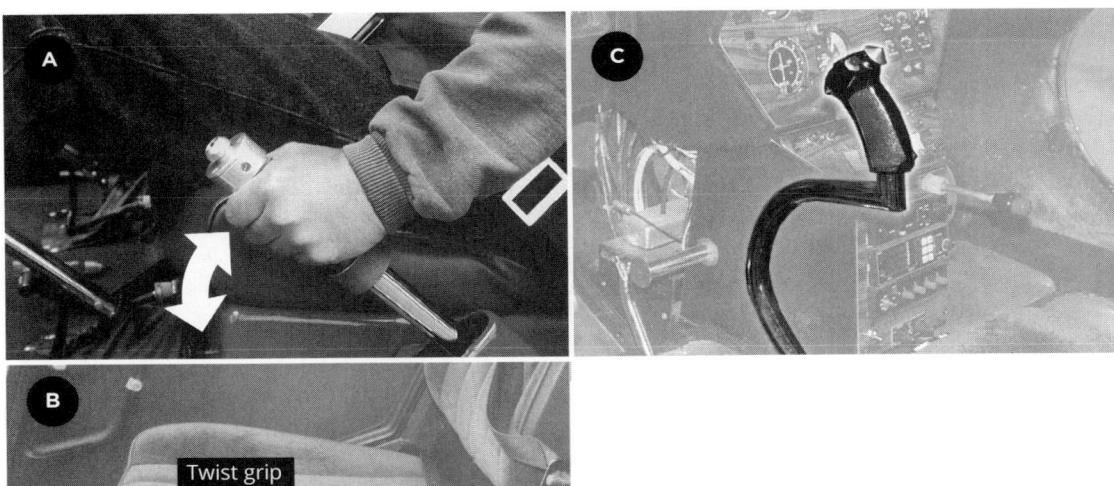

(FAA-H-8083-21B)

ANSWER KEYS
CHAPTER 2

LESSON 1, Activity 1 and Activity 3
Parts of an Airplane Pre-Test and Post-Test (Student Notebook)

1. The fuselage is the section of the airplane that consists of the cabin and/or cockpit, containing seats for the occupants and the controls for the airplane.
   a. Most modern single-engine aircraft feature all-metal construction. For example, in the Piper Archer II, the basic airframe, except for a tubular steel engine mount, steel landing gear struts, and other miscellaneous steel parts, is of aluminum alloy construction. The extremities (wing tips, cowling, tail surfaces) are of fiberglass or ABS thermoplastic.
2. An airfoil is the cross-section of any surface, such as a wing, propeller, rudder, or even a trim tab, which provides aerodynamic force when it interacts with a moving stream of air.
3. Flaps are the hinged portion of the trailing edge of the wing between the ailerons and fuselage. In some aircraft, ailerons and flaps are interconnected to produce full-span "flaperons." In either case, flaps change the lift and drag on the wing.
4. The ailerons are the primary flight control surfaces mounted on the trailing edge of an airplane wing, near the tip. Ailerons control roll about the longitudinal axis.
5. An empennage is the section of the airplane that consists of the vertical stabilizer, the horizontal stabilizer, and the associated control surfaces.
   a. Stabilizer—There are horizontal stabilizers and vertical stabilizers. The vertical stabilizer provides stability for the aircraft, preventing side-to-side (yawing) motion of the aircraft's nose. The rudder can be found on the vertical stabilizer (only the rudder moves). The horizontal stabilizer prevents up-and-down, or pitching, motion of the aircraft's nose. The elevator is found on the rear of the horizontal stabilizer.
   b. Stabilator—A single-piece horizontal tail surface on an airplane that pivots around a central hinge point. A stabilator serves the purposes of both the horizontal stabilizer and the elevators.
   c. Elevator—The horizontal, movable primary control surface in the tail section, or empennage, of an airplane. The elevator is hinged to the trailing edge of the fixed horizontal stabilizer. When the elevator moves, it varies the amount of force generated by the tail surface and is thus used to generate and control the pitching motion of the aircraft.
6. Trim is used to adjust the aerodynamic forces on the control surfaces so that the aircraft maintains the set attitude without any control input.

7. Landing gear supports the weight of the aircraft and supports the aircraft during landing.
8. The two types of landing gear configurations are conventional (tail wheel) and tricycle gear.
9. Rudder pedals
10. The powerplant is a complete engine and propeller combination with accessories.
    a. The powerplant can also serve as a source of heat, source for the vacuum system, alternator for the electrical system.
11. Parts of an airplane.

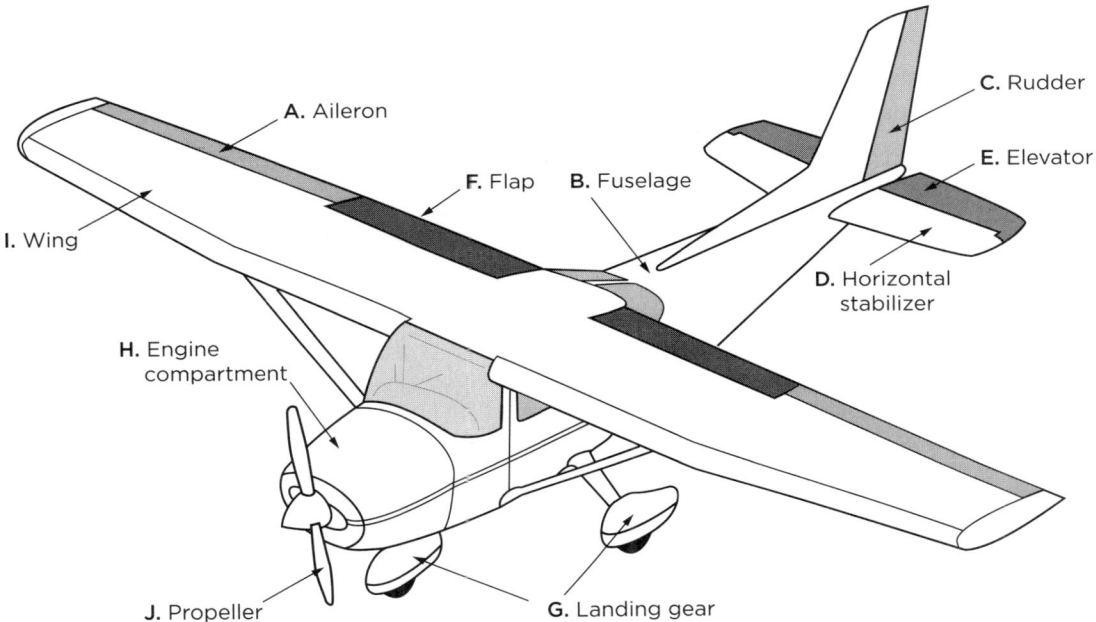

LESSON 2, Activity 1
Aircraft Flight Instruments—Round Dial Cockpit

1. A. Airspeed indicator—A differential pressure gauge that measures the dynamic pressure of the air through which the aircraft is flying. Displays the aircraft's airspeed, typically in knots, to the pilot.

   B. Attitude indicator—The foundation for all instrument flight, this instrument reflects the airplane's attitude in relation to the horizon.

   C. Altimeter—A flight instrument that indicates altitude by sensing pressure changes.

   D. Turn coordinator—A rate gyro that senses both roll and yaw due to the gimbal being canted. Has largely replaced the turn-and-slip indicator in modern aircraft. (The turn-and-slip indicator is a flight instrument consisting of a rate gyro to indicate the rate of yaw and a curved glass inclinometer to indicate the relationship between gravity and centrifugal force. The turn-and-slip indicator indicates the relationship between angle of bank and rate of yaw. Also called a turn-and-bank indicator.)

E. Heading indicator—An instrument which senses airplane movement and displays heading based on a 360° azimuth, with the final zero omitted. The heading indicator, also called a directional gyro (DG), is fundamentally a mechanical instrument designed to facilitate the use of the magnetic compass. The heading indicator is not affected by the forces that make the magnetic compass difficult to interpret.

F. Vertical speed indicator (VSI)—A rate-of-pressure change instrument that gives an indication of any deviation from a constant pressure level. The VSI indicates whether the aircraft is climbing, descending, or in level flight.

G. Magnetic compass—displays the current magnetic heading of the aircraft, *i.e.*, the aircraft's directional orientation relative to the Earth's magnetic field. The magnetic heading is used by the pilot for navigational purposes.

2. These instruments are located on the instrument panel in the aircraft's cockpit.

3. See answers to question 1 above.

LESSON 8

Chapter 2 Exam

1. Straight-and-level flight, turns, climbs, and descents
2. (c) Attitude indicator, altimeter, airspeed indicator
3. (c) 3,040 feet
4. (a) 075
5. (b) Nose of the aircraft is above the horizon
6. (c) The left wing is below the horizon and the right wing is above the horizon
7. (b) Horizontal component of lift
8. (a) Relieve
9. a. Heading indicator
   b. An instrument which senses airplane movement and displays heading based on a 360° azimuth, with the final zero omitted. The heading indicator, also called a directional gyro (DG), is fundamentally a mechanical instrument designed to facilitate the use of the magnetic compass. The heading indicator is not affected by the forces that make the magnetic compass difficult to interpret.
10. a. Altimeter
    b. A flight instrument that indicates altitude by sensing pressure changes.
11. a. Airspeed indicator
    b. A differential pressure gauge that measures the dynamic pressure of the air through which the aircraft is flying. Displays the aircraft's airspeed, typically in knots, to the pilot.
12. a. Attitude indicator
    b. The foundation for all instrument flight, this instrument reflects the airplane's attitude in relation to the horizon.

13. a. Vertical speed indicator (VSI)
    b. A rate-of-pressure change instrument that gives an indication of any deviation from a constant pressure level. The VSI indicates whether the aircraft is climbing, descending, or in level flight.
14. a. Turn coordinator
    b. A rate gyro that senses both roll and yaw due to the gimbal being canted. Has largely replaced the turn-and-slip indicator in modern aircraft.
15. a. Magnetic compass
    b. A device for determining direction measured from magnetic north
16. a. White arc: Flap operating speeds
    b. Green arc: Normal operating speeds
    c. Yellow arc: Caution range/speeds
    d. Red line: Never exceed speed
17. a. aileron
    b. fuselage
    c. rudder
    d. horizontal stabilizer
    e. elevator
    f. flaps
    g. landing gear
    h. engine compartment
    i. wing
    j. propeller
18. a. collective
    b. throttle
    c. cyclic

CHAPTER 3
AIRPORT OPERATIONS

Introduction

STANDARDS & OBJECTIVES

North Dakota Aviation Content Standards (Grades 10–12)
- 3.1.1—Discuss the five legs of a standard traffic pattern.
- 3.1.2—Describe how runway numbers are determined.
- 3.1.3—Recognize various types of airports.
- 3.1.4—Explain the purpose of a displaced threshold.
- 3.1.5—Explain the purpose of a blast pad.
- 3.1.6—Recognize visual aids and their purpose (e.g., signs, lights, and markings).

Physical Science—Next Generation Science Standards (Grades 9–12)
- HS-ETS1-2—Design a solution to a complex real-world problem by breaking it down into smaller, more manageable problems that can be solved through engineering.
- HS-ETS1-3—Evaluate a solution to a complex real-world problem based on prioritized criteria and trade-offs that account for a range of constraints, including cost, safety, reliability, and aesthetics, as well as possible social, cultural, and environmental impacts.

Language Arts—CCSS.ELA-LITERACY.CCRA
- L.1—Demonstrate command of the conventions of standard English grammar and usage when writing or speaking.
- L.2—Demonstrate command of the conventions of standard English capitalization, punctuation, and spelling when writing.
- SL.1—Prepare for and participate effectively in a range of conversations and collaborations with diverse partners, building on others' ideas and expressing their own clearly and persuasively.
- SL.2—Integrate and evaluate information presented in diverse media and formats, including visually, quantitatively, and orally.
- SL.4—Present information, findings, and supporting evidence such that listeners can follow the line of reasoning and the organization, development, and style are appropriate to task, purpose, and audience.
- SL.5—Make strategic use of digital media and visual displays of data to express information and enhance understanding of presentations.

- **W.2**—Write informative/explanatory texts to examine and convey complex ideas and information clearly and accurately through the effective selection, organization, and analysis of content.
- **W.4**—Produce clear and coherent writing in which the development, organization, and style are appropriate to task, purpose, and audience.
- **W.7**—Conduct short as well as more sustained research projects based on focused questions, demonstrating understanding of the subject under investigation.
- **W.8**—Gather relevant information from multiple print and digital sources, assess the credibility and accuracy of each source, and integrate the information while avoiding plagiarism.
- **W.9**—Draw evidence from literary or informational texts to support analysis, reflection, and research.

ESSENTIAL QUESTIONS

- How do the different operations at an airport work together effectively?
- What are the essential features of an airport complex?
- How is safety ensured for those operating on or in the vicinity of an airport?

LESSONS

Lesson	Topic	Student Notebook Activities
Lesson 1	Introduction to Airports	1. Airport Operations Questions 2. Video Guided Notes 3. Summary Prompt
Lesson 2	Airports	1. PHAK Airport Operations Questions
Lesson 3	Marking and Signage	1. Compass Rose Questions 2. Airport Signs and Markings Graphic Organizer 3. Airport Diagrams 4. Runway Layout Activity
Lesson 4	Airport Lighting	1. Airport Lighting Chart 2. Chart Supplement Example 3. Chart Supplement Research 4. Chart Supplement Airport Homework
Lesson 5	Guest Speaker—Operations	1. Double Entry Notes 2. Inquiry Question

Lessons 6 & 7	Airport Design Project—Introductory and Work Days (Days 1 and 2)	1. Building Hong Kong's Airport Notes
		2. Engineering Design Graphic
		3. Design Process Example Graphic Organizer
		4. Airport Design Project Assignment
		  • Assignment Description
		  • Airport Design Planning Guide
		  • Airport Design Grading Checklist
		  • Self-Evaluation Rubric

Lesson 8	Airport Design Project—Presentations (Day 3)	1. Presentation Viewing Graphic Organizer
Lesson 9	Airport Operations Review Study Guide	1. Study Guide Questions
Lesson 10	Review: Airport Operations	1. Chapter Review Notes
Lesson 11	Chapter 3 Exam	1. Article Response and Rubric

LESSON 1

INTRODUCTION TO AIRPORTS

PURPOSE

The purpose of this lesson is to introduce students to the operations of an airport.

ACCOMMODATIONS FOR LEARNING DIFFERENCES

It is important that lessons accommodate the needs of every learner. These lessons may be modified to accommodate your students with learning differences by referring to **www.pacer.org/parent/php/PHP-c267.pdf**.

PREPARATION

- Copy of or streaming access to City in the Sky, Episode 1, "Departure," produced by PBS (52m 59s).[1]

DIRECTIONS

Introductory Activity: Show four pictures of different sizes and kinds of airports to spark conversation. Pose the discussion questions to students in small groups.

- What is an airport?
- Why are they designed so differently?
- What kind of jobs are at an airport?
- What does it take to get a million people off the ground and up in the air?

Students will record their initial ideas in the Student Notebook, Activity 1 (Airport Operations Questions).

Step 1: Watch *City in the Sky,* Episode 1, "Departure."[2] Stop the video every 10–15 minutes during natural scene transitions to allow for active processing. Students will complete Activity 2 (Video Guided Notes) in their Student Notebooks while watching the video and during processing breaks.

Step 2: When the video has finished, students will compare video guided notes, adding any additional information classmates recorded that they did not. The facilitator will monitor the group discussions and prompt thinking to include the most important details about airport operations highlighted in the *Pilot's Handbook of Aeronautical Knowledge*.

Concluding Activity: Students will individually complete Activity 3 (Summary Prompt) in their Student Notebooks: "Explain how an airport facilitates social, economic, scientific and/or cultural exchange/change? They should provide a detailed example for each topic area.

LESSON 2

AIRPORTS

PURPOSE
The purpose of this lesson is to examine airport infrastructure.

ACCOMMODATIONS FOR LEARNING DIFFERENCES
It is important that lessons accommodate the needs of every learner. These lessons may be modified to accommodate your students with learning differences by referring to www.pacer.org/parent/php/PHP-c267.pdf.

PREPARATION
- Student copies of the *Pilot's Handbook of Aeronautical Knowledge* (FAA-H-8083-25)
- FAR/AIM or **eCFR.gov**
- Class copies of Twin Cities sectional chart (or access to sectional online)

DIRECTIONS
Introductory Activity: Display pictures of 3–4 different sized airports: make sure to show an airport with multiple paved runways, an airport with only one paved runway, and another with a grass runway. Ask students to describe the differences and similarities they observe.

Step 1: Students will individually read Chapter 14 of the *Pilot's Handbook of Aeronautical Knowledge*.

Step 2: Students will answer the questions individually on the worksheet in their Student Notebooks under Activity 1 (PHAK Airport Operations Questions). (An answer key is provided at the end of the chapter.) Monitor students as they work individually, answering questions and guiding them to the appropriate sections of the *Pilot's Handbook of Aeronautical Knowledge* (Chapter 14) and *Aeronautical Information Manual* (Chapter 2) as reference and for color images of airport signs and markings.

Step 3: Correct the worksheet together as a class. Display visual representations from Chapter 14 in the *Pilot's Handbook of Aeronautical Knowledge* to further demonstrate and answer each of the worksheet questions. Explain why incorrect answers are incorrect. Clarify student misconceptions and answer questions as necessary.

Concluding Activity: Students will turn and talk to a partner, answering the following inquiry-based question in regard to runways: "Why is it important that each type of runway marking and sign is the same across the world?"

LESSON 3
MARKING AND SIGNAGE

PURPOSE

The purpose of this lesson is to examine markings and signs that provide direction to pilots and assist in airport operations.

ACCOMMODATIONS FOR LEARNING DIFFERENCES

It is important that lessons accommodate the needs of every learner. These lessons may be modified to accommodate your students with learning differences by referring to www.pacer.org/parent/php/PHP-c267.pdf.

PREPARATION

- Use sticky notes to label the classroom with directions, degrees, and headings. For example:
  - N, 180
  - S, 360
  - E, 270
  - W, 90
- Compass rose for each student (printed in the Student Notebook)
- Computers/devices and internet access for students
- Sticky notes

DIRECTIONS

Introductory Activity: Have each student refer to the compass rose printed in Activity 1 (Compass Rose Questions) in their Student Notebooks. You may have them answer the following questions, on the cardinal directions to identify directionality of classroom landmarks, in written form in the Student Notebook or using a digital response system (such as Quizlet or Kahoot).

Have the students gather in the center of the room and then answer the following questions by giving the direction in degrees of each specific object's location in relation to where they are. You may fill in the last three questions with additional objects in your specific classroom.

Example questions:

1. Where is the teacher's desk? _____
2. Where is the projector or smart board? _____
3. Where is the wall clock? _____
4. Where is the garbage can? _____
5. Where is the _____?
6. Where is the _____?
7. Where is the _____?

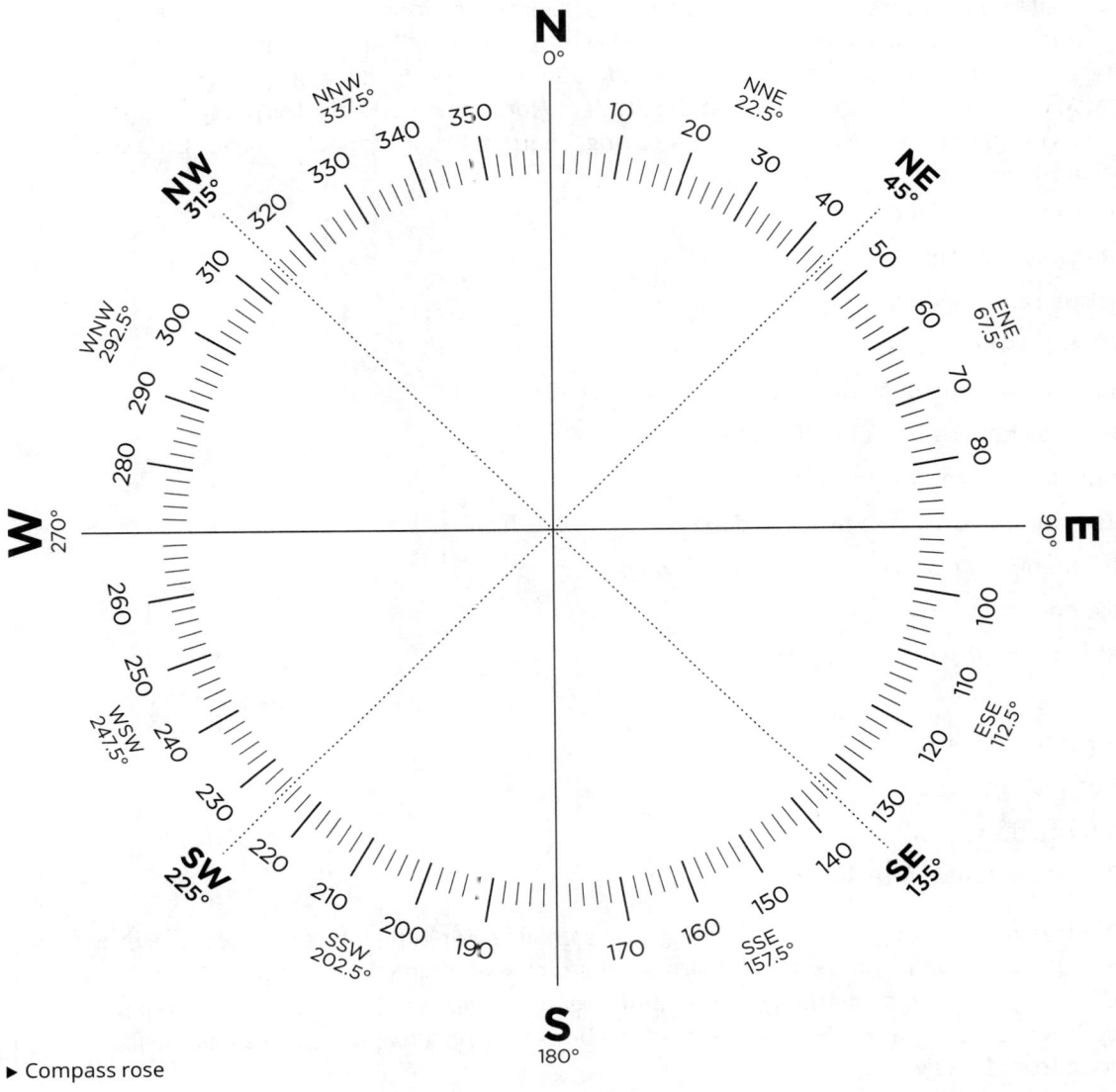

▶ Compass rose

Review responses as a whole class for accuracy or re-teaching. Now that they know the directions, have the students lay out rectangular pieces of paper that represent runways in various configurations and directions.

1. Runway 36 – 18
2. Runway 31 – 13
3. Runway 09 – 27

Runway 36-18 | 36 | | 18 |
Runway 31-13 | 31 | | 13 |
Runway 09-27 | 09 | | 27 |

Step 1: Facilitate an interactive lecture using visual representations and pictures in the presentation that clarifies and demonstrates key concepts from Chapter 14 and Appendix C of the *Pilot's Handbook of Aeronautical Knowledge*. Students will follow along with the facilitator, using the graphic organizer in the Student Notebook, Activity 2 (Airport Signs and Markings Graphic Organizer), completing it during frequent breaks for active processing of the information.

Airport markings and signs:
- Runway threshold
- Displaced threshold
- Runway safety area
- Runway holding position sign
- Runway holding position marking
- Runway designation marking
- Temporarily closed runways and taxiways
- Permanently closed runways and taxiways
- No entry
- Mandatory instruction signs
- Location signs
- Direction signs
- Destination signs
- Information signs
- Runway distance remaining

Step 2: After going through airport markings and signage during the interactive lecture, draw on the board or show an example of an airport diagram, explaining the signage. The student should add signage and or markings in the appropriate locations in the diagrams printed in Activity 3 (Airport Diagrams) in their Student Notebooks. Airport diagrams are available for download from FAA's website.

- Simple example: Aspen, Colorado (KASE)
- More complicated example: Honolulu, Hawaii (PHNL)

Step 3: Assign Activity 4 (Runway Layout Activity) located in the Student Notebook to students to complete for homework.

Concluding Activity: Students will go online to work on the Grand Forks International Airport Signage Trainer created by the University of North Dakota (UND) at **avitmedia.aero.und.edu/airportSignageTrainer/**. Students will put the number of attempts and signs correct from the Airport Signage Trainer on a sticky note with their name and place it on the facilitator's desk as they leave the classroom.

CHAPTER 3 AIRPORT OPERATIONS

LESSON 4
AIRPORT LIGHTING

PURPOSE
The purpose of this lesson is to examine airport lighting that provides information to pilots and assists in airport operations.

ACCOMMODATIONS FOR LEARNING DIFFERENCES
It is important that lessons accommodate the needs of every learner. These lessons may be modified to accommodate your students with learning differences by referring to www.pacer.org/parent/php/PHP-c267.pdf.

PREPARATION
- Student Notebook two-column notes for interactive lecture
- Flashlight
- Access to *Chart Supplements* (online through the FAA's website, or paper copies)
- Computers/devices and internet access for students (if applicable)

DIRECTIONS
Before the lesson begins, review the homework from Lesson 3 with students, checking for accuracy and correcting misconceptions.

Introductory Activity: Turn off the lights in the class and ask the students to imagine that they are piloting an aircraft and that they must land on a runway located at the front of the classroom. Ask them what would help them with this task.

Step 1: Facilitate an interactive lecture using visual representations and pictures in the presentation that clarify and demonstrate key concepts from Chapter 14 of the *Pilot's Handbook of Aeronautical Knowledge* about airport lighting, including various types and how to turn them on. As you present this material, the students will fill in the Airport Lighting Chart in Activity 1 in their Student Notebooks. Types of lighting covered should include:

- Airport beacons
- Approach lighting systems
- Visual glideslope indicators
- Runway lighting
- Taxiway lighting
- Obstruction lighting
- New lighting technologies

Note: There are many videos and pictures available online that can be used for this lesson.

Step 2: Display the Park Rapids Municipal Airport, Minnesota (KPKD) *Chart Supplement* as an example. (It is provided in the Facilitator Information at the end of this lesson.) Refer to the Airport/Facility Directory Legend in the *Chart Supplement* or display the legend in class to demonstrate where to find specific airport information. Identify the following information while the students label the *Chart Supplement* example in Activity 2 in the Student Notebook.

1. Pilot-controlled or air traffic-controlled lighting
2. Frequency for pilot-controlled lighting
3. Intensity of pilot-controlled lighting
4. Visual slope indicators at the airport
5. Approach lighting systems at the airport
6. Location of the airport beacon

While looking at the *Chart Supplement*, show the students all of the other information they can find on that document, such as:

- Field elevation
- Time zones
- Runway information
- Airport remarks
- Weather reporting systems

Step 3: Have the students pick a local airport and look it up in the *Chart Supplements* (online through FAA's Aeronautical Information Services Digital Products, or on paper copies, if applicable). The students will then be able to answer the questions about their chosen airport's lighting in Activity 3 (Chart Supplement Research) in their Student Notebooks.

Step 4: Assign Activity 4 (Chart Supplement Airport Homework) from the Student Notebook for homework. (An answer key is provided at the end of the chapter.)

Concluding Activity: Turn the lights off and have the students again imagine that they are piloting an aircraft and they have to land on a runway that is at the front of the class room. Ask them the same question from the introduction: what would help them with this task? Turn the lights back on and have students list (on an exit slip) the specific types of lighting that they would want to have at an airport to land at night.

FACILITATOR INFORMATION

Chart Supplement Airport Homework

(An answer key is provided at the end of the chapter.)

Reference Anoka County Airport (KANE) in the North Central U.S. *Chart Supplement* for questions 1–4.

1. What is the field elevation?
2. What is the traffic pattern altitude?
3. What is runway 09-27 light intensity?
4. What is the frequency to turn on the lights?

Reference Brainerd Lakes Regional Airport (KBRD) it in the North Central *U.S. Chart Supplement* for questions 5–9.

5. What is the field elevation?
6. What is the traffic pattern altitude?
7. What is runway 05-23 light intensity?
8. What is the frequency to turn on the lights?
9. Is runway 05 left or right traffic?

Reference West Fargo Municipal Airport (D54) in the North Central *U.S. Chart Supplement* for questions 10–17.

10. What is the field elevation for West Fargo, ND (D54)?
11. Runway 18 at D54 has what direction of traffic pattern?
    a. Standard
    b. Non-standard
12. Runway 36 at D54 has what direction of traffic pattern?
    a. Standard
    b. Non-standard
13. What is the width and length of runway 18-36?
14. What is the traffic pattern altitude?
15. What is the CTAF frequency?
16. What type of pilot-controlled lighting does runway 18 have?
17. How many clicks will turn on the lighting for runway 18?

Chart Supplement for Park Rapids, Minnesota (KPKD)

PARK RAPIDS MUNI–KONSHOK FLD (PKD)(KPKD) 2 S UTC–6(–5DT) N46°54.07′ W95°04.39′ **TWIN CITIES** H–2J, L–14H IAP
 1445 B NOTAM FILE PKD
 RWY 13–31: H5497X100 (ASPH) S–20, D–36 HIRL
  RWY 13: REIL. PAPI(P4L)—GA 3.0º TCH 48′.
  RWY 31: MALSR. PAPI(P4L)—GA 3.0º TCH 48′.
 RWY 18–36: H3500X75 (ASPH)   MIRL
  RWY 18: REIL. PAPI(P4L)—GA 3.0º TCH 40′.
  RWY 36: REIL. PAPI(P4R)—GA 3.0º TCH 40′.
 SERVICE: S4 FUEL 100LL, JET A LGT HIRL Rwy 13–31 low intst SS–SR; to incr intst & ACTIVATE MIRL Rwy 18–36; REIL Rwys 13, 18 & 36; PAPI Rwys 13, 31, 18 & 36; MALSR Rwy 31—CTAF.
 AIRPORT REMARKS: Attended Mon–Fri 1400–2300Z‡. Call 218–237–8528 for svc after hrs. Fuel: 100LL avbl 24 hrs with credit card. Rwy 13–31 markings faded.
 AIRPORT MANAGER: 218-237-2713
 WEATHER DATA SOURCES: ASOS 110.6 PKD (218) 732–0920.
 COMMUNICATIONS: CTAF/UNICOM 123.0
  RCO 122.1R 110.6T (PRINCETON RADIO)
 ®MINNEAPOLIS CENTER APP/DEP CON 134.75
 RADIO AIDS TO NAVIGATION: NOTAM FILE PKD.
  (L) VOR/DME 110.6 PKD Chan 43 N46°53.89′ W95°04.25′ at fld. 1441/4E. ASOS
  SPIDA NDB (LOMW) 269 PK N46°50.04′ W94°58.53′ 311º 5.7 NM to fld. 1413/4E.
  ILS 110.9 I–PKD Rwy 31. Class IC. LOM SPIDA NDB.

(FAA)

LESSON 5

GUEST SPEAKER—OPERATIONS

PURPOSE

The purpose of this lesson is to introduce students to real-world life experiences in airport operations and career opportunities in the aviation industry.

ACCOMMODATIONS FOR LEARNING DIFFERENCES

It is important that lessons accommodate the needs of every learner. These lessons may be modified to accommodate your students with learning differences by referring to **www.pacer.org/parent/php/PHP-c267.pdf**.

PREPARATION

- Make arrangements for a guest speaker, such as an airport manager, civil engineer who works with airport construction, or someone who works in airport operations.
- Logistics/preparation for guest speaker: Send inquiry questions (see page 6), double entry notes worksheet (Activity 1 in Student Notebook), and airport design project instructions and rubric in advance.
- Ask the guest speaker to present dressed for their profession (e.g., pilot uniform, flight suit, military uniform); this will stimulate curiosity and questions from students.

DIRECTIONS

Introductory Activity: Introduce the presenter to the class. Choose one or two things that you truly admire about the speaker to share. The more specific, the better. Emphasize the importance of their role in aviation to establish credibility and interest.

Step 1: Have the speaker give their prepared presentation.

Step 2: While the speaker is presenting, students will actively process using the Double Entry Notes in Activity 1 in the Student Notebook. Allow students to think of and ask the speaker any additional questions.

- Be sure to highlight key issues about airport operations investigated by the students.
- Direct the conversation to things that students may be interested in.
- Make explicit connections to the airport design project (Lessons 6–8).

Step 3: Ask the students and the speaker if there are any last questions or issues. Thank the guest speaker for his/her time.

Concluding Activity: Students will compare information from their Double Entry Notes graphic organizers with a partner. Next, students will complete the summary prompt in Activity 2 (Inquiry Question) to answer at least one inquiry question. (See list of inquiry questions in the Student Notebook and at the beginning of this guide on page 6). Collect these when completed, or have students return them the next class period.

LESSONS 6 AND 7

AIRPORT DESIGN PROJECT—INTRODUCTORY AND WORK DAYS (DAYS 1 AND 2)

PURPOSE

The purpose of this lesson is to demonstrate knowledge of airport operations and the functions of various airport factors (i.e., signage, lights, markings, design, etc.).

ACCOMMODATIONS FOR LEARNING DIFFERENCES

It is important that lessons accommodate the needs of every learner. These lessons may be modified to accommodate your students with learning differences by referring to www.pacer.org/parent/php/PHP-c267.pdf.

PREPARATION

- Technology to display examples for students
- Airport Design Project Assignment Description and Grading Checklist (from Student Notebook)
- Poster board for each group
- Materials for creating the airport (rulers, colored tape, access to print pictures, words and symbols, markers, colored paper, etc.)

DIRECTIONS

In these lessons, the facilitator will introduce the Airport Design Project assignment to students. Students will also be introduced to the Engineering Design Process and will apply that process to their airport designs.

Introductory Activity: Display pictures of recent innovations in airport design. Ask students how these innovations will affect the future of aviation.

Step 1: Show the Discovery Channel video *Extreme Engineering*, Season 1, Episode 6, "Building Hong Kong's Airport" (44 min) (available online through various platforms/outlets).[3] While watching the video, students should record answers to the questions about the challenges to the engineering design process in their Student Notebooks under Activity 1 (Building Hong Kong's Airport Notes).

Step 2: Using the graphic found in the Student Notebook Activity 2 (Engineering Design Graphic), review the engineering design process. Consider finding a video that explains the engineering design process to show the class.

Step 3: Model the engineering design process for students by using a familiar topic, such as making a cake. In the Student Notebook, the third column of the Design Process Example Graphic Organizer (Activity 3) is blank. To facilitate a discussion, potential answers are shared below.

THE DESIGN PROCESS EXAMPLE Making a cake		
ASK	What is the problem? What do you already know? What are the limits or controls of the task?	I am hosting a birthday party and need to make a cake. I have having 20 people over. The birthday boy likes chocolate cake.
IMAGINE	What are some solutions to the problem? Research. Brainstorm.	Need access to a kitchen, ingredients, measuring devices, and a cake pan. Must be able to follow directions.
PLAN	Draw a diagram. What supplies will you need? Who will do the jobs? Make a list of the steps you will take.	Make a list of all the items required for the recipe and for the baking process. Write out the steps of the recipe.
CREATE	Follow your plan. Collaborate with your team. Work. Test your design.	Bake the cake!
IMPROVE	Learn from mistakes. Make your design better. Test it again and redesign.	Did it turn out? What was right or wrong about the result? What changes will you make before you bake another cake?
PRESENT	Share your design.	Bake another cake; share it with friends and family.

Step 4: To familiarize students with the assignment and explain expected levels of performance, review the following items with students (all documents are found under Activity 4 [Airport Design Project Assignment] in the Student Notebook):

- Airport Design Project—Assignment Description
- Airport Design Planning Guide
  > Have students complete the third column as they apply the engineering design process to their project.
- Airport Design Grading Checklist
  > Students will use this to peer-evaluate projects as groups present in Lesson 8.
- Self-Evaluation Rubric
  > This is the rubric you will use to evaluate students' design projects and which students will use for self-evaluation.

Be sure to take time to explain how this project applies the engineering design process.

Step 5: Monitor students as they begin working on their airport design. Correct any misconceptions or incorrect application as students work. They have the rest of the class period and the next to work on it.

Concluding Activity: Use a few minutes at the end of the class for students to self-evaluate their progress on completing the project. Ask students to plan what tasks they will complete during the following work times: homework and during the next class period.

LESSON 8

AIRPORT DESIGN PROJECT—PRESENTATIONS (DAY 3)

PURPOSE
The purpose of this lesson is to demonstrate knowledge of airport operations and the functions of various airport factors (i.e., signage, lights, markings, design, etc.) and to apply language arts literacy skills.

ACCOMMODATIONS FOR LEARNING DIFFERENCES
It is important that lessons accommodate the needs of every learner. These lessons may be modified to accommodate your students with learning differences by referring to **www.pacer.org/parent/php/PHP-c267.pdf**.

PREPARATION
- Technology required for students to share their airport designs
- Copies of the assignment rubrics for facilitator, peer, and self-evaluation (from Lessons 6 and 7).

DIRECTIONS

Introductory Activity: Have the students share with the class what they thought was the most interesting part of this airport design project.

Step 1: Student groups will present their airport design and explain why they designed the airport the way they did.

Step 2: Groups watching the presentations will record information in their Student Notebooks in Activity 1 (Presentation Viewing Graphic Organizer) while the facilitator notes feedback and evaluation on the rubric. Once all presenters are done, the students should rank the airport designs from best to least. The facilitator can look at all of the results and then provide the group with the best airport design an appropriate reward (e.g., extra credit, additional simulator time).

Concluding Activity: Students will peer-evaluate projects as they are presented using copies of the Airport Design Grading Checklist and self-evaluate their own project using the Self-Evaluation Rubric, found in the Student Notebook in Lessons 6 and 7. Make as many copies as necessary.

FACILITATOR INFORMATION

AIRPORT DESIGN GRADING CHECKLIST

Group Members: _____

Engineering Design Process	Checklist	Comments
Ask: Carefully considers prior knowledge, limits, and controls that impact the project outcome.	/5	
Imagine: Generate and explore multiple ideas and options for airport design. Consideration is given to recent innovations and technological advances in aviation.	/5	
Plan: Critically evaluate each of the design requirements. Work to generate different design possibilities and keep record of plans and revisions.	/5	
Create: Creatively and responsibly uses materials and resources	/5	
Improve: Self-critique the prototype and analyze the design for accuracy and areas for improvement	/5	

Airport Design Requirements	Checklist	Comments
Location, name, and identifier (unique to location) of airport are clearly marked	/5	
1 paved runway identified and correctly marked	/5	
1 grass runway identified and correctly marked	/5	
2 major taxiways with two connections at the ends and one midpoint, correctly marked	/5	
Ramp with FBO correctly marked	/5	
Segmented circle correctly marked	/5	
Greenspace (e.g., trees/landscape)	/5	
Runway End Identifier Lights (REILS)	/5	
Airport beacon	/5	

Chart Supplement Insert Requirements	Checklist	Comments
Organization/accuracy	/5	
Pilot controlled lighting	/5	
CTAF frequency (HIRL, MIRL or LIRL)	/5	
Field elevation	/5	
Traffic pattern altitude	/5	
Runway dimensions	/5	
Runway surface	/5	

Presentation Requirements	Checklist	Comments
Explanation of airport design is presented clearly and logically so the audience can follow your line of reasoning.	/5	
While presenting, keep eye contact with the audience and speak in a clear, precise manner.	/5	
Answer audience questions accurately.	/5	
Total	/120	

SELF-EVALUATION RUBRIC

Student's name: _____ Date: _____

Project: _____ Average: _____ out of 4

KEY 1 = **Beginning**—experiences difficulty even with teacher prompting 2 = **Developing**—inconsistent and/or requires teacher prompting 3 = **Accomplished**—consistent with little or no teacher prompting 4 = **Exemplary**—consistent and independent	Student Evaluation	Teacher Evaluation
Ask		
Carefully consider the investigation guidelines.		
Thoughtfully discuss multiple relevant and interesting questions for further exploration.		
Determine multiple team or individual goals in response to your questions.		
Imagine		
Without teacher guidance, generate and explore numerous ideas, responses, and solutions.		
Independently generate clever, unique, or unusual ideas.		
Work with teammates to imagine many different possible solutions to the team's questions and the design challenge.		
Independently perceive and accept the team's many differing positions and points of view.		
Plan		
Critically evaluate the purpose of every detail of the design.		
Keep detailed records and sketches of design possibilities, plans, and revisions.		
Conduct research and use prior knowledge as a foundation for prototype plans		
Create		
Persevere to create a functioning prototype.		
Creatively and responsibly use materials and resources.		
Improve		
Without teacher guidance, self-critique the prototype and analyze all design flaws.		
Suggest multiple solutions to problems, or multiple ways to improve the efficiency or quality of the prototype.		

CHAPTER 3 AIRPORT OPERATIONS

LESSON 9

AIRPORT OPERATIONS REVIEW STUDY GUIDE

PURPOSE

The purpose of this lesson is to synthesize information and assess student knowledge of airport operations.

ACCOMMODATIONS FOR LEARNING DIFFERENCES

It is important that lessons accommodate the needs of every learner. These lessons may be modified to accommodate your students with learning differences by referring to www.pacer.org/parent/php/PHP-c267.pdf.

PREPARATION

- Copies of the Airport Design Grading Checklist (from Lesson 8) for peer and self-evaluation
- Student copies of the *Pilot's Handbook of Aeronautical Knowledge* (FAA-H-8083-25)
- Access to *Chart Supplements* (online through the FAA's website, or paper copies)
- Previous Chapter 3 graded assignments

DIRECTIONS

Introductory Activity: Begin the class by reviewing the rubric for the airport design project. Students will turn and talk to a partner, explaining what a project that meets expectations would contain.

Step 1: Remaining groups will present their airport design project. Students will engage in peer-evaluation and self-evaluation using the rubric in the Student Notebook. If this requires additional time, Step 2 can be moved to Lesson 10.

Step 2: Arrange students into facilitator-selected pairs or triads. Students will work together to share initial answers (from what they learned, without using resources) to the questions listed in Activity 1 (Study Guide Questions) in their Student Notebooks. This activity is completed without referring to books or other resources. Each student records the answers on their own study guide. The facilitator will monitor student work, noting common areas of misunderstanding or information that requires re-teaching to the whole class. (An answer key is provided at the end of the chapter.)

Concluding Activity: There is no formal summary activity. Students will work to complete the Chapter 3 study guide questions in preparation for the exam in Lesson 11.

CHAPTER 3 AIRPORT OPERATIONS

LESSON 10

REVIEW: AIRPORT OPERATIONS

PURPOSE
The purpose of this lesson is to synthesize information and assess student knowledge of airport operations.

ACCOMMODATIONS FOR LEARNING DIFFERENCES
It is important that lessons accommodate the needs of every learner. These lessons may be modified to accommodate your students with learning differences by referring to **www.pacer.org/parent/php/PHP-c267.pdf**.

PREPARATION
- Student copies of the *Pilot's Handbook of Aeronautical Knowledge* (FAA-H-8083-25)

DIRECTIONS

Introductory Activity: Students will watch the short news clip "Air traffic congestion lengthens flight times" (CNBC Nightly Business Report) about how airline operations are impacted by air traffic congestion.[4] Lead a short discussion about the video based on the inquiry question: "How does the airport impact social, economic, scientific, and/or cultural factors?"

Step 1: Arrange students into facilitator-selected pairs or triads. Students will work to supplement the group's initial responses from the study guide completed in the previous lesson. They will find the correct answers to the questions by utilizing their aviation resources: *Pilot's Handbook of Aeronautical Knowledge*, FAA regulations and websites, class notes, past assignments, and other key resources for more information.

Step 2: Review correct answers with the whole class to ensure accuracy in answers before ending class for the day and in preparation for the exam that occurs in the next lesson.

Concluding Activity: Explain the structure and expectations for the exam in the next lesson (number of questions, format, and what to do after the exam).

CHAPTER 3 AIRPORT OPERATIONS

LESSON 11

CHAPTER 3 EXAM

PURPOSE

The purpose of this lesson is to assess student knowledge of airport operations.

ACCOMMODATIONS FOR LEARNING DIFFERENCES

It is important that lessons accommodate the needs of every learner. These lessons may be modified to accommodate your students with learning differences by referring to **www.pacer.org/parent/php/PHP-c267.pdf**.

PREPARATION

- Exam copies
- Article assigned to class, "Should passengers pay extra if they are overweight?" from **news.com.au**[5]
- Computer/device access for each student or paper copies of the article and questions
- Response writing rubric (in Student Notebook)

DIRECTIONS

Introductory Activity: Re-engage the students on aviation operations by sharing a relevant occurrence about weight and balance and performance close to the date of the exam from the website This Day in Aviation (**www.thisdayinaviation.com**). Display relevant pictures as you share the story. Have students turn and talk with a partner about what impact this historical event had on modern day aviation.

Provide instructions on what students are to do after the exam before it commences.

Step 1: Students will complete the Chapter 3 Exam on Airport Operations. Sample questions are included under Facilitator Information at end of the lesson. (An answer key is provided at the end of the chapter.)

Step 2: When students have turned in the exam, make the **news.com.au** article "Should passengers pay extra if they are overweight?" available to them to read independently.[6] In Activity 1 (Article Response and Rubric) in the Student Notebook, students will write a two-paragraph response that includes a summary and reflection on the prompts below:

"How does the importance of weight and balance technology in conducting safe and efficient flight impact aircraft passengers?"

"What is your opinion: Should passengers pay for two seats if they're overweight or naturally large or even be forced to sit in 'fat zones' so airlines can work out a more exact weight and balance of aircraft and in turn cut operating costs?"

The two-paragraph response will be graded using the rubric provided in the Student Notebook.

Concluding Activity: There is no formal summary activity. Students will work independently to finish the exam at different times and begin reading the provided article as an introductory activity to Chapter 4 on weight and balance and performance.

The facilitator may decide to review the correct answers to address incorrect responses and/or misconceptions prior to beginning Chapter 4.

FACILITATOR INFORMATION
Chapter 3 Exam: Airport Operations

(This exam is available in the online Instructor Resources in a format ready for use in the classroom. An answer key is provided at the end of the chapter.)

Read each question carefully. There is only one correct answer for each question.

1. The numbers 8 and 26 on the approach ends of a runway indicate that the runway is orientated approximately
    a. 008 and 026 degrees true
    b. 080 and 260 degrees true
    c. 008 and 026 degrees magnetic
    d. 080 and 260 degrees magnetic

2. What color are taxiway edge lights?
    a. White
    b. Amber
    c. Red
    d. Blue

3. What color are taxiway markings?
    a. White
    b. Yellow
    c. Blue
    d. Red

4. What color are runway markings?
    a. White
    b. Yellow
    c. Red
    d. Blue

5. Taxiways are labeled with numbers, for example: "Taxiway 32"
    a. True
    b. False

6. An airport's rotating beacon operated during daylight hours indicates which of the following?
   a. There are obstructions on the airport.
   b. The weather at the airport is below basic VFR weather minimums.
   c. The air traffic control tower is not in operation.
   d. The beacon is never on during the daylight hours.

7. A land and hold short clearance means that you are cleared to land but must stop before crossing the intersecting runway.
   a. True
   b. False

8. Draw in the dashed hold short lines on the correct side in the drawing below.

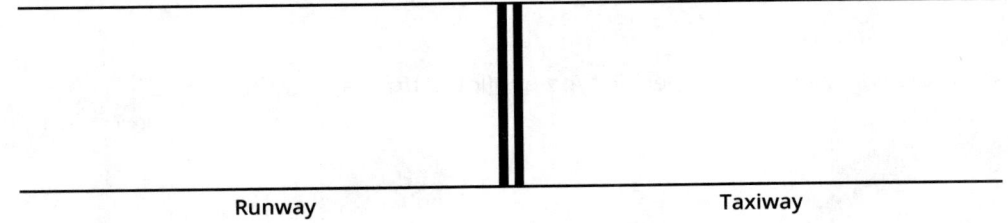

9. You are landing on a runway with a VASI. What is the indication for "above glide path"?
   a. White over white
   b. Red over white
   c. Red over red
   d. None of the above (the lights are all in a single row)

You may use the North Central *Chart Supplement* for the following questions.

10. What is the field elevation for Bismarck Municipal Airport (KBIS) in North Dakota?

11. Runway 31 at KBIS has what direction of traffic pattern?
    a. Standard
    b. Non-Standard

12. What is the width and length of runway 31 at KBIS?

13. What is the traffic pattern altitude for Park Rapids, MN (KPKD)?

14. What is the CTAF frequency for Park Rapids?

15. How high above the traffic pattern altitude should you be when overflying the airport to check on the wind sock?
    a. 1,000 feet
    b. 500 feet

For questions 16–19: You are conducting a night flight to Bottineau Municipal Airport, North Dakota (D09). The winds are 190 at 10 knots. It is 10:00 p.m.

16. What runway are you planning on landing on at Bottineau?
    a. 03
    b. 13
    c. 21
    d. 31

17. What frequency do you activate the pilot-controlled lighting on at D09?
    a. 119.6
    b. 122.8
    c. 125.875
    d. 127.6

18. How many clicks will activate the specific type of pilot-controlled lighting at D09?
    a. 3
    b. 5
    c. 7
    d. 9

19. What is the traffic pattern altitude for D09?
    a. 2,480
    b. 2,580
    c. 2,680
    d. 2,780

ANSWER KEYS
CHAPTER 3

LESSON 2, Activity 1
PHAK Airport Operations Questions (Student Notebook)

1. Federal Aviation Regulations, enforced by the Federal Aviation Administration
2. whole numbers; white
3. magnetic
4. 16
5. 04
6. the runway heading
7. magnetic compass, heading indicator
8. three five
9. zero four
10. Runways should appear as shown:

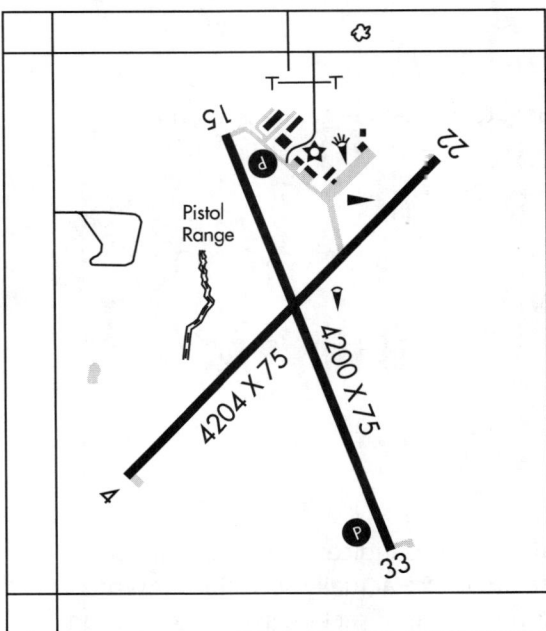

11. white
12. green
13. red

14. red; end
15. in-runway
16. white
17. Letters (e.g., A, B, C)
18. Airport diagram
19. Yellow
20. yellow, solid
21. black
22. black
23. blue; seen from all directions
24. green
25. holding position
26. taxiway side
27. Yes
28. Runway side
29. No
30. the hold short line
31. Common Traffic Advisory Frequency
32. white; red
33. Runway 31
34. is not (this is a blast pad)
35. displaced threshold; this can be used for taxiing, takeoff, emergency operations. It cannot be used for landing.
36. indicate it is night time
37. white; green
38. white; white; green
39. No
40. Yes

LESSON 3, Activity 3
Airport Diagrams (Student Notebook)

1. The student should place the three types of airport signs indicated (see examples in Aspen airport diagram on the next page). Note: there are actually six different types of airport signs: mandatory instruction signs, location signs, direction signs, destination signs, information signs, and runway distance remaining signs. (Reference *AIM* ¶2-3-7–¶2-3-13)

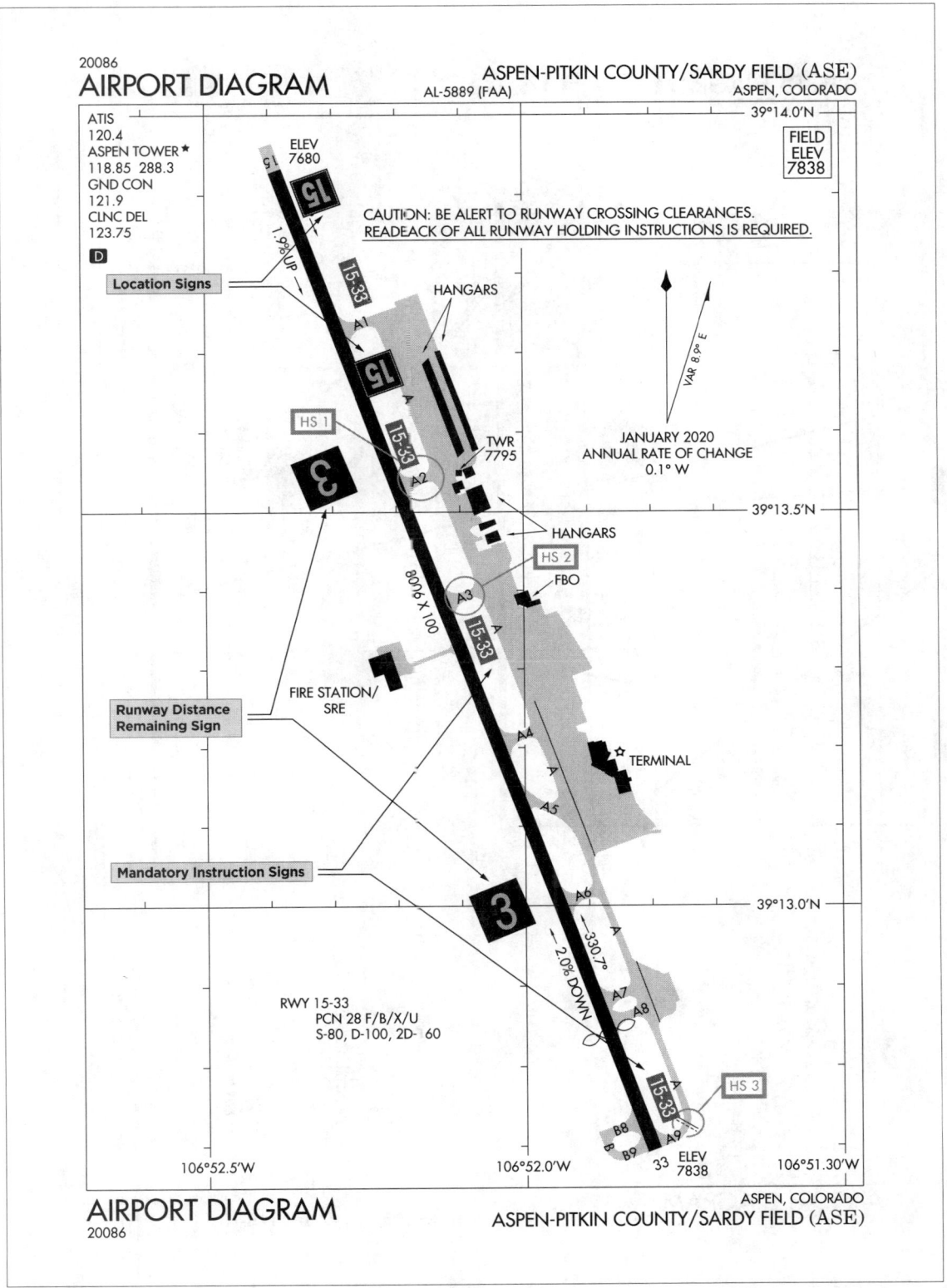

▶ Airport diagram for Aspen-Pitkin County Airport (KASE). *(FAA)*

CHAPTER 3 Answer Keys / Facilitator Guide

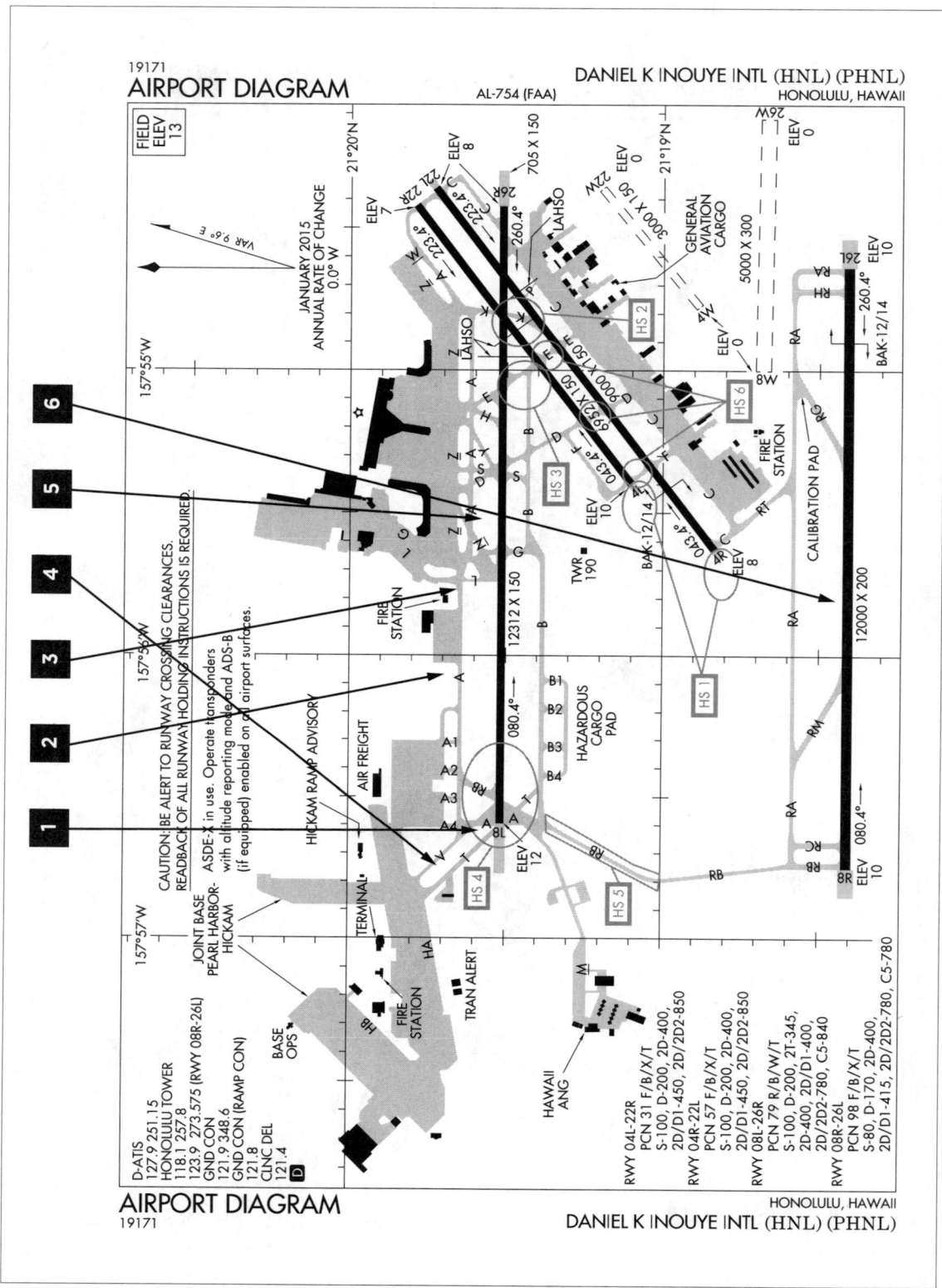

▶ Airport diagram for Daniel K. Inouye International Airport (PHNL) in Honolulu, Hawaii. *(FAA)*

2. See the airport diagram for Daniel K. Inouye International Airport (PHNL) on the previous page for possible locations of the fo lowing signs. You may also refer to the *Aeronautical Information Manual* (AIM), ¶2-3-7–¶2-3-13, for details about these signs and their possible locations.

   1. Mandatory instruction sign
   2. Location sign
   3. Direction sign
   4. Destination sign
   5. Information sign
   6. Runway distance remaining sign

LESSON 4, Activity 4
Chart Supplement Airport Homework (Student Notebook)

1. 912 feet
2. 1,912 feet
3. High intensity
4. 132.4
5. 1,232 feet
6. 2,232 feet
7. High intensity
8. 122.7
9. Left
10. 896 feet
11. (b) Non-standard
12. (a) Standard
13. 3,300 feet (length) × 50 feet (width)
14. 1,896 feet
15. 122.7
16. Low Intensity
17. 3 clicks

LESSON 9, Activity 1
Study Guide Questions (Student Notebook)

1. **Departure (Upwind)**—you should continue on the departure leg of the traffic pattern until you are past the departure end of the runway and within 300 feet of traffic pattern altitude.

   Crosswind—you should be completing your climb to traffic pattern altitude and planning for your downwind leg.

   Downwind—you should be level, and at midfield downwind you need to start preparing for the landing. Abeam your touchdown point, you should pull some power out, add the first notch of flaps (depending on weather/wind), and begin a stabilized descent. When 45 degrees from the approach end of the runway, begin your turn onto the base leg.

   Base leg—add second notch of flaps and continue your stabilized descent. Your base to final turn should be made no closer than ¼ mile from the runway.

   Final—add remaining flaps and continue your stabilized approach to the runway.

   Entry Leg—Entering into the traffic pattern (1) should be made while at traffic pattern altitude at the midfield downwind point on a 45-degree angle or as instructed by ATC.

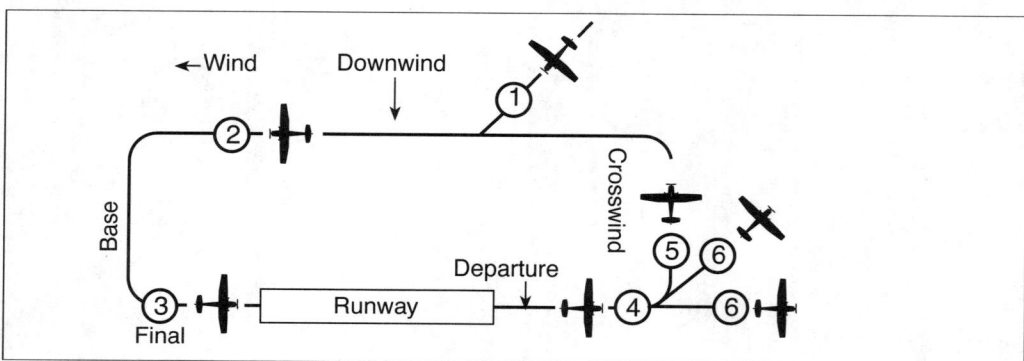

Key to traffic pattern operations

1. Enter pattern in level flight, abeam the midpoint of the runway, at pattern altitude.
2. Maintain pattern altitude until abeam approach end of the landing runway on downwind leg.
3. Complete turn to final at least 1/4 mile from the runway.
4. Continue straight ahead until beyond departure end of runway.
5. If remaining in the traffic pattern, commence turn to crosswind leg beyond the departure end of the runway within 300 feet of pattern altitude.
6. If departing the traffic pattern, continue straight out, or exit with a 45 degree turn (to the left when in a left-hand traffic pattern) beyond the departure end of the runway, after reaching pattern altitude.

▶ Standard left-hand traffic pattern. *(Adapted from FAA FAR/AIM)*

2. Left
3. 1,000 feet
4. Common Traffic Advisory Frequency
5. 1,500 feet
6. (a) Standard

7. Width 100 feet, length 6,502 feet
8. 2,500 feet
9. Runway 22
10. 123.0
11. (b) 500 feet
12. HIRL (high intensity runway lights)
13. 7 clicks
14. The painted runway marking located at the hold-short point between taxiways and runways.
15. The solid line is the taxiway side and the dashed line is the runway side.
16. Taxi and take off
17. Direction signs: taxiway direction, runway exit, outbound destination, inbound destination
18. Location sign: taxiway location and runway location
19. Runway hold position, runway intersection, runway approach end
20. If weather conditions are less than VFR.
21. White and green
22. White, white, and green
23. You are on glide path.
24. You are too high.
25. Runway end identifier lights
    a. White
26. Blue
27. White
28. Into the wind
    a. We want air to flow over the wings, creating more lift.
29. Into the wind
    a. If landing with a tailwind, the wind will push the aircraft further down the runway.
30. If too slow, the aircraft will not have enough lift to support the weight of the aircraft and then it will stall or settle back down to the ground.
31. If the speed is too slow, the aircraft might stall and there may not be sufficient altitude to recover. If the speed is too fast, the aircraft may overshoot the landing spot on the runway.
32. V_X is best angle-of-climb speed. The airspeed at which an airplane gains the greatest amount of altitude in a given distance. It is used during a short-field takeoff to clear an obstacle.
33. V_Y is best rate-of-climb speed. This airspeed provides the most altitude gain in a given period of time.

LESSON 11
Chapter 3 Exam

1. (d) 080 and 260 degrees magnetic
2. (d) Blue
3. (b) Yellow
4. (a) White
5. (b) False
6. (b) The weather at the airport is below basic VFR weather minimums.
7. (a) True
8.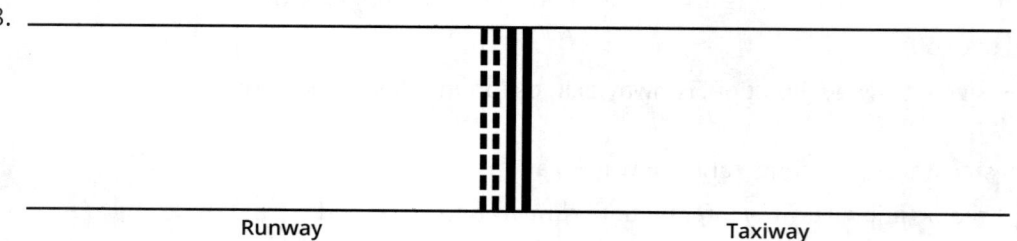
9. (a) White over white
10. 1,661 feet
11. (a) Standard
12. 8,794 feet (length) × 150 feet (width)
13. 2,445 feet
14. 123.0
15. (b) 500 feet
16. (b) 13
17. (b) 122.8
18. (b) 5 clicks
19. (c) 2,680 feet

CHAPTER 4
WEIGHT & BALANCE AND PERFORMANCE

Introduction

STANDARDS & OBJECTIVES
North Dakota Aviation Content Standards (Grades 10–12)
- **2.4.1**—Define weight and balance terms (e.g., center of gravity, basic empty, weight and useful load).
- **2.4.2**—Identify the methods of calculating weight and balance.
- **2.4.3**—Explain the effects of weight on aircraft performance.
- **2.4.4**—Explain the effects of forward/aft center of gravity on aircraft performance.
- **A.2.4.4**—Explain the effects of weight on aircraft performance, takeoff, climb, cruise and landing.
- **2.4.5**—Determine the center of gravity using the computation method.

Note: Standards beginning with "A" indicate the objectives align with but do not exactly match the identified ND Aviation Standards.

Science—Next Generation Science Standards (Grades 9–12)
- **HS-PS2-1**—Analyze data to support the claim that Newton's second law of motion describes the mathematical relationship among the net force on a macroscopic object, its mass, and its acceleration.
- **HS-ETS1-3**—Evaluate a solution to a complex real-world problem based on prioritized criteria and trade-offs that account for a range of constraints, including cost, safety, reliability, and aesthetics, as well as possible social, cultural, and environmental impacts.

Math—CCSS.MATH.CONTENT (Grades 10–12)
- **HS.N-Q.1**—Use units as a way to understand problems and to guide the solution of multi-step problems; choose and interpret units consistently in formulas; choose and interpret the scale and the origin in graphs and data displays.
- **HS.N-Q.2**—Define appropriate quantities for the purpose of descriptive modeling
- **HS.N-Q.3**—Choose a level of accuracy appropriate to limitations on measurement when reporting quantities.
- **HS.A-SSE.1**—Interpret expressions that represent a quantity in terms of its context
- **HS.A-CED.1**—Create equations and inequalities in one variable and use them to solve problems.
- **MP.2**—Reason abstractly and quantitatively.

Language Arts—CCSS.ELA-LITERACY.CCRA

- **L.1**—Demonstrate command of the conventions of standard English grammar and usage when writing or speaking.
- **L.2**—Demonstrate command of the conventions of standard English capitalization, punctuation, and spelling when writing.
- **SL.1**—Prepare for and participate effectively in a range of conversations and collaborations with diverse partners, building on others' ideas and expressing their own clearly and persuasively.
- **SL.2**—Integrate and evaluate information presented in diverse media and formats, including visually, quantitatively, and orally.
- **SL.4**—Present information, findings, and supporting evidence such that listeners can follow the line of reasoning and the organization, development, and style are appropriate to task, purpose, and audience.
- **SL.5**—Make strategic use of digital media and visual displays of data to express information and enhance understanding of presentations.
- **W.2**—Write informative/explanatory texts to examine and convey complex ideas and information clearly and accurately through the effective selection, organization, and analysis of content.
- **W.4**—Produce clear and coherent writing in which the development, organization, and style are appropriate to task, purpose, and audience.
- **W.7**—Conduct short as well as more sustained research projects based on focused questions, demonstrating understanding of the subject under investigation.
- **W.8**—Gather relevant information from multiple print and digital sources, assess the credibility and accuracy of each source, and integrate the information while avoiding plagiarism.
- **W.9**—Draw evidence from literary or informational texts to support analysis, reflection, and research.

ESSENTIAL QUESTIONS

- What patterns can you see across topics in aviation?
- How does weight and balance affect flight safety?
- What impact would taking off over maximum takeoff weight have on an aircraft? What impacts would it have on the flight?
- Have you ever been weighed before going on an airline flight? Why not? How do the airlines calculate weight and balance?

LESSONS

Lesson	Topic	Student Notebook Activities
Lesson 1	Weight and Balance Introduction	1. Comprehension Questions 2. Vocabulary Chart 3. True or False Statements

Lesson 2	Weight and Balance Computation	1. Weight and Balance Reference Charts
		  • *Weight and Balance Loading Form*
		  • *Weight vs. CG Envelope Chart*
		2. Weight and Balance Worksheet
		3. Weight and Balance Exercises
		  • *Weight and Balance Exercise 1*
		  • *Weight and Balance Exercise 2*
		  • *Weight and Balance Exercise 3*
		  • *Weight and Balance Exercise 4*

Lesson 3	Current Event	1. Current Event Outline and Rubric

Lesson 4	Performance Introduction	1. Factors that Affect Performance Chart
		2. Takeoff Charts
		  • *Flaps Up Takeoff Performance Chart*
		  • *Flaps 25 Degrees Takeoff Performance Chart*
		  • *Flaps Up Takeoff Ground Roll Chart*
		  • *Flaps 25 Degrees Takeoff Ground Roll Chart*
		3. Landing Charts
		  • *Landing Performance Chart*
		  • *Landing Ground Roll Chart*
		4. Performance Worksheet

Lesson 5	Enroute, Climb, and Descent Performance Charts	1. Aspen, Colorado Airport
		  • *Picture of Aspen, Colorado, Airport*
		  • *Airport Information for Aspen-Pitkin County Airport*
		2. Climb Performance Chart
		3. Time, Fuel, Distance to Climb
		  • *Time, Fuel, Distance to Climb Chart*
		  • *Time, Fuel, Distance to Climb Example*
		  • *Time, Fuel, Distance to Climb Practice Problems*
		4. Time, Fuel, Distance to Descend
		  • *Time, Fuel, Distance to Descend Chart*
		  • *Time, Fuel, Distance to Descend Practice Problems*
		5. Engine/Cruise Performance
		  • *Engine/Cruise Performance (55%) Chart*
		  • *Engine/Cruise Performance (65%) Chart*
		  • *Engine/Cruise Performance (75%) Chart*
		  • *Engine/Cruise Performance Practice Problems*

Lesson	Topic	Student Notebook Activities
Lesson 6	Range, Endurance, and Glide Charts	1. Range, Endurance, and Glide Range Charts • *Range Chart (No Reserve)* • *Range Chart (45 min. Reserve)* • *Endurance Chart (No Reserve)* • *Endurance Chart (45 min. Reserve)* • *Glide Range Chart* 2. Range, Endurance, and Glide Practice Problems
Lesson 7	Guest Speaker: Aviation Professional	1. Two-Column Notes
Lessons 8 & 9	Review: Weight & Balance and Performance	1. Exam Review Problems
Lesson 10	Chapter 4 Exam	1. Current Events Notes

CHAPTER 4 WEIGHT & BALANCE AND PERFORMANCE

LESSON 1
WEIGHT AND BALANCE INTRODUCTION

PURPOSE
The purpose of this lesson is to explore the concepts of weight and balance in an aircraft.

ACCOMMODATIONS FOR LEARNING DIFFERENCES
It is important that lessons accommodate the needs of every learner. These lessons may be modified to accommodate your students with learning differences by referring to www.pacer.org/parent/php/PHP-c267.pdf.

PREPARATION
- Presentation with basic information about weight and balance
- Rulers
- Paper clips
- String
- Small pieces of green and red paper

DIRECTIONS
Introductory Activity: Ask students to picture a teeter-totter and then to think-pair-share (think about the questions, pair up with a partner, and share with each other) and discuss how a teeter-totter is similar to an aircraft as it relates to weight and balance. Next, display pictures of aircraft that have been loaded improperly. Ask students to discuss with their partners what may have caused the incidents shown in the pictures. Lead a discussion to answer questions and address misconceptions. If time allows, find videos that show the results of what happens when an aircraft is not loaded correctly.

Step 1: Hand out two small pieces of paper, one green and one red, to each student. Read the following statements to students, asking them to hold up the green paper if they agree with the statement and the red paper if they disagree. After students indicate their agreement or disagreement with the statement, follow up with a brief discussion. An expanded discussion will take place later in the lesson. Whether or not the statement is true or false is indicated after each statement:

- Pilots should compute weight and balance before every flight. (*Answer:* True)
- An aircraft will have a shorter takeoff distance when it's heavily loaded than when it's lightly loaded. (*Answer:* False)
- A heavily loaded aircraft will have a shorter landing distance than if that same aircraft were lightly loaded. (*Answer:* False)

- For a pilot to compute takeoff and landing distances, the pilot must first compute the aircraft's weight. (*Answer:* True)
- A light aircraft will have reduced fuel economy (rate of fuel burned) as compared to a heavy aircraft. (*Answer:* False)
- The starting point for every weight and balance calculation is the standard empty weight. (*Answer:* False)

Step 2: The facilitator should prepare a presentation using Chapter 10 in the *Pilot's Handbook of Aeronautical Knowledge* along with a Piper Archer or Cessna 172 Pilot's Operating Handbook (refer to section 6 for weight and balance). Present information discussing foundational information in understanding weight and balance. Guide the students in defining terms and answering the following questions. Students can record answers to these questions in their Student Notebooks in Activity 1 (Comprehension Questions).

- Why do we compute weight and balance before every flight?
  (*Answer:* The aircraft could carry a different number of passengers and bags. We might have a different amount of fuel in the aircraft. We might fly a different aircraft.)
- What do the Federal Aviation Regulations (FARs) say about weight and balance?
  (*Answer:* 14 CFR §91.103—if time allows, have the students go to **faa.gov** and search for §91.103.)

  §91.103 Preflight action.

  Each pilot in command shall, before beginning a flight, become familiar with all available information concerning that flight. This information must include—

  > (a) For a flight under IFR or a flight not in the vicinity of an airport, weather reports and forecasts, fuel requirements, alternatives available if the planned flight cannot be completed, and any known traffic delays of which the pilot in command has been advised by ATC;

  > (b) For any flight, runway lengths at airports of intended use, and the following takeoff and landing distance information:

  >> (1) For civil aircraft for which an approved Airplane or Rotorcraft Flight Manual containing takeoff and landing distance data is required, the takeoff and landing distance data contained therein; and

  >> (2) For civil aircraft other than those specified in paragraph (b)(1) of this section, other reliable information appropriate to the aircraft, relating to aircraft performance under expected values of airport elevation and runway slope, aircraft gross weight, and wind and temperature.

  Note: In order to compute the takeoff and landing distances the pilot must know the weight of the aircraft.
- How do we figure out the aircraft's useful load?
  (*Answer:* Maximum ramp weight − Basic empty weight = Useful load)
- Why might there be a difference between the maximum ramp weight and maximum takeoff weight?
  (*Answer:* Aircraft burn fuel while taxiing from the ramp to the end of the runway.)

Next, students should write the definitions for the following terms, as they are presented in class, in their Student Notebooks under Activity 2 (Vocabulary Chart). Definitions for vocabulary words can be found in the *Pilot's Handbook of Aeronautical Knowledge* or by using a simple internet search.

Weight and balance terms:

- Basic empty weight
- Standard empty weight
- Useful load
- Payload
- Center of Gravity (CG)
- Datum
- Moment
- Maximum ramp weight
- Maximum taxi weight
- Maximum takeoff weight
- Maximum landing weight

Step 3: To help illustrate the importance of proper weight and balance loading, students will conduct the following experiment:

1. Give each student a ruler, string, and paper clips.
2. Have each student tie the string onto the middle of the ruler (held horizontally and perpendicular to the string) and then set one paper clip on either end of the ruler (the goal is to make the ruler balance).
3. Have them move the string to different positions along the ruler and add paper clips to make the ruler balanced.
4. Ask students: What does the string represent? How does moving the string affect the stability/balance of the ruler?

Concluding Activity: Revisit the true and false statements from the beginning of the lesson. Students will complete Student Notebook Activity 3 (True or False Statements). Ask students to complete an exit slip (quick assessment of learning by writing a response to a question or orally answering) to correct one of the statements they got incorrect (or guessed on) the first time through. Students will explain what they learned about the statement through their written or oral exit slip. If time allows, review students' exit slips as a class, answering questions and clarifying misconceptions.

LESSON 2

WEIGHT AND BALANCE COMPUTATION

PURPOSE

The purpose of this lesson is to introduce students to a variety of weight and balance charts.

ACCOMMODATIONS FOR LEARNING DIFFERENCES

It is important that lessons accommodate the needs of every learner. These lessons may be modified to accommodate your students with learning differences by referring to www.pacer.org/parent/php/PHP-c267.pdf.

PREPARATION

- Note cards
- Calculators
- Piper Archer and/or Cessna 172 Pilot's Operating Handbook (POH) charts (found below and in the Student Notebook)
- Class copies of *Pilot's Handbook of Aeronautical Knowledge* (FAA-H-8083-25)

DIRECTIONS

Introductory Activity: Ask one student to come to the front of the classroom. Direct the student to raise his or her arms straight out to the sides. Set a heavy book on one hand and explain that the hand represents the nose of the airplane. The other arm is the tail of the airplane. Place another book on top of the first book. Ask students, "How is this heavier weight impacting the airplane (student)?" (*Answer:* The nose of the airplane is going down and the tail is going up.) Add books to either side, continually asking the students, "How is this affecting the balance of the airplane?" Students should be connecting this information to the ruler/paper clip activity from Lesson 1.

Step 1: Direct students' attention to the weight and balance charts found in Student Notebook Activity 1 (Weight and Balance Reference Charts). Now that an actual aircraft is being referenced, highlight the maximum allowable fuel (48 gallons), maximum baggage weight (200 lbs), maximum ramp weight (2,558 lbs), takeoff weight (2,550 lbs), and landing weight (2,550 lbs) for that specific aircraft from the Weight and Balance Loading Form (found in the Student Notebook and reproduced below under Facilitator Information). Have students circle or highlight this important information. Also, the conversation should include how much a gallon of gas weighs in pounds (1 gallon weighs 6 pounds).

Step 2: Model how to compute a weight and balance calculation using the computational method (example below). Make the modeling interactive by asking students to assist with filling in the chart. As the facilitator is modeling, students can record information in their

Student Notebooks in the Weight and Balance Loading Form in Activity 1. More information on how to conduct the computational method can be found in Chapter 10 of the *Pilot's Handbook of Aeronautical Knowledge*.

Following are the steps in the computational method:

1. Reference the aircraft's POH for the basic empty weight and moment and enter these values in the chart.
2. Find out how much the pilot and passengers weigh and enter that data into the chart in the appropriate locations (passengers can sit in the front or the back).
    - For each, multiply the weight by the arm, and that equals the pilot's or passenger's moment (Weight × Arm = Moment).
3. Enter the baggage weight if applicable.
    - Multiply the weight by the arm to calculate the baggage moment.
4. Enter the amount (in pounds) of fuel you plan to take.
    - Multiply the weight by the arm to calculate the fuel moment.
5. Add all of the weights up to determine the Ramp Weight.
6. Add all of the moments up to determine the Ramp Moment.
7. The aircraft burns fuel on engine start, taxi, and runup; therefore, the POH states that we need to subtract 8 pounds of fuel.
    - Multiply that by the fuel arm and that is the fuel moment for engine start, taxi, and runup.
8. Take the Ramp Weight and subtract the fuel used for start, taxi, and runup to determine the takeoff weight.
    - Subtract the fuel moment for engine start, taxi, and runup from the ramp moment to determine the takeoff moment.
9. To find the takeoff center of gravity (CG), divide the Takeoff Moment by the Takeoff Weight.
10. Verify that the Takeoff CG is within the limits.
11. To compute the Landing Weight, CG, and Moment, calculate how much fuel you will burn during your flight (for example, at 75% best power the Archer burns 11 gallons per hour).
    - Subtract the fuel weight from the takeoff weight to calculate the Landing Weight.
    - Multiply the landing weight by the fuel arm to get the landing moment.
    - Divide the landing moment by the landing weight to calculate the landing CG.

Here are the numbers you will need to model the next weight and balance scenario/problem:

- Basic empty weight is 1,659.2 lbs and the Moment is 146,344.8 in-lbs
  Note: These numbers are specific to each aircraft's weight. The example is based on the weight of an actual Piper Archer.
- Pilot: 130 lbs
- Front Passenger: 155 lbs
- Rear Passengers: 170 lbs
- Baggage: 100 lbs
- Fuel: 30 gallons (180 lbs)

Have the students fill in the chart in Student Notebook Activity 2 (Weight and Balance Worksheet) with the numbers above, and then refer to the Weight and Balance Loading Form (provided below under Facilitator Information and for reference in Activity 1 in the Student Notebook) to help students fill out the "Arm" column of the example weight and balance worksheet. Finish the weight and balance problem and then have the students reference the Weight vs. CG Envelope Chart to verify that the calculated takeoff CG is within limits. A completed chart is included below for reference.

Weight and Balance Loading Form Example

Key: ▢ = Numbers given to you
       ▢ = Numbers provided by the pilot
       ▢ = Calculated numbers

	Weight	Arm	Moment
Basic Empty Weight (BEW)	1,659.2		146,344.8
Pilot	130	80.5	10,465
Front Passenger	155	80.5	12,477.5
Rear Passengers	170	118.1	20,077
Baggage	100	142.8	14,280
Fuel	180	95	17,100
Ramp Weight	2,394.2	92.2	220,744.3
Run-up	−8	95	−760
Takeoff Weight	2,386.2	92.19	219,984.3

Step 3: Continue to lead students through several different examples of using the computational method to calculate weight and balance. Three practice problems can be found in the Student Notebook in Activity 3 (Weight and Balance Exercises). For reference: Exercise 1 is within limits, Exercise 2 is overweight, in Exercise 3 the CG is aft of limits, and Exercise 4 is a blank worksheet that can be used for additional practice. (Complete answers are provided in the answer key at the end of the chapter.) Problems not completed in class can be assigned as homework. When completing the practice problems in class, follow up questions should include:

- If the aircraft is overweight, how can you get that aircraft under the maximum weight? (*Answer:* Take out fuel, baggage, or people.)

- If the center of gravity (CG) is too far forward, what can you do to move it back or aft? (*Answers include:* Put more weight in the back, or put heavy person in the back and move the light person to the front.)

- If the CG is too far aft, what can you do to bring it forward? (*Answers include:* Put less weight in the back, or put light person in the back and move the heavy person to the front.)

If time permits, introduce students to the Graph Method and Table Method for calculating weight and balance found in Chapter 10 of the *Pilot's Handbook of Aeronautical Knowledge*. If the students need more practice, consider extending this lesson for another day.

Concluding Activity: Use the 3-2-1 summary activity to wrap up the lesson. On a blank piece of paper or a note card, have students write down 3 points to remember from today's chart analysis, 2 things they liked about the lesson, and 1 question they still have. Call on several students, ask them to share their questions, and address the questions as time allows.

FACILITATOR INFORMATION

Weight and Balance Reference Charts

(The following form and chart are from the Piper Archer III PA-28-181 POH. For example only; do not use for flight planning.)

Weight and Balance Loading Form

SECTION 6
WEIGHT AND BALANCE   **PA-28-181, ARCHER III**

	Weight (Lbs)	Arm Aft Datum (Inches)	Moment (In-Lbs)
Basic Empty Weight			
Pilot and Front Passenger		80.5	
Passengers (Rear Seats)*		118.1	
Fuel (48 Gallon Maximum)		95.0	
Baggage (200 Lbs. Maximum)*		142.8	
Ramp Weight (2558 Lbs. Normal, 2138 Lbs. Utility Maximum)			
Fuel Allowance For Engine Start, Taxi and Run Up	-8	95.0	-760
Takeoff Weight (2550 Lbs. Normal, 2130 Lbs. Utility Maximum)			

Totals must be within approved weight and C.G. limits. It is the responsibility of the airplane owner and the pilot to ensure that the airplane is loaded properly. The Basic Empty Weight C.G. is noted on the Weight and Balance Data Form (Figure 6-5). If the airplane has been altered, refer to the Weight and Balance Record for this information.

*Utility Category Operation - No baggage or rear passengers allowed.

Weight vs. CG Envelope Chart

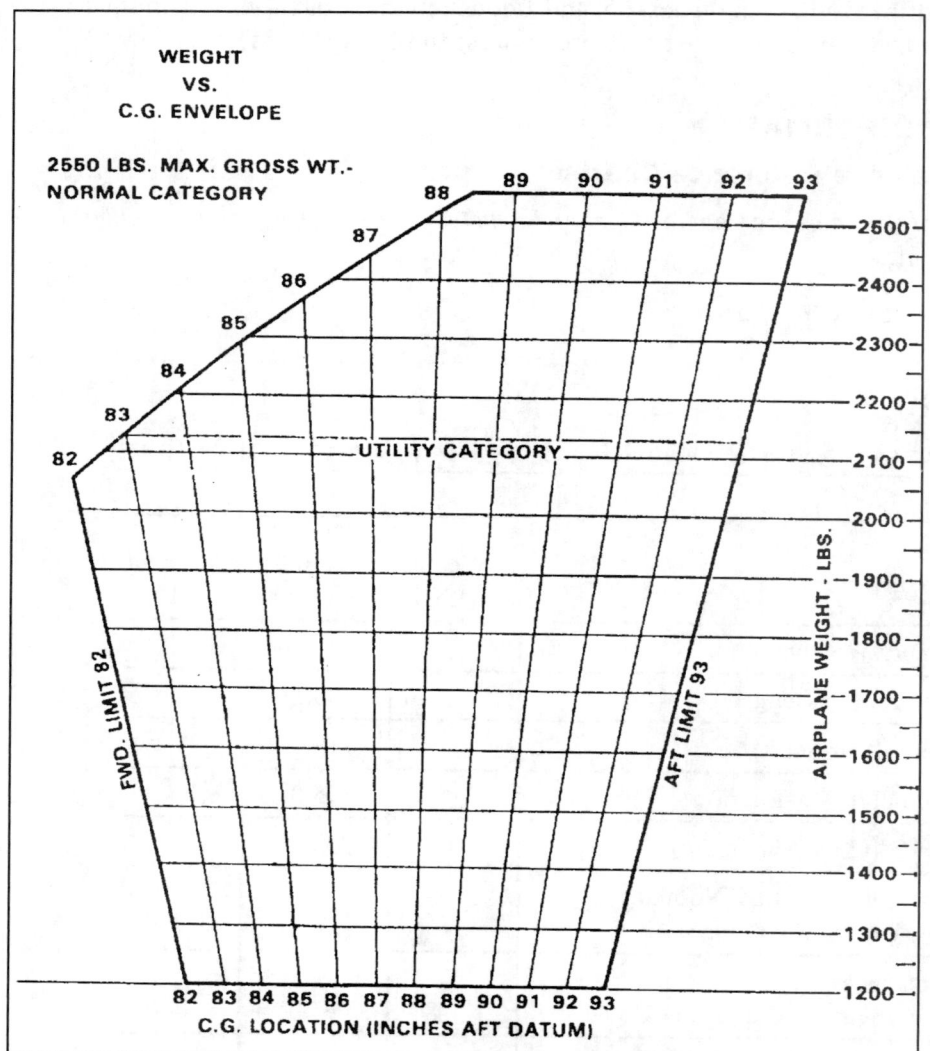

C.G. RANGE AND WEIGHT

CHAPTER 4   WEIGHT & BALANCE AND PERFORMANCE

LESSON 3
CURRENT EVENT

PURPOSE
The purpose of this lesson is to explore current events related to aviation.

ACCOMMODATIONS FOR LEARNING DIFFERENCES
It is important that lessons accommodate the needs of every learner. These lessons may be modified to accommodate your students with learning differences by referring to www.pacer.org/parent/php/PHP-c267.pdf.

PREPARATION
- Computers/devices and internet access for students to research current event articles
- Inquiry questions
- Paper and pen

DIRECTIONS
Introductory Activity: Have students go on the internet and choose an article of approximately 250 words in length from a major news magazine, newspaper, or radio/TV segment. To ensure the information is current, the article/segment should have been published within the past three months and should address weight & balance and performance. If a weight and balance current event is not available, feel free to choose an applicable aviation current event topic. Have them briefly share their current events with a few of their peers.

Step 1: Ask students to carefully read their current event and summarize the main point(s) of the article in their own words. This summary should clearly demonstrate understanding of the material and can be written in the first space found under Activity 1 in the Student Notebook.

Step 2: Have students write a reflective response to the article that addresses at least two of the course inquiry questions, listed below and in the Student Notebook. A few prompts for reflective writing can also guide the response.

Inquiry Questions:
- How does this article relate to the key concepts and big ideas we have studied this year, or to big ideas from your other classes?
- What did you learn from the article that you did not previously know? What additional questions do you now have about the topic?
- Identify a problem that needs to be solved within this situation.

- What is your opinion of what you are reading and the issue being discussed? Do you agree/disagree with the writer/creator of this news item? Why or why not?
- How could the knowledge you gained from the event be used in your future aviation career?
- What are some questions you still have regarding this topic?

Step 3: Have students select and write down two of their own questions (question creation should be guided by the inquiry question prompts) about the issues or events mentioned in the article. These will be used for class discussion in the concluding activity.

Step 4: Remind students that their current event assignment will be graded using the provided rubric (printed below and in the Student Notebook) in the areas of article selection, summary, response, and conventions.

Concluding Activity: Have the students share several of their questions, and lead the class in a discussion to answer the students' questions.

FACILITATOR INFORMATION
Current Events Rubric

(See next page.)

CURRENT EVENTS RUBRIC

	Exceeds Expectation (4)	Proficient (3)	Partially Proficient (2)	Novice (1)	Non-Performance (0)
Article	Article is well-chosen given topic and inquiry questions from relevant website or news source. All the required information is cited clearly and correctly in MLA format. Article is handed in with the assignment.	Article is from relevant web source and related to aviation. The required citation information is complete. Article is handed in with the assignment.	Article may not be from relevant or appropriate source. The title, source, or one other piece of information may be missing from the citation. Article is handed in with the assignment.	Article may be inappropriate for course topics and important information about the article is missing.	No article submitted.
Summary	Information is clearly summarized and demonstrates understanding of the topic. Includes strong supporting details addressing the who, what, where, when, why or how questions.	Information from source is summarized and general comprehension is demonstrated. Includes supporting details addressing the who, what, where, when, why, or how questions.	Summary may be unclear, incomplete, copies the article, or is inaccurate. There is a need for more supporting details. Summary is only a few sentences.	Summary is vague, too much information was copied from the article or important details are left out. Details or summary may be confusing.	No summary included.
Response	Student is able to relate article content to class material. Insightfully gives personal response with extremely strong thoughts and ideas. Two thoughtful, inquiry related questions are present.	General connection made between article and class material. Tells what their thoughts of the article are, with detail and description. Attempts to push thinking with some prompts. Two questions are submitted that relate to the field of aviation.	Simple or brief connection made between article and class material. Attempts to tell thoughtful ideas about the article. Lacks thoughtful ideas that relate to the article. Only one question present and/or are not applicable.	Attempt made to relate article content to class material. Response is inappropriate to the content of the article. Questions attempted.	No response written.
Conventions	Writer makes little or no errors in grammar or spelling that distract the reader from the content. Paragraphs contain sentences that are well-constructed. There are varied beginnings and rich and appropriate vocabulary.	Writer makes very few errors in grammar or spelling that distract the reader from the content. Most sentences are well-constructed with varied beginnings and vocabulary.	Writer makes some major errors in grammar or spelling. Some sentences may not be well-constructed. Similar words are used too often.	Writer makes many errors in grammar or spelling. Sentences lack structure and appear incomplete or are confusing.	No writing submitted or is illegible.

Suggested grading conversion scale: A = 16–14   B = 13–10   C = 9–8   D = 7–4   F = 3–0

Total _____ / 16 pts

Comments

CHAPTER 4 WEIGHT & BALANCE AND PERFORMANCE

LESSON 4

PERFORMANCE INTRODUCTION

PURPOSE

The purpose of this lesson is to explore factors that affect the performance of an aircraft and to see how these factors impact an aircraft for both takeoff and landing.

ACCOMMODATIONS FOR LEARNING DIFFERENCES

It is important that lessons accommodate the needs of every learner. These lessons may be modified to accommodate your students with learning differences by referring to www.pacer.org/parent/php/PHP-c267.pdf.

PREPARATION

- Video
- 14 CFR §91.103 (FAR/AIM or eCFR.gov)
- Piper Archer (PA-28-181) Pilot's Operating Handbook (POH), Section 5
- *Pilot's Handbook of Aeronautical Knowledge* (FAA-H-8083-25)

DIRECTIONS

Introductory Activity: Locate a video on the internet that shows what happens when all aspects of performance are not considered. A sample video can be found listed in the Instructor Resources (Disclaimer: This video ends in a crash and all 3 people on board do survive. There is a disclaimer on the video so be sure to preview it before sharing with students.)

Facilitate a class discussion to explain the factors that can affect aircraft performance (examples include weight, CG location, temperature, pressure, air density, and pilot technique). List these factors on the board. Have the students pick which of the factors just listed on the board may have had an impact on the crash in the video.

Step 1: In the Student Notebook Activity 1 (Factors that Affect Performance Chart), have students record the factors that affect performance in the first column of the table. In the second column, lead a discussion so that students can record *how* each of these factors affect performance. Explanations for each of the following factors can be found in Chapter 11 of the *Pilot's Handbook of Aeronautical Knowledge* (2016). The areas to focus on include:

- Atmospheric pressure
- Pressure altitude
- Air density
- Weight
- CG location
- Wind
- Runway slope
- Runway condition
- Aircraft configuration
- Turbulence
- Pilot technique

Step 2: Watch the videos about landing at St. Barts Airport (see Instructor Resources). The first video shows the pilot's view of landing at St. Barts. After watching the first video, facilitate a class discussion to lead students to the factors that can affect aircraft performance at this specific airport. List these factors on the board. Watch the second video of a landing at St. Barts where the pilot is not able to stop and crashes into the sand/water. Have the students pick which of the factors that were just listed on the board may have had an impact on the crash (i.e., runway slope, wind, and pilot techniques/decision-making).

Step 3: Direct students' attention to Activity 2 (Takeoff Charts) found in their Student Notebooks. Discuss why the Piper Archer has four different takeoff charts (with flaps and with no flaps for both takeoff ground roll and takeoff distance over a 50-foot barrier). Describe the meaning of takeoff ground roll and takeoff distance over a 50-foot barrier found in the *Pilot's Handbook of Aeronautical Knowledge*, Chapter 11.

Step 4: Review the associated conditions found at the top of the Piper Archer charts printed in the Student Notebook (and provided below under Facilitator Information) and relate this back to the performance (full throttle before brake release, runway conditions, liftoff speed, flap configuration, air temperature, weight, wind, and pressure altitude). Again, reference the *Pilot's Handbook of Aeronautical Knowledge*, Chapter 11, for more information.

Step 5: Before modeling how to use the charts, have the following information available to students:

- **Weather:** The weather can be found online at the Aviation Weather Center website (**www.aviationweather.gov**). Reference the Observation/METAR for the local airport and find the altimeter setting and winds. Here is a sample METAR:

  KGFK 011553Z 15004KT 10SM SCT120 OVC200 01/M02 A2998 RMK AO2 SLP143 T00061022

  › The wind is coming from 150 degrees at 4 knots.
  › The temperature today is 1°C.
  › The current altimeter setting is 29.98.

- **Field Elevation:** Find the airport's field elevation by using the *Chart Supplement*, either paper or online.

```
328                              NORTH DAKOTA
GRAND FORKS INTL  (GFK)(KGFK)  5 NW  UTC–6(–5DT)  N47°56.84′ W97°10.43′      TWIN CITIES
   845   B  AOE  LRA  ARFF Index—See Remarks  NOTAM FILE GFK  MON Airport   H–2I, L–14G
   RWY 17R–35L: H7351X150 (ASPH–GRVD)  S–75, D–160, 2S–175,                  IAP, AD
      2D–270, 2D/D1–438, C5–840 PCN 35 R/C/W/T  HIRL
      RWY 17R: REIL. PAPI(P4L)—GA 3.0° TCH 53′. RVR–R Rgt tfc.
```

▶ Grand Forks International (KGFK) *Chart Supplement* Excerpt. *(FAA)*

› Grand Forks Field Elevation is 845 feet.

- **Weight of Loaded Aircraft:** For this example, we can use a takeoff weight of 2,249 lbs.
- **Pressure Altitude:** Take time to elaborate on how to compute pressure altitude by using the following equation (29.92 inches of Mercury (inHg) = standard atmospheric pressure):

  Pressure Altitude = (29.92 inHg − current altimeter setting) × 1,000 + field elevation

CHAPTER 4 Lesson 4 / Facilitator Guide

Once the above information is shared, model for students how to find the takeoff ground roll and takeoff distance over a 50-foot barrier using the takeoff charts from the POH found below and in their Student Notebooks. Reference the *Pilot's Handbook of Aeronautical Knowledge* and POH for clarification on how to use the charts. Here are the steps to using the takeoff charts:

1. Start on the lower left part of the chart with the temperature.
2. Go up to the pressure altitude (which you just computed).
3. Go straight over to the weight reference line.
    a. Follow the sloping lines down to the weight of the aircraft.
4. Then go over to the wind reference line.
    a. Follow the sloping lines down to the wind.
5. Go straight across to the right, and that number is your takeoff distance or ground roll.

Step 6: With guidance and modeling, students can complete practice problems 1–4 found in Activity 4 (Performance Worksheet) in their Student Notebooks. (An answer key is provided at the end of the chapter.)

Step 7: Determining landing distance is an identical process to determining takeoff distance. For this reason, takeoff and landing distances can easily be taught in the same lesson. To determine landing distance, define landing ground roll and landing distance over a 50-foot barrier. Model at least two examples with students. Then, have them work on the landing distance examples in practice problems 5–7 in Activity 4 (Performance Worksheet) in their Student Notebooks.

If time allows, consider modeling how to compute takeoff distances using another aircraft's takeoff charts, such as a Cessna 172. Computing the takeoff and landing distances requires using a chart, and to get the exact takeoff and landing distances requires interpolation. This can be found in the *Pilot's Handbook of Aeronautical Knowledge*, Chapter 11.

Concluding Activity: Have students share one thing they learned from this lesson on performance. Answer additional questions as time allows.

FACILITATOR INFORMATION
Takeoff and Landing Charts

(The following charts are from the Piper Archer III PA-28-181 POH. For example only; do not use for flight planning.)

Flaps Up Takeoff Performance Chart

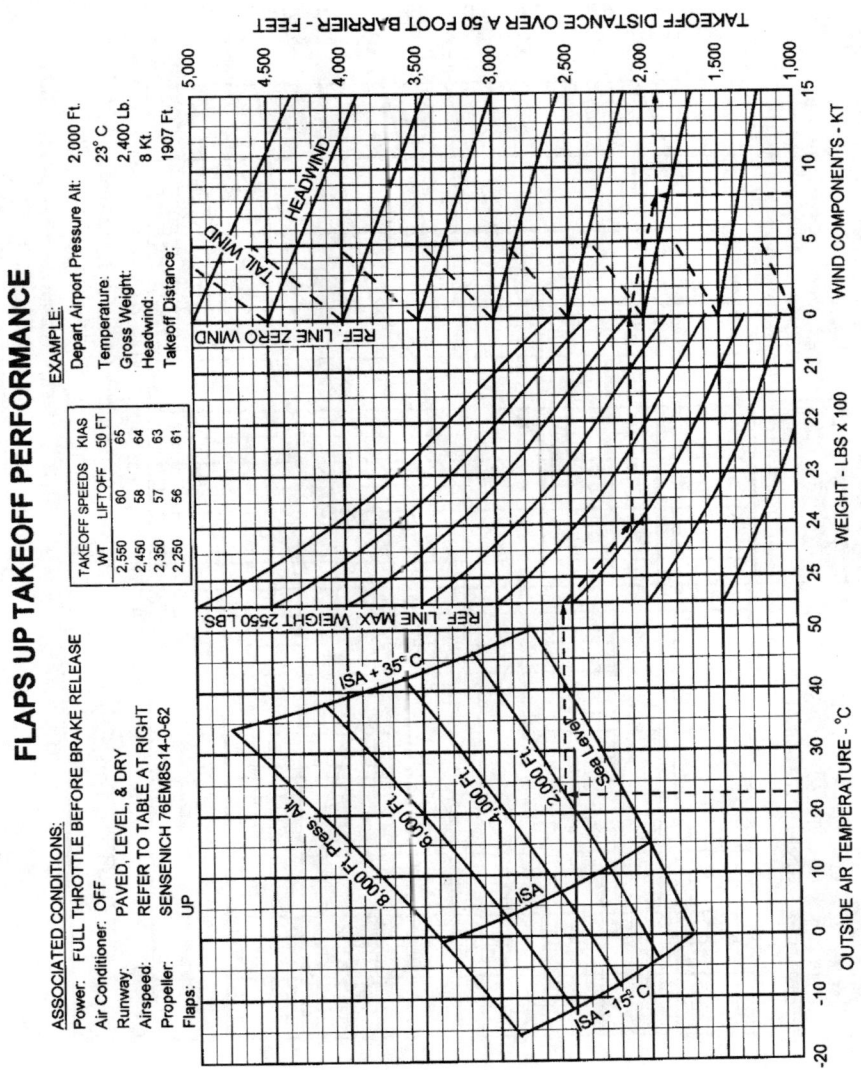

FLAPS UP TAKEOFF PERFORMANCE
Figure 5-7

Flaps 25 Degrees Takeoff Performance Chart

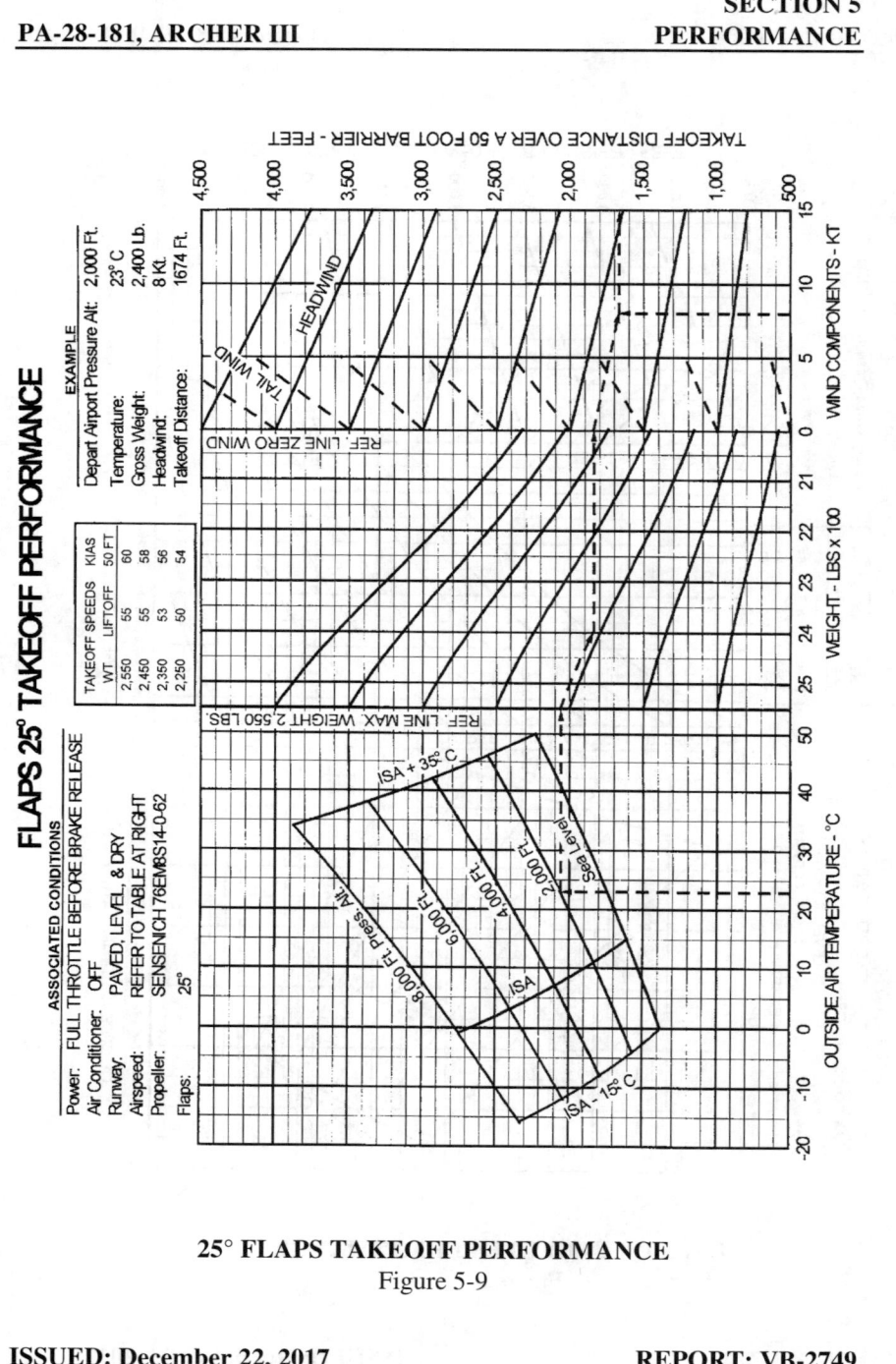

25° FLAPS TAKEOFF PERFORMANCE
Figure 5-9

Flaps Up Takeoff Ground Roll Chart

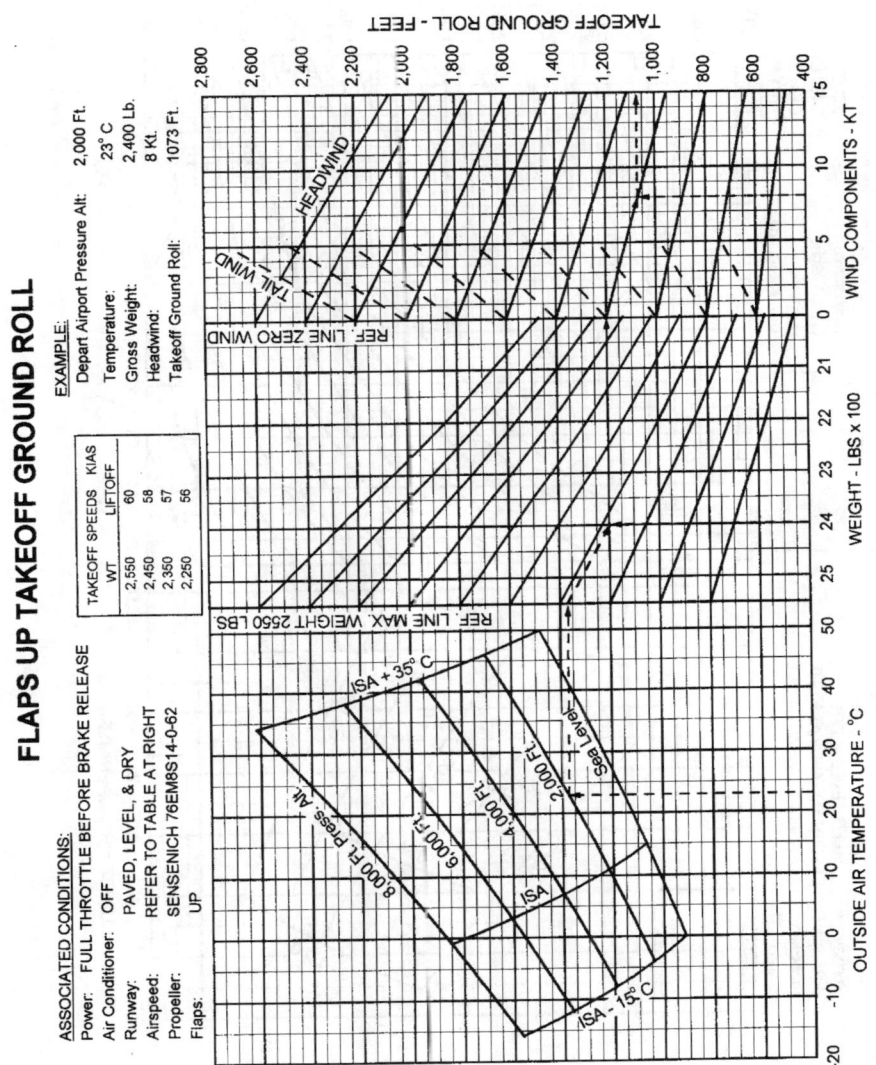

FLAPS UP TAKEOFF GROUND ROLL
Figure 5-11

Flaps 25 Degrees Takeoff Ground Roll Chart

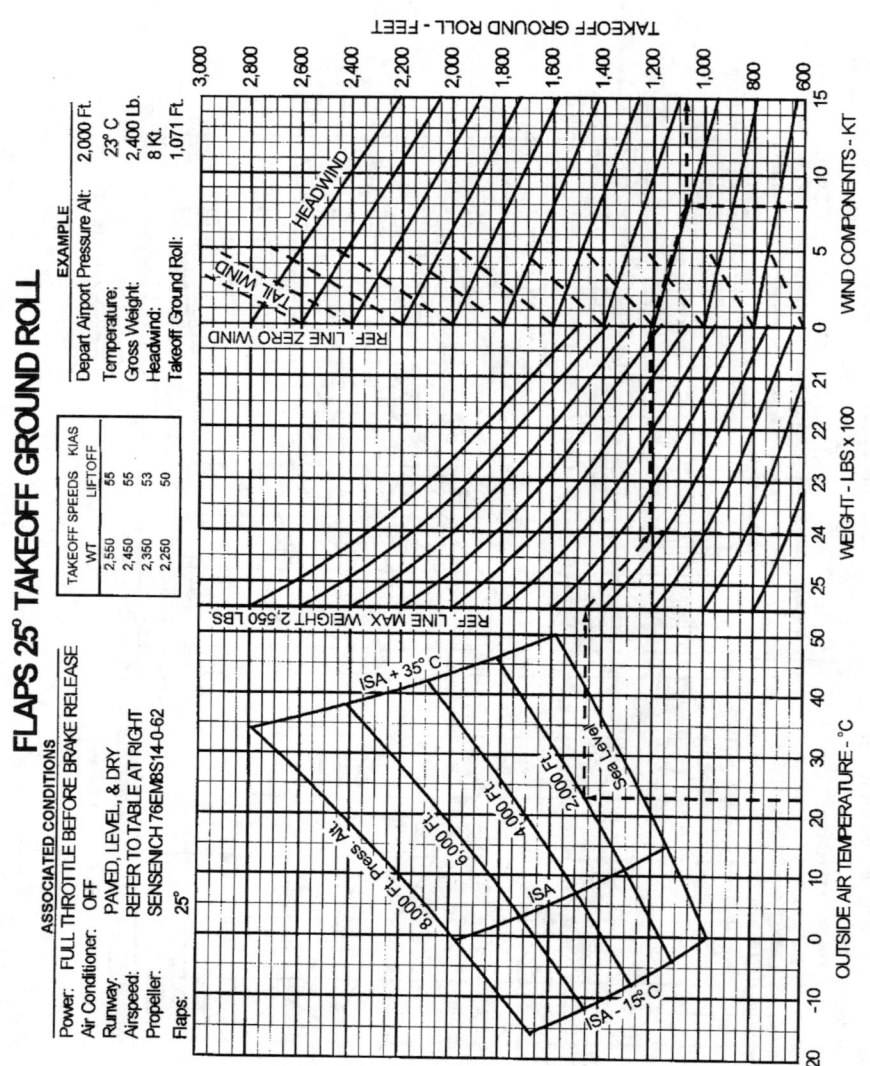

25° FLAPS TAKEOFF GROUND ROLL
Figure 5-13

Landing Performance Chart

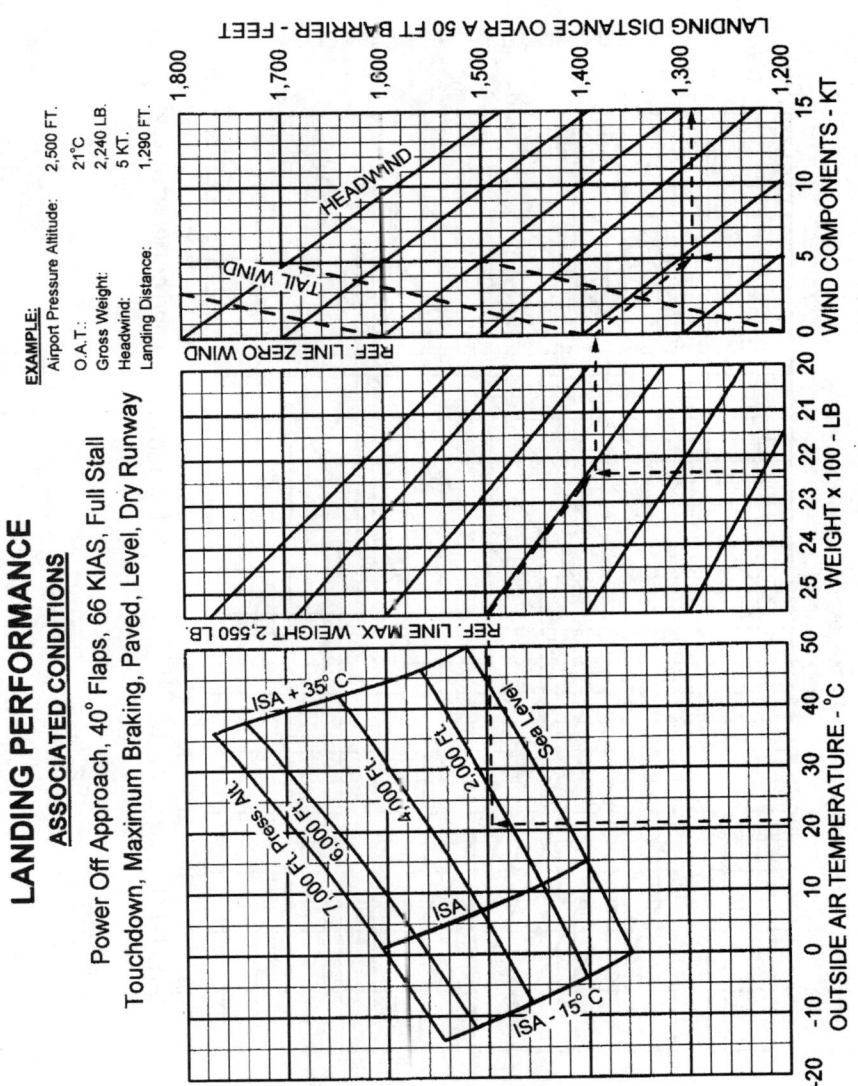

LANDING PERFORMANCE
Figure 5-41

Landing Ground Roll Chart

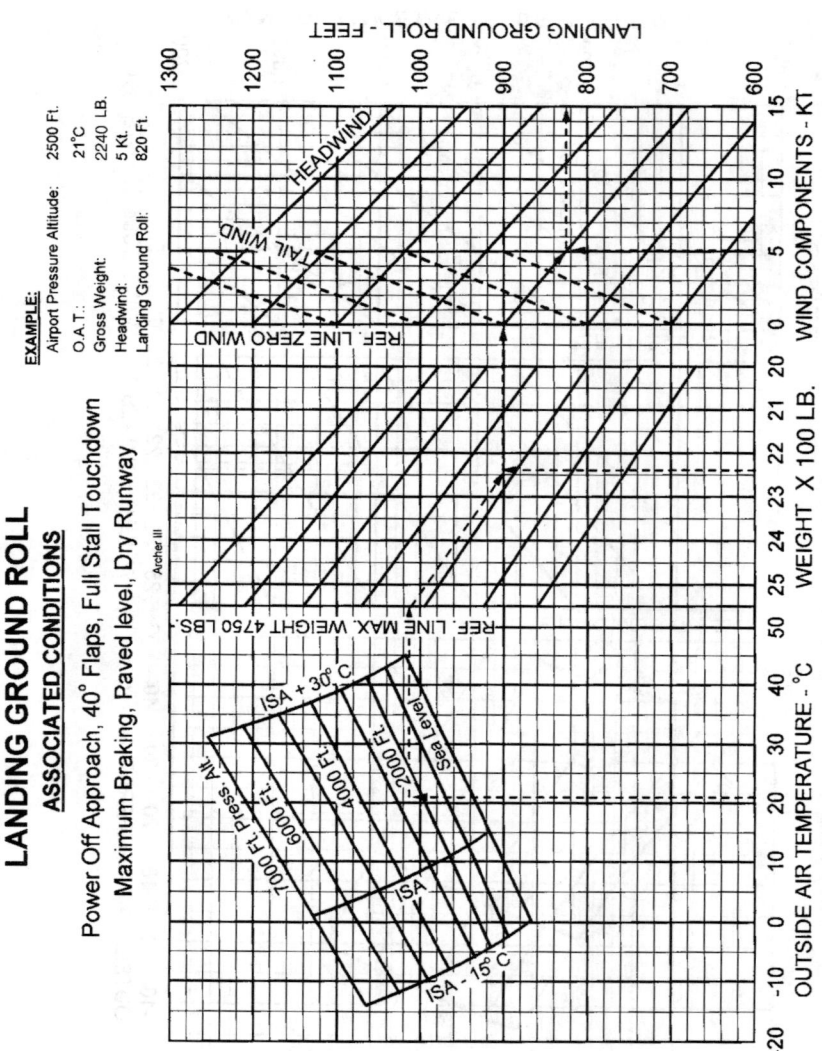

LANDING GROUND ROLL
Figure 5-43

LESSON 5

ENROUTE, CLIMB, AND DESCENT PERFORMANCE CHARTS

PURPOSE

The purpose of this lesson is to explore how to use climb, enroute, and descent aircraft performance charts.

ACCOMMODATIONS FOR LEARNING DIFFERENCES

It is important that lessons accommodate the needs of every learner. These lessons may be modified to accommodate your students with learning differences by referring to www.pacer.org/parent/php/PHP-c267.pdf.

PREPARATION

- Piper Archer (PA-28-181) Pilot's Operating Handbook (POH)
- *Pilot's Handbook of Aeronautical Knowledge* (FAA-H-8083-25)

DIRECTIONS

Introductory Activity: Direct students' attention to the picture of the Aspen, Colorado, airport in the Student Notebook under Activity 1 (Aspen, Colorado, Airport). Ask students to identify what they notice about the picture in regard to factors that affect the performance of an aircraft. Next, review the airport information for Aspen-Pitkin County Airport (KASE) from the *Chart Supplement*, reproduced in the Student Notebook. Discuss factors that make this airport a difficult one to fly in and out of (examples include high density altitude, mountainous terrain, rapidly changing weather conditions, etc.).

Step 1: Locate a video on the internet that indicates how weather can affect performance for an aircraft. A few sample videos are listed in the Instructor Resources. Facilitate a class discussion to explain which factors affected the performance of the aircraft in the videos.

Step 2: Define "rate of climb" and discuss why it should be an important factor to consider for takeoff and landing by recording the term and definition on the board. Building on students' knowledge of takeoff and landing charts from the previous lesson, model for students how to use the climb performance chart printed in Activity 2 in the Student Notebook (and under Facilitator Information below). Reference Chapter 11 in the *Pilot's Handbook of Aeronautical Knowledge* for more information about climb performance. Steps to using the climb performance chart are as follows:

1. Start at the bottom of the chart with temperature.
2. Go up to the climb pressure altitude (the altitude to which you are climbing).
3. Go over to the right side of the chart and that is your rate of climb in feet per minute.

Step 3: The next step will be to explain to students why we use the Time, Fuel, Distance to Climb chart, found in Student Notebook Activity 3 (Time, Fuel, Distance to Climb) and under Facilitator Information below. Again, referring back to what they learned and know about performance, lead the class in a discussion about whether the aircraft burns more gas in cruise, a climb, or a descent. (*Answer:* the aircraft will typically burn more fuel in a climb, so when trying to compute how much fuel will be used for a given flight, it is important to know how much will be used for the climb.) More information can be found in the *Pilot's Handbook of Aeronautical Knowledge*, Chapter 11. Prior to modeling how to use this chart, give the students either a weather scenario where they have to compute a pressure altitude, or provide them with a starting pressure altitude, PA (e.g., 1,000) and an altitude that you are going to climb to (e.g., 3,500 feet). Once this information is shared, model how to use the Time, Fuel, Distance to Climb chart to compute how much time, fuel, and distance it takes an aircraft to climb to a given altitude. Steps to using this chart are as follows:

1. Start at the lower left side of the chart with the cruise altitude's temperature.
2. Go up to the cruise altitude pressure altitude.
3. Go over to the time line and then straight down. Note that time in the chart below.
4. Go over to the fuel reference line and then straight down. Note that fuel in the chart below.
5. Go over to the distance reference line and then straight down. Note that distance in the chart below.
6. Repeat this process for the departure temperature and pressure altitude.
7. Subtract the departure numbers from the cruise numbers and that is your time, fuel, and distance to climb numbers.

Students can record the answers in the Time, Fuel, Distance to Climb Example table provided in the Student Notebook.

	Time	Fuel	Distance
Cruise Pressure Altitude			
Departure Pressure Altitude	–	–	–

Step 4: Direct students' attention to the Time, Fuel, Distance to Climb practice problems found in their Student Notebooks. Complete these as a class or have students work independently, depending on the students' understanding. (An answer key is provided at the end of the chapter.)

Step 5: Determining time, fuel, and distance for climb is an identical process to determining time, fuel, distance to descend. For this reason, takeoff and descending can easily be taught in the same lesson. Using the chart in Student Notebook under Activity 4 (Time, Fuel, Distance to Descend), model at least two examples of time, fuel, and distance to descend with students. Then, have them work on the time, fuel, distance to descend practice problems in the Student Notebook. (An answer key is provided at the end of the chapter.)

Step 6: The final charts used for this lesson will be the Engine/Cruise Performance charts found in Activity 5 (Engine/Cruise Performance) in the Student Notebook and reproduced under Facilitator Information below. Before practicing with the charts, be sure to define 55%, 65%, and 75% power as they relate to engine performance and explain why a pilot would pick one over the other. (*Answer:* At 55% the aircraft is going slower but saving fuel, at 75% the aircraft is going faster and burning lots of fuel, and at 65% the aircraft is going only a few knots slower than 75% but saving more fuel.) When using this chart, give an enroute altitude such as 4,000 to start and a standard temperature. Before using this chart, review the section on International Standard Atmosphere (ISA) found in Chapter 11 of the *Pilot's Handbook of Aeronautical Knowledge*.

Step 7: With guidance and modeling, students can complete the engine/cruise performance practice problems found in the Student Notebook. (An answer key is provided at the end of the chapter.) Steps to using the chart are as follows:

1. Determine which chart to use: 55%, 65%, or 75%.
2. Start on the left side of the chart with the enroute or cruise pressure altitude.
3. Go across to the right and find the appropriate temperature.
4. In the same row, read across to find the engine speed and the true air speed.

Note: Reference the *Pilot's Handbook of Aeronautical Knowledge* for a more in-depth description of the use of the charts.

Concluding Activity: Have students "quiz" the teacher by asking questions about enroute, climb, and descent performance that could be answered by today's lesson. Answer additional questions as time allows.

FACILITATOR INFORMATION

Enroute, Climb, and Descent Performance Charts

(The following charts are from the Piper Archer III PA-28-181 POH. For example only; do not use for flight planning.)

Climb Performance Chart

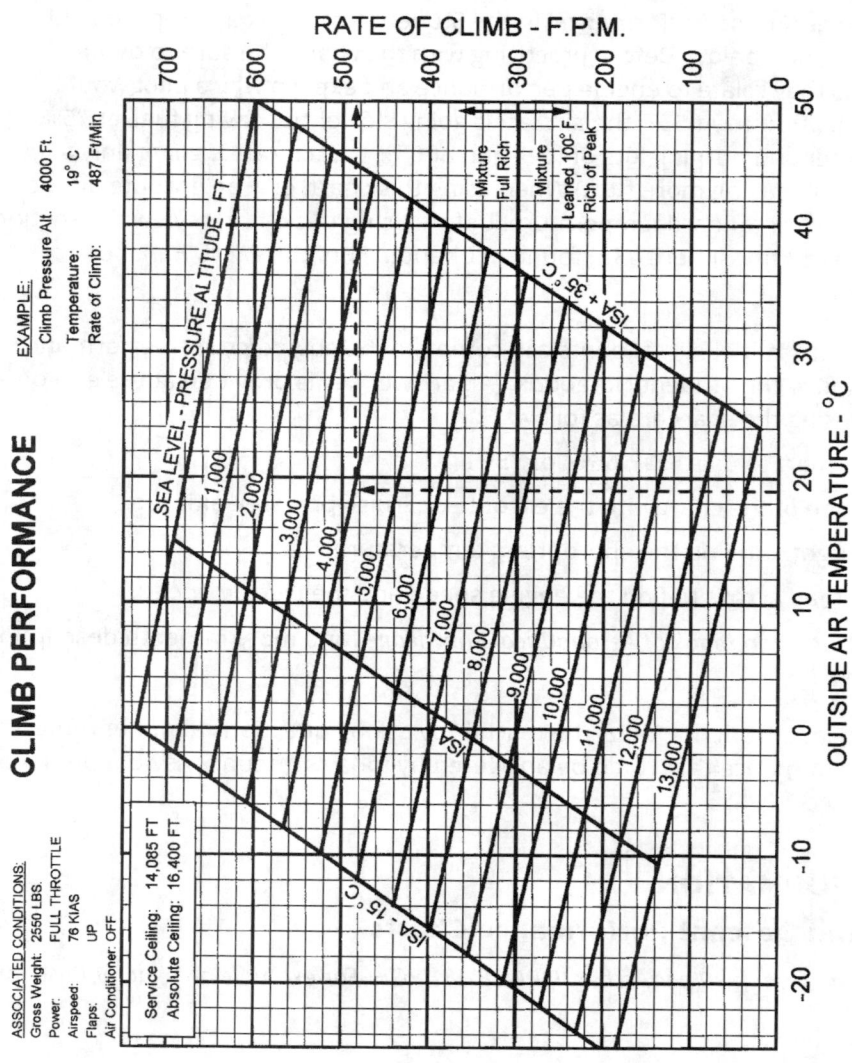

CLIMB PERFORMANCE
Figure 5-15

Time, Fuel, Distance to Climb Chart

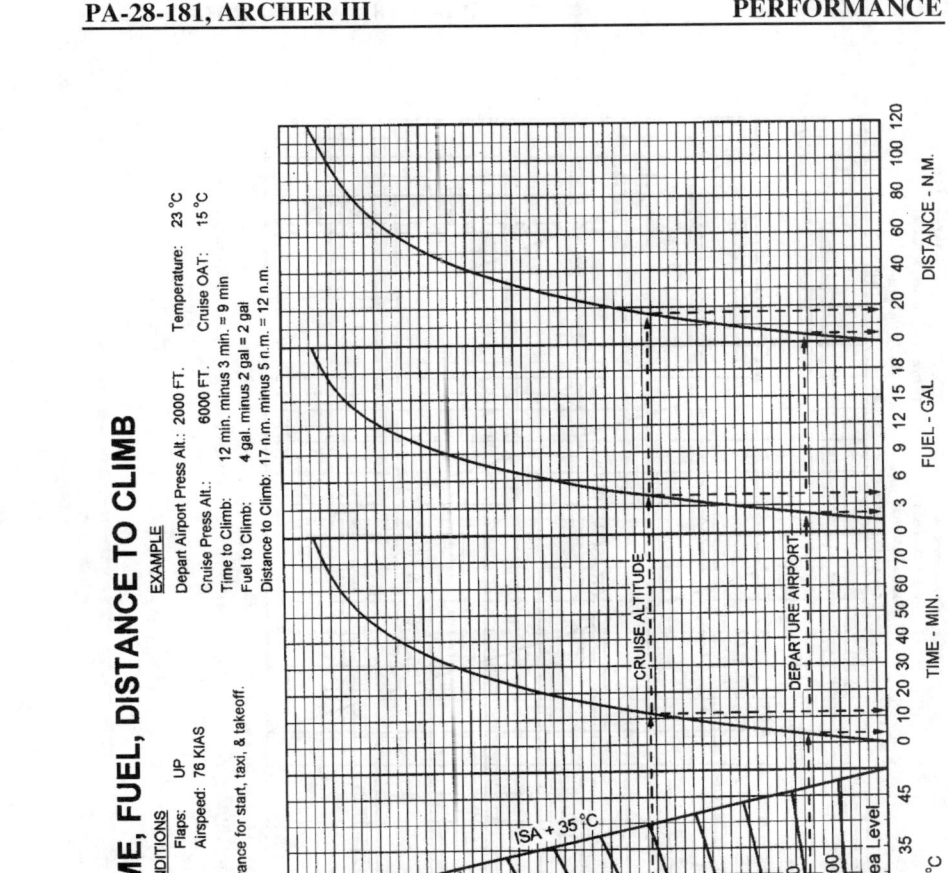

TIME, DISTANCE AND FUEL TO CLIMB
Figure 5-17

Time, Fuel, Distance to Descend Chart

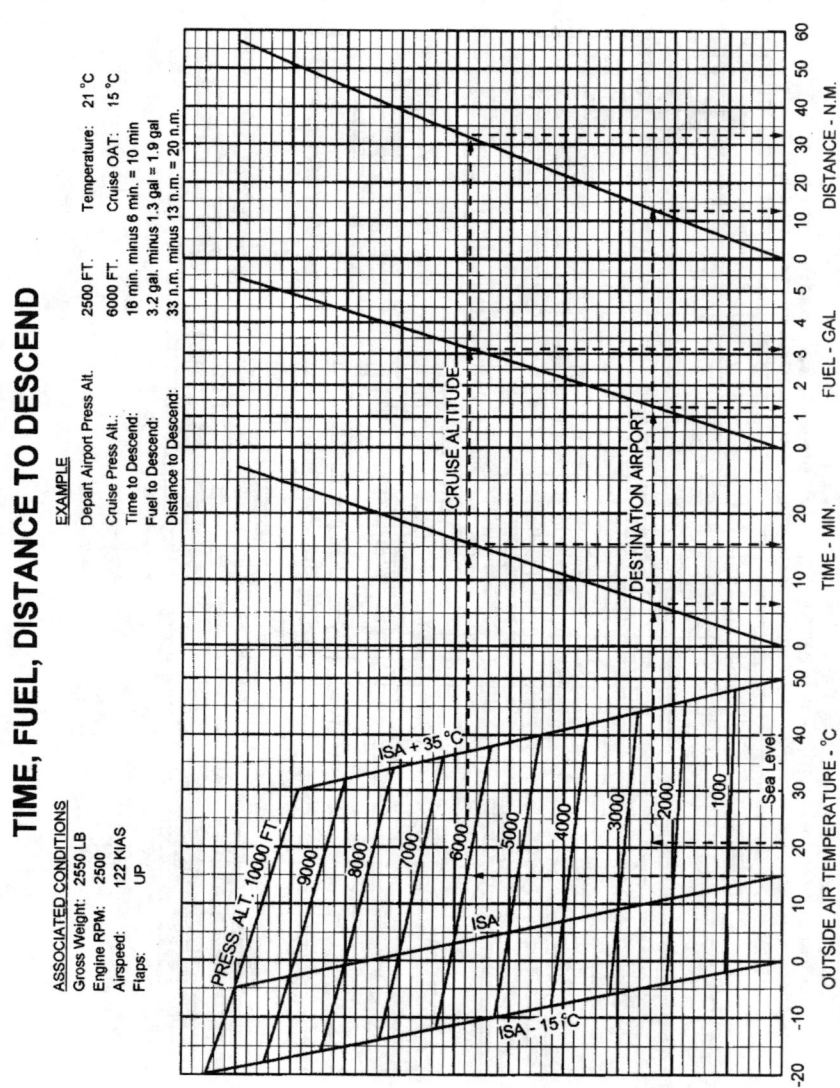

TIME, DISTANCE AND FUEL TO DESCEND
Figure 5-37

Engine/Cruise Performance (55%)

PA-28-181, ARCHER III

SECTION 5
PERFORMANCE

Engine / Cruise Performance for Non-ISA OAT*
RPM for Constant 55% Power
Fuel Flow: Best Economy Mixture, 8.2 GPH

Pressure Altitude Feet	Indicated Outside Air Temperature °C	°C	°F	Engine Speed RPM	True Air Speed Knots **
Sea Level	ISA-15	0	32	2245	105
	ISA	15	59	2265	
	ISA +10	25	77	2275	
	ISA +20	35	95	2285	
	ISA +30	45	113	2295	106
2000	ISA -15	-4	25	2265	106
	ISA	11	52	2280	
	ISA +10	21	70	2295	
	ISA +20	31	88	2305	
	ISA +30	41	106	2315	107
4000	ISA -15	-8	18	2285	106
	ISA	7	45	2300	
	ISA +10	17	63	2315	
	ISA +20	27	81	2325	
	ISA +30	37	99	2335	108
6000	ISA -15	-12	10	2305	107
	ISA	3	37	2320	
	ISA +10	13	55	2330	
	ISA +20	23	73	2345	
	ISA +30	33	91	2355	108
8000	ISA -15	-16	3	2320	107
	ISA	-1	30	2340	
	ISA +10	9	48	2350	
	ISA +17.5	15.5	62	2360	108
9000	ISA -15	-18	0	2330	107
	ISA	-3	27	2350	
	ISA +8.5	5.5	42	2360	108
10000	ISA - 15	-20	-4	2340	107
	ISA	-5	23	2360	108

NOTE: * Aircraft weight 2550 Lbs., Wheel pants and strut fairings installed
** Subtract 3 KTAS if wheel pants are removed.

ENGINE/CRUISE PERFORMANCE (55%)
Figure 5-21

ISSUED: December 22, 2017

REPORT: VB-2749
5-21

Engine/Cruise Performance (65%)

SECTION 5
PERFORMANCE   PA-28-181, ARCHER III

Engine / Cruise Performance for Non-ISA OAT*
RPM for Constant 65% Power
Fuel Flow: Best Economy Mixture, 9.5 GPH

Pressure Altitude Feet	Indicated Outside Air Temperature			Engine Speed RPM	True Air Speed Knots **
	°C	°C	°F		
Sea Level	ISA -15	0	32	2385	113
	ISA	15	59	2405	
	ISA +10	25	77	2415	
	ISA +20	35	95	2430	
	ISA +30	45	113	2440	116
2000	ISA -15	-4	25	2405	114
	ISA	11	52	2425	
	ISA +10	21	70	2440	
	ISA +20	31	88	2450	
	ISA +30	41	106	2465	117
4000	ISA -15	-8	18	2430	115
	ISA	7	45	2450	
	ISA +10	17	63	2460	
	ISA +20	27	81	2475	
	ISA +30	37	99	2485	118
6000	ISA -15	-12	10	2450	116
	ISA	3	37	2470	
	ISA +10	13	55	2485	
	ISA +20	23	73	2495	
	ISA +30	33	91	2510	119
8000	ISA -15	-16	3	2475	117
	ISA	-1	30	2495	
	ISA +10	9	48	2505	
	ISA +17.5	16.5	62	2515	119
9000	ISA -15	-18	0	2485	117
	ISA	-3	27	2505	
	ISA +8.5	5.5	42	2515	119
10000	ISA -15	-20	-4	2495	118
	ISA	-5	23	2515	119

NOTE: * Aircraft weight 2550 Lbs., Wheel pants and strut fairings installed
** Subtract 3 KTAS if wheel pants are removed.

ENGINE/CRUISE PERFORMANCE (65%)
Figure 5-23

REPORT: VB-2749   **ISSUED: December 22, 2017**

Engine/Cruise Performance (75%)

PA-28-181, ARCHER III

SECTION 5
PERFORMANCE

Engine / Cruise Performance for Non-ISA OAT*
RPM for Constant 75% Power
Fuel Flow: Best Economy Mixture, 11.0 GPH

Pressure Altitude Feet	Indicated Outside Air Temperature			Engine Speed RPM	True Air Speed Knots **
	°C	°C	°F		
Sea Level	ISA -15	0	32	2485	119
	ISA	15	59	2515	
	ISA +10	25	77	2535	
	ISA +20	35	95	2550	
	ISA +30	45	113	2565	124
2000	ISA -15	-4	25	2520	121
	ISA	11	52	2545	
	ISA +10	21	70	2565	
	ISA +20	31	88	2580	
	ISA +30	41	106	2600	126
3000	ISA -15	-6	21	2535	122
	ISA	9	48	2560	
	ISA +10	19	66	2580	
	ISA +20	29	84	2595	
	ISA +30	39	102	2615	127
4000	ISA -15	-8	18	2550	123
	ISA	7	45	2575	
	ISA +10	17	63	2595	
	ISA +20	27	81	2610	
	ISA +30	37	99	2630	128
5000	ISA -15	-10	14	2565	124
	ISA	5	41	2590	
	ISA +10	15	59	2610	
	ISA +20	25	77	2625	
	ISA +25	30	86	2635	128
6000	ISA -15	-12	10	2580	125
	ISA	3	37	2605	
	ISA +10	13	55	2625	
	ISA +15	18	64	2635	128
7000	ISA -15	-14	6.8	2595	126
	ISA	1	34	2625	
	ISA +7.5	8.5	47	2635	128

NOTE: * Aircraft weight 2550 Lbs., Wheel pants and strut fairings installed
** Subtract 3 KTAS if wheel pants are removed.

ENGINE/CRUISE PERFORMANCE (75%)
Figure 5-25

ISSUED: December 22, 2017

REPORT: VB-2749
5-23

CHAPTER 4 WEIGHT & BALANCE AND PERFORMANCE

LESSON 6

RANGE, ENDURANCE, AND GLIDE CHARTS

PURPOSE

The purpose of this lesson is for students to learn how to use the range and endurance charts and to practice using the weight and balance and performance charts covered in previous lessons.

ACCOMMODATIONS FOR LEARNING DIFFERENCES

It is important that lessons accommodate the needs of every learner. These lessons may be modified to accommodate your students with learning differences by referring to www.pacer.org/parent/php/PHP-c267.pdf.

PREPARATION

- Piper Archer (PA-28-181) Pilot's Operating Handbook (POH)
- *Pilot's Handbook of Aeronautical Knowledge* (FAA-H-8083-25)

DIRECTIONS

Introductory Activity: Pose the following question for students: You are lost; how long will you be able to remain aloft, i.e., how much time do you have to find a place to land before running out of fuel? Allow time for student responses. To address the question posed, discuss the factors that affect range, endurance, and glide. (*Examples include*: altitude, weight of the aircraft, density altitude, wind, etc.)

Step 1: Create and describe a scenario where the student has to use a variety of performance charts. The scenario should have enough information about a flight in a few hours so they have to compute a weight and balance and use that to figure out takeoff, landing, rate of climb, fuel time, distance to climb and descend, cruise, endurance, range, and landing distances. (*Example Scenario*: You are planning for a couple hour sightseeing flight around the local area and you are departing KABC airport, which has a field elevation of 900 feet. Use the weight of the aircraft from previous lessons, with two passengers that weigh 150 and 127, and have the students use their own weight or a common weight of 130. The temperature today is 20 degrees C, the wind is 250 at 11 knots, and the altimeter setting is 29.95.)

Step 2: Referencing the charts in Activity 1 (Range, Endurance, and Glide Range Charts) in the Student Notebook (and below under Facilitator Information), ask students to define range, endurance, and glide and describe how they are different from each other. (*Answer:* range is how far the aircraft will fly, endurance is how long the aircraft can remain in flight, and glide is how far the aircraft will descend without engine power.)

Pose the following question to the students as they are looking at the charts in their Student Notebooks: "Why are there two endurance charts and two range charts for the Piper Archer?" (*Answer:* One is with the fuel reserves and the other is without the fuel reserves.)

Reference Chapter 11 in the *Pilot's Handbook of Aeronautical Knowledge* for more information about these topics.

Step 3: Building on students' knowledge of aircraft performance from the previous lessons, model how to use the range and endurance charts by creating a scenario that includes the altitude you will be cruising at (enroute altitude) and what percent power you will be using for the flight (55%, 65%, or 75%). Once the enroute altitude and power setting are indicated, model how to use the charts to compute the endurance and range for that given flight. Examples showing how to use the charts are provided on the actual Piper Archer performance charts in the Student Notebook, and generic examples can be found in the *Pilot's Handbook of Aeronautical Knowledge*, Chapter 11.

Steps to using the range and endurance charts are as follows:

1. Start on the left side of each of the charts at your cruise pressure altitude.
2. Go straight over to the percent power at which you will be flying.
3. Go straight down, and that will give you the range or endurance information.

Step 4: With guidance and modeling, students can complete the range and endurance practice problems (questions 1–4) found in Activity 2 in the Student Notebook. (An answer key is provided at the end of the chapter.)

Step 5: Direct students' attention to the glide range performance chart found in the Student Notebook. Model how to use the glide chart by creating a scenario that includes the altitude you will be cruising at (enroute altitude) and field or ground elevation. Once the altitudes are indicated, model how to use the chart to compute the glide range for that given flight. Again, an example of how to use the chart is provided on the actual Piper Archer glide range chart provided in the Student Notebook (also reproduced under Facilitator Information at the end of this lesson), and generic examples can be found in the *Pilot's Handbook of Aeronautical Knowledge*, Chapter 11. Steps to using the glide chart are as follows:

1. Start on the left side of the chart at your cruise pressure altitude.
2. Go straight across to the reference line.
3. Go straight down and note that distance.
4. Do the same 3 steps using the terrain pressure altitude.
5. Subtract the terrain distance from the cruise and that is your glide distance.

Step 6: With guidance and modeling, students can complete the remainder of the glide range practice problems (questions 5–6) found in Activity 2 in the Student Notebook.

Concluding Activity: Have students share/reflect how the answers to the above scenarios would change if they were flying a Boeing 747 or any other much larger and heavier aircraft that flies at a higher altitude (all aircraft regardless of size will have performance charts and limitations). Answer additional questions as time allows.

FACILITATOR INFORMATION

Range, Endurance, and Glide Range Charts

(The following charts are from the Piper Archer III PA-28-181 POH. For example only; do not use for flight planning.)

Range Chart (No Reserve)

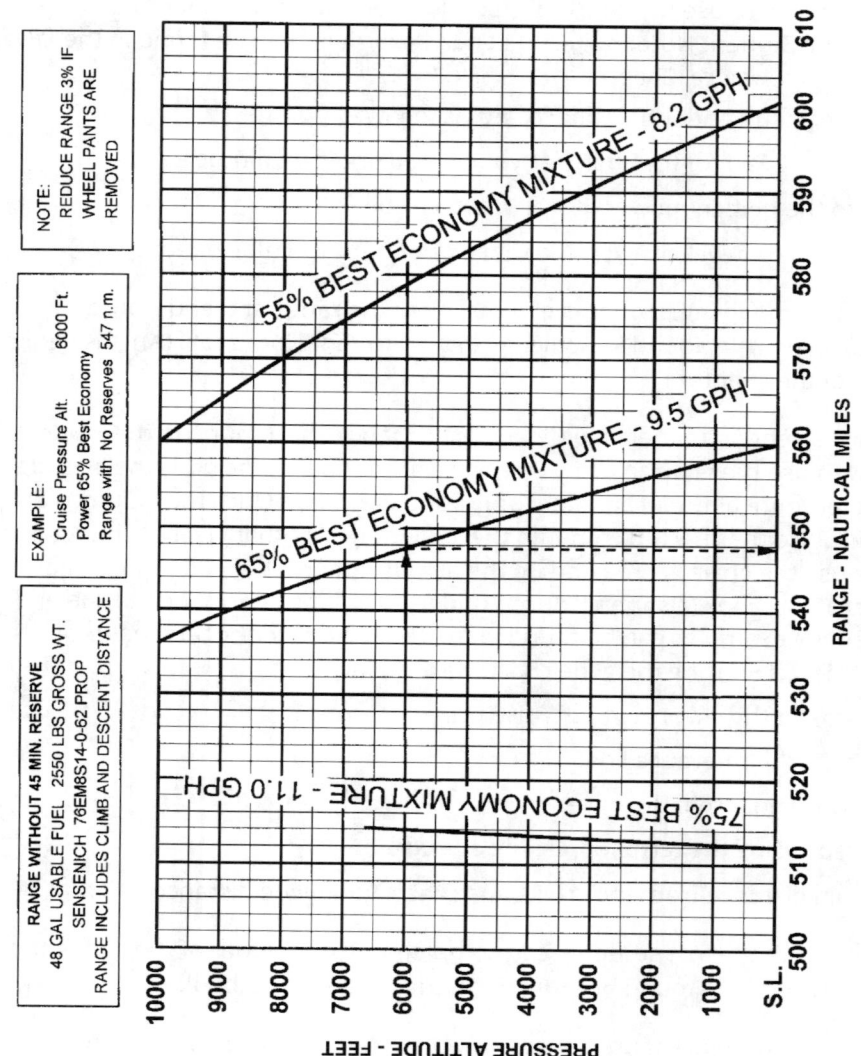

RANGE (NO RESERVE)
Figure 5-29

Range Chart (45 min. Reserve)

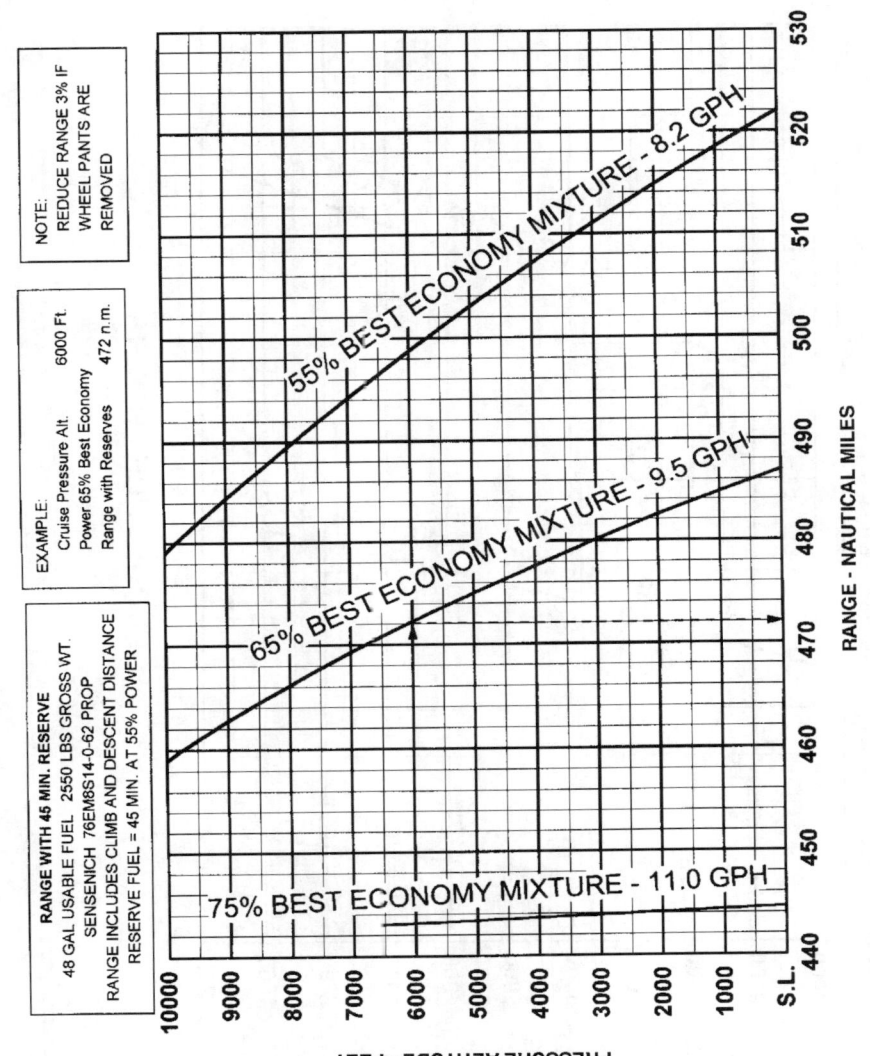

RANGE (45 MIN. RESERVE)
Figure 5-31

Endurance Chart (No Reserve)

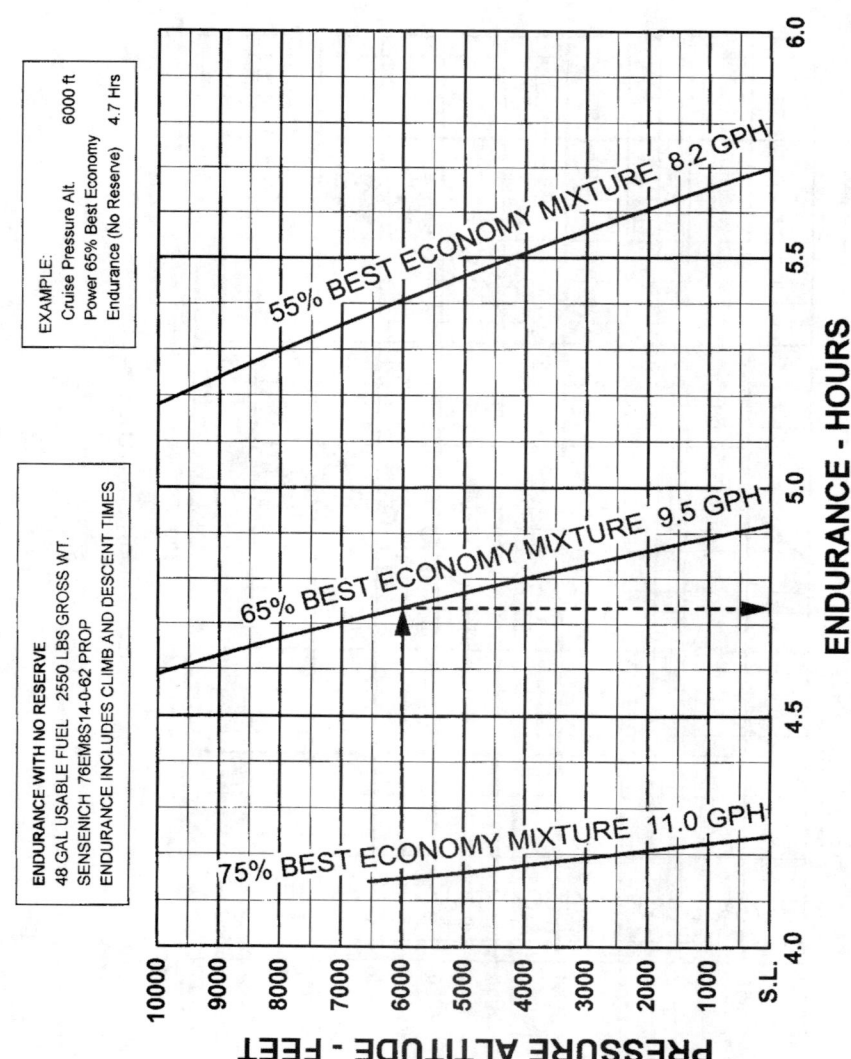

ENDURANCE (NO RESERVE)
Figure 5-33

Endurance Chart (45 min. Reserve)

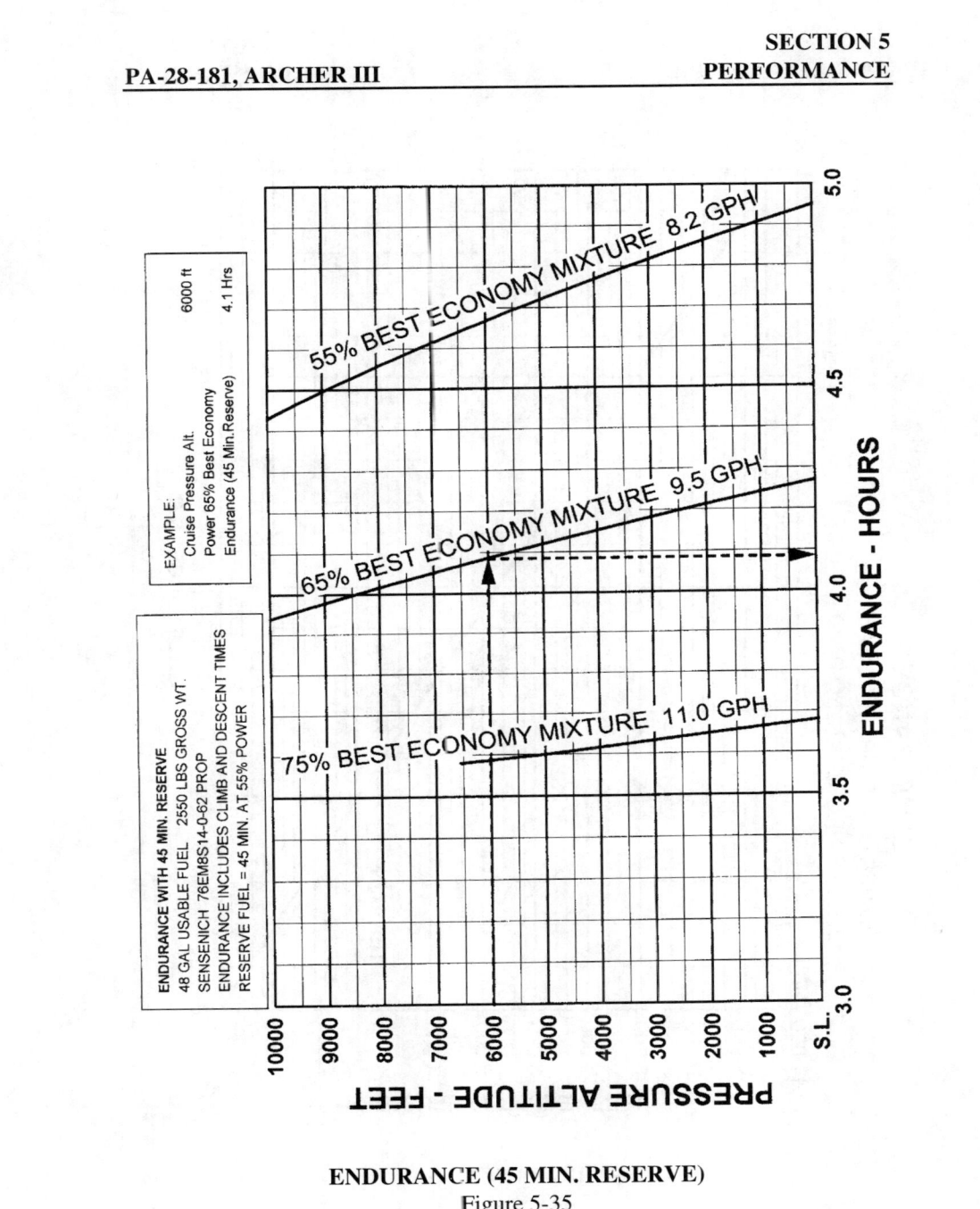

ENDURANCE (45 MIN. RESERVE)
Figure 5-35

Glide Range Chart

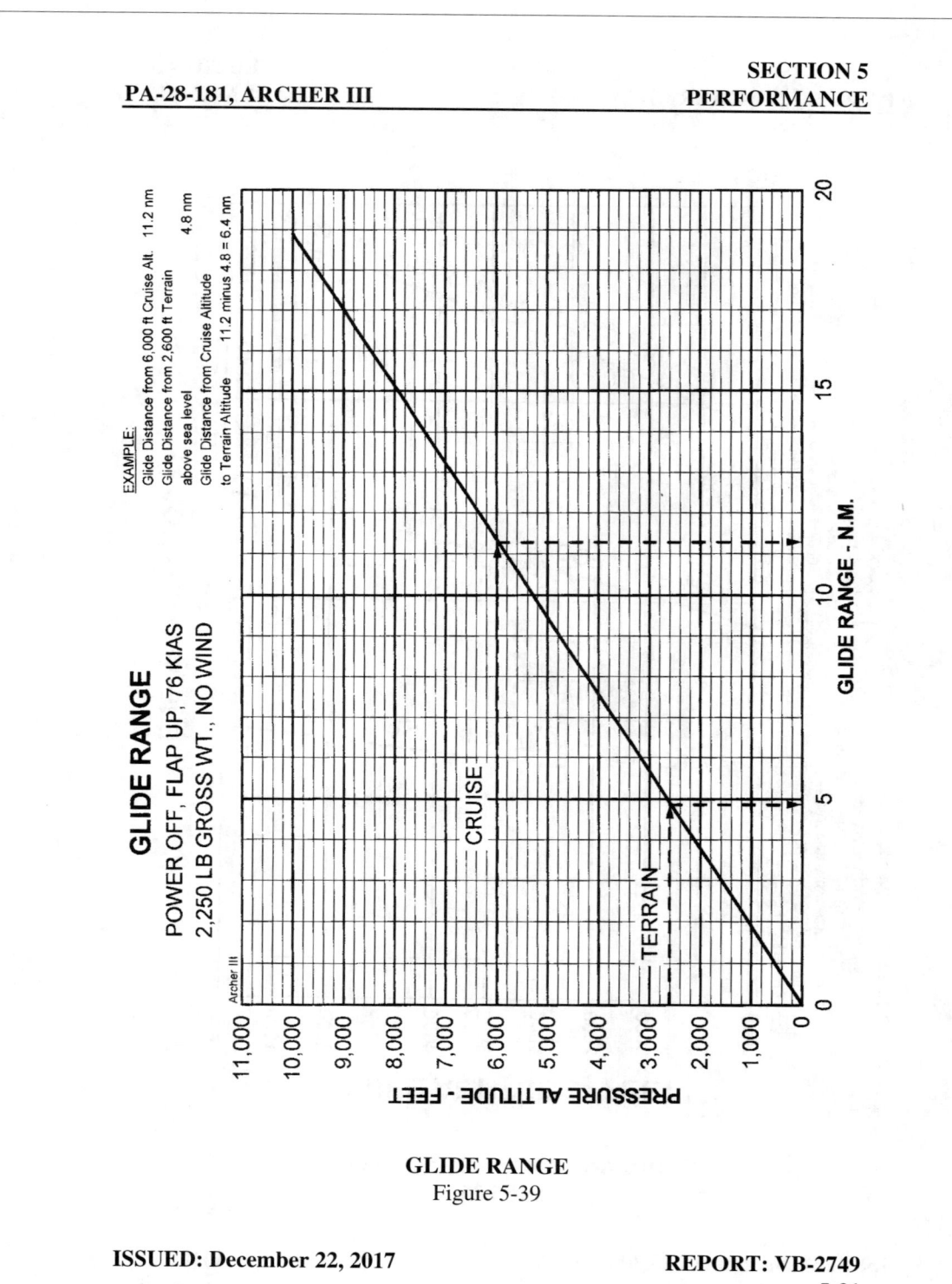

GLIDE RANGE
Figure 5-39

CHAPTER 4 WEIGHT & BALANCE AND PERFORMANCE

LESSON 7

GUEST SPEAKER: AVIATION PROFESSIONAL

PURPOSE

The purpose of this lesson is to expose students to real-world life experiences and career opportunities in aviation.

ACCOMMODATIONS FOR LEARNING DIFFERENCES

It is important that lessons accommodate the needs of every learner. These lessons may be modified to accommodate your students with learning differences by referring to www.pacer.org/parent/php/PHP-c267.pdf.

PREPARATION

- Send any relevant preparation materials to the guest speaker in advance (e.g., purpose, description of students' prior knowledge, Student Notebook pages).
- Ask the guest speaker to present dressed for their profession (e.g., pilot uniform, flight suit, military uniform); this will stimulate curiosity and questions from students.

DIRECTIONS

Introductory Activity: Introduce the presenter to the class. State: "Today we will be listening and talking to _____ about their aviation career." Choose one or two things that you truly admire about the speaker to share. The more specific, the better. Emphasize the importance of their role in aviation to establish credibility and interest.

Step 1: Have the speaker give their prepared presentation.

Step 2: While the speaker is presenting, students will actively process using the graphic organizer provided in Activity 1 (Two-Column Notes) in the Student Notebook. Allow students to think of and ask the speaker any additional questions.

- Be sure to highlight key issues that have been investigated by the students.
- Direct the conversation to things that students may be interested in.

Step 3: Ask the students and the speaker if there are any last questions or issues. Thank the guest speaker for his/her time.

Concluding Activity: Students will compare notes on the graphic organizer with a partner. Next, students will complete the summary prompt at the end of the two-column notes to answer at least one inquiry question. (See list of inquiry questions at the beginning of this guide on page 6.) Ask several students to share aloud. As a facilitator, be sure to highlight important information and clear up any misconceptions.

FACILITATOR INFORMATION
Guest Speaker Options
- Military pilots
- Airline pilots
- Aircraft mechanics
- GA pilot who built his or her own aircraft
- Aviation lawyer
- Airport manager

CHAPTER 4 WEIGHT & BALANCE AND PERFORMANCE

LESSONS 8 AND 9

REVIEW: WEIGHT & BALANCE AND PERFORMANCE

PURPOSE
The purpose of these lessons is to review exam questions.

ACCOMMODATIONS FOR LEARNING DIFFERENCES
It is important that lessons accommodate the needs of every learner. These lessons may be modified to accommodate your students with learning differences by referring to www.pacer.org/parent/php/PHP-c267.pdf.

PREPARATION
- Note cards

DIRECTIONS
Consideration: This lesson can take 1–2 days depending on how well your students know the content. You may take one day to complete the review/scenario questions and the next day to go over the answers and allow time for students' questions. Or you can have students complete the review questions, go over them in class, and assign the summative assessment for Weight & Balance and Performance for the next class period.

Introductory Activity: To begin the review session, write several weight, balance, and performance exam review questions on note cards (one for each student). Pass out questions and ask students to answer the questions independently by using the resources presented throughout the chapter. Answers can be recorded on the question cards. If students need additional questions, consider having several extras prepared. After a few minutes, call on each student to share their question and answer. Confirm responses and clear up any misconceptions.

Step 1: Exam review can be found in the Student Notebook in Activity 1 (Exam Review Problems). Allow students to complete the review questions independently or with a partner. (An answer key is provided at the end of the chapter.)

Step 2: Provide students with the correct answers to the exam review problems, answering questions as they arise.

Concluding Activity: Ask students to share the components of the content that are the most challenging. Address their questions and clear up misconceptions as necessary.

LESSON 10

CHAPTER 4 EXAM

PURPOSE

The purpose of this lesson is to assess students' knowledge of weight and balance and performance.

ACCOMMODATIONS FOR LEARNING DIFFERENCES

It is important that lessons accommodate the needs of every learner. These lessons may be modified to accommodate your students with learning differences by referring to **www.pacer.org/parent/php/PHP-c267.pdf**.

PREPARATION

- Student copies of Weight & Balance and Performance Exam
- Piper Archer (PA-28-181) Pilot's Operating Handbook (POH) charts for students to reference during exam.

DIRECTIONS

Introductory Activity: Review the total number of exam questions with students and remind them of the class's grading scale. This will focus students' attention on doing their best on the exam.

Step 1: Create an exam using the test bank below. Make copies of the exam and pass out one to each student.

Step 2: Remind students to listen to and read instructions carefully, making sure they understand the instructions. Encourage them to ask a question if they have one. Students should answer questions completely and with detail, checking to ensure they have not skipped anything and have proofread their answers.

Step 3: If students finish early, they can begin searching for current events for Chapter 5, which covers aviation communication.

Concluding Activity: Be sure to evaluate students' work and provide them with a summative score for the exam. (An answer key is provided at the end of the chapter.) If time allows, students can share a brief overview of the current events they located.

FACILITATOR INFORMATION

Chapter 4 Exam: Weight & Balance and Performance

(This exam is available in the online Instructor Resources in a format ready for use in the classroom. An answer key is provided at the end of the chapter.)

Read each question carefully and give exact answers; do not round.
(Reference the Piper Cherokee Archer POH)

1. Reference the Piper Cherokee Archer (PA 28-181) charts to compute a weight and balance using the following chart. The weights are as follows: the pilot is 180 pounds, the front passenger is 165 pounds, the rear passenger is 100 pounds, baggage is 25 pounds, and you plan to take full fuel.

	Weight	Arm	Moment
Basic Empty Weight (BEW)	1,658.40		146,518.99
Pilot			
Front Passenger			
Rear Passengers			
Baggage			
Fuel			
Ramp Weight			
Run-up	−8		−760
Takeoff Weight			

   Are you within limits?

2. Calculate the pressure altitude if the current altimeter setting is 29.74 and the field elevation is 942 feet.

3. Calculate the pressure altitude if the current altimeter setting is 30.22 and the field elevation is 1,564 feet.

4. What is the flaps up takeoff ground roll distance if the pressure altitude is 2,000 feet, temperature is 20°C, there is a 5-knot headwind, and the aircraft weighs 2,450 pounds?

5. What is the flaps 25 degrees takeoff ground roll distance if the pressure altitude is 3,000 feet, the temperature is 0°C, there is a 9-knot headwind, and the aircraft weighs 2,500 pounds?

6. What is the flaps up takeoff distance over a 50-foot barrier if the pressure altitude is 2,000 feet, the temperature is 10°C, there is a 5-knot headwind, and the aircraft weighs 2,350 pounds?

7. What is the flaps 25 degrees takeoff distance over a 50-foot barrier if the pressure altitude is 3,500 feet, the temperature is 5°C, there is a 15-knot headwind, and the aircraft weighs 2,400 pounds?

8. What is the lift-off speed at 2,500 pounds?

9. What is the landing ground roll distance if the pressure altitude is 1,500 feet, the temperature is 10°C, there is no wind, and the weight of the aircraft is 2,400 pounds?

10. What is the landing distance over a 50-foot barrier if the pressure altitude is 2,500 feet, the temperature is 10°C, there is a 7-knot headwind, and the weight of the aircraft is 2,450 pounds?

11. You plan to go on a flight today at 5,500 feet. The temperature is 4° C. You are planning to use 75% power.
    a. What is your engine RPM?
    b. What is your KTAS?
    c. What is your GPH?

12. You plan to go on a flight today at 4,000 feet. The temperature is −8°C. You are planning to use 65% power.
    a. What is your engine RPM?
    b. What is your KTAS?
    c. What is your GPH?

13. You are planning to fly to 5,500 feet today and the temperature is −5°C. What is your rate of climb?

14. You are planning to depart KGFK and climb to 3,500 feet. Today's pressure altitude upon departure is 1,000 feet.
    a. How long will it take you to climb?
    b. How much fuel will you use in the climb?
    c. How many miles will it take you to climb?

15. You are planning to depart KGFK and climb to 6,500 feet. Today's pressure altitude upon departure is 2,000 feet.
    a. How long will it take you to climb?
    b. How much fuel will you use in the climb?
    c. How many miles will it take you to climb?

16. You are planning to cruise at 7,500 feet. The field elevation is 1,500 feet.
    a. How long will it take you to descend?
    b. How much fuel will you use in the descent?
    c. How many miles will it take you to descend?
    d. What would your range be if you were flying at 5,500 feet and at 75% with reserve?
    e. What would your endurance be if you were flying at 3,000 feet at 55% with no reserve?

17. You are flying at 6,500 feet and experience an engine failure. How far will you glide in NM? The field elevation in this area is 1,200 feet.

ANSWER KEYS
CHAPTER 4

LESSON 2, Activity 3
Weight and Balance Exercises

Weight and Balance Exercise 1

	Weight	Arm	Moment
Basic Empty Weight (BEW)	1,662.78		146,840.14
Pilot	125	80.5	10,062.5
Front Passenger	110	80.5	8,855
Rear Passengers	200	118.1	23,620
Baggage	20	142.8	2,856
Fuel	288	95	27,360
Ramp Weight	2,405.78		219,593.64
Run-up	−8	95	−760
Takeoff Weight	2,397.78		218,833.64

CG = 91.26

Are you within limits? Yes.

Why or why not? Center of gravity and weights are within limits of the center of gravity envelope.

Weight and Balance Exercise 2

	Weight	Arm	Moment
Basic Empty Weight (BEW)	1,658.4		146,361.59
Pilot	300	80.5	24,150
Front Passenger	200	80.5	16,100
Rear Passengers	125	118.1	14,762.5
Baggage	50	142.8	7,140
Fuel	288	95	27,360
Ramp Weight	2,621.4		235,874.09
Run-up	−8	95	−760
Takeoff Weight	2,613.4		235,114.09

CG = 89.96
Are you within limits? No.
Why or why not? Maximum ramp and takeoff weights have been exceeded.
If not, what could you do to bring the aircraft back within limits? Reduce aircraft weight.

Weight and Balance Exercise 3

	Weight	Arm	Moment
Basic Empty Weight (BEW)	1,661.4		146,454.59
Pilot	125	80.5	10,062.5
Front Passenger	125	80.5	10,062.5
Rear Passenger	200	118.1	23,620
Rear Passenger	175	118.1	20,667.5
Baggage	50	142.8	7,140
Fuel	180	95	17,100
Ramp Weight	2,516.4		235,107.09
Run-up	−8	95	−760
Takeoff Weight	2,508.4		234,347.09

CG = 93.42
Are you within limits? No.
Why or why not? Center of gravity is aft of limits.
If not, what could you do to bring the aircraft back within limits? Reduce aft weight.

LESSON 4, Activity 4
Performance Worksheet (Student Notebook)

1. a. 815 feet
   b. 645 feet
   c. 925 feet
2. a. ~1,550 feet
   b. ~1,150 feet
   c. ~1,225 feet
   d. ~1,350 feet
3. a. ~1,750 feet
   b. ~1,950 feet
   c. ~2,200 feet
4. a. ~900 feet
   b. ~1,300 feet
   c. ~1,125 feet
5. a. ~920 feet
   b. ~910 feet
   c. ~910 feet
   d. ~980 feet
6. a. ~1,320 feet
   b. ~1,380 feet
   c. ~1,400 feet
7. a. ~800 feet
   b. ~1,040 feet
   c. ~920 feet
   d. ~920 feet

LESSON 5, Activity 3
Time, Fuel, Distance to Climb Practice Problems (Student Notebook)

1. a. ~4 minutes
   b. ~1 gallon
   c. ~8.0 miles
2. a. ~6 minutes
   b. ~1 gallon
   c. ~8 miles
3. a. ~12 minutes
   b. ~5 gallons
   c. ~18 minutes

LESSON 5, Activity 4
Time, Fuel, Distance to Descend Practice Problems (Student Notebook)

1. a. ~5 minutes
   b. ~0.9 gallons
   c. ~8 miles
2. a. ~20 minutes
   b. ~2.5 gallons
   c. ~38 miles
3. a. ~15 minutes
   b. ~3.0 gallons
   c. ~31 miles

LESSON 5, Activity 5
Engine/Cruise Performance Practice Problems (Student Notebook)

1. a. ~2575 RPM
   b. ~123 knots
   c. ~11.0 GPH
2. a. ~2485 RPM
   b. ~118 knots
   c. ~9.5 GPH
3. a. ~2587 RPM
   b. ~125 knots
   c. ~11 GPH

LESSON 6, Activity 2
Range, Endurance, and Glide Practice Problems (Student Notebook)

1. ~547 miles
2. ~443 miles
3. ~5.48 hours
4. ~4.0 hours
5. ~8.0 miles
6. ~10 miles

LESSONS 8 & 9, Activity 1
Exam Review Problems (Student Notebook)

Weight and balance for this flight:

	Weight	Arm	Moment
Basic Empty Weight (BEW)	1,658.40		146,518.99
Pilot	175	80.5	14,087.5
Front Passenger	140	80.5	11,270
Rear Passengers	190	118.1	22,439
Baggage	50	142.8	7,140
Fuel	288	95	27,360
Ramp Weight	2,501.4	91.75	228,815.49
Run-up	−8		−760
Takeoff Weight	2,493.4		228,055.49

1. Yes
2. ~1,000 feet taking off runway 27
3. ~840 feet
4. ~8 minutes
5. ~1.5 gallons
6. ~10 miles
7. ~11 minutes
8. 1.0 gallon
9. 23 miles
10. ~2,635 RPM
11. ~128 knots
12. ~11.0 gallons
13. ~443 miles
14. 3.6 hours
15. 9 NM

LESSON 10, Chapter 4 Exam
Weight & Balance and Performance

1.

	Weight	Arm/CG	Moment
Basic Empty Weight (BEW)	1,658.40		146,518.99
Pilot	180	80.5	14,490
Front Passenger	165	80.5	13,282.5
Rear Passengers	100	118.1	11,810
Baggage	25	142.8	3,570
Fuel	288	95	27,360
Ramp Weight	2,416.4	89.816	217,031.49
Run-up	−8		−760
Takeoff Weight	2,408.4	89.798	216,271.49

Are you within limits? Yes

2. 1,122 feet pressure altitude
3. 1,264 feet pressure altitude
4. 1,150 feet
5. 1,150 feet
6. 1,500 feet
7. 1,600 feet
8. 55 knots
9. 900 feet
10. 1,380 feet
11. a. 2,595 RPM
    b. 124.5 KTAS
    c. 11.0 GPH
12. a. 2,430
    d. 115 knots
    e. 9.5 GPH
13. ~500 fpm
14. a. ~5 minutes
    b. ~1.5 gallons
    c. ~7 miles
15. a. ~5 minutes
    b. ~2 gallons
    c. ~14 miles
16. a. ~15 minutes
    b. ~3.0 gallons
    c. ~29 miles
    d. 445 miles
    e. 5.6 hours
17. 10 NM

CHAPTER 5

COMMUNICATION

Introduction

STANDARDS & OBJECTIVES

North Dakota Aviation Content Standards (Grades 10–12)
- 3.3.1—Demonstrate use of the phonetic alphabet and numbers.
- 3.3.2—Convert local times to Zulu time and vice versa.
- 3.3.3—Discuss the purpose of the following facilities/frequencies: ground control, tower, CTAF, Unicom, FSS, approach/departure control, ATIS and en route center.
- 3.3.4—Describe the purpose of an airplane's transponder.
- 3.3.5—Explain the standard and emergency squawk codes.
- 3.3.6—Explain light gun signals and their purpose.

Science—Next Generation Science Standards (Grades 9–12)
- HS-PS4-2—Evaluate questions about the advantages of using a digital transmission and storage of information.

Language Arts—CCSS.ELA-LITERACY.CCRA
- L.1—Demonstrate command of the conventions of standard English grammar and usage when writing or speaking.
- L.2—Demonstrate command of the conventions of standard English capitalization, punctuation, and spelling when writing.
- R.1—Read closely to determine what the text says explicitly and to make logical inferences from it; cite specific textual evidence when writing or speaking to support conclusions drawn from the text.
- R.10—Read and comprehend complex literary and informational texts independently and proficiently.
- SL.1—Prepare for and participate effectively in a range of conversations and collaborations with diverse partners, building on others' ideas and expressing their own clearly and persuasively.
- SL.2—Integrate and evaluate information presented in diverse media and formats, including visually, quantitatively, and orally.
- SL.4—Present information, findings, and supporting evidence such that listeners can follow the line of reasoning and the organization, development, and style are appropriate to task, purpose, and audience.

- **W.2**—Write informative/explanatory texts to examine and convey complex ideas and information clearly and accurately through the effective selection, organization, and analysis of content.
- **W.4**—Produce clear and coherent writing in which the development, organization, and style are appropriate to task, purpose, and audience.
- **W.7**—Conduct short as well as more sustained research projects based on focused questions, demonstrating understanding of the subject under investigation.
- **W.8**—Gather relevant information from multiple print and digital sources, assess the credibility and accuracy of each source, and integrate the information while avoiding plagiarism.
- **W.9**—Draw evidence from literary or informational texts to support analysis, reflection, and research.

ESSENTIAL QUESTIONS

- What do you notice about how things work in this aviation topic?
- What are some things we could not do without understanding this topic in aviation?
- If we changed one thing about how this works, what do we think would happen?
- How do small changes in aviation affect the larger system?
- How do you think technology might change how we do this in the future?
- How will automation and/or autonomous operations change how this is accomplished in the future?

LESSONS

Lesson	Topic	Student Notebook Activities
Lesson 1	Air Traffic Control History	1. Shocking Facts 2. ATC History Timeline 3. ATC History Quiz
Lesson 2	Effective Communication	1. Take Home Communication Activity
Lesson 3	Air Traffic Control Jobs	1. Air Traffic Control Job Graphic Organizer 2. Air Traffic Control Jobs List
Lesson 4	Air Traffic Control Field Trip	1. News Report Outline
Lesson 5	Radio Transmissions	1. Phonetic Alphabet Pre-Test 2. Phonetic Alphabet Graphic Organizer 3. Phonetic Alphabet Post-Test
Lesson 6	Air Traffic Control Simulation	1. Airport Layout Graphic
Lesson 7	Current Events in Air Traffic Control	1. Double Entry Chart
Lessons 8, 9, 10	Air Traffic Management Group Research Project	1. ATM Assignment • ATM Assignment Description • Grading Criteria for ATM Research Presentation
Lesson 11	Review: Communication	1. Review Notes
Lesson 12	Chapter 5 Exam	1. Current Events

LESSON 1
AIR TRAFFIC CONTROL HISTORY

PURPOSE
The purpose of this lesson is to introduce students to the purpose and importance of air traffic control.

ACCOMMODATIONS FOR LEARNING DIFFERENCES
It is important that lessons accommodate the needs of every learner. These lessons may be modified to accommodate your students with learning differences by referring to **www.pacer.org/parent/php/PHP-c267.pdf**.

PREPARATION
- National Air Traffic Controller Association (NATCA) Presentation, "A History of Air Traffic Control"
- Video showing global air traffic volume over 24-hour period
- Video: "A Day in the Life of Air Traffic Over the United States"
- ATC History quiz

DIRECTIONS

Introductory Activity: Display several of the photos found in the National Air Traffic Controllers Association (NATCA) presentation, "A History of Air Traffic Control"[1] (see online Instructor Resources). After discussion of the photos, have students state what they already know about Air Traffic Control (ATC).

Or, visit the FAA's webpage "Air Traffic By the Numbers"[2] (**www.faa.gov/air_traffic/by_the_numbers/**) and have the students identify 1–2 of the statistics that they are most shocked by and write them down in Activity 1 (Shocking Facts) in the Student Notebook. Have students share why they think those are the most shocking statistics. The numbers/statistics illustrate how busy the aviation industry is.

Step 1: Pose the following question to the students: "Why do we need air traffic controllers?" Show the class videos that illustrate the volume of air traffic over the course of a day both globally and within the United States.

Then pose the following questions to the students: "Now imagine what would happen if there weren't air traffic controllers? How would that impact this industry?"

Step 2: The NATCA resource referenced above (in the Introductory Activity) can be used to share information on the history of ATC, or facilitators may create their own presentation related to ATC focusing on the following content:

- Name of the first air traffic controller and where he worked
- How ATC was conducted in the early years
- Why and when the federal government became responsible for ATC
- Equipment and displays used by ATC
- Technology advancements in ATC
- Job outlook, placement, and retirement age of air traffic controllers

Step 3: While you conduct an interactive lecture on the ATC history presentation, students will be filling in the graphic organizer under Activity 2 (ATC History Timeline) found in their Student Notebooks.

Step 4: Lead a discussion to review students' responses according to notes in their ATC History Timeline graphic organizers.

Step 5: Instruct students to complete the ATC History Quiz found in Activity 3 in the Student Notebook. (An answer key is provided at the end of the chapter.)

Concluding Activity: Review quiz answers while students grade their responses. If applicable, have students turn in their quizzes to be recorded in the gradebook.

LESSON 2
EFFECTIVE COMMUNICATION

PURPOSE
The purpose of this lesson is to explain the importance of effective communication in the operation of aircraft.

ACCOMMODATIONS FOR LEARNING DIFFERENCES
It is important that lessons accommodate the needs of every learner. These lessons may be modified to accommodate your students with learning differences by referring to www.pacer.org/parent/php/PHP-c267.pdf.

PREPARATION
- Divide students into groups
- Piece of paper for each group
- Piece of paper and pen for each student
- Take Home Communication Activity (Activity 1 in Student Notebook)

DIRECTIONS
Introductory Activity: Write the following sentence on the board: "enoyreve, yadot ssalc ot emoclew" (Note: It is in reverse order to make a point that effective communication is key! If written forward, the sentence would read: "Welcome to class today, everyone!") Lead a brief discussion on the importance of communicating effectively to get your point across. Split students into groups and have them complete the effective communication activities outlined below.

Step 1: *Communication Activity 1:* Give each student one piece of paper. Explain that you will be giving students instructions on how to fold the paper to create an origami shape. Let students know that they must keep their eyes closed and cannot ask any questions during the origami activity. Instruct students to fold the paper in specific ways and rip in several spots. The order that students fold and rip is not as important as the students keeping their eyes closed. When they are done folding and ripping, have students unfold their papers and open their eyes.

Step 2: Begin asking questions. Explain that each student's paper looks different even though they were all given the same instructions. What does that mean? Ask the group if you think the results would have been better if they kept their eyes open or were allowed to ask questions. The purpose of this activity is to reinforce the idea that communicating clearly is not easy and that everyone interprets the given information differently, and that is why it's very important to ask questions and confirm understanding to ensure the communicated message is not distorted.

Step 3: *Communication Activity 2:* Give all students a piece of paper and ask them to follow the drawing steps found below as you read the steps aloud. (This activity could easily be modified to describe the drawing of any simple object.) The students are not allowed to ask questions or to talk during this step of the activity.

1. Draw a large circle.
2. Draw two triangles on top of the big circle.
3. Draw two smaller circles inside the bigger circle.
4. Color in the inside circles.
5. Draw a triangle inside the big circle.
6. Draw three lines on each side of the top point of the inner triangle.

Step 4: After students have completed their drawings, have students compare their drawings with each other and ask, "How are the drawings the same and how are they different? Why are they the same or different?" Reinforce the need for effective communication.

Step 5: *Communication Activity 3:* Review expectations for Student Notebook Activity 1 (Take Home Communication Activity), which will be taken home as homework. Specific directions can be found in the Student Notebook. Have students work either in groups or by themselves to complete Part A of the activity in class. Part B should be completed at home as homework.

Concluding Activity: Search online for more activities that help illustrate the importance of effective communication. To summarize the lesson, have students share in writing the main reason that effective communication is essential in ATC.

LESSON 3

AIR TRAFFIC CONTROL JOBS

PURPOSE
The purpose of this lesson is to introduce students to air traffic control jobs.

ACCOMMODATIONS FOR LEARNING DIFFERENCES
It is important that lessons accommodate the needs of every learner. These lessons may be modified to accommodate your students with learning differences by referring to **www.pacer.org/parent/php/PHP-c267.pdf**.

PREPARATION
- Computers/devices and internet access for students
- Marker board and marker
- FAA webpage about aviation careers

DIRECTIONS
Before starting today's lesson, review the Take Home Communication Activity from the previous lesson to clarify misconceptions and answer students' questions.

Introductory Activity: Watch the video "A Flight Across America" on the FAA's website.[3] While the students are watching the video, have them write down as many of the jobs/positions that they see related to air traffic control. Examples of these positions may include: flight service station, ground controllers, tower controllers, approach controllers, departure controller, En route controllers, control specialist, operations, tower technician, operations supervisor, software engineer, supervisor, etc. Have the students share the positions and the facilitator should write them on the board.

Step 1: Using the list on the board, cross out jobs that are not related to air traffic control and lead a discussion about why those jobs are or are not related to air traffic control, providing a brief description of each.

Step 2: Once all careers have been reviewed, assign students ATC jobs in small groups. Their charge will be to develop and create an infographic related to their assigned ATC job. An infographic is a visual representation of information using a variety of images, charts, and pictures with minimal use of text. Infographics provide a concise overview of a particular topic. There are various websites that students can utilize to create their infographics, such as Piktochart, Venngage, and Canva. Students will be given time in class to complete their infographics. They can use the space provided in Activity 1 (Air Traffic Control Job Graphic Organizer) in the Student Notebook to organize their information. An example infographic may look like the following:

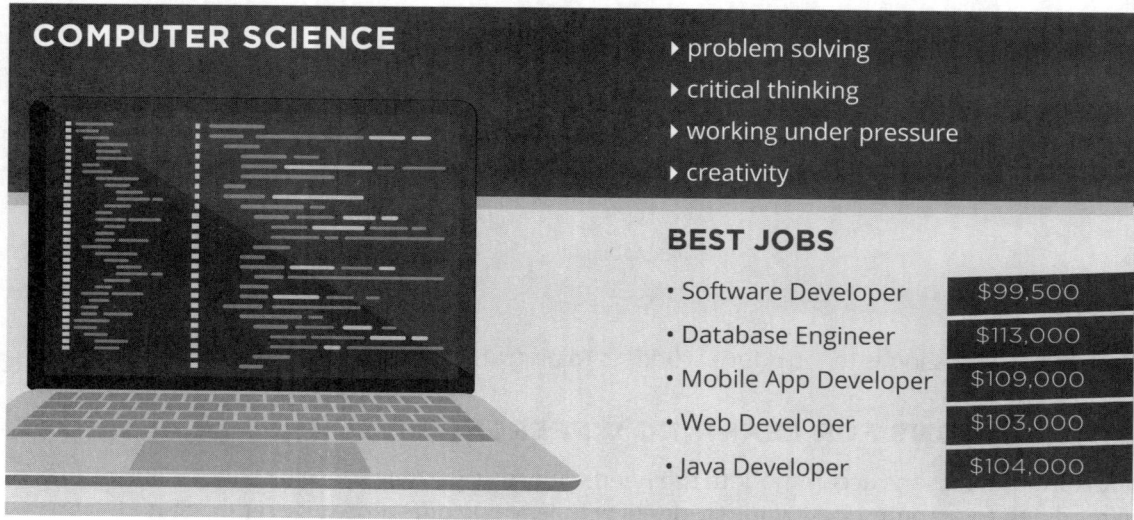

▶ Example Infographic

Step 3: Students will be asked to share their infographics with their peers. As students are presenting, the remaining students should record the airspace control and responsibilities of each particular ATC job in their Student Notebooks under Activity 2 (Air Traffic Control Jobs List).

Step 4: Included below under Facilitator Information is a sample of an ATC quiz that can be completed if time allows. The quiz would help the facilitator gauge the students' understanding of the various air traffic control roles. (An answer key is provided at the end of the chapter.)

Concluding Activity: Finally, print and display the infographics around the classroom and allow class time for students to share what they learned from creating and viewing the infographics.

FACILITATOR INFORMATION
ATC Quiz

(This exam is available in the online Instructor Resources in a format ready for use in the classroom. An answer key is provided at the end of this chapter.)

1. What does ground control do?
2. What does tower/local do?
3. What does approach do?
4. What does departure do?
5. What does a center do?
6. What does flight service station (FSS) do?

CHAPTER 5 COMMUNICATION

LESSON 4

AIR TRAFFIC CONTROL FIELD TRIP

PURPOSE
The purpose of this lesson is to explore an air traffic control tower, virtually or in person.

ACCOMMODATIONS FOR LEARNING DIFFERENCES
It is important that lessons accommodate the needs of every learner. These lessons may be modified to accommodate your students with learning differences by referring to **www.pacer.org/parent/php/PHP-c267.pdf**.

PREPARATION
- Determine whether you will take a real field trip (Option A) *or* virtual field trip (Option B) and plan accordingly.
- Notebook for students to make notes
- Notify parents of field trip and seek permission forms (Option A).
- Video clip on ATC tower (Option B)
- Paper and clipboards (Option A) or computers (Option B) for students to record observations during the field trip.
- News Report Outline (in Student Notebook)
- Thank you letters and envelopes

DIRECTIONS
Option A: Real Field Trip
If at all possible, schedule a field trip to a local Air Traffic Control Tower or Center Facility (ARTCC).* This allows students to observe the overall function and intricate details of the topic they are studying.

*Air traffic control centers are at all large airports. If you are located at or near a city with a population of approximately 30,000 people or near a military base with a runway, most likely there is an air traffic control tower. If you are unsure of who to contact, call the airport managers at your local airport who will be able to assist you in contacting the nearest air traffic control facility. If you are unable to contact an airport manager, contact the FAA at **www.faa.gov**.*

Step 1: Explain to students that you will be taking a field trip. Discuss the purpose of the field trip and how it relates to the current unit of air traffic control.

Step 2: As a class, brainstorm a set of behaviors and expectations to adhere to during the field trip. Also, brainstorm a list of open-ended questions that will help students gather information during the visit. You may assign students questions or allow students to naturally ask the questions during the field trip.

Step 3: While at the field trip site, encourage students to take notes, answering the questions that they brainstormed as a class. Students should note particular points of interest, items that surprised them, and questions they still have regarding air traffic control.

Step 4: Students will create a short news report about what happened on the field trip. This reinforces important concepts and allows the students an opportunity to summarize their learning. Have students work in small groups to complete the template in Activity 1 (News Report Outline) found in their Student Notebooks. Give students an authentic audience by publicizing the news report via an article in your local newspaper, school paper, school bulletin board, etc.

Concluding Activity: Have students share their news reports with the rest of the class. If possible, have the class compose and send thank you letters to the field trip site hosts. Include favorite items or special information learned during the field trip.

Option B: Virtual Field Trip

If a field trip is not possible in your area, conduct a virtual field trip with your students.

Introductory Activity: Have six students in the class stand up, and tell them all to run to the door right now. Have the class observe what happened. As the facilitator, bring up the fact that the students most likely adjusted the speed in which they were walking/running to exit the classroom in a certain order. Ask the students why they did that. This happens every day with aircraft, but the difference is the aircraft can't see each other. Aircraft have ATC to separate them as they fly into and out of airports.

Step 1: Explain to students that you will be taking a virtual field trip. Discuss the purpose of the field trip and how it relates to the current unit about air traffic control. Potential resources to use to find a virtual field trip that is right for you and your students include online videos about ATC, news stories, and arranging a video chat with an air traffic controller. (See Instructor Resources for several specific ideas.)

Step 2: Brainstorm a list of open-ended questions that will help students gather information during the virtual field trip. You may assign students questions or allow students to naturally ask questions that arise during the virtual field trip.

Step 3: During the virtual field trip, encourage students to take notes, answering the questions brainstormed as a class. Have students note particular points of interest, items that surprised them, and questions they still have regarding air traffic control.

Step 4: Student will create a short news report about what happened during the virtual field trip. This reinforces important concepts and allows the students an opportunity to summarize their learning. Have students work in small groups to complete the template in Activity 1 (News Report Outline) found in their Student Notebooks. Give students an authentic audience by publicizing the news report via an article in your local newspaper, school paper, school bulletin board, etc.

Concluding Activity: Have students share their news reports with the rest of the class. Include favorite items or special information learned during the virtual field trip.

LESSON 5

RADIO TRANSMISSIONS

PURPOSE
The purpose of this lesson is to learn and practice using the phonetic alphabet.

ACCOMMODATIONS FOR LEARNING DIFFERENCES
It is important that lessons accommodate the needs of every learner. These lessons may be modified to accommodate your students with learning differences by referring to **www.pacer.org/parent/php/PHP-c267.pdf**.

PREPARATION
- Video demonstrating radio transmissions between pilot and ATC
- Technical Aviation Communication Interactive Trainers, University of North Dakota Aviation
- Phonetic Alphabet Graphic Organizer (in Student Notebook)
- Radio transmission, cut into slips (optional; found below)
- Computers/devices and internet access for students

DIRECTIONS

Introductory Activity: Set up the computer and projector so students can listen and watch a video to hear radio transmissions between pilots and air traffic control. While students are watching and listening, have them pay attention to the letters and numbers they are hearing. Encourage them to identify what those numbers might mean by asking them questions once the video is over.

Step 1: Once students have watched the video and been exposed to the terminology, have them complete the pre-test found in their Student Notebooks, Activity 1 (Phonetic Alphabet Pre-Test). Students will make predictions as to what words represent certain letters of the phonetic alphabet. (An answer key is provided at the end of the chapter.)

Step 2: After the pre-test, take time to explain the phonetic alphabet with students. Discuss why it is used and how it was developed. Ask them if they can think of a time where the use of the phonetic alphabet would have helped them. List other examples of how it is used in the real world. The phonetic alphabet is used to help communicate on the radio when there may be multiple aircraft call signs similar to one another. If an aircraft's N-number is "123SP" and another aircraft is "123TD", the call signs could be confused resulting in a pilot accepting a clearance from air traffic control that would be dangerous. "123 Sierra-Papa" and "123 Tango-Delta" ensures effective communication between the sender and the receiver.

Step 3: Give students time to conduct research on the internet to fill in Activity 2 (Phonetic Alphabet Graphic Organizer) in their Student Notebooks. Once students have filled in the answers, review the correct phonetic alphabet letter representations with them (found under Facilitator Information below).

Step 4: Show students a video that demonstrates a person saying each of the letters in the phonetic alphabet. Have students practice the alphabet and its associated words with a partner. One partner will say the letter and the other partner will say the phonetic alphabet word associated with that letter.

Step 5: Have students complete the Phonetic Alphabet Post-Test found in Activity 3 in the Student Notebook and then discuss results as a class. (An answer key is provided at the end of the chapter.) Provide correct letter associations as aligned to the phonetic alphabet. If they finish the post-test early, have them create their own sentences using the phonetic alphabet.

Step 6: If you have additional time, split students into small groups of three or four students. Give each group a copy of the radio transmission (from the Facilitator Information section below) cut up into slips. Allow students to sort them in the correct order. Once the groups have divided the transmission slips into the correct order, assign speaking parts to various students in the class. Have the students read out the radio transmissions and explain throughout what each transmission means and help the students with the proper phraseology. For example, instead of saying "N245ND" the pilot should say "November 2-4-5 November Delta."

Concluding Activity: Pull up the radio transmissions video that was played at the beginning of the lesson. Pause the video on a scene that depicts several examples of practical application related to the phonetic alphabet. Have students discuss and share what those letters represent and state why the phonetic alphabet is so important to pilots.

FACILITATOR INFORMATION
Phonetic Alphabet

Phonetic Alphabet	
A — Alpha	N — November
B — Bravo	O — Oscar
C — Charlie	P — Papa
D — Delta	Q — Quebec
E — Echo	R — Romeo
F — Foxtrot	S — Sierra
G — Golf	T — Tango
H — Hotel	U — Uniform
I — India	V — Victor
J — Juliet	W — Whiskey
K — Kilo	X — X-ray
L — Lima	Y — Yankee
M — Mike	Z — Zulu

Radio Transmission

Directions: Make enough copies so each small group has a copy. Before the sorting activity, cut up transmissions into slips and have students sort them, in order, in their small groups.

Pilot: Miami Ground N245ND is at the FBO we are ready to taxi for a NE departure and we have information Lima.

Miami Ground: N245ND, Miami Ground, you are cleared to taxi to RWY 36 via Uniform, Bravo, Bravo 1, squawk 0129.

Pilot: Taxi to RWY 36 via Uniform, Bravo, Bravo 1, squawk 0129, N245ND.
(Now at the runway) Miami Tower, N245ND is holding short of RWY 36, ready for takeoff.

Miami Tower: N245ND, Miami Tower, hold short of the RWY, traffic 1 mile final.

Pilot: Hold short of the RWY, N245ND.

Miami Tower: N245ND, cleared for takeoff RWY 36, fly runway heading.

Pilot: Runway heading, cleared for takeoff, N245ND.

Miami Tower: N245ND, contact Miami Departure on 132.3.

Pilot: Contact Miami Departure on 132.3, N245ND.

Pilot: Miami Departure, N245ND is climbing through 2,500 ft.

Miami Departure: N245ND, radar contact 4 miles N of the airport at 2,700 ft. Cleared on course to Boston.

Pilot: Cleared on course to Boston, N245ND.

Miami Departure: Contact Miami Center on 118.1.

Pilot: Contact Miami Center on 118.1, N245ND
(switched to Miami Center frequency)
Miami Center, this is N245ND level at 7,500.

Miami Center: N245ND, Miami Center, radar contact 30 miles NE of Miami. The current altimeter setting at Daytona Beach is 29.98.

Pilot: Roger. N245ND

Pilot: Boston Approach, N245ND is descending through 5,600 ft inbound to Boston International for a full stop landing with information Foxtrot.

Boston Approach: N245ND, radar contact, descend at pilot's discretion to 3,000 ft, report when you have the field in sight.

Pilot: Descend to 3,000 ft and will report the field in sight, N245ND.
Field in sight, N245ND.

Boston Approach: Contact Boston Tower on 124.5.

Pilot: Boston Tower, N245ND is 5 miles S of the field for a full stop.

Boston Tower: N245ND, follow traffic on a 2 miles final for RWY 22, expect RWY 22.

Pilot: Boston tower, N245ND is looking for traffic and expect RWY 22.
Traffic in sight. N245ND.

Boston Tower: N245ND, cleared to land RWY 22.

Pilot: N245ND cleared to land RWY 22.

Boston Tower: N245ND turn right on Kilo 4 and contact ground.

Pilot: Right on Kilo 4 and contact ground, N245ND *(to Boston Tower)*
(they have switched to Boston Ground's frequency now)
Boston Ground, N245ND is on Kilo 4, ready to taxi to the FBO.

Boston Ground: N245ND, taxi to parking via Kilo, Juliet and Alpha.

Pilot: Taxi to parking via Kilo, Juliet and Alpha, N245ND.

LESSON 6
AIR TRAFFIC CONTROL SIMULATION

PURPOSE
The purpose of this lesson is for students to practice communicating as pilots to controllers and as controllers to pilots in a simulated environment.

ACCOMMODATIONS FOR LEARNING DIFFERENCES
It is important that lessons accommodate the needs of every learner. These lessons may be modified to accommodate your students with learning differences by referring to **www.pacer.org/parent/php/PHP-c267.pdf**.

PREPARATION
- Picture of an airport layout, on projector screen
- Masking tape
- Student role cards
- Paper and markers or whiteboard and markers
- Evaluation checklist for each student
- Exit slip

DIRECTIONS
Introductory Activity: Show students a picture of an airport layout (select one with multiple runways or even intersecting runways). Ask students to turn to someone sitting next to them and discuss some of the challenges an air traffic controller would potentially face given that airport/runway layout. Have several partners share what they noticed and lead a discussion to clarify any misconceptions and validate students' accurate thinking.

Step 1: Direct students to review the airport layout graphic shown in Activity 1 in the Student Notebook. From there, ask the class to make room in the classroom to create this layout on the floor with masking tape. Give students several minutes to create the runways, taxiways, departure and arrival corridors, control towers, etc., offering assistance as necessary.

Direct the students to discuss what challenges an air traffic controller would potentially face given that airport/runway layout. Ask students to record their thoughts about the airport design in their Student Notebooks.

Step 2: In order for air traffic controllers to tell pilots where to go, they need to have a great understanding of directions. The facilitator should review with the class where North is in reference to the classroom. Then ask them to locate South, East, and West. The facilitator will put post-it notes on the 4 walls with cardinal directions in degrees on them (unless the post-it notes are still there from covering this material in Chapter 3).

Step 3: Now that the students have reviewed their directions, they are ready to take on the roles of controllers. Create two sets of role cards (one card per student). Half the role cards should state "Aircraft" and the other half "Controller." Pass out the role cards to students. Split students into the two assigned groups and have each group brainstorm their responsibilities as an "Aircraft" or as a "Controller." Have them write their responsibilities on a piece of paper or the whiteboard. Lead the discussion to ensure that students have accurate responsibilities written on their role cards.

Step 4: Using the examples below, model for students how to use proper terminology when leading the plane into and out of the airport. A good rule of thumb is that conversations always include who they are talking to, who they are, where they are, and what they want to do.

Example:

    Pilot: "Grand Forks Ground, N274ND *(November-2-7-4-November Delta)* is on the Charlie Ramp, would like to taxi for a Northeast departure with information Alpha."

    Ground: "N274ND *(November-2-7-4-November Delta)* Grand Forks Ground, taxi to runway 35R (35-right) via Charlie, Charlie 2."

Remember to use the phonetic alphabet when saying these statements.

Another Example:

    Tower: "N342TJ, Grand Forks Tower, you are cleared for takeoff."

    Pilot: "Grand Forks Tower, N342TJ is cleared for Takeoff."

The facilitator is there to help with requests and offer further directions. The website LiveATC.net (**www.liveatc.net**) can be used to provide sample conversations between air traffic controllers and aircraft.

Step 5: After ample practice, have students conduct ATC simulations in which those in different roles (aircraft and controller) communicate with each other during various phases of flight (taxi, takeoff, landing, etc.). The simulation can last several days if you so choose.

Step 6: When students have demonstrated mastery, use the checklist below to evaluate students' ability to use and apply ATC communication. Prior to the evaluation, display the checklist so students know how they will be evaluated.

Concluding Activity: Ask students to list five things learned in class during the air traffic control simulation through an exit slip (a quick assessment of learning by writing a response to a question or orally answering). If time allows, review students' exit slips as a class, answering questions and clarifying misconceptions.

FACILITATOR INFORMATION

Airport Simulation Evaluation Checklist

Use the checklist below to evaluate students' performance on the airport simulation activity.

Student Name: _____

Skill		Points
Phraseology	Did they use the correct phraseology?	____/10
Appropriate clearance	For their given role (controller, aircraft), did they come up with an actual clearance that would be given by someone in their role? If a pilot, did they have a correct response?	____/15
Clearance order	Did they state who they are, where they are, and what they want to do as a pilot? As a controller, did they state who they are, who they are talking to, and what they want them to do?	____/10
Effort	Were they serious and did they put effort into this activity?	____/10
Participation	Did they actively participate in the activity (not just sit on the side of the classroom)?	____/5
Total points		____/50

LESSON 7

CURRENT EVENTS IN AIR TRAFFIC CONTROL

PURPOSE

The purpose of this lesson is to explore current events related to air traffic control.

ACCOMMODATIONS FOR LEARNING DIFFERENCES

It is important that lessons accommodate the needs of every learner. These lessons may be modified to accommodate your students with learning differences by referring to www.pacer.org/parent/php/PHP-c267.pdf.

PREPARATION

- Current event article
- Double Entry Chart (in Student Notebook)

DIRECTIONS

Introductory Activity: Select an appropriate current event related to air traffic control for students to read and discuss. You may find current events by searching the internet, news websites, or the sites of aviation-related organizations. Read the title together and have students predict what they think the story will be about.

Step 1: Have students independently read the article and complete Activity 1 (Double Entry Chart) in the Student Notebook, including notable quotes from the text supported by the students' personal observations, comments, or questions.

Step 2: Once students have completed their Double Entry Chart, lead a discussion on the current events article. As a facilitator, draw students' attention to the key ideas in the article and connections to air traffic control and other areas of aviation.

Concluding Activity: Have students share one entry from their chart. If time allows, ask students to find another article related to the original current events article.

LESSONS 8, 9, AND 10

AIR TRAFFIC MANAGEMENT GROUP RESEARCH PROJECT

PURPOSE
The purpose of these lessons is to conduct research on air traffic management.

ACCOMMODATIONS FOR LEARNING DIFFERENCES
It is important that lessons accommodate the needs of every learner. These lessons may be modified to accommodate your students with learning differences by referring to **www.pacer.org/parent/php/PHP-c267.pdf**.

PREPARATION
- Marker board and markers
- ATM Assignment Description (in Student Notebook)
- Grading rubric

DIRECTIONS
These lessons will take three days to complete.

Introductory Activity: As a class, brainstorm big topics in air traffic management (ATM) today. Facilitate the conversation to generate a comprehensive list. List the ideas on the board. Some topics could include:

- Next Generation Technology
- Privatization of air traffic control
- Congested airspace
- Integrating unmanned aircraft into the National Airspace System
- Crew resource management (CRM)
- Finding qualified personnel to work
- Preparing for flying cars
- User fees
- Free flight
- Duty periods
- ATC safety programs

Step 1: Split students into groups and assign each group a different topic relating to air traffic management (ATM). Review the Assignment Description and Grading Criteria provided in Activity 1 in the Student Notebook. Answer any questions students may have about the assignment.

Step 2: Identify 5–10 presentation modalities students can choose from (e.g., PowerPoint, Prezi, Google Slides, Powtoon, paper poster, iMovie, etc.). Spend a few minutes modeling for students how to collect accurate information for their presentation using the assignment description.

Step 3: Allow students class time to work on their presentations in small groups, providing support and clarification where necessary.

Step 4: Students will present their presentations during day 3 of this lesson. Before presentations, remind students of the grading criteria. Depending on class size, allow students 5–10 minutes to present their topic about ATM. Consider inviting individuals in the field of ATM or aviation in general to be a part of an authentic audience for student presentations.

Concluding Activity: As a facilitator, provide oral feedback on the presentations while students are presenting, highlighting key information you wanted the students to share. Also, print or copy the grading checklist below to formally provide students with feedback on their ATM presentations.

FACILITATOR INFORMATION
Grading Criteria for ATM Research Presentation

Prepare a presentation to explain the ATM topic assigned to your group. You will need to present this material to the class. Each group member will need to talk. Following are the grading criteria.

Student Name: _____

Skill	Points
Spoke during the presentation	____/20
Presentation included: • Explanation of the topic • How the topic impacts ATC • How the topic impacts pilots	____/20 ____/20 ____/20
Overall presentation (pictures, flow, duration)	____/20
Total points	____/100

LESSON 11

REVIEW: COMMUNICATION

PURPOSE

The purpose of this lesson is to review concepts related to air traffic control.

ACCOMMODATIONS FOR LEARNING DIFFERENCES

It is important that lessons accommodate the needs of every learner. These lessons may be modified to accommodate your students with learning differences by referring to www.pacer.org/parent/php/PHP-c267.pdf.

PREPARATION

- Communication/air traffic control exam questions (from the exam in Lesson 12)

DIRECTIONS

Introductory Activity: Ahead of time, select exam questions to review with students that you anticipate will be difficult for them. Show students a video clip of the game show Family Feud. Ask students to list what they notice about the rules of the game.

Step 1: Divide students into two teams, similar to Family Feud, and review the rules of the game with students. One person from each team will compete against each other to answer a review question, chosen and read by the facilitator. To be able to answer the question, students need to "buzz in." This could be the first student to raise their hand, first to grab an object placed between them, etc. If the first student to buzz in gets the question right, their team gets a point. If the first student gets the answer incorrect, the other student has a chance to answer and earn a point. To engage the other students on each team while they are not directly answering the question, have them write the answers to the questions in their Student Notebooks under Activity 1 (Review Notes).

Concluding Activity: Ask students to list one concept, idea, or vocabulary term they will study to ensure they do well on the exam during the next lesson.

LESSON 12
CHAPTER 5 EXAM

PURPOSE
The purpose of this lesson is to assess students' understanding of air traffic control and effective communication.

ACCOMMODATIONS FOR LEARNING DIFFERENCES
It is important that lessons accommodate the needs of every learner. These lessons may be modified to accommodate your students with learning differences by referring to **www.pacer.org/parent/php/PHP-c267.pdf**.

PREPARATION
- Communication exam
- Computers/devices and internet access for students

DIRECTIONS
Introductory Activity: Create an exam using the test bank provided under Facilitator Information and make copies of it for each student. (An answer key is provided at the end of the chapter.) Pass out exams and review the directions, highlighting questions that may challenge students.

Step 1: Remind students where they are expected to hand in their exam once it is complete. Allow time and provide a quiet space for students to complete the exam.

Step 2: When students finish the exam and are waiting for others to finish, have them preview current events for Chapter 6 (People, Events, and Trends in Aviation) by finding a recent article relating to this topic. The *General Aviation News* website (**generalaviationnews.com**) is an example of a potential resource.

Step 3: Have students write a one-paragraph reflective response to the article in their Student Notebooks under Activity 1 (Current Events). A few prompts for reflective writing can also guide the response. The following prompts are also provided for reference in the Student Notebook.

Prompts:
- How does this article relate to the key concepts and big ideas we have studied this year, or to big ideas from your other classes?
- What did you learn from the article that you did not previously know? What additional questions do you now have about the topic?
- Identify a problem that needs to be solved within this situation.

- What is your opinion of what you are reading and the issue being discussed? Do you agree/disagree with the writer/creator of this news item? Why or why not?
- How could the knowledge you gained from the event be used in one of the many aviation professions?
- What are some questions you still have regarding this topic?

Concluding Activity: Review correct exam answers with students once everyone has completed the exam. Students can share general findings from their preview of the Chapter 6 current events.

FACILITATOR INFORMATION
Chapter 5 Exam: Communication

(This exam is available in the online Instructor Resources in a format ready for use in the classroom. An answer key is provided at the end of the chapter.)

1. Generally speaking, what altitude does a Center Facility control?
    a. High
    b. Low

2. The Professional A_____ T_____ C_____ Organization, or PATCO, encouraged workers to go on _____ in 19_____. President _____ fired all workers who did not go back to work. Workers were seeking better _____.

3. The first air traffic controller at St. Louis Airport was _____.

4. The first air traffic controller controlled aircraft using _____.

5. Before the air traffic control system, pilots used to navigate via _____ to get to their destinations.

6. Controllers look at a screen called a _____ to view the radar information.

7. Within a tower facility, there are multiple ATC positions such as clearance delivery, ramp, ground, and tower. A ground controller can clear an aircraft to take off.
    a. True
    b. False

8. When controlling aircraft, it is important for the person to know what thing(s) about the aircraft they are controlling. List at least one of these things.

9. List two different jobs (positions) within the ATC field.

10. At what age does an air traffic controller need to retire?
    a. By their 56th birthday
    b. By their 57th birthday
    c. By their 58th birthday

11. Where do you go for training once you have been hired as an air traffic controller?
    a. Tulsa
    b. Oklahoma City
    c. Pensacola

12. List two benefits of being an air traffic controller.

13. List two cons or potential negatives about being an air traffic controller.

14. What is the name of the book that contains all of the ATC regulations?
    a. 8710
    b. 7110.65T
    c. ATC guide book

15. The purpose of an air traffic controller is to:
    a. Organize traffic
    b. Expedite traffic
    c. Prevent collisions
    d. All of the above

16. Who gets the first priority from ATC?
    a. Presidential flights
    b. Commercial airlines
    c. Lifeguard flights

17. What does "CRM" stand for as an air traffic controller?
    a. Crew resource management
    b. Client relationship management
    c. Customer relations management

18. Free Flight is expected to reduce air traffic controllers' workload.
    a. True
    b. False

19. The Air Traffic Safety Action Program (ATSAP) is designed to be a punitive program.
    a. True
    b. False

20. What heading is each of the letters in the text boxes from the center of the star?

    a. Letter A = heading _____
    b. Letter B = heading _____
    c. Letter C = heading _____
    d. Letter D = heading _____
    e. Letter E = heading _____

    HEADINGS
    110
    050
    235
    340
    170

21. When is it appropriate for a pilot not to follow ATC instructions?

22. When a pilot reads back a clearance to ATC, what does that tell the controller?

23. What is the phonetic word for the following letters?

    a. L _____   F _____
    b. U _____   P _____
    c. J _____   H _____

For questions 24–28, find the correct answer from the list below and place the corresponding letter (a, b, c, d, or e) after the question in the space provided.

Answer options:

   a. It is the en route control as well as into and out of airports without a control tower.
   b. It controls the area 4–5 NM away from an airport for aircraft landing and departing at the airport
   c. It is the command center that oversees possible traffic congestion situations.
   d. It provides pre-flight and in-flight briefings, filing flight plans, and search and rescue operations.
   e. It controls the area 5–40 NM away from an airport for aircraft arriving or departing the airport.

24. What is the duty of a Flight Service Station?_____

25. What is the duty of an Air Traffic Control Tower facility?_____

26. What is the duty of a Terminal Radar Approach Control facility?_____

27. What is the duty of an Air Route Traffic Control Center facility?_____

28. What is the duty of a Flow Control facility?_____

Bonus Questions:

29. The distance between two cities is 400 miles. What maximum speed will UPS285 have to maintain in order to fly this route in under 2.5 hours?

30. If a plane is traveling 270 knots with a 30-knot tailwind, how many miles will the plane fly in 3 hours and 15 minutes?

ANSWER KEYS

CHAPTER 5

LESSON 1, Activity 3
ATC History Quiz (Student Notebook)

1. (b) Archie League
2. (a) St. Louis
3. (c) Shrimp boats
4. (c) 1950s
5. (a) An aircraft midair collision
6. (c) A scope
7. (a) Reagan
8. (b) fired
9. (a) IBM
10. (a) By their 56th birthday

LESSON 3
ATC Quiz

1. Ground control controls the aircraft and vehicles while in operation on the ground.
2. Tower/local controls the approximately 4–5 NM radius around an airport for landing and departing aircraft at the airport.
3. Approach controls the area approximately 5–40 NM away from an airport for aircraft arriving at the airport.
4. Departure controls the area approximately 5–40 NM from an airport for aircraft departing the airport.
5. A center provides the en route control as well as into and out of airports without a control tower.
6. Flight Service communicates directly with pilots for pilot briefings, flight plans, inflight advisory services, search and rescue initiation, aircraft emergencies, and Notices to Airmen (NOTAMs).

LESSON 5, Activity 1
Phonetic Alphabet Pre-Test (Student Notebook)

A = Alpha   H = Hotel
D = Delta   L = Lima
I = India   P = Papa
T = Tango   V = Victor

LESSON 5, Activity 2
Phonetic Alphabet Graphic Organizer (Student Notebook)

A	Alpha	H	Hotel	O	Oscar	V	Victor
B	Bravo	I	India	P	Papa	W	Whiskey
C	Charlie	J	Juliett	Q	Quebec	X	Xray
D	Delta	K	Kilo	R	Romeo	Y	Yankee
E	Echo	L	Lima	S	Sierra	Z	Zulu
F	Foxtrot	M	Mike	T	Tango		
G	Golf	N	November	U	Uniform		

LESSON 5, Activity 3
Phonetic Alphabet Post-Test (Student Notebook)

Triple 0 is the number to ring for police assistance.

LESSON 12
Chapter 5 Exam: Communication

1. (a) High
2. Air Traffic Controllers Organization; strike; 1981; Reagan; pay and working conditions
3. Archie League
4. flags
5. bonfires, railroad tracks
6. scope
7. (b) False
8. Speed, size, destination
9. Tower controller, approach controller, center controller, departure controller, manager
10. (a) By their 56th birthday
11. (b) Oklahoma City
12. Good pay, mandated rest periods, job is always changing, comfortable work conditions
13. Shift work, may be stressful/really busy at times, may be very boring or slow at times

14. (b) 7110.65T
15. (d) All of the above
16. (c) Lifeguard Flight
17. (a) Crew resource management
18. (a) True
19. (b) False
20. a. 235°
    b. 340°
    c. 050°
    d. 110°
    e. 170°
21. In an emergency or when doing so will cause the pilot to break a regulation.
22. It tells the controller that they understand and will follow the instructions.
23. a. L = Lima; F = Foxtrot
    b. U = Uniform; P = Papa
    c. J = Juliet; H = Hotel
24. (d)
25. (b)
26. (e)
27. (a)
28. (c)
29. 160 knots
30. 975 NM

CHAPTER 6

PEOPLE, EVENTS, AND TRENDS IN AVIATION

Introduction

STANDARDS & OBJECTIVES

North Dakota Aviation Content Standards (Grades 10–12)
- 4.1.1—Discuss important people in aviation history and their contribution to the field of aviation.
- 4.1.2—Determine the progression of aviation technology.
- 4.1.3—Identify and explain current issues in aviation.
- 4.1.4—Describe how events in aviation history are changing the future of aviation.
- 4.4.2—Identify current career trends in aviation.

Science—Next Generation Science Standards (Grades 9–12)
- HS-PS3-3—Design, build, and refine a device that works within given constraints to convert one form of energy into another form of energy.
- HS-PS3-5—Develop and use a model of two objects interacting through electric or magnetic fields to illustrate the forces between objects and the changes in energy of the objects due to the interaction.

Language Arts—CCSS.ELA-LITERACY.CCRA
- L.1—Demonstrate command of the conventions of standard English grammar and usage when writing or speaking.
- L.2—Demonstrate command of the conventions of standard English capitalization, punctuation, and spelling when writing.
- R.1—Read closely to determine what the text says explicitly and to make logical inferences from it; cite specific textual evidence when writing or speaking to support conclusions drawn from the text.
- R.10—Read and comprehend complex literary and informational texts independently and proficiently.
- SL.2—Integrate and evaluate information presented in diverse media and formats, including visually, quantitatively, and orally.
- SL.4—Present information, findings, and supporting evidence such that listeners can follow the line of reasoning and the organization, development, and style are appropriate to task, purpose, and audience.
- SL.5—Make strategic use of digital media and visual displays of data to express information and enhance understanding of presentations.

- **W.2**—Write informative/explanatory texts to examine and convey complex ideas and information clearly and accurately through the effective selection, organization, and analysis of content.
- **W.4**—Produce clear and coherent writing in which the development, organization, and style are appropriate to task, purpose, and audience.
- **W.7**—Conduct short as well as more sustained research projects based on focused questions, demonstrating understanding of the subject under investigation.
- **W.8**—Gather relevant information from multiple print and digital sources, assess the credibility and accuracy of each source, and integrate the information while avoiding plagiarism.
- **W.9**—Draw evidence from literary or informational texts to support analysis, reflection, and research.

ESSENTIAL QUESTIONS

1. Why is the history of aviation important to know?
2. How has experimentation changed design, navigation, and regulation over time?
3. What impact on aviation have key people had?

LESSONS

Lesson	Topic	Student Notebook Activities
Lesson 1	Aviation Pioneers	1. Picture Response 2. Notes Outline 3. Quick-Think Questions 4. Summary Quote Response
Lesson 2	Aviation History—World War I through the Golden Age	1. Introduction Photo Analysis 2. Skeletal Notes Timeline 3. Quick-Think Questions 4. Influential Person/Event Comparison
Lesson 3	Aviation History—World War II, the Cold War, and the Jet Age to Today	1. Introduction Photo and Video Prompts 2. Cornell Notes Outline 3. Quick-Think Questions 4. Summary Activity Prompt
Lesson 4	Famous People in Aviation—Introduction	1. Famous People in Aviation List 2. Biography Template
Lesson 5	Famous People in Aviation—FakeBook	1. Fakebook Template 2. Venn Diagram
Lessons 6 & 7	Famous People in Aviation—Research Paper Workshop	1. Whip Share Prompts 2. Research Paper Rubric 3. One-Minute Paper
Lessons 8, 9 & 10	Hot Air Balloons	(None)
Lesson 11	Review: People, Events, and Trends in Aviation	(None)
Lesson 12	Chapter 6 Exam	1. Article Response and Rubric

CHAPTER 6 PEOPLE, EVENTS, AND TRENDS IN AVIATION

LESSON 1

AVIATION PIONEERS

PURPOSE

The purpose of this lesson is to explore the prehistory of early flight, identify the pioneers in the field, and make connections to the modern-day aviation industry.

ACCOMMODATIONS FOR LEARNING DIFFERENCES

It is important that lessons accommodate the needs of every learner. These lessons may be modified to accommodate your students with learning differences by referring to www.pacer.org/parent/php/PHP-c267.pdf.

PREPARATION

- Aviation history slideshow for pre-history, aviation pioneers up to World War I
- Student notebooks—notes outline

DIRECTIONS

Introductory Activity: Display 2–3 pictures of early aviation from the Library of Congress's "The Dream of Flight" timeline to the students.[1] Students will write down their response to the following statement about the pictures under Activity 1 (Picture Response) in the Student Notebook:

- I notice... so I wonder...

Step 1: Use an interactive lecture to provide direct instruction of early aviation history (up to dirigibles). Explain each new content element to be learned. Provide sufficient examples, and pair visual and auditory instruction.

Step 2: Have students complete Activity 2 (Notes Outline) in their Student Notebooks during the interactive lecture for active processing.

Step 3: Insert "quick-thinks" about every 10 minutes that function both as checks for understanding and as brief student engagement tasks. Have students record their responses under Activity 3 (Quick-Think Questions) in the Student Notebook.

- *Quick Think 1:* Turn to a partner next to you and complete this statement.: "The most similar part of early historical aviation that we still see evident in modern aviation is..."
- *Quick Think 2:* To encourage dialogue, ask students to find a new partner. Have students explain whether they think the following statement is true or false and explain why: "Leonardo da Vinci was the first true aviator."

- *Quick Think 3:* Ask students to explain how the Montgolfier brothers applied the engineering design method with their balloon.
  - Ask—What problem were they trying to solve?
  - Imagine—How did they propose to solve the problem?
  - Plan—What supplies did they need and what steps did they take?
  - Create—What did they create? (include dimensions)
  - Improve—What did they learn from their mistakes? How did they improve the design?
  - Present—How did they present their findings?

Concluding Activity: Write the following quote on the board or display it on a projection screen:

> "Man must rise above the Earth—to the top of the atmosphere and beyond—for only thus will he fully understand the world in which he lives."[2]

After reading the quote, ask students the following question: How does this quote by Socrates connect to/explain the importance of modern-day aviation? Students will record answers individually in Activity 4 (Summary Quote Response) in their Student Notebooks and then compare responses with a partner.

CHAPTER 6   PEOPLE, EVENTS, AND TRENDS IN AVIATION

LESSON 2

AVIATION HISTORY—WORLD WAR I THROUGH THE GOLDEN AGE

PURPOSE

The purpose of this lesson is to examine how and why aviation changed from World War I through the Golden Age of aviation and to introduce the history of unmanned aircraft.

ACCOMMODATIONS FOR LEARNING DIFFERENCES

It is important that lessons accommodate the needs of every learner. These lessons may be modified to accommodate your students with learning differences by referring to www.pacer.org/parent/php/PHP-c267.pdf.

PREPARATION

- Aviation history slideshow for World War I to the Golden Age
- Computers/devices and internet access for students
- Backchannel Chat discussion setup (or other online discussion tool)

DIRECTIONS

Introductory Activity: Have students view the picture in Activity 1 (Introduction Photo Analysis) in their Student Notebooks, or display an alternative photo involving World War I aircraft or historical unmanned aircraft used as a drone. Students will analyze the photo and record their responses to the prompts in Activity 1 (Introduction Photo Analysis) in the Student Notebook using the photo analysis process from the U.S. National Archives.[3]

Step 1: Use an interactive lecture to provide direct instruction of events on the timeline of flight from World War I through the Golden Age. Refer to the aviation history timeline under Facilitator Information on the next page for reference. Explain each event to show how and why aviation changed during that time period. Provide sufficient examples, and pair visual and auditory instruction.

Step 2: Have students complete Activity 2 (Skeletal Notes Timeline) to create a timeline of key events and people in the Student Notebook during the interactive lecture. See the correct timeline events under Facilitator Information at the end of this lesson.

Step 3: About every 10 minutes, insert "quick thinks" that function both as checks for understanding and as brief student engagement tasks. These are provided under Activity 3 (Quick-Think Questions) in the Student Notebook.

- *Quick Think 1:* Turn to a partner near you and compare completion of the timeline for accuracy up to this point.

- *Quick Think 2:* Turn to a new partner. Answer the following question together. "The most important lasting implication for aviation from World War I was…." Have students add their answers to Backchannel Chat or another online discussion tool.
- *Quick Think 3:* Students will take a class vote, recording which country's approach to aviation during the time of World War I is most like that of the United States today: Britain, Germany, or France. Students in each group should discuss the reasons for their answer in a way that convinces the other groups so that the class comes to consensus on one answer (use tally marks on the board or an interactive voting mechanism, such as Poll Everywhere).

Concluding Activity: Pose the following questions to students: "Who or what do you think is the most influential person or event in aviation history so far? Explain three reasons why that person or event is the most influential." Students will record answers individually in Activity 4 (Influential Person/Event Comparison) and then compare their responses with a partner. Students will turn in written answers.

FACILITATOR INFORMATION
Aviation History Timeline

Date	Name or Event	Description or Accomplishment
BC	Daedalus	Made wings of feathers and attached them to his arms with wax. His son flew too close to the sun, the wax melted from the heat of the sun, the feathers fell off, and the son fell out of the sky.
875 AD	Abbas ibn Firnas	Designed a flying machine capable of carrying a human being.
1452	Leonardo da Vinci	Sketched lots of flying machines including one with a screw link design.
1783	Montgolfier brothers	First hot air balloon flight
1849	Sir George Cayley	Father of aviation. First to think of four aerodynamic forces. Lots of manned glider designs. Used modern engineering terms.
1887	E.D. Archibald	Kite aerial photography by this British meteorologist.
1893	Otto Lilienthal	Studied birds. He built lots of gliders and logged more than 2,000 glider flights.
1898	Nicola Tesla	Demonstrated radio control of a small boat to the U.S. Navy.
1900	Ferdinand von Zeppelin	The prototype LZ1 took flight and carried people for almost 4 miles. He went on to create more successful rigid dirigible airships.
1903	Wright brothers	First manned flight in the Wright Flyer.
1908	Glenn Curtis	Man from the U.S. who championed for the development of aircraft. Created the "June Bug." Flew the first public flight over 5,000 feet, the longest flight to date.
1909	Louis Blériot	First man to fly across the English Channel.

Date	Name or Event	Description or Accomplishment
1914	World War I	Development of aircraft, bombers, and seaplanes. Lots of engine trouble. Aircraft were used in war for the first time, mostly for manned photographic reconnaissance.
1916	William Boeing	Created Pacific Airplane Company and a year later the company was renamed Boeing Airplane Company.
1916	Manfred von Richthofen	Recorded his first of many "kills" during aerial combat for Russia.
1917	Archibald Montgomery Low	He began work on an unmanned aircraft, which included the use of a gyroscope to maintain stability. He was labeled the "father of radio guided systems."
1918	Hewitt-Sperry Automatic Airplane	The first pilotless aircraft (drone) was developed after World War 1, flying in 1918. It was developed by the U.S. to be used for "aerial torpedoes."
1919	William "Billy" Mitchell	He is referred to as the "Father of the US Air Force." He advocated for the strengthening of air power in the U.S. military.
1924	Collett Woolman	He was one of the founders of Delta Airlines.
1925	Jimmy Doolittle	First pilot to complete an outside loop. First to fly completely IFR. Lots of records.
1927	Charles Lindbergh	First nonstop flight between New York and Paris.
1928	Amelia Earhart	First woman to fly across the Atlantic. Many records. Disappeared in 1937 during an attempt to fly around the world.
1930	Archie League	First air traffic controller. Controlled traffic by waving flags.
1932	Wernher von Braun	He went to work for the German army to develop liquid-fuel rockets.
1937	Jackie Cochran	Lots of air races. First woman to enter some of them. Set numerous speed records in various aircraft. First woman to land on an aircraft carrier. First woman to fly faster than the speed of sound. Best female aviator in 1938.
1940s	World War II	Increased the size of the Army's and Navy's aircraft presence. Lots of developments to aircraft—P-51 Mustang, P-38 Lightning, Corsair. Better engines, increased weapon-carrying capacity since WWI, increased maneuverability and speed. Jet engines were introduced. Pilot training became very important.
1940s	Radioplane Company	15,000 drones manufactured by this company for training UAS Army anti-aircraft gunners. The company was owned by Reginald Denny and later purchased by Northrop Corporation in 1952.
1942–1944	WASP—Women Air Service Pilots	Jacki Cochran had a big influence in the creation of this service opportunity for women. They ferried aircraft, provided aircraft training, and provided towing of artillery targets.
1944	V-1 flying bomb (buzz bomb)	10,000 of these drones were launched at London in 1944. It was an early cruise missile used by the Germans.

Date	Name or Event	Description or Accomplishment
1947	Howard Hughes	His work on the "Spruce Goose" was completed. It made its first and only flight that year. This idea led to further development of large transport aircraft designs.
1947	Chuck Yeager	First pilot to fly faster than the speed of sound in the Bell X-1. Was a P-51 pilot, then became a test pilot. Many other records.
1950s	Robert Hoover	Military pilot who began flying in airshows with both military and civilian aircraft. Very famous airshow performer.
1953	Scott Crossfield	Test pilot who was hired by NACA. First pilot to fly Mach 2, over 1,320 mph. Flew lots of rocket planes, X-15. He logged over 100 flights in these types of aircraft. He was an aerospace engineer who felt that flying was integral to designing the best aircraft.
1961	Yuri Gagarin	Test pilot. Was the first man in outer space. From Russia.
1969	Neil Armstrong	First man on the moon.
1969	Michael Collins	One of the three Apollo 11 Astronauts. He was the one who stayed in the shuttle.
1970s	Vietnam War	Aviation changed the way war was fought. New tactics were developed. Helicopters were used for both reconnaissance and attacks. Jet bombers and fighters were used extensively.
1980s	Abraham Karem	Aeronautical engineer is credited with designing various UAS platforms (Albatross and Amber) that laid the foundation for today's Predator.
1982	Bekaa Valley War	Use of UAS by Israeli Air Force.
1990s	Gulf Wars	Lots of missiles and bombs were used. Improved technology and changes in use of aerial tactics. Threat of chemical weapons. Apache helicopter fired the first air shot of the war. Increased knowledge about how aircraft perform in desert conditions—for example, how to care for aircraft/helicopter engines after a sandstorm.
2000s	Unmanned Aircraft Systems (UAS)	Military and civilian use. Military uses include collecting surveillance and dropping bombs. Civilian uses include aerial photography, surveillance, and recreation. Sizes range from as small as a hummingbird to as large as a full-size, four-seat GA aircraft.
2000s	Northrop Grumman Global Hawk	This UAS aircraft set endurance record of 33.1 hours in 2008.
2000s	Boeing Insitu	This UAS manufacturer has flown the ScanEagle UAS more than 1,000,000 hours.
2000s	Curiosity and Opportunity	NASA's Mars Rovers. They completed the journey to Mars and have been collecting samples and sending back data and pictures.

CHAPTER 6 PEOPLE, EVENTS, AND TRENDS IN AVIATION

LESSON 3

AVIATION HISTORY—WORLD WAR II, THE COLD WAR, AND THE JET AGE TO TODAY

PURPOSE

The purpose of this lesson is to define how aviation evolved to what it is today.

ACCOMMODATIONS FOR LEARNING DIFFERENCES

It is important that lessons accommodate the needs of every learner. These lessons may be modified to accommodate your students with learning differences by referring to www.pacer.org/parent/php/PHP-c267.pdf.

PREPARATION

- Aviation history slideshow covering World War II through the Cold War and Jet Age to today's aviation industry
- Video showing global air traffic volume over 24-hour period
- Cornell notes (in Student Notebook)

DIRECTIONS

Introductory Activity: Display the picture that appears in the Student Notebook, Activity 1 (Introduction Photo and Video Prompts) showing intriguing current/modern aviation trends. Be careful not to display the title/caption of the photo. Next, play a video showing air traffic volume across the globe over a 24-hour period. Students will use visual thinking strategies by writing down their responses to the following statements about the pictures and video:

- What's going on in this picture/video?
- What do you see that makes you say that?
- What evidence supports your observations?

Step 1: Use an interactive lecture to provide direct instruction about events on the timeline of flight from World War II through the Cold War and Jet Age to today's aviation industry. Explain each new content element to be learned. Provide sufficient examples, and pair visual and auditory instruction.

Step 2: Have students complete the Cornell Notes in Activity 2 (Cornell Notes Outline) in the Student Notebook during the interactive lecture.

Step 3: About every 10 minutes, insert "quick-thinks" that function both as checks for understanding and as brief student engagement tasks. Have students record responses in Activity 3 (Quick-Think Questions) in the Student Notebook.

- *Quick Think 1:* Do a two-minute writing response to the following prompt: "The most similar part of World War II aviation that we still see evident in modern aviation is …"
- *Quick Think 2:* Turn to a partner next to you. Explain whether you think the following statement is true or false, and why: "The Douglas DC-3 and DC-6 aircraft are significantly different than modern-day airliners."
- *Quick Think 3:* Students will choose which of the following they think is the most important issue in modern aviation (based on personal experience/general knowledge):
  › Airports
  › Air traffic control/management
  › Pilot supply
  › Free flight or flight paths
  › Integrating UAS with manned aircraft into the National Airspace System
  › Aviation security

Concluding Activity: Reveal the title/caption of the photo from the beginning of the lesson and explain what is actually occurring in the image. (*Answer:* Map of scheduled airline traffic around the world, circa June 2009.) Have students share with a partner their own thoughts from the beginning of the lesson and discuss how closely their ideas match what is actually shown in the photo.

CHAPTER 6   PEOPLE, EVENTS, AND TRENDS IN AVIATION

LESSON 4

FAMOUS PEOPLE IN AVIATION—INTRODUCTION

PURPOSE

The purpose of this lesson is to define specific contributions of important individuals in the aviation industry.

ACCOMMODATIONS FOR LEARNING DIFFERENCES

It is important that lessons accommodate the needs of every learner. These lessons may be modified to accommodate your students with learning differences by referring to www.pacer.org/parent/php/PHP-c267.pdf.

PREPARATION

- Pre-determined student groups
- Devices with internet access
- Blank paper for taking notes about students' conversations
- Note cards

DIRECTIONS

Note: This is the first of four lessons dedicated to researching an influential person in aviation.

Introductory Activity: In Activity 1 (Famous People in Aviation List) in the Student Notebook, have students read through the names of influential people in aviation. Students should guess and record the inventions or events that led each person to become famous in aviation history. Have 2–3 students share their guesses. This process introduces students to individuals who may be the focus of their research papers.

Step 1: Explain to students that as a group, you can learn a lot about the aviation industry by taking a closer look at the people who had a hand in making the aviation industry what it is today. For this project, they are to research a famous or influential person in aviation history.

Step 2: List eight potential individuals who have made significant contributions to the field of aviation (using the list of people in Student Notebook Activity 1). Break students into small groups. Assign each group an influential person and have them complete the graphic organizer in their interactive notebook in Activity 2 (Biography Template).

Step 3: Have students take a "museum walk" around the classroom to read other groups' graphic organizers. This means hanging their Biography Templates around the room and allowing students to view and enjoy each template to learn something new.

Step 4: Pair students up with someone who was assigned a different influential person. Have students use the biography template prompts in their Student Notebooks to have a conversation about the influential person they were assigned. Walk around and observe interactions, recording notes to share with the class once the activity is done. Focus on recording interactions where students are accurately conveying their influential person's perspective.

Concluding Activity: On the board, write example conversation lines that you heard as you walked around the room. Discuss the importance of really getting to know your influential person before the next class period as students will be completing a "Fakebook" activity (see next lesson for more information). Have each student share one thing they learned from this activity.

CHAPTER 6   PEOPLE, EVENTS, AND TRENDS IN AVIATION

LESSON 5

FAMOUS PEOPLE IN AVIATION—FAKEBOOK

PURPOSE
The purpose of this lesson is to share information about a students' influential person in aviation.

ACCOMMODATIONS FOR LEARNING DIFFERENCES
It is important that lessons accommodate the needs of every learner. These lessons may be modified to accommodate your students with learning differences by referring to **www.pacer.org/parent/php/PHP-c267.pdf**.

PREPARATION
- Two pictures of influential people in aviation history
- Computers/devices and internet access for students
- Masking tape
- FakeBook Template (from Student Notebook)
- Venn Diagram (from Student Notebook)

DIRECTIONS
Note: This is the second of four lessons dedicated to researching an influential person in aviation.

Introductory Activity: Print off two pictures of influential people in aviation history. Tape the pictures to the board and draw speech bubbles next to each person. Have students brainstorm two sentences, one for each person, which would potentially be the start of a conversation between the two of them. For example:

Amelia Earhart, 1935: "I just signed up to compete in the Bendix race. It appears that I am the first women to ever enter in the race."

After today's lesson, the student will be able to share several examples of conversations that could occur between famous people in the field of aviation.

Step 1: Ask students to turn to Activity 1 (FakeBook Template) in their Student Notebooks. This page contains a template for students to use when creating their "FakeBook" page. Select a famous person in aviation and model for students how to brainstorm information for the FakeBook page. Discuss each section (information, friends, photos, wall, etc.) and have students give examples of what might fall in that section.

Step 2: Now that students have had the opportunity to read about many different influential people, have each student select one person to be the topic of their research paper. Keep a list of which influential person each student selects for your reference, or display it for the class, showing each student's assigned influential person. Students will record this person's name and information in the FakeBook template in the Student Notebook. Students will then spend a majority of the class period collecting pictures and information to be added to the templates.

Step 3: Monitor student work and clear up any misconceptions that may be occurring. Following are possible question prompts to ask students as you walk around:
- What else was going on throughout the country during that time? What did/would this person think about that?
- How did your person's aviation accomplishment impact others?
- Was your person friends with other famous people in aviation? If so, what kinds of conversations would/might they have had?

Step 4: Pair students up and have them share their FakeBook template with each other. After 3–4 minutes of sharing, have students come up with one thing their famous people have in common and one thing that was unique for each person. They will record these similarities and differences using the Venn Diagram under Activity 2 in their Student Notebooks.

Concluding Activity: Students will share one similarity and difference with the group. After all groups have had a chance to share, the teacher will state one common theme that was mentioned throughout each Venn Diagram presentation. An example of a common theme might be: "How did the country or people react to their accomplishments?"

During this lesson, students dug deeper into the historical contexts surrounding famous people in aviation. During the next class period, students will begin work on writing a 2–3 page research paper in an effort to learn more about famous people in aviation and their contributions.

CHAPTER 6 PEOPLE, EVENTS, AND TRENDS IN AVIATION

LESSONS 6 AND 7

FAMOUS PEOPLE IN AVIATION—RESEARCH PAPER WORKSHOP

PURPOSE
The purpose of these lessons is to provide time for students to work on their research papers.

ACCOMMODATIONS FOR LEARNING DIFFERENCES
It is important that lessons accommodate the needs of every learner. These lessons may be modified to accommodate your students with learning differences by referring to www.pacer.org/parent/php/PHP-c267.pdf.

PREPARATION
- Excerpts from students' papers
- Copies of research paper rubric

DIRECTIONS
Note: These are the final lessons dedicated to researching an influential person in aviation and are designed to span two days.

Step 1: Allow students time to work on their research papers. You could create small writing groups for students who need specific practice on citing sources or locating accurate resources. Students could quietly work on their own as well.

Step 2: Have students complete the prompts about their research in Activity 1 (Whip Share Prompts) in the Student Notebook. Ask students to share this information about the influential person they researched with a partner or the entire class. This activity is called a "whip share" because students quickly share their responses to the prompts, and the sharing "whips" around the room.

Step 3: If time allows at the end of the first day, students can swap papers with a small group of peers for the last five minutes of class. Make a list on the board of similar contributions to aviation that are emerging as a result of students' research. Consider having students submit a rough draft of their paper. Provide written, oral, or audio-recorded feedback and have it ready for students before the beginning of the next class period.

Step 4: At the beginning of the second day, pull excerpts from the students' rough drafts that you collected at the end of the last lesson. Keeping them anonymous, post these excerpts around the room. Refer students to the research paper rubric (Activity 2 in their Student Notebooks) and ask students to evaluate their classmates' work using the rubric, which the facilitator will eventually also use to evaluate each student's work. As a group, discuss the strengths and challenges the class is observing after viewing excerpts from each other's papers. The lesson today will allow time for students to finish up research papers using the feedback from their peers and from the teacher. This will be the last day to work on the paper in class. Remind students of the due date and how you would like them to submit the paper.

Concluding Activity: Have students write a one-minute summary in Activity 3 (One-Minute Paper) in their Student Notebooks, addressing the following: "Does your paper have details about the person? Are you making sure you are answering the questions in the assignment description or rubric?" Give students 60 seconds to complete this one-minute paper.

Research papers will be submitted to the facilitator who will use the Research Paper Rubric provided under Facilitator Information below to evaluate student work.

FACILITATOR INFORMATION
Research Paper Rubric

(See next page.)

RESEARCH PAPER RUBRIC

	Exemplary (4)	Proficient (3)	Basic (2)	Unacceptable (1)
Thesis	Clearly and concisely states the paper's purpose in a single sentence, which is engaging and thought-provoking.	Clearly states the paper's purpose in a single sentence.	States the paper's purpose in a single sentence.	Incomplete and/or unfocused.
Introduction	Strong introduction of topic's key question(s), terms. Clearly delineates subtopics to be reviewed. Specific thesis statement.	Conveys topic and key question(s). Clearly delineates subtopics to be reviewed. General thesis statement.	Conveys topic, but no key question(s). Describes subtopics to be reviewed. General thesis statement.	Does not adequately convey topic. Does not describe subtopics to be reviewed. Lacks adequate thesis statement.
Body x2	All material clearly related to subtopic, main topic. Strong organization and integration of material within subtopics. Strong transitions linking subtopics, and main topic.	All material clearly related to subtopic, main topic, and logically organized within subtopics. Clear, varied transitions linking subtopics and main topic.	Most material clearly related to subtopic, main topic. Material may not be organized within subtopics. Attempts to provide variety of transitions.	Little evidence material is logically organized into topic, subtopics or related to topic. Many transitions are unclear or nonexistent.
Conclusion	Strong review of key conclusions. Strong integration with thesis statement. Insightful discussion of impact of the researched material on topic.	Strong review of key conclusions. Strong integration with thesis statement. Discusses impact of researched material on topic.	Review of key conclusions. Some integration with thesis statement. Discusses impact of researched material on topic.	Does not summarize evidence with respect to thesis statement. Does not discuss the impact of researched material on topic.
Grammar & Mechanics	The paper is free of errors in grammar, spelling, & punctuation.	Grammatical errors or spelling & punctuation errors are rare and do not detract from the paper.	Very few grammatical, spelling, or punctuation errors interfere with reading the paper.	Grammatical errors or spelling & punctuation errors substantially detract from the paper.
MLA Style	No errors in MLA style. Scholarly style. Writing is flowing and easy to follow.	Rare errors in MLA style that do not detract from the paper. Scholarly style. Writing has minimal awkward or unclear passages.	Errors in MLA style are noticeable. Word choice occasionally informal in tone. Writing has a few awkward or unclear passages.	Errors in MLA style detract substantially from the paper. Word choice is informal in tone. Writing is choppy, with many awkward or unclear passages.
References	All references and citations are correctly written and present.	One reference or citation missing or incorrectly written.	Two references or citations missing or incorrectly written.	Reference and citation errors detract significantly from paper.
Deadlines	5 points for rough draft, 5 points for submitting on time, and 50 points for final paper.			
Comments				Total _____ / 60 pts

CHAPTER 6 PEOPLE, EVENTS, AND TRENDS IN AVIATION

LESSONS 8, 9, AND 10
HOT AIR BALLOONS

PURPOSE

The purpose of these lessons is to learn the basics of flight through the creation of hot air balloons.

ACCOMMODATIONS FOR LEARNING DIFFERENCES

It is important that lessons accommodate the needs of every learner. These lessons may be modified to accommodate your students with learning differences by referring to **www.pacer.org/parent/php/PHP-c267.pdf**.

PREPARATION

- Hot air balloon lesson from the Space Foundation
- Tissue paper
- Butcher paper
- Glue sticks
- Scissors
- Straight pins
- Cellophane tape
- Additional materials needed to launch the balloons, listed in the Space Foundation's lesson
- Medium-sized ball
- Marker board and marker

DIRECTIONS

Introductory Activity: State the following: "How do hot air balloons work? And how does that relate to what we've learned about the field of aviation?" Show a video explaining how hot air balloons work, and tell students they will need to watch the video to learn tips in order to build their own hot air balloons.

Step 1: Access the Paper Hot Air Balloon lesson from the Space Foundation (**www.yumpu.com/en/document/view/12146386/paper-hot-air-balloon-space-foundation**).[4] This lesson plan guides students through the creation of a hot air balloon and the science behind how they work.

Step 2: As a teacher, you may want to dedicate 2–3 days to this project, depending on how much time you have.

Concluding Activity: Have everyone stand up and form a circle where everyone is facing toward the center, looking at each other. Toss a ball to a person and ask what they thought was the most important thing they learned through the hot air balloon activity. They then toss the ball to someone else who explains what they thought was the most important thing learned. Continue the exercise until everyone has caught the ball at least once and explained an important concept learned in the hot air balloon activity. The teacher should jot down memorable points on the board for reference and reinforcement.

LESSON 11

REVIEW: PEOPLE, EVENTS, AND TRENDS IN AVIATION

PURPOSE
The purpose of the lesson is to review people, events, and trends in aviation.

ACCOMMODATIONS FOR LEARNING DIFFERENCES
It is important that lessons accommodate the needs of every learner. These lessons may be modified to accommodate your students with learning differences by referring to **www.pacer.org/parent/php/PHP-c267.pdf**.

PREPARATION
- Mural paper or poster board
- Markers
- Create four large signs. On one sign, write a large letter A. Write a large letter B on the second sign, a C on the third sign, and a D on the fourth. Post one of the signs in each corner of your classroom.
- Obtain one index card for each student in the class. Write the word "Player" on about three-fourths of the cards; write the word "Fibber" on the remaining cards.
- Prepare in advance at least 25 multiple-choice questions relating to a unit or skill students have been studying. All questions should have four possible answers: A, B, C, or D.
- Follow-up worksheet with questions for summary activity

DIRECTIONS

Introductory Activity: Re-engage the students on aviation history by sharing a relevant historical occurrence that happened on the same date as today's lesson from the website This Day in Aviation (**www.thisdayinaviation.com**). Display relevant pictures as you share the story. Have students turn and talk with a partner about what impact this historical event had on modern-day aviation.

Step 1: To begin the lesson, place one of the index cards face down on each student's desk. Instruct students to look at their cards privately to find out if their role in the game is that of a "Player" or a "Fibber." Tell students to not reveal their roles to their classmates.

Step 2: Run through a couple of practice questions before beginning the game. Pose the first question and four possible responses. Ask students which response they think is the correct one. Have students who think the correct answer is A stand by the A sign. Students who think the correct answer is B, C, or D gather near those respective signs hung in each corner of the classroom.

Step 3: Students who hold the Player cards go to their appropriate corners while students who hold the Fibber cards are free to go to any corner. The Fibber's movements are intended to throw off the other students. Perhaps some of the brightest students are Fibbers and some players will be tempted to follow those students to the wrong corners. This approach encourages students to think for themselves, not just follow the flock.

Step 4: When all students have taken their corners, reveal the correct answer to the question. Ask students who chose the correct answer to explain why they selected that answer. Clarify any errors or misconceptions when they arise. Then you're ready to pose the next question.

Concluding Activity: Provide a follow-up worksheet with the same questions used in the above activity or with different, yet similar, questions. This will help students prepare for the exam being administered in the next lesson.

CHAPTER 6   PEOPLE, EVENTS, AND TRENDS IN AVIATION

LESSON 12

CHAPTER 6 EXAM

PURPOSE

The purpose of this lesson is to assess students' knowledge of aviation history.

ACCOMMODATIONS FOR LEARNING DIFFERENCES

It is important that lessons accommodate the needs of every learner. These lessons may be modified to accommodate your students with learning differences by referring to www.pacer.org/parent/php/PHP-c267.pdf.

PREPARATION

- Exam copies
- Newsela teacher account with article assigned to class
- Computers/devices and internet access for students, or paper copies of the article and questions
- Non-fiction writing rubric (in Student Notebook)

DIRECTIONS

Introductory Activity: Re-engage the students on aviation history by sharing a relevant historical occurrence that happened on the same date as today's lesson from the website This Day in Aviation (www.thisdayinaviation.com). Display relevant pictures as you share the story. Have students turn and talk with a partner about what impact this historical event had on modern day aviation. Before the exam commences, provide instructions on what students are to do after they have completed it.

Step 1: Students will complete the Chapter 6 exam. The exam should include questions and prompts covering the information shown in the test bank provided under Facilitator Information at the end of this lesson. (An answer key is provided at the end of the chapter.)

Step 2: When students have turned in their exams, have them independently read the article, "Is that pilot in the cockpit human or a robot, and does it matter?" by the *Associated Press* on Newsela.[5] Students will complete the four-question automated quiz with the article on Newsela. Students will then complete Activity 1 (Article Response) in the Student Notebook, writing a two-paragraph response that includes a summary and reflection on the prompts: "How will robotic pilots impact the number of human pilots?" and "What is your opinion on replacing human co-pilots with robot pilots? Does it matter which is used?" It will be graded using the non-fiction writing rubric provided in the Student Notebook.

Concluding Activity: No formal summary activity. Students will work independently to finish the exam at different times and begin reading the article as an introductory activity to Chapter 7 on aviation careers.

FACILITATOR INFORMATION
Chapter 6 Exam: People, Events, and Trends in Aviation

(This exam is available in the online Instructor Resources in a format ready for use in the classroom. An answer key is provided at the end of the chapter.)

1. List the names of at least five famous aviators.

2. Name at least five important discoveries or developments in aerospace.

3. Name at least one event or accomplishment prior to the advent of heavier-than-air aircraft.

4. What is one (or more) of the Wright brothers' accomplishments?

5. Name at least one other event/accomplishment that occurred in the early 1900s prior to World War I.

6. Name at least one significant event, aircraft, or advancement in aviation that occurred during World War I.

7. Name at least one significant event, aircraft, or advancement in aviation that occurred during World War II.

8. Name at least one significant event, aircraft, or advancement in aviation that occurred during the Vietnam War.

9. Name at least one significant event, aircraft, or advancement in space travel.

10. Name at least one modern-day accomplishment or advancement in aviation.

11. Place the correct letters (A–F) from the list on the left next to the correct name on the right.

A	He made many sketches of flying machines by studying birds.	Jean-Pierre Blanchard
B	In June 1783, brought a hot air balloon to Paris. First public display of a hot air balloon.	Rozier and d'Arlandes
C	People who built wings, strapped them to their arms, and jumped off of various surfaces trying to sustain flight.	Leonardo da Vinci
D	First to make balloon flights in North America.	Tower Jumpers
E	In November 1783, first manned ascent in the hot air balloon.	Daedalus
F	Made wings of feathers and wax so he and his son could escape from imprisonment.	Montgolfier Brothers

12. List a benefit of a hot air balloon.

13. List a drawback of a hot air balloon.

14. List a benefit of a dirigible/airship.

ANSWER KEYS
CHAPTER 6

LESSON 12
Chapter 6 Exam

Questions 1–10: Answers will vary. Refer to the aviation history timeline in Lesson 2.

11. A = Leonardo da Vinci
    B = Montgolfier Brothers
    C = Tower Jumpers
    D = Jean-Pierre Blanchard
    E = Rozier and d'Arlandes
    F = Daedalus
12. It allowed people to fly. First uses include: mail, communication, war benefits such as aerial guns, and better bird's-eye view of areas.
13. People had very little control over where it went. It could not carry a lot of weight.
14. A person could control it. It could carry more passengers/cargo.

CHAPTER 7

AVIATION CAREERS

Introduction

STANDARDS & OBJECTIVES
North Dakota Aviation Content Standards (Grades 10–12)
- 4.4.1—Identify career opportunities n aviation.
- A.4.4.1—Learn about different career paths based on interests.
- 4.4.2—Identify current career trends in aviation.
- A.4.4.2—Determine the importance of aviation careers.
- 4.4.3—Discuss pathways to an aviation career.
- A.4.4.3—Develop aviation scholarship applications.
- A.4.4.3—Discuss ways students can get exposure to careers of interest.

Note: Standards beginning with "A" indicate the objectives align with but do not exactly match the identified ND Aviation Standards.

Language Arts—CCSS.ELA-LITERACY.CCRA
- L.1—Demonstrate command of the conventions of standard English grammar and usage when writing or speaking
- L.2—Demonstrate command of the conventions of standard English capitalization, punctuation, and spelling when writing.
- R.1—Read closely to determine what the text says explicitly and to make logical inferences from it; cite specific textual evidence when writing or speaking to support conclusions drawn from the text.
- SL.1—Prepare for and participate effectively in a range of conversations and collaborations with diverse partners, building on others' ideas and expressing their own clearly and persuasively.
- SL.2—Integrate and evaluate information presented in diverse media and formats, including visually, quantitatively, and orally.
- SL.3—Evaluate a speaker's point of view, reasoning, and use of evidence and rhetoric.
- SL.4—Present information, findings, and supporting evidence such that listeners can follow the line of reasoning and the organization, development, and style are appropriate to task, purpose, and audience.
- SL.5—Make strategic use of digital media and visual displays of data to express information and enhance understanding of presentations.

- **W.2**—Write informative/explanatory texts to examine and convey complex ideas and information clearly and accurately through the effective selection, organization, and analysis of content.
- **W.4**—Produce clear and coherent writing in which the development, organization, and style are appropriate to task, purpose, and audience.
- **W.7**—Conduct short as well as more sustained research projects based on focused questions, demonstrating understanding of the subject under investigation.
- **W.8**—Gather relevant information from multiple print and digital sources, assess the credibility and accuracy of each source, and integrate the information while avoiding plagiarism.
- **W.9**—Draw evidence from literary or informational texts to support analysis, reflection, and research

ESSENTIAL QUESTIONS
- How can you prepare yourself to follow your career choice?
- What types of preparation must you complete to achieve your goals?
- What personal goals must you set for yourself?

LESSONS

Lesson	Topic	Student Notebook Activities
Lesson 1	Career Article and Introduction	1. List of Potential Aviation Careers 2. Aviation Career Graphic Organizer
Lesson 2	Career Investigation/ Education & Training (Day 1)	1. Aviation Careers 2. Aviation-Related Job Templates 3. Grading Checklist for Graphic Organizer Responses 4. Concept Map 5. Concluding Activity
Lesson 3	Career Investigation/ Education & Training (Day 2)	1. Personal Characteristics 2. Interview Q and A
Lesson 4	Career Investigation/ Education & Training (Day 3)	1. Top Three Careers in Aviation 2. Top Three Careers in Aviation Rubric
Lesson 5	Current Events	1. Current Events Assignment Description 2. Current Events Rubric
Lesson 6	University, Community College, and Training Options	1. Training Options Worksheet 2. Training Options Matrix 3. Research Summary
Lessons 7 & 8	Scholarship Applications	1. Aviation Scholarship Worksheet 2. Scholarship Reflection
Lesson 9	Guest Speaker	1. Two-Column Notes Graphic Organizer

LESSON 1

CAREER ARTICLE AND INTRODUCTION

PURPOSE
The purpose of this lesson is to identify career opportunities in aviation.

ACCOMMODATIONS FOR LEARNING DIFFERENCES
It is important that lessons accommodate the needs of every learner. These lessons may be modified to accommodate your students with learning differences by referring to www.pacer.org/parent/php/PHP-c267.pdf.

PREPARATION
- Note cards
- Whiteboard and marker

DIRECTIONS

Introductory Activity: Review student responses to the article from the last lesson of Chapter 6. Allow students the opportunity to share their responses to the following questions:
- How will autonomous flight impact the number of human pilots needed in the cockpit?
- What is your opinion on replacing human co-pilots with autonomy or artificial intelligence; does it matter?

Step 1: Hand each student a note card. Ask them to record one aviation career they are familiar with on the front of the note card and one unfamiliar career on the back, keeping it hidden from their classmates.

Step 2: Have students share the aviation careers on their note cards. Students will shout these out when called upon. The facilitator will then write all of these careers on the board (a sample list can be found at the end of this lesson under Facilitator Information or through searching online) and students will record careers in their Student Notebooks under Activity 1 (List of Potential Aviation Careers). The facilitator will help to lead this discussion to include a wide variety of aviation careers (more than what was written on students' note cards).

Step 3: Once a thorough list has been created, conduct a sorting activity with the class, asking students to help you sort the careers into categories (i.e., flight—manned vs. flight—unmanned, flight operations support, service provider, etc.).

Step 4: After students and facilitator have completed the sorting activity, the facilitator will briefly describe several of the uncommon aviation careers using an interactive lecture and opportunities for active processing; answer students' questions and clarify misconceptions.

Step 5: Model how to research a career in aviation by demonstrating how to complete the graphic organizer as an example, and support students on how to find accurate information. Students will be expected to record the example written on the board by the facilitator in their Student Notebooks in Activity 2 (Aviation Career Graphic Organizer). Students will conduct research and complete another graphic organizer independently in the next lesson.

Concluding Activity: On a note card, have students record their top three aviation career choices with a sentence describing each choice. Use this information to assign students aviation careers to research the following day.

FACILITATOR INFORMATION
List of Aviation Careers

- Accountant
- Aerial application
- Aerial firefighter
- Aerospace engineer
- Air ambulance
- Air traffic controller
- Aircraft manufacturing
- Aircraft marshal
- Aircraft sales
- Airport manager
- Airport operations
- Airport: Crash, fire, rescue
- Astronaut
- Aviation high school teacher
- Aviation Medical Examiner
- Aviation professor
- Baggage handler
- Charter/bush pilot
- Customs and Border Protection pilot
- Dispatcher
- FAA safety inspector
- FBO manager
- Flight attendant
- Flight data analyst
- Flight instructor
- Flight service station
- Helicopter pilot
- Human resources
- Law enforcement pilot
- Lawyer
- Manager
- Mechanic
- Meteorologist
- Mission planner
- Natural resources pilot
- NTSB
- Pilot
- Ramp agent
- Safety officer
- Search and rescue pilot
- Test pilot
- TSA
- UAS pilot operator
- UAS sensor operator

LESSON 2

CAREER INVESTIGATION/EDUCATION & TRAINING (DAY 1)

PURPOSE

The purpose of this lesson is to further investigate aviation careers of student interest.

ACCOMMODATIONS FOR LEARNING DIFFERENCES

It is important that lessons accommodate the needs of every learner. These lessons may be modified to accommodate your students with learning differences by referring to www.pacer.org/parent/php/PHP-c267.pdf.

PREPARATION

- Online access for survey and research or printed copy of survey for each student
- List of careers from Chapter 7, Lesson 1
- Aviation-related jobs templates (in Student Notebook)
- Individual checklists for grading
- Completed graphic organizer from Lesson 1, for reference

DIRECTIONS

Introductory Activity: Take 10 minutes to have each student take the UCanGo2 Career Interest Survey.[1] Students will calculate their scores and identify their career cluster area, highlighting that explanation and the corresponding occupations that interest them. Students will then complete Student Notebook Activity 1 (Aviation Careers) to record their top three career interest areas and two occupations within each category they would consider. Discuss student interest results and how their skills align with a variety of aviation careers.

Step 1: Divide students into groups of 3 or 4 (or students can work independently). Assign a career or multiple careers in aviation (cover all careers brainstormed in Lesson 1) and direct students to research the careers. Give students time (10–15 minutes) to research their assigned aviation career online, fielding questions as necessary. You may provide students with a list of example websites that would be useful in their research, and they can also use their career titles as search terms online. Answers may not be available from just one source. Note that for some careers, "probationary periods" (found on the graphic organizer) may not be applicable.

Step 2: Direct students to complete the graphic organizers found in Activity 2 (Aviation-Related Job Templates) while conducting their research. At this point, it would benefit students to review how their graphic organizers will be assessed. The grading checklist can be found at the end of this lesson.

Step 3: After several minutes of research, students will informally share out their findings. Call on students, as time allows, to summarize what they wrote on their completed templates. Students will record information from their peers' presentations in their Student Notebooks in Activity 4 (Concept Map).

Concluding Activity: Have students think back to the results of the career interest survey they took at the beginning of this lesson. Ask students to consider what aviation career most closely aligns with their current interests and skills. Consider asking the following questions; students can record their responses in Activity 5 (Concluding Activity) in the Student Notebook.

a. What are subjects in school you should pursue now to have a particular career in aviation?

b. What are some clubs/organizations or activities you could pursue now to become involved in the field of aviation?

c. What are some questions that you would like to ask someone who is working in that career? Do you know someone who is currently working in that career?

This sharing will highlight aviation careers for the next two lessons, where students will complete mock interviews to learn more about specific aviation careers.

FACILITATOR INFORMATION

GRADING CHECKLIST FOR GRAPHIC ORGANIZER RESPONSES	
Name: _____ Job: _____	
Type of education required	___/5
Where to receive education	___/5
Time required for education	___/5
Job duties	___/5
Potential employer	___/5
Starting salary	___/5
Ending salary	___/5
Total points	___/35

LESSON 3

CAREER INVESTIGATION/EDUCATION & TRAINING (DAY 2)

PURPOSE

The purpose of this lesson is to consider personal characteristics that may impact students' future work in an aviation career.

ACCOMMODATIONS FOR LEARNING DIFFERENCES

It is important that lessons accommodate the needs of every learner. These lessons may be modified to accommodate your students with learning differences by referring to **www.pacer.org/parent/php/PHP-c267.pdf**.

PREPARATION

- Computers/devices and internet access for students

LESSON DIRECTIONS

Introductory Activity: Have students turn to Activity 1 (Personal Characteristics) in their Student Notebooks. Have students record personal characteristics (organization, time management, ability to handle stressful situations, etc.) that may affect their future career choice in aviation. If students are having a difficult time identifying characteristics, guide them to reference an online list of personality traits. Students record their ideas independently. After a minute or two, students can stand up, walk around, and share their ideas with a partner or small group of students. Remind students to record personal characteristics that they did not come up with but that their classmates recorded. The lesson today focuses on coming up with several factors, including "personal characteristics" that may affect a student's future as a person who works in the field of aviation. As a class, you will look at these factors in the form of interview questions.

Step 1: Students can be assigned new careers, different than those they have been studying in Lessons 1 and 2, or the teacher can decide to allow them to continue studying a career of their choice.

Step 2: Divide students into groups of 3 to 4. In small groups, students will develop questions that would be appropriate to ask of different individuals in a variety of aviation careers. Below is a list of sample questions to help lead the discussion:

    a. How long have you worked as a _____?
    b. What other careers did you engage in prior to your current career?
    c. What do you like most about your job?
    d. What are the biggest challenges of your job?

e. What personal characteristics do you feel are needed to be successful as a _____?
f. Where did you get your education from?
g. What was your college degree in?
h. What type of training did you receive once you were hired?
i. What changes in your career have you seen occur?
j. What types of technology do you use in your line of work?
k. How have you had to adjust to changes in technology in your line of work?

Step 3: Each student should record similar questions in the left column of the table in Activity 2 (Interview Q and A) found in the Student Notebook.

Step 4: Students will work independently to answer the interview questions their group came up with according to the aviation career they were assigned. For example, small groups may come up with six interview questions and one student is assigned air traffic controller. That individual writes the answers to the interview questions as if he or she is an air traffic controller. This allows students to think about various aviation careers from a different perspective.

Step 5: Allow students time to research and practice the answers to the interview questions, as they will be interviewed by classmates in Lesson 4.

Concluding Activity: Summarize the lesson by asking several students to state one thing they learned from developing and answering interview questions. Have them state their thoughts out loud, making note of any student summaries that highlight key information or misconceptions for you, as a facilitator, to clear up.

CHAPTER 7 AVIATION CAREERS

LESSON 4

CAREER INVESTIGATION/EDUCATION & TRAINING (DAY 3)

PURPOSE

The purpose of this lesson is for students to examine available career paths in aviation.

ACCOMMODATIONS FOR LEARNING DIFFERENCES

It is important that lessons accommodate the needs of every learner. These lessons may be modified to accommodate your students with learning differences by referring to **www.pacer.org/parent/php/PHP-c267.pdf**.

PREPARATION

- Large open space with chairs and tables in interview positions
- Previously created interview questions (from Lesson 3)
- Top Three Careers in Aviation table (in Student Notebook)
- Note cards for concluding activity

DIRECTIONS

Introductory Activity: Ask students to turn and talk to a partner, discussing if they have ever been interviewed for anything before. Ask them to discuss things to remember when being interviewed (e.g., make eye contact, answer the questions being asked, avoid using fillers such as "um" or "ah," etc.). As an additional resource, find and show students a video covering interview skills. Record students' answers on the board and discuss them as a group, encouraging students to remember these factors as they are interviewers and interviewees throughout today's lesson. State the purpose of the lesson, which is continuing research on aviation careers by answering interview questions through the lens of an air traffic controller, a UAS pilot operator, an aircraft mechanic, etc.

Step 1: Students form two circles—an inner circle and an outer circle—with chairs, tables, or desks. Make sure students are far enough apart as to not distract one another during the interviewing process. Pair students up so you have one from the inner circle and one from the outer circle as partners.

Step 2: The student on the outside circle of each pair asks the interview questions while the person on the inner circle answers the interview questions.

Step 3: Rotate the students in the outer circles and reverse roles so the inner student asks the questions and the outer student answers the questions.

Step 4: Continue this process until students have learned a few things about several different aviation careers.

Step 5: Have students complete Activity 1 (Top Three Careers in Aviation) in the Student Notebook. For this activity, students will record the top three careers in aviation that they are currently considering. They will also include a three-sentence summary explaining why they're interested in each particular aviation career. The rubric for how their work will be evaluated is included in the Student Notebook (and below under Facilitator Information).

Step 6: Give students an opportunity to share their top aviation career choice and justify why. Assess the top three list using the rubric below (and in the Student Notebook).

Concluding Activity: Pass one note card to each student. On the note card, have students write one thing they learned and one question they still have about careers in aviation. Have students share their questions and lead a brief discussion to answer them, if possible. If those questions will be addressed in the chapters to come, let students know that.

To end the lesson, assign students the Current Events Assignment (Lesson 5, Activity 1) in the Student Notebook as homework, requesting that they find and select a current event that interests them, particularly from the field of aviation. Instructions for the current event one-page writing assignment are found in the Student Notebook.

FACILITATOR INFORMATION

TOP THREE CAREERS IN AVIATION RUBRIC		
Criteria	Earned Points	Points per Criteria
Are responses in-depth, thorough, and connected to the interview activity?		___/5
Were all boxes of the Top Three Careers in Aviation table filled in?		___/4
Is the writing clear and easy to read?		___/1
Total points		___/10

CHAPTER 7 AVIATION CAREERS

LESSON 5
CURRENT EVENTS

PURPOSE
The purpose of this lesson is to recognize the consistent role aviation plays in society and to keep up to date on global developments.

ACCOMMODATIONS FOR LEARNING DIFFERENCES
It is important that lessons accommodate the needs of every learner. These lessons may be modified to accommodate your students with learning differences by referring to www.pacer.org/parent/php/PHP-c267.pcf.

PREPARATION
- Current event article—copies or digital format displayed
- White board
- List of course inquiry questions (provded at the beginning of this guide on page 6).
- If expectations for group roles have not previously been discussed, provide clear instructions for the responsibilities that come with the assignment. You might want to make lists of what it looks like when the role is performed well and when it is not performed well. Assigning roles helps to distribute responsibility among group members and ensures accountability for all students' participation. As students practice different roles, they have the opportunity to develop a variety of skills.

DIRECTIONS
Introductory Activity: Share a current event that interests you (the facilitator) from the aviation field. Since this unit is on careers, selecting an event on this topic will reinforce learning. Model for students a summary, a personal response, and inquiry questions through a think-aloud (describing your thinking and purpose).

Step 1: Organize students in groups of four. Assign group roles: facilitator, recorder, presenter, and timekeeper. Explain expectations of each role.

The facilitator will lead the group and keep the conversation on track. The recorder will write down the information for the prompts asked in the Student Notebook, encouraging his or her peers to do the same. The presenter will be responsible for summarizing the group's discussion and sharing it with the class. The timekeeper will keep the conversation moving and ensure the group completes all required assignment components in the allotted time.

Step 2: Direct students' attention to the current events assignment in the Student Notebook. Using their assigned roles, students will complete the responses in their Student Notebook. After the allotted time, the student assigned as the presenter will share their prepared summary and personal response (see the Current Events Rubric provided in the Student Notebook)—approximately 5 minutes per student. Presenters will then ask their inquiry questions to the whole group and all students and the facilitator will attempt to answer the questions. Encourage students to record inquiry questions and responses in their student notebook.

Step 3: When all students have shared and the inquiry questions have been answered, the recorder for each group will turn in the answers to the facilitator. Consider using a digital discussion/submission platform (i.e., Padlet, Flipgrid, etc.) for students to submit these questions and responses.

Step 4: Collect each individual student's one-page current event assignments (see the Current Events Rubric in the Student Notebook) so feedback can be provided and grades recorded, if applicable.

Concluding Activity: Each group will choose the one most important point about aviation they learned in relation to aviation careers through the discussion (paraphrasing skill). The group will develop a "headline" statement that captures the essence of the most important point. The group presenter will share the headline with the class.

CHAPTER 7 AVIATION CAREERS

LESSON 6

UNIVERSITY, COMMUNITY COLLEGE, AND TRAINING OPTIONS

PURPOSE
The purpose of this lesson is to discuss the importance of making an informed decision about a university/training program to pursue a career in aviation.

ACCOMMODATIONS FOR LEARNING DIFFERENCES
It is important that lessons accommodate the needs of every learner. These lessons may be modified to accommodate your students with learning differences by referring to **www.pacer.org/parent/php/PHP-c267.pdf**.

PREPARATION
- Computers/devices and internet access for students
- Marketing video from a university aviation program
- In-classroom support from the school guidance counselor

DIRECTIONS

Introductory Activity: Show the students a marketing video from one of the universities listed in Step 1 below for exploration, or use the *We'll See You Up Here!* video from the University of North Dakota.[2] The video provides an overview of one university's aviation program. Have students share their initial thoughts on how the video relates to other training programs across the region, tri-state area, nation, etc.? How are they the same? How are they different? Discuss the importance of choosing a university/training program, and if relevant, share how you selected your educational path.

Step 1: Explain the Student Notebook Activity 1 (Training Options Worksheet) to students. Display the worksheet and model two examples, filling in the chart with the information.

- *Example 1:* University of North Dakota (http://fly.und.edu/). Demonstrate how to navigate around the website to find where information might be located. Find the webpages for Costs and Tuition and follow the links to find course cost and individual program cost.

- *Example 2:* Search "Embry-Riddle Aeronautical University" using an internet search engine to find its website. In the search bar, type "tuition." Follow the links to explore undergraduate estimated costs.

Step 2: Students will conduct their own research, choosing at least 2–5 university/community college options according to their area of interest in aviation, ensuring all students have selected a different training option. The facilitator will strategically move around the classroom, observe, and provide feedback in order to maximize engagement and achievement during independent work.

Step 3: After students have completed research on the aviation university or community college training program options, they should explore the websites for other factors that would make each university or community college an attractive option to them (back-up plans, sports, other areas of interest, job placement, internships, reputation, scholarships, etc.). Ask them to consider the question, "What factors, other than aviation programs, makes this university or community college an attractive option to you?" Students will compare and contrast the programs, evaluating and deciding on which one they would apply for. They should record their choice by completing Activity 3 (Research Summary) in the Student Notebook.

Step 4: As students share their research, instruct each student to record information on five options for training in their Student Notebooks in Activity 2 (Training Options Matrix).

Concluding Activity: At the end of the lesson, students will share their choices in groups of 2 to 3, explaining why they chose the particular program they did.

CHAPTER 7 AVIATION CAREERS

LESSONS 7 AND 8
SCHOLARSHIP APPLICATIONS (DAYS 1 AND 2)

PURPOSE
The purpose of the lesson is to apply for scholarships to successfully complete aviation training.

ACCOMMODATIONS FOR LEARNING DIFFERENCES
It is important that lessons accommodate the needs of every learner. These lessons may be modified to accommodate your students with learning differences by referring to **www.pacer.org/parent/php/PHP-c267.pdf**.

PREPARATION
- Computers/devices and internet access for students
- Aviation Scholarship Worksheet (in the Student Notebook)
- In-classroom support from the school guidance counselor

DIRECTIONS
Introductory Activity: Display an example of total costs for earning an aviation degree. Discussing the following points:
- There are thousands of scholarships that go unclaimed every year
- Since scholarships do not have to be repaid, they are an effective way to reduce your college or other postsecondary expenses.
- Discuss what scholarships or ways to reduce expenses you received during college

Step 1: Explain the table in Activity 1 (Aviation Scholarship Worksheet) to students. Display the worksheet and model one example, filling in the chart with the first scholarship available for aviation on **scholarships.com**. Other websites with aviation scholarship listings to guide students to include Airline Owners and Pilots Association (AOPA), CollegeScholarships.com, Federal Aviation Administration (FAA), UND Aerospace, and University Aviation Association.

Tip: An additional resource for facilitators is the *Collegiate Aviation Scholarship Listing*, which consolidates the publicly available information concerning collegiate aviation scholarships. The publication describes how to obtain applications for more than 700 aviation scholarship awards with a total value in excess of one million dollars. The most recent edition is available for purchase in the University Aviation Association (UAA) online bookstore.

Step 2: Students will conduct their own research, choosing scholarships applicable to their area of interest in aviation. The teacher will strategically move around the classroom, observe, and provide feedback in order to maximize engagement and achievement during independent work.

Step 3: After students have completed research on their three scholarships, they will choose one to actually apply for. Students who are eligible at this time to officially submit the completed application will do so and submit a copy to the facilitator. Students who are not yet eligible will simulate completing the application by sending it to the guidance counselor for review and feedback. If applications are extensive and more time consuming, collaborate with the guidance counselor to provide support for students to fully complete the application outside of class time.

Concluding Activity: At the end of Day 2 of the lesson, students will share their scholarship information with one other student to compare and contrast what they found. They will complete Activity 2 (Scholarship Reflection) in the Student Notebook to answer the following questions, which they will share with their partners:

- What special personal qualities, skills, talents, or abilities do you have?
- How can you highlight those qualities when applying for a scholarship?

CHAPTER 7 AVIATION CAREERS

LESSON 9
GUEST SPEAKER

PURPOSE
The purpose of this lesson is to expose students to real-world life experiences and career opportunities in aviation.

ACCOMMODATIONS FOR LEARNING DIFFERENCES
It is important that lessons accommodate the needs of every learner. These lessons may be modified to accommodate your students with learning differences by referring to www.pacer.org/parent/php/PHP-c267.pdf.

PREPARATION
- Two-column notes graphic organizer (in Student Notebook)
- Logistics/preparation for guest speaker—send inquiry questions and relevant preparation materials to the guest speaker in advance.
- If guest speaker is a sUAS operator, ask them to demonstrate their sUAS in class.

DIRECTIONS
Introductory Activity: Ask the guest speaker(s) to present dressed for their profession (e.g., pilot uniform, flight suit, military uniform); this will stimulate curiosity and questions from students.

Step 1: Introduce the presenter to the class. Choose one or two things that you truly admire about the speaker to share. The more specific, the better. Emphasize the importance of their role in aviation to establish credibility and interest.

Step 2: Have the speaker give their prepared presentation. For basic guidance, you can use the graphic organizer titled "Aviation Related Job Template" from Lesson 2 to inform the presenter what to discuss as he or she feels comfortable.

Step 3: While the speaker is presenting, students will actively process using the Two-Column Notes Graphic Organizer in Activity 1 in their Student Notebooks. Allow students to think of and ask the speaker any additional questions.
- Be sure to highlight key issues that have been investigated by the students.
- Direct the conversation to things that students may be interested in.

Step 4: Ask the students and the speaker if there are any last questions or issues. Thank the guest speaker for his/her time.

Concluding Activity: Students will compare notes from the graphic organizer with a partner. Next, students will complete the summary prompt at the end of the two-column notes to answer at least one inquiry question. Collect these when completed, or have students return them the next class period. Consider pulling key ideas and share them in a thank you note addressed to the guest speaker.

FACILITATOR INFORMATION
Guest Speaker Ideas

For a list of ideas for guest speakers, refer to the "List of Aviation Careers" provided in Chapter 7, Lesson 1, under Facilitator Information.

CHAPTER 8
AERODYNAMICS OF FLIGHT

Introduction

STANDARDS & OBJECTIVES

North Dakota Aviation Content Standards (Grades 10–12)
- 2.1.1—Explain and describe the relationship the four forces of flight.
- A.2.1.1—Identify and describe meaningful relationships between variables of flight
- 2.1.2—Define the angle of attack and critical angle of attack.
- 2.1.3—Describe the types of drag, both parasite and induced.
- 2.1.4—Explain various wing shapes and how wing tip vortices are created.
- 2.1.5—Discuss and compare the four main types of wing flaps and the advantages and disadvantages to their uses.
- 2.1.6—Explain how Newton's Third Law and Bernoulli's principle affect lift.
- 2.1.7—Identify the parts of an airfoil (e.g., chord line, relative wind, camber, leading edge, trailing edge).
- 2.1.8—Describe the aerodynamics of a stall.
- 2.1.9—Define static and dynamic stability.

Note: Standards beginning with "A" indicate the objectives align with but do not exactly match the identified ND Aviation Standards.

Science—Next Generation Science Standards (Grades 9–12)
- HS-PS2-1—Analyze data to support the claim that Newton's second law of motion describes the mathematical relationship among the net force on a macroscopic object, its mass, and its acceleration.
- HS-PS2-2—Use mathematical representations to support the claim that the total momentum of a system of objects is conserved when there is no net force on the system.
- HS-PS2-6—Communicate scientific and technical information about why the molecular-level structure is important in the functioning of designed materials.
- HS-PS3-3—Design, build, and refine a device that works within given constraints to convert one form of energy into another form of energy.

Math—CCSS.MATH.CONTENT (Grades 10–12)
- HS.S-ID.1—Represent data with plots on the real number line (dot plots, histograms, and box plots).

Language Arts—CCSS.ELA-LITERACY.CCRA

- **L.1**—Demonstrate command of the conventions of standard English grammar and usage when writing or speaking.
- **L.2**—Demonstrate command of the conventions of standard English capitalization, punctuation, and spelling when writing.
- **SL.2**—Integrate and evaluate information presented in diverse media and formats, including visually, quantitatively, and orally.
- **W.7**—Conduct short as well as more sustained research projects based on focused questions, demonstrating understanding of the subject under investigation.
- **W.8**—Gather relevant information from multiple print and digital sources, assess the credibility and accuracy of each source, and integrate the information while avoiding plagiarism.
- **W.9**—Draw evidence from literary or informational texts to support analysis, reflection, and research.

ESSENTIAL QUESTIONS

- How do the four forces of thrust, drag, lift, and weight affect flight?
- How does a pilot control these forces with the use of power and flight controls?
- How do Newton's third law and Bernoulli's principle affect lift?
- Why is it important to be at appropriate airspeed when on the base to final turn in a traffic pattern?
- What is a change that could be made to an aircraft and how would that change impact (either positively or negatively) the performance of that aircraft?

LESSONS

Lesson	Topic	Student Notebook Activities
Lesson 1	Forces of Flight	1. The Four Forces 2. Aerodynamics Graphic Organizer 3. Home Group Questions 4. Acrostic
Lesson 2	Introduction to Airfoils	1. Airfoil Definitions 2. Labeling Airfoil Parts 3. Wing Experiment Questions
Lesson 3	Lift—Newton & Bernoulli	1. Label Diagrams 2. Comprehension Questions Homework
Lesson 4	Drag and Design	1. Semi-Truck Comparison 2. Three-Column Organizer 3. Interactive Lecture Diagram and Notes
Lesson 5	Stalls and Spins	1. Stalls Outline Table 2. Spins Outline Table
Lesson 6	Review: Aerodynamics of Flight	1. Study Guide
Lesson 7	Chapter 8 Exam	1. Article Response and Rubric

CHAPTER 8 AERODYNAMICS OF FLIGHT

LESSON 1
FORCES OF FLIGHT

PURPOSE
The purpose of this lesson is to comprehend the relationship of forces as they act on an aircraft.

ACCOMMODATIONS FOR LEARNING DIFFERENCES
It is important that lessons accommodate the needs of every learner. These lessons may be modified to accommodate your students with learning differences by referring to **www.pacer.org/parent/php/PHP-c267.pdf**.

PREPARATION
- Class copies of *Pilot's Handbook of Aeronautical Knowledge* (FAA-H-8083-25)

DIRECTIONS
Introductory Activity: Show students the figure below or Figure 5-1 from the *Pilot's Handbook of Aeronautical Knowledge* with the terms and arrows removed or covered up. In pairs or triads, direct students to label the directional arrows with each of the terms—lift, weight, thrust, and drag—in the drawing in Activity 1 (The Four Forces) in the Student Notebook. Within their groups, have students explain to each other what term they placed in each location and the reasons for the placement (for example, lift is put on top of the aircraft because it makes the aircraft go up).

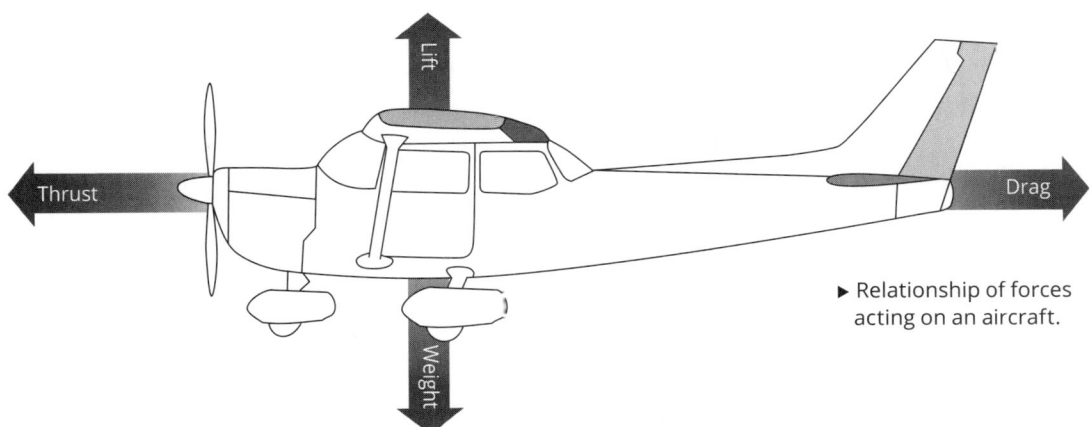

▶ Relationship of forces acting on an aircraft.

Step 2: Show students the correct labels and directions according to the figure shown above and have them self-correct their own labels. Provide a simple explanation of each of the four forces by showing a video that explains how airplanes fly.

Step 3: Students will participate in a jigsaw activity to become experts on one of the four forces and then teach their classmates about it.

1. Divide students into four jigsaw groups of roughly equal numbers of students. These groups will be the "home groups" of the jigsaw. (For additional explanation on the jigsaw activity, see the link to instructions in the online Instructor Resources.)
2. Tell students that they are responsible for teaching one force (lift, weight, drag, or thrust) to their home group they are sitting with now.
3. Now students will leave their home group to sit in a group with the other students assigned to the same force (lift, weight, drag, or thrust); this will be the "expert group" for that force. Ask students to begin reading to themselves or to take turns reading aloud about their assigned force in the *Pilot's Handbook of Aeronautical Knowledge*. When students are finished reading, the group should discuss their segment, fill out the section for their assigned force in Student Notebook Activity 2 (Aerodynamics Graphic Organizer), and decide how they should present to their home groups.
4. Students will regroup with their home groups and work together to answer the questions in Activity 3 (Home Group Questions) in the Student Notebook. Each student is then responsible for teaching their force to their home group. All students are responsible for learning all material, and as other students present information on the forces, they should fill in the other columns in Activity 2 (Aerodynamics Graphic Organizer) to complete it.
5. The facilitator should review all columns collectively to ensure accuracy of the four forces of flight.

Concluding Activity: Give each "home group" of students one of the four forces from the lesson. They must then write a detail or descriptor that starts with each of the letters of the force to form an acrostic. Have students write these on the board and record each in Activity 4 (Acrostic) in their Student Notebooks.

T	L	D	W
H	I	R	E
R	F	A	I
U	T	G	G
S			H
T			T

Example:
Turning tendency
High performance aircraft
RPM
Unaccelerated flight
Speed
Torque

LESSON 2

INTRODUCTION TO AIRFOILS

PURPOSE

The purpose of this lesson is to examine the design of an airfoil and note how it creates lift.

ACCOMMODATIONS FOR LEARNING DIFFERENCES

It is important that lessons accommodate the needs of every learner. These lessons may be modified to accommodate your students with learning differences by referring to **www.pacer.org/parent/php/PHP-c267.pdf**.

PREPARATION

- Class copies of *Pilot's Handbook of Aeronautical Knowledge* (FAA-H-8083-25)
- Sticky notes
- Scrap paper for the wing experiment

DIRECTIONS

Introductory Activity: Show the class a picture of a Northrop Grumman B-2 aircraft. Ask students to write down on sticky notes the first word that comes to mind when they see this picture. Have them also answer yes or no to the following question: "Do the four forces act differently on this aircraft than on the one you saw in the previous lesson?" Have students bring their notes up to the front of the class and stick them on the board. Organize the sticky notes into groups of similar answers and discuss any answers that relate to the aircraft's aerodynamic airfoil-looking shape. Read and discuss students' yes or no answers to the earlier question. (*Answer:* The forces still act the same.)

Extra credit or critical thinking question: "Why was this aircraft designed this way?"

Step 1: Ask the class to define the term "airfoil." Ask students to give examples both in and outside of aviation. (Example in aviation: pull up a picture of an aircraft and have students list the parts of the aircraft that are shaped like an airfoil; *Answer:* fuselage, wings, propellers, wheel covers, and vertical and horizontal stabilizers. Examples outside of aviation include sports cars, spoilers on cars, windmill blades, etc.)

Step 2: Have the students define the following terms by looking them up in the *Pilot's Handbook of Aeronautical Knowledge* Chapter 5 and recording their answers in the Student Notebook in Activity 1 (Airfoil Definitions): Leading edge, trailing edge, chord line, camber, angle of attack, relative wind, high-pressure area, and low-pressure area.

Once students have defined the terms, have them draw and label the parts of an airfoil in their Student Notebooks in Activity 2 (Labeling Airfoil Parts). Go over the definitions to verify the students have a practical understanding of the terms. Call students up to draw and label the parts of the airfoil on the board.

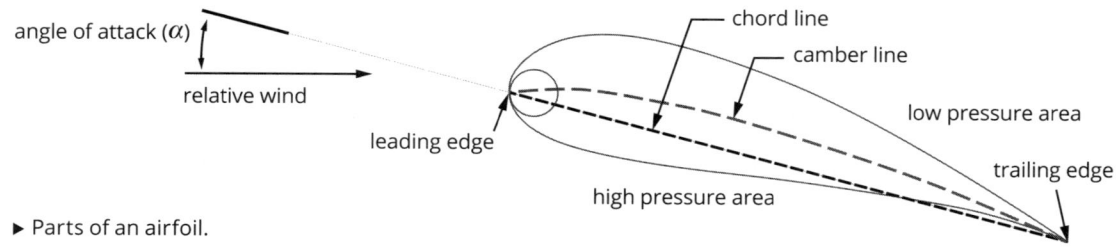

▶ Parts of an airfoil.

Step 3: Have the class break up into small groups. Students will work in their groups to conduct the wing experiment and record their answers in Activity 3 (Wing Experiment Questions) in their Student Notebooks.

Step 4: Ask a representative from each group to share their selected wing design out loud with the class. As the facilitator, lead a discussion about how their designs did or did not produce lift. Note the different camber of each wing. Aircraft are designed for certain purposes. Compare by showing side-by-side pictures of a fighter jet (pick any fighter) and a training/aerobatic aircraft (e.g., Cessna 172, Piper Archer). Ask students the question, "How do their wings compare?" (*Answers include:* differences in size, camber, the thickness of leading edge. Fighters are designed for maneuverability and speed; they need an airfoil for lift, but they also have a large engine to add thrust for any loss of lift. Training aircraft do not have engines that are big as those in fighters; therefore, the wings need to be sufficient to produce adequate lift for the weight and drag of the aircraft.)

Concluding Activity: Have the students answer the following question on an exit slip: "When looking at a wind farm, why are some windmills turning and others are not? What is different about their angles of attack?" (*Answer:* On some windmills, the blades are feathered, or their angle of attack is zero so the blades are not producing lift.)

FACILITATOR INFORMATION
Directions for Wing Experiment

Directions: Cut your paper to create two pieces that are each 4 by 5 inches. Keep one piece of paper flat and form a slight arch, loop, or hill on top with the other. Tape the two pieces together.

1. Draw what your wing looks like.
2. How does it react when you blow over the top of the wing?
3. How does it react when you blow across the bottom of the wing?
4. Why is there a difference?

Create another wing with a different camber.

5. Draw what your wing looks like.
6. How does it react when you blow over the top of the wing?
7. Which wing performed better?
    a. Why?

CHAPTER 8 AERODYNAMICS OF FLIGHT

LESSON 3

LIFT—NEWTON & BERNOULLI

PURPOSE

The purpose of this lesson is to comprehend aerodynamic forces for flying a controlled, safe flight.

ACCOMMODATIONS FOR LEARNING DIFFERENCES

It is important that lessons accommodate the needs of every learner. These lessons may be modified to accommodate your students with learning differences by referring to www.pacer.org/parent/php/PHP-c267.pdf.

PREPARATION

- Class copies of *Pilot's Handbook of Aeronautical Knowledge* (FAA-H-8083-25)
- Paper of various thicknesses
- Scissors
- Sticky notes or small pieces of paper
- Computers and internet access for students

DIRECTIONS

Introductory Activity: Place a sticky note or small scrap of paper on each student's desk. Write on the board the following question: "Of the four forces—lift, thrust, weight and drag—which one is not exerted on a paper airplane, actually making it a glider and not a plane?" Have students record the answer on their sticky notes and compare their responses. Poll the class using a show of hands for which force students think it is. Explain the correct response. (*Answer:* Paper airplanes are actually "gliders," as they do not provide themselves any thrust throughout their flight.) Review the key concepts of the four forces and airfoil structure from the previous lessons.

Step 1: Watch the short video, "Principles of Flight" (start to 5:31), produced by Embry-Riddle Aeronautical University Special VFR Productions,[1] or another similar video that demonstrates principles of flight and lift.

Step 2: Facilitate an interactive lecture on lift discussing Newton's Third Law and Bernoulli's Principle as they impact lift using visual representations and pictures in the presentation that clarify and demonstrate the key concepts. Refer to the figures under Facilitator Information below. During the lesson, students will label and take notes on their diagrams under Activity 1 (Label Diagrams) in the Student Notebook.

Step 3: Have the students research and design a wind tunnel that they could build to test Bernoulli's principle and Newton's Law. Have students report back on their findings.

Concluding Activity: Assign students Activity 2 (Comprehension Questions) in the Student Notebook for homework. (An answer key is provided at the end of the chapter.) They may use the *Pilot's Handbook of Aeronautical Knowledge* and may work on the assignment for the remainder of the class time.

FACILITATOR INFORMATION
Figures for Step 2

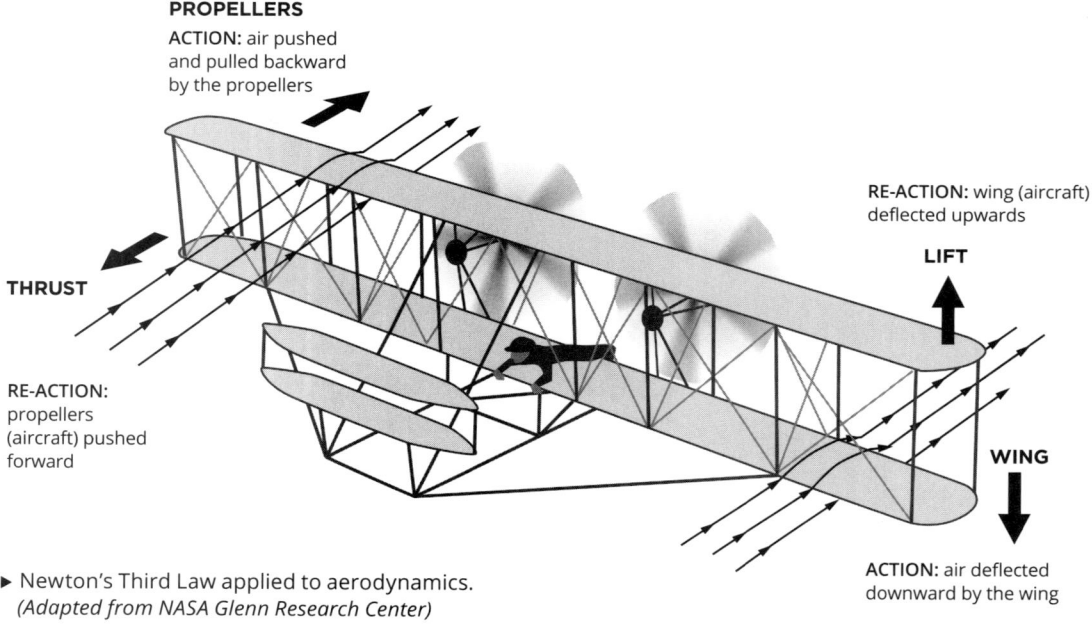

▶ Newton's Third Law applied to aerodynamics.
(Adapted from NASA Glenn Research Center)

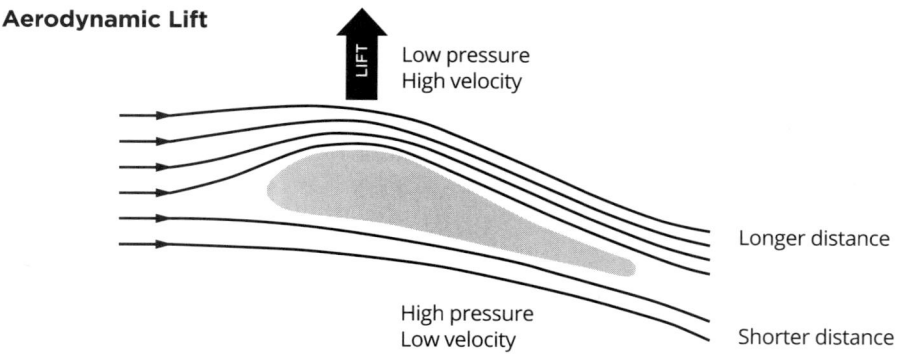

▶ Bernoulli's Principle and aerodynamic lift.

CHAPTER 8   AERODYNAMICS OF FLIGHT

LESSON 4

DRAG AND DESIGN

PURPOSE

The purpose of this lesson is to explain drag and identify the variables that influence drag.

ACCOMMODATIONS FOR LEARNING DIFFERENCES

It is important that lessons accommodate the needs of every learner. These lessons may be modified to accommodate your students with learning differences by referring to www.pacer.org/parent/php/PHP-c267.pdf.

PREPARATION

- *Aeronautics for Introductory Physics* file (by NASA & American Association of Physics Teachers)[2]
- Four station cards (print from *Aeronautics for Introductory Physics*, pages 103–106)
- Electronic balance
- Ping-pong balls
- Golf balls
- Regular coffee filters
- Industrial-sized coffee filters (and/or muffin cups)
- Long translucent containers
- Corn syrup
- Water
- Stapler
- Marbles

DIRECTIONS

Introductory Activity: Show students the pictures of semi-trucks and trailers provided under Facilitator Information, and have them write down the differences they see in Activity 1 (Semi-Truck Comparison) in their Student Notebooks. Ask the students why the fronts of the semi-trucks are different, why the gaps between the trucks and trailers are so different, and why one has material below the trailer between the tires. These are all drag-reducing strategies that have been implemented by this industry to improve truck performance. Reference the website on semi-truck aerodynamics (see online Instructor Resources) for examples of the drag-reduction strategies used on semi-trucks and trailers. How does this relate to aircraft? (*Answer:* When engineers and manufacturers are designing aircraft, they need to think of ways in which to reduce drag as well.)

Step 1: Have students complete Activity 2 (Three-Column Organizer) in the Student Notebook. The questions include: "What do you think causes drag?" "How does it work?" (Drawing) "How does it work?" (Explanation)

Have students compare and contrast their explanations in the three columns with their observations in the semi-truck comparison activity.

Step 2: Facilitate an interactive lecture about drag using visual representations and pictures in the presentation that clarify and demonstrate the key concepts. A drag curve is provided under Facilitator Information at the end of this lesson. Short videos are available online to illustrate the concept of parasite drag. Students will take notes during the lesson in their Student Notebooks in Activity 3 (Interactive Lecture Diagram and Notes). Be sure to include the following concepts:

- Drag
- Parasite drag
  › Form drag
  › Interference drag
  › Skin friction drag
- Induced drag
- Lift-to-drag ratio

Step 3: Prepare and conduct the Air Friction Stations Discovery Lab: Drag and Aircraft Design experiment from the NASA *Aeronautics for Introductory Physics* file (pages 99–106).[3] All station instructions and handouts to print are included in PDF file (see Instructor Resources for link).
   Note: Stations could take more than one day of instructional time.

Concluding Activity: Display a picture of the NASA concept aircraft from the "Will It Work" webpage in NASA's online gallery (see Facilitator Information below). In pairs or triads, ask students the questions, "Will it work? Will this concept aircraft be more efficient than a conventional craft? Explain using aerodynamics of flight concepts."

FACILITATOR INFORMATION
Semi-Truck Images for Introductory Activity

(See next page.)

(iStock.com/mokee81)

(by Korbitr, commons.wikimedia.org/wiki/File:Tesla_Semi_3.jpg, public domain)

(iStock.com/grandriver)

Drag Curve for Step 2

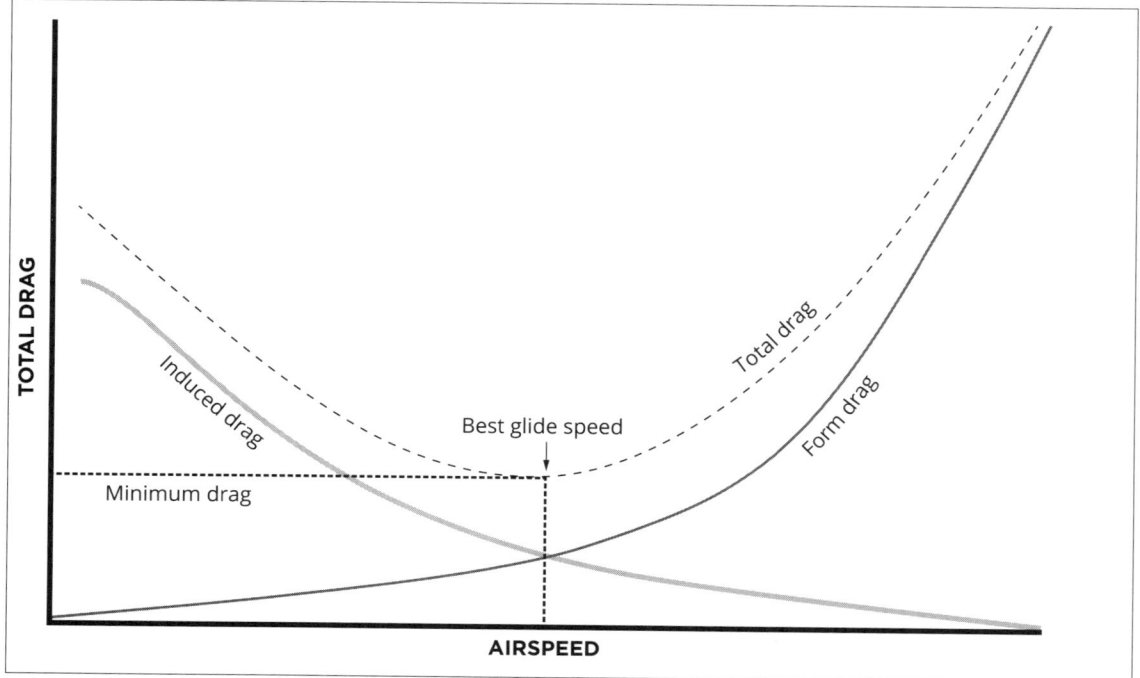

▶ Drag curve.

Concept Aircraft Photo for Concluding Activity

▶ Scale model of a potential future aircraft concept inside the Subsonic Wind Tunnel at NASA's Langley Research Center in Hampton, Virginia. *(NASA Langley/David C. Bowman)*

CHAPTER 8   AERODYNAMICS OF FLIGHT

LESSON 5

STALLS AND SPINS

PURPOSE

The purpose of this lesson is to examine the causes and recovery procedures of stalls and spins to facilitate safe flight.

ACCOMMODATIONS FOR LEARNING DIFFERENCES

It is important that lessons accommodate the needs of every learner. These lessons may be modified to accommodate your students with learning differences by referring to **www.pacer.org/parent/php/PHP-c267.pdf**.

PREPARATION

- Class copies of *Pilot's Handbook of Aeronautical Knowledge* (FAA-H-8083-25)
- Visual display for interactive lecture
- Video and audio capabilities

DIRECTIONS

Introductory Activity: Display to students the following statistics from the AOPA article, "The Spin Training Story—And Why It's Still Important," by Ken Medley.[4]

- About 9% of general aviation accidents are stall/spin accidents.
- 29% of these accidents are fatal.
- Stall/spin accidents kill almost 13% of all people lost in general aviation aircraft.

Ask students, "What do you think about these facts and statistics? Given what you know about aerodynamic forces, discuss with a partner what might cause a stall or spin to occur."

Step 1: Facilitate an interactive lecture about stalls and spins using visual representations, videos, and pictures in the presentation that clarify and demonstrate the key concepts. Use videos to demonstrate and explain the key concepts, interspersing the videos throughout the interactive lecture. Demonstrate stalls and spins using flight simulation or unmanned aircraft (UAS) or refer to Chapter 10.

During the lesson, students will label and take notes using Activity 1 (Stalls Outline Table) and Activity 2 (Spins Outline Table) in their Student Notebooks. Be sure to include the following concepts:

Stalls
- When does it occur?
- Indications of a stall
- Recovery procedures
- Factors affecting stall speed
    › Weight
    › CG location
    › Angle of bank and load factor
    › Flaps
    › Power and thrust
    › Frost/snow/ice
    › Turbulence

Spins
- What is a spin?
- Causes
- Phases of a spin
- Spin recovery

Step 2: Have students independently take notes on the listed key concepts from the *Pilot's Handbook of Aeronautical Knowledge*, Chapter 5. Students will add information from the FAA publication to the middle column of the outline tables in Activities 1 and 2.

Step 3: Group students into pairs or triads. Have students compare notes taken from the interactive lecture and FAA handbook reading. Students will add any additional information from their partner's information that was not already included in their own notes in the last column of the Stalls Outline Table and Spins Outline Table.

Concluding Activity: Ask students to list questions they would still like clarified on the board. Answer the questions and reteach concepts as time allows, and consider adding additional instruction at the beginning of Lesson 6 based on questions.

LESSON 6
REVIEW: AERODYNAMICS OF FLIGHT

PURPOSE
The purpose of this lesson is to review key principles and concepts of the aerodynamics of flight.

ACCOMMODATIONS FOR LEARNING DIFFERENCES
It is important that lessons accommodate the needs of every learner. These lessons may be modified to accommodate your students with learning differences by referring to **www.pacer.org/parent/php/PHP-c267.pcf**.

PREPARATION
- Class copies of *Pilot's Handbook of Aeronautical Knowledge* (FAA-H-8083-25)

DIRECTIONS

Introductory Activity: Re-engage the students on aviation history by sharing a relevant occurrence close to today's date from the website This Day in Aviation (**www.thisdayinaviation.com**). Display relevant pictures as you share the story. Have students turn and talk with a partner about what impact this historical event had on modern day aviation.

Step 1: In pairs, have students complete the review in Activity 1 (Study Guide) in the Student Notebook. (An answer key is provided at the end of the chapter.) Students may use the *Pilot's Handbook of Aeronautical Knowledge* (Chapter 5) and class notes for reference. The facilitator will circulate through the room, answering questions and checking for understanding.

Step 2: Ask students to look through their course material and write down anything that they don't remember, missed, or are unclear on. Take turns answering their questions and clarifying; chances are that several students will have the same questions, so this will be a very productive time for all.

Step 3: Review the study guide questions with the students for accuracy. Correct any misconceptions or inaccuracies. Reteach as needed.

Concluding Activity: No formal concluding activity. Students can continue to work on the study guide due for the next day prior to the exam.

LESSON 7
CHAPTER 8 EXAM

PURPOSE
The purpose of this lesson is to assess student knowledge of the aerodynamics of flight.

ACCOMMODATIONS FOR LEARNING DIFFERENCES
It is important that lessons accommodate the needs of every learner. These lessons may be modified to accommodate your students with learning differences by referring to www.pacer.org/parent/php/PHP-c267.pdf.

PREPARATION
- A copy of the exam for each student
- Access to online *Wired* article or printouts of the article for students

DIRECTIONS

Introductory Activity: Re-engage the students on aerodynamics by showing the clip of a fighter jet stall. In pairs, have students explain to each other how the four forces of flight (lift, weight, thrust, and drag) are demonstrated by the jet in the video clip.

Provide instructions on what students are to do after the test before it commences.

Step 1: Students will complete the aerodynamics of flight exam; questions are available at the end of this lesson for the facilitator's reference. (An answer key is provided at the end of the chapter.)

Step 2: When students have turned in the exam, have them independently read the *Wired* article, "July 19, 1989: Human Heroics Overcome Aircraft Failure in Sioux City."[5] In Activity 1 (Article Response and Rubric) in the Student Notebook, students will write a one-paragraph response that includes a summary and reflection on the prompts: (1) Explain the systems and aerodynamic principles the crew worked with to maneuver the plane. (2) Explain which systems failed and how they failed. (3) What mistake was made and what was learned from it? What changes were made in aviation as a result?

Student responses will be graded using the rubric provided in the Student Notebook.

Concluding Activity: No formal summary activity. Students will work independently to finish the exam at different times and begin reading the article as an introductory activity to Chapter 9 on aircraft systems.

The facilitator may decide to review the correct exam answers to address incorrect responses and/or misconceptions prior to beginning Chapter 9.

FACILITATOR INFORMATION

Chapter 8 Exam: Aerodynamics of Flight

(This exam is available in the online Instructor Resources in a format ready for use in the classroom. An answer key is provided at the end of the chapter.)

Directions: Read each question carefully and circle the correct answer or respond in the space provided.

1. The four forces acting on an airplane in flight are:
    a. Lift, weight, thrust, and drag
    b. Lift, weight, gravity, and thrust
    c. Lift, gravity, power, and friction

2. When are the four forces that act on an airplane in equilibrium?
    a. During straight-and-level, unaccelerated flight
    b. When the aircraft is accelerating
    c. When the aircraft is decelerating

3. Which lift principle relates to the statement "As the airspeed increases the pressure decreases"?
    a. Newton
    b. Bernoulli

4. Which lift principle deals with airflow striking the bottom of the wing and bouncing off?
    a. Newton
    b. Bernoulli

5. The chord line is an imaginary line connecting which of the following?
    a. Wing root with wing tip
    b. Leading edge to the trailing edge of the wing
    c. Wing tip to wing tip

6. Draw an airfoil and label the following. (8 pts)
    a. Leading edge
    b. Trailing edge
    c. Chord line
    d. Camber
    e. Angle of attack
    f. Relative wind
    g. High pressure
    h. Low pressure

7. Define critical angle of attack.

8. What are two indications that an aircraft is approaching a stall?

9. If the wing stalls, what is the most important action to recover?
   a. Apply back pressure.
   b. Reduce the angle of attack to less than its critical value.
   c. Let go of the controls.

10. Induced drag is drag caused by the same factors that produce
    a. lift
    b. airspeed
    c. thrust

11. What is the difference between interference, form, and skin friction drag? (3 pts)

12. If you are flying along at 95 knots and you lower the landing gear, what will happen to your airspeed if you do not touch the controls?
    a. It will increase.
    b. It will decrease.
    c. Nothing—airspeed will not change.

13. Extending or retracting flaps changes the wing's _____ and _____ characteristics.
    a. weight, thrust
    b. lift, drag
    c. thrust, drag

14. In order for an airplane to spin, it must be stalled first.
    a. True
    b. False

15. Stall recovery is harder for an aircraft with an aft CG.
    a. True
    b. False

16. Lowering flaps increases the overall camber of the wing, resulting in increased air velocity of the wing's upper surface.
    a. True
    b. False

17. Load factor is greater in straight-and-level flight than when in a 60-degree turn.
    a. True
    b. False

18. When conducting a power-on stall, an aircraft typically has a higher angle of attack as compared to a power-off stall.
    a. True
    b. False

19. A pilot can climb and fly faster just by pitching the nose of the aircraft up and not increasing the throttle.

    a. True
    b. False

20. What are some adverse effects of flying an airplane at max gross weight?

21. Why does the airplane want to roll/turn left after takeoff?

22. A pilot misjudged his altitude and is on a collision course with a mountain. In order to climb rapidly, he must increase throttle to full and move which flight control for increased pitch?

    a. elevator
    b. aileron
    c. rudder
    d. trim

23. The upward angle of both wings creates more stability. This is called:

    a. adverse yaw
    b. dihedral
    c. aspect ratio

24. Label parasite drag, induced drag, total drag, and best glide speed on the following drawing (3 pts):

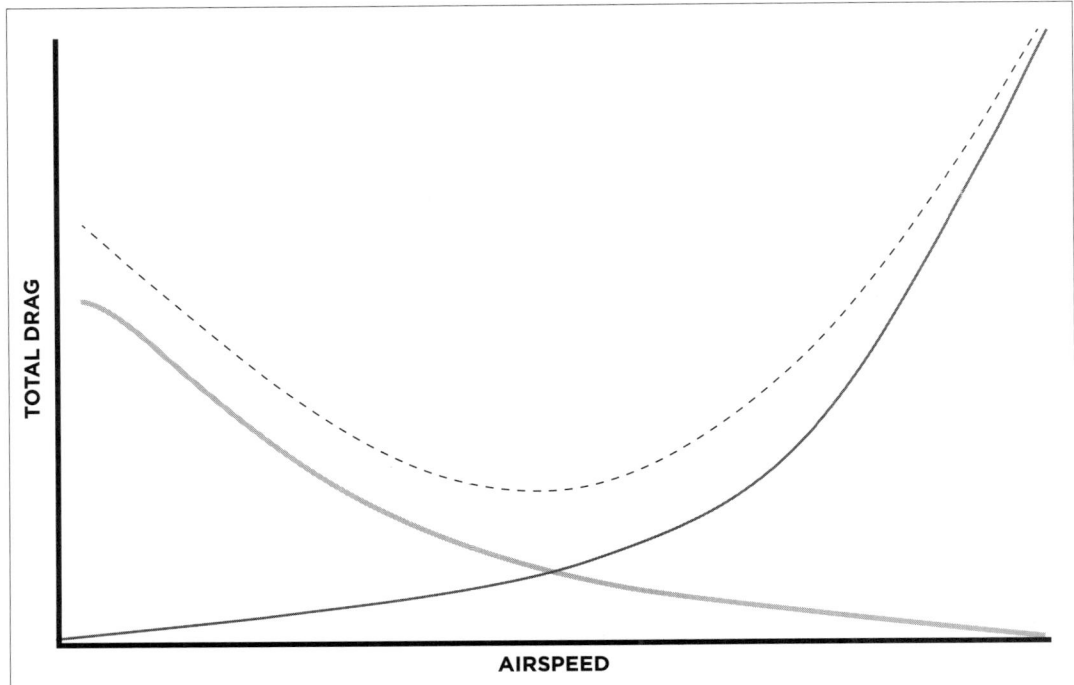

25. When on final approach to land, about 300 feet above ground level, you notice that you are a little too low. Why is it not a good idea to just pitch the nose of the aircraft up?

26. If you increase the payload, the takeoff distance _____.
    a. increases
    b. decreases

27. If you increase the payload, the speed required to take off _____.
    a. increases
    b. decreases
    c. stays the same regardless of weight

28. What part of the wing do manufacturers design to stall first?
    a. The wing root
    b. The midsection
    c. The wing tip
    d. None of the above

29. There is a lot of thinking that goes on when designing and engineering an aircraft. Even the slightest change can impact performance. Give an example of a change that could be made to an aircraft and describe how that would impact (either positively or negatively) the performance of that aircraft.

ANSWER KEYS
CHAPTER 8

LESSON 3, Activity 2
Comprehension Questions Homework (Student Notebook)

1. (b) Bernoulli
2. (a) Newton
3. Increase throttle or decrease angle of climb.
4. No. If you go into a climb, your thrust and lift must counteract your drag and weight. You will need to increase throttle to equalize the forces and not lose airspeed.
5. Your takeoff distance will increase because it takes longer to overcome opposing forces.
6. (a) increased. Excessive weight reduces the flight performance in almost every respect.

LESSON 6, Activity 1
Study Guide (Student Notebook)

1. Flaps are the most common high-lift devices used on aircraft. These surfaces, which are attached to the trailing edge of the wing, increase both lift and induced drag for any given angle of attack (AOA). Flaps allow a compromise between high cruising speed and low landing speed because they may be extended when needed and retracted into the wing's structure when not needed.
2. The rudder is attached to the back of the vertical stabilizer. During flight, it is used to move the airplane's nose left and right.
3. Lift, drag, weight, thrust.
4. For the aircraft to remain in steady, level flight, equilibrium must be obtained by a lift equal to the aircraft weight and a powerplant thrust equal to the aircraft drag.
5. Bernoulli's Principle states that as the velocity of a moving fluid (liquid or gas) increases, the pressure within the fluid decreases. This principle explains what happens to air passing over the curved top of the airplane wing.
6. Newton's Third Law: "For every action, there is an equal and opposite reaction." In an airplane, the propeller moves and pushes back the air; consequently, the air pushes the propeller (and thus the airplane) in the opposite direction—forward. In a jet airplane, the engine pushes a blast of hot gases backward; the force of equal and opposite reaction pushes against the engine and forces the airplane forward.
7. The angle of attack (AOA) is defined as the acute angle between the chord line of the airfoil and the direction of the relative wind.
8. The chord line is an imaginary line drawn through the blade from its leading edge to its trailing edge.

9. The relative wind is the airflow opposite to the flight path of the aircraft.
10. Critical angle of attack.
11. Answers may vary—sluggish controls, a buffeting of the aircraft, and stall warning horn may alert the pilot.
12. Reduce the angle of attack, maintain coordination.
13. (a) Root of the wing
14. (a) Power on
15. **Takeoff distance** would be increased. Frost on an aircraft will increase drag and possibly weight, resulting in decreased performance. Frost disrupts the flow of air over the wing and can drastically reduce the production of lift. It also increases drag, which when combined with lowered lift production can adversely affect the ability to take off. An aircraft must be thoroughly cleaned and free of frost prior to beginning a flight. **Cruise flight**—Due to the increased weight and drag and the loss of lift, the aircraft will require more power to maintain normal cruise flight. That increase in power increases fuel flow. **Landing**—Due to the loss in lift, the pilot will need to carry more power into the landing. This will increase the landing distance.
16. Skin friction drag
17. a. Interference drag: The intersection of the wing and the fuselage at the wing root has significant interference drag.

    b. Form drag: Examples include the engine cowlings, antennas, and the aerodynamic shape of other components.

    c. Skin friction drag: Frost or dirt on the wing.
18. Induced drag is drag caused by the same factors that produce lift; its amount varies inversely with airspeed. As airspeed decreases, the angle of attack must increase, in turn increasing induced drag.
19.

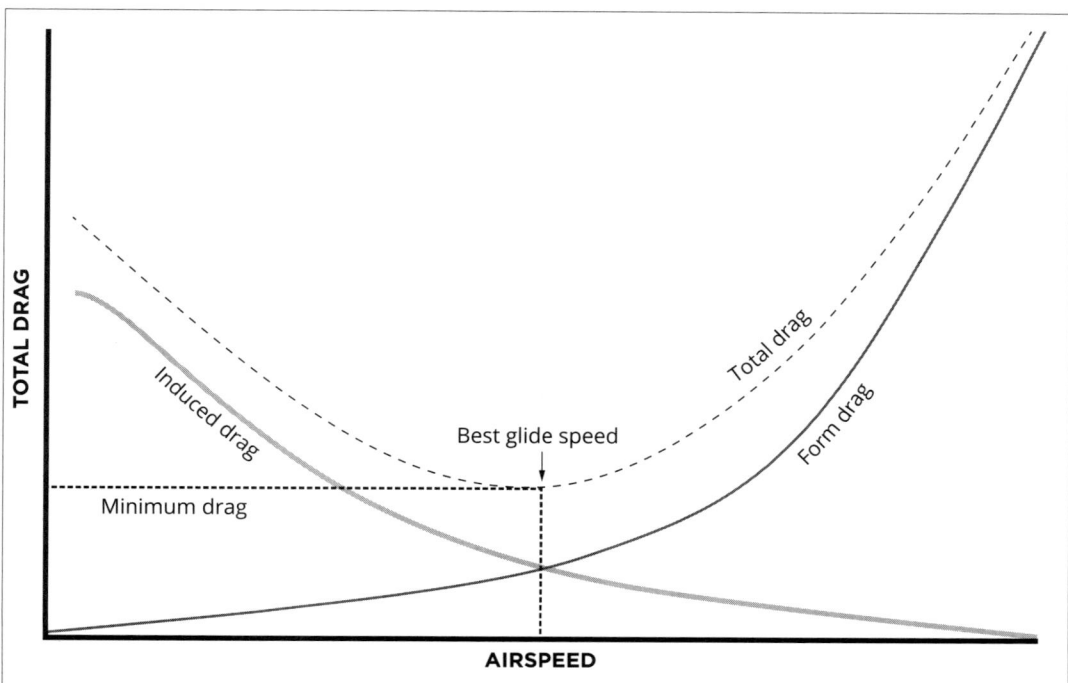

20. The recovery from a stall in any aircraft becomes progressively more difficult as its CG moves aft. The airplane may feel as if it is tail heavy and therefore when trying to recover from a stall it may be difficult to push the nose of the aircraft forward enough to reduce the angle of attack.

21. Torque: It is a left-turning tendency. In the Piper Archer, the propeller rotates to the right or clockwise, so the aircraft has the tendency to roll to the left.

22. Load factor: The ratio of a specified load to the total weight of the aircraft.

23. Turn.

24. Your airspeed will decrease and you could stall.

25. It decreases performance due to drag.

26. You can push the nose forward or down.

27. You will still be able to climb, but the rate at which you can will depend on the thrust you have available to climb. You will be unable to climb with an increase in airspeed without increasing thrust. If you want to fly faster without increasing throttle, you will have to pitch the aircraft's nose down and hold it in a descent.

28. An increase in payload results in a decrease in performance; more lift is required for straight-and-level flight, resulting in more drag.

29. A spin is an aggravated stall that results in an airplane descending in a helical, or corkscrew, path. It may occur when a pilot is distracted during an emergency or during landing when the pilot slows the aircraft down and inadvertently stalls the aircraft while being uncoordinated or causing a yawing force.

LESSON 7
Chapter 8 Exam

1. (a) Lift, weight, thrust, and drag
2. (a) During straight-and-level, unaccelerated flight
3. (b) Bernoulli
4. (a) Newton
5. (b) Leading edge to the trailing edge of the wing
6. Parts of an airfoil.

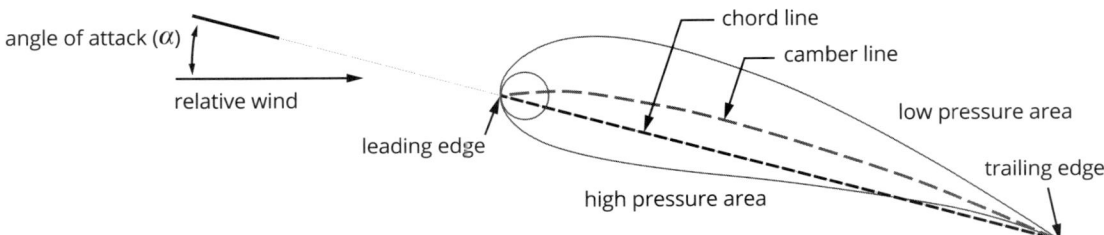

7. The critical angle of attack is the angle of attack at which a wing stalls regardless of airspeed, flight attitude, or weight.

8. Answers may vary: Stall horn, buffeting of aircraft, sluggish controls.

9. (b) Reduce the angle of attack to less than its critical value.

10. (a) lift

11. Skin friction drag is drag generated between air molecules and the solid surface of the aircraft. Form drag is the portion of parasite drag generated by the aircraft due to its shape and airflow around it. Interference drag comes from the intersection of airstreams that creates eddy currents, turbulence, or restricts smooth airflow.

12. (b) It will decrease.

13. (b) lift, drag

14. (a) True

15. (a) True

16. (a) True

17. (b) False

18. (a) True

19. (b) False

20. Answers may vary: A heavier gross weight results in a longer takeoff run and shallower climb, and a faster touchdown speed and longer landing roll. Even a minor overload may make it impossible for the aircraft to clear an obstacle that normally would not be a problem during takeoff under more favorable conditions. The detrimental effects of overloading on performance are not limited to the immediate hazards involved with takeoffs and landings. Overloading has an adverse effect on all climb and cruise performance, which leads to overheating during climbs, added wear on engine parts, increased fuel consumption, slower cruising speeds, and reduced range.

21. Due to left-turning tendencies of the airplane.

22. (a) elevator

23. (b) dihedral

24.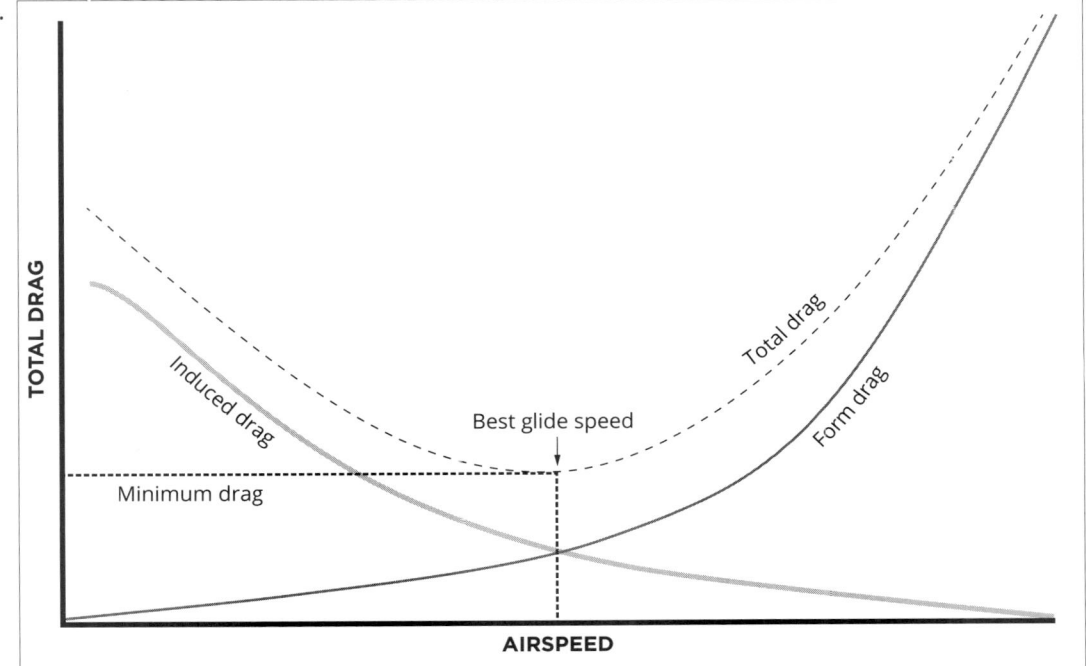

25. The aircraft's airspeed will decrease and you could stall. Since you are low to the ground, you don't have room to recover. The best practice for this situation is to add power and adjust pitch as needed and if you still aren't "stabilized," you should plan to go around.

26. (a) increases

27. (a) increases

28. (a) The wing root

29. Answers will vary:
    - The manufacturer could increase the size of the wings. They will most likely produce more lift; however, they will also increase the weight of the aircraft.
    - The manufacturer could increase the size of the fuselage to allow for more people and cargo to be carried onboard the aircraft. This size and shape of the new fuselage could increase the drag and the additional weight will add to the overall weight of the aircraft. A more powerful engine may also be needed.

CHAPTER 9
AIRCRAFT SYSTEMS

Introduction

STANDARDS & OBJECTIVES
North Dakota Aviation Content Standards (Grades 10-12)
- **1.3.1**—Explain the function of the battery, alternator, and magneto.
- **1.3.2**—Discuss fuel systems.
- **1.3.3**—Explain the cycle of an internal combustion engine.
- **1.3.4**—Describe common errors with the induction system.
- **1.3.5**—Compare differences between fixed pitch and constant speed propellers.

Science—Next Generation Science Standards (Grades 9-12)
- **HS-PS3-3**—Design, build, and refine a device that works within given constraints to convert one form of energy into another form of energy.

Language Arts—CCSS.ELA-LITERACY.CCRA
- **L.1**—Demonstrate command of the conventions of standard English grammar and usage when writing or speaking.
- **L.2**—Demonstrate command of the conventions of standard English capitalization, punctuation, and spelling when writing.
- **SL.1**—Prepare for and participate effectively in a range of conversations and collaborations with diverse partners, building on others' ideas and expressing their own clearly and persuasively.
- **SL.2**—Integrate and evaluate information presented in diverse media and formats, including visually, quantitatively, and orally.
- **SL.4**—Present information, findings, and supporting evidence such that listeners can follow the line of reasoning and the organization, development, and style are appropriate to task, purpose, and audience.
- **SL.5**—Make strategic use of digital media and visual displays of data to express information and enhance understanding of presentations.
- **W.2**—Write informative/explanatory texts to examine and convey complex ideas and information clearly and accurately through the effective selection, organization, and analysis of content.
- **W.4**—Produce clear and coherent writing in which the development, organization, and style are appropriate to task, purpose, and audience.

- **W.7**— Conduct short as well as more sustained research projects based on focused questions, demonstrating understanding of the subject under investigation.
- **W.8**—Gather relevant information from multiple print and digital sources, assess the credibility and accuracy of each source, and integrate the information while avoiding plagiarism.
- **W.9**—Draw evidence from literary or informational texts to support analysis, reflection, and research.

ESSENTIAL QUESTIONS

- What are the relationships amongst the functions of the battery and the alternator?
- How does a fuel-injected fuel system compare to a carbureted fuel system?
- What is happening in the power stroke of a reciprocating engine?
- What are the key differences in flight between fixed-pitch and constant-speed propellers?

LESSONS

Lesson	Topic	Student Notebook Activities
Lesson 1	Introduction to Aircraft Systems	1. Skeleton Notes for Aircraft Systems, Part 1
Lesson 2	Engine	1. Cylinder Diagram 2. Four Square Graphic Organizer
Lesson 3	Fuel Systems	1. Fuel Systems Diagram 2. Skeleton Notes for Aircraft Systems, Part 2 3. Denver Centennial Airport (KAPA) Chart Supplement
Lesson 4	Flight Instruments Review	1. Flight Instruments Graphic Organizer 2. Pitot-Static Instruments Diagram 3. Gyroscopic Flight Instrument Definitions
Lesson 5	Vacuum and Electrical Systems	1. Discussion Prompts 2. Electrical Systems Graphic Organizer 3. Glass Cockpit Flight Instruments
Lesson 6	Review: Aircraft Systems	1. Preview Questions 2. Research Conclusions Graphic Organizer 3. Two-Sentence Summary
Lesson 7	Chapter 9 Exam	1. Article Response and Rubric

CHAPTER 9 AIRCRAFT SYSTEMS

LESSON 1

INTRODUCTION TO AIRCRAFT SYSTEMS

PURPOSE
The purpose of this lesson is to introduce aircraft systems and to focus on the importance of troubleshooting during flight.

ACCOMMODATIONS FOR LEARNING DIFFERENCES
It is important that lessons accommodate the needs of every learner. These lessons may be modified to accommodate your students with learning differences by referring to **www.pacer.org/parent/php/PHP-c267.pdf**.

PREPARATION
- Class copies of *Pilot's Handbook of Aeronautical Knowledge* (FAA-H-8083-25)
- Aircraft pilot's operating handbook (POH), Section 7, if possible

DIRECTIONS
Introductory Activity: Give students a scenario: "You're driving down the road and your car makes a weird noise. What do you do?" (*Potential answer:* Stop your car, investigate, go to a gas station, call your parents, etc.). Allow time for an open-ended discussion. Now, provide the following flight scenario: "You're in flight and you look at your tachometer and you notice that instead of the power being at 2,500 RPM, it is now at 1,800 RPM. You reach over and increase the throttle and there is no change in the RPMs. What do you do? What could possibly be wrong?" (*Potential answers:* Problem with one of the two magnetos, running out of gas, engine failing, etc.). The purpose of this lesson is to introduce aircraft systems and to focus on the importance of troubleshooting during flight.

Step 1: The facilitator will need to direct students to Activity 1 (Skeleton Notes for Aircraft Systems, Part 1) found in the Student Notebook. Information to complete these notes can be found in the *Pilot's Handbook of Aeronautical Knowledge*, Chapter 7: Aircraft Systems. Monitor and guide student work as necessary. Allow students time to complete the skeleton notes independently or in small groups.

Step 2: Use the remainder of class time to complete the notes. Students can be assigned any notes they do not finish as homework. The completed skeleton notes will be reviewed in class during the next lesson.

Concluding Activity: Now that students have researched a little on various aircraft systems, lead a discussion to decide which system seems the most complicated and ask why it would be important to know a little about it as a pilot.

LESSON 2
ENGINE

PURPOSE

The purpose of this lesson is to review the parts of an aircraft engine.

ACCOMMODATIONS FOR LEARNING DIFFERENCES

It is important that lessons accommodate the needs of every learner. These lessons may be modified to accommodate your students with learning differences by referring to **www.pacer.org/parent/php/PHP-c267.pdf.**

PREPARATION

- *Pilot's Handbook of Aeronautical Knowledge* (FAA-H-8083-25)
- Aircraft pilot's operating handbook (POH) for Piper Archer (PA-28-181)

DIRECTIONS

Introductory Activity: Ask a question to engage students in thinking about aircraft engines: "Does anyone work on or have snowmobiles or a boat? Is that engine a two-stroke or four-stroke cycle? Can anyone guess how many strokes are in the engine cycle in the Piper Archer aircraft?" (*Answer:* 4 strokes). The purpose of today's lesson is to review the parts of an aircraft's reciprocating engine.

Step 1: Explain to students that most small general aviation aircraft have what is called a reciprocating engine. Define the word "reciprocating." (*Answer:* a back-and-forth motion; in aviation, a reciprocating engine has one or more pistons moving up and down in cylinders.)

Step 2: Direct students to turn to Activity 1 (Cylinder Diagram) in their Student Notebooks. Have students use their skeleton notes from the previous lesson to label the parts of the cylinder while you guide the discussion, provide more information about how each part of the cylinder works, and clear up misconceptions. Refer to the engine diagram under Facilitator Information.

Step 3: Show videos and/or animations to explain the 4-stroke engine cycle to students. Explain each section by referring to the four-stroke engine information from students' skeleton notes. Have students complete Activity 2 (Four Square Graphic Organizer) in the Student Notebook to record the names of the strokes and what happens in each stroke.

Step 4: Prepare an interactive lecture to lead a discussion on the following systems, using pictures and/or videos to describe each one. Students can add to their skeleton notes from Lesson 1 during the interactive lecture.

I. Exhaust system
   a. Aircraft heater
II. Ignition system
   a. Magnetos
   b. Selecting left, right, and off
   c. Why have dual magnetos?

III. Oil Systems
   a. Purpose
   b. Oil changes
   c. Oil system emergencies

Concluding Activity: Have students turn and talk to a partner about one thing they learned from the lesson that was not in their skeleton notes from the previous lesson. Select several students to share their answers out loud.

FACILITATOR INFORMATION
Engine Diagram

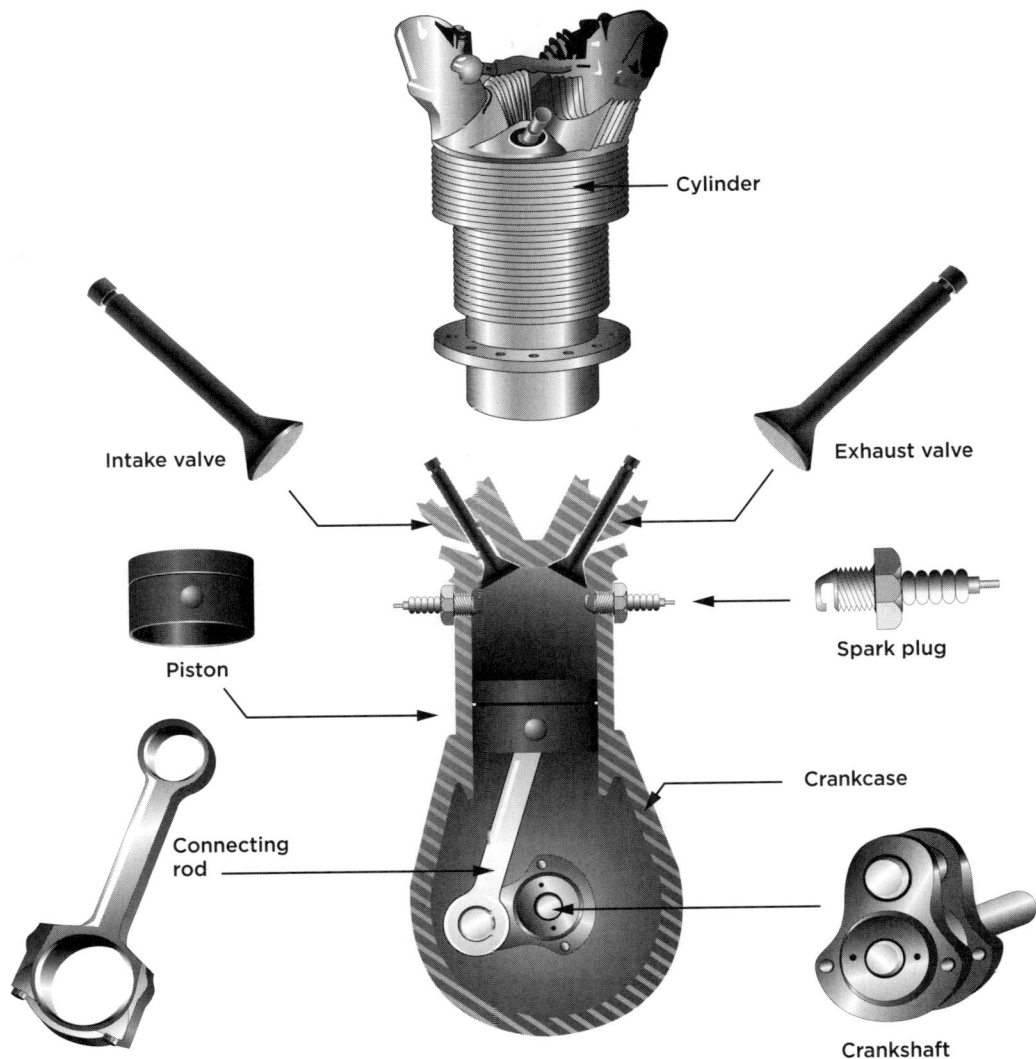

▶ Main components of a spark ignition reciprocating engine. *(FAA-H-8083-25B)*

CHAPTER 9 AIRCRAFT SYSTEMS

LESSON 3

FUEL SYSTEMS

PURPOSE

The purpose of this lesson is to understand the differences between fuel-injected and carburetor fuel systems.

ACCOMMODATIONS FOR LEARNING DIFFERENCES

It is important that lessons accommodate the needs of every learner. These lessons may be modified to accommodate your students with learning differences by referring to www.pacer.org/parent/php/PHP-c267.pdf.

PREPARATION

- Clear, red, blue, and green pieces of paper
- Note cards
- *Pilot's Handbook of Aeronautical Knowledge* (FAA-H-8083-25)
- Aircraft pilot's operating handbook (POH) Section 7, Piper Archer (PA 28-181)
- Computers and internet access for students

DIRECTIONS

Introductory Activity: Display four pieces of paper on the whiteboard, one of each of the following colors: clear (perhaps a transparency or cellophane), purple, blue, and green (these colors represent the colors of fuel). Pose the question, "Why are these colors important to me as a pilot? How do they relate to fuel systems?" (*Answers:* Fuel has dye added to it so that it is easy to tell what type of fuel has been added to the fuel tanks. On preflight, pilots need to inspect the aircraft to determine if it is ready for flight and one of the items they check is the fuel. They look at the color, check the amount, and check to determine if there is any debris in the fuel. The Piper Archer uses what is called Aviation Grade [AVGAS] 100 Low Lead or 100LL. It is dyed blue. Green is for AVGAS 100, Colorless is for Jet A, and purple is for AVGAS 82UL [unleaded].)

Step 1: Create a presentation to discuss various fuel systems. Just as with the previous lessons, ask the students if they have heard of carburetors or fuel-injected systems. Encourage them to share what they know about the systems. Refer back to their responses throughout the lesson. Reference the *Pilot's Handbook of Aeronautical Knowledge* (Chapter 7) and the information below to create the presentation.

The students should follow along in their Student Notebooks, labeling the parts of the two systems diagrams in Activity 1 (Fuel Systems Diagrams) and recording notes in Activity 2 (Skeleton Notes for Aircraft Systems, Part 2).

Fuel Systems

- Gravity-feed system
- Fuel-pump system
- Components
  › Fuel primer
  › Fuel gauges
  › Fuel selectors
  › Strainers, sumps and drains
- Fuel
  › Types
  › Colors
- Straining
- Controls
  › Mixture control
- Leaning
- Fuel system emergencies

Step 2: After students have labeled the diagrams, break students into small groups. Print the fuel system picture found under Facilitator Information below and make it larger, if possible. Cut the picture into small pieces, each with a different part of the fuel system on it. Give each group one of the smaller pictures. Have groups of students research the purpose of their assigned fuel system component and write a few facts on the back of the card.

Step 3: The class will work together to build the entire fuel system schematic on the floor or table using their cards. As the students build the schematic, they should be describing what each particular part is for. The facilitator should add questions or bring up topics either during or after to see if the students fully understand what they are describing. For example, one such topic would be, "How would this schematic be different for a high-wing aircraft?" (*Answer:* A gravity-fed system may only have one fuel pump; reference Figure 7-30 in the *Pilot's Handbook of Aeronautical Knowledge.*) Other topics would be, "Why do we need to check for contamination in the fuel?" (*Answer:* The engine runs off of fuel, so imagine what would happen if there was water in the tanks—would the engine run? No, it might sputter or quit completely.) "What is the difference between usable and unusable fuel?" (*Answer:* Unusable fuel is fuel that is in the lines and bottom of the tanks that cannot be used.)

Step 4: Now that the students have a basic knowledge of the fuel systems, time should be spent discussing how to refuel the aircraft. Show students a video that explains how to refuel an aircraft.

Have the students look up an airport (Denver Centennial, KAPA) in the *Chart Supplement* to see if it has self-service gas (see figure provided in the Student Notebook Activity 3 and under Facilitator Information below). (*Answer:* Under "Service" and "Airport Remarks," it notes that the airport has 100LL and Jet A and that 100LL is available via self service.) Have each of the students look up another airport to see what fuel it has and report their findings back to the class.

At the end of the lesson, hand each student two note cards. Have the students write a separate question related to the chapter on their index cards (see sample questions below). Create enough question cards so each student can have at least two cards (i.e., 10 students = 20 question cards). Lay the cards, written question side down, on the table. Put students in groups of 2–3. Have one group select a question card. Read the question card aloud and have students work in their small groups to answer the question. Students can write their responses on paper or a small whiteboard. Ask students to share their thinking out loud, perhaps awarding points to groups that respond with the correct answer. This activity can be used to review the content that was presented in today's lesson.

Concluding Activity: To wrap up the lesson, pick one of the following questions to pose to the class and allow several students the opportunity to share:

- What color is the fuel that is used in the Piper Archer? (*Answer:* 100LL is blue, which is the preferred fuel; 100 can be used and it is green.)
- What type of fuel is used in the Piper Archer? (*Answer:* 100LL, 100 low lead.)
- What are some of the advantages of the fuel-injected system? (*Answer:* Advantages include reduction in evaporative icing, better fuel flow, better fuel distribution, easier cold weather starts.)
- What are some of the advantages of the carburetor system? (*Answer:* relatively inexpensive, very common in training aircraft)
- Why do we need to sump the fuel prior to every flight? (*Answer:* to check for debris or contamination [like water] in the fuel and to confirm the correct fuel color.)
- What would happen if the fuel selector is not in the Left/Right or On position? (*Answer:* The engine would quit, because the fuel line would not be open and therefore no fuel would get from the tank to the engine.)
- What aircraft would use Jet A fuel? (*Answer:* an aircraft with a turbine engine.)

FACILITATOR INFORMATION

Piper Archer III Fuel System Information from the Pilot's Operating Handbook

7.15 FUEL SYSTEM

Two twenty-five gallon (24 gallons usable) fuel tanks are secured as the leading edge of each wing by screws and nut plates. Each tank contains an indicator tab in the filler neck to determine fuel status. 17 gallons of usable fuel is measured at the bottom of each indicator tab.

The minimum fuel grade is 100 or 100LL. There is one float type fuel sensor in each wing. The signal corresponding to the position of the floats is sent to the Garmin Engine Airframe (GEA) interface unit where it is converted into fuel quantity. The fuel quantity information is then sent to the MFD for display.

After power-up of the avionics system, the Fuel On Board (FOB) should be synchronized with the corresponding fuel quantity sensed in each tank. This can be done by pressing the FOB SYNC softkey on the MFD's AUX-WEIGHT PLANNING page. The gallons remaining will be set to the current fuel quantity in the tanks and the gallons used will be set to zero as shown in the FUEL CALC window of the ENGINE page of the MFD. Pressing FOB SYNC softkey is required to make calculated parameters such as range, endurance, fuel over destination (FOD) and the fuel range ring accurate.

The fuel selector control contains three positions: "OFF", "L" (left tank), and "R" (right tank). To turn the fuel off, rotate selector handle counter-clockwise to the "OFF" position while depressing the button. Rotate the selector handle clockwise to either "L" or "R" positions to permit fuel flow. The button will release automatically preventing accidental selection of the fuel to the off position.

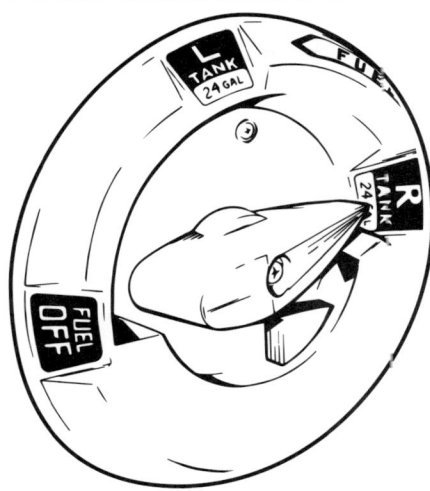

FUEL SELECTOR
Figure 7-5

An auxiliary electric fuel pump is provided in case of failure of the engine driven pump. The electric pump should be on for all takeoffs and landings, and when switching tanks. The pump switch is located in the switch panel above the throttle quadrant.

The fuel drain is provided at the lowest, inboard corner of each wing tank. An engine fuel strainer is accessible through the exterior, lower, left nose section. Each fuel drain and strainer should be opened and the fuel checked for contamination prior to the first flight of the day or after each refueling. Refer to paragraph 8.21e for fuel draining procedure.

(From the Piper Archer III PA-28-181 POH. For example only)

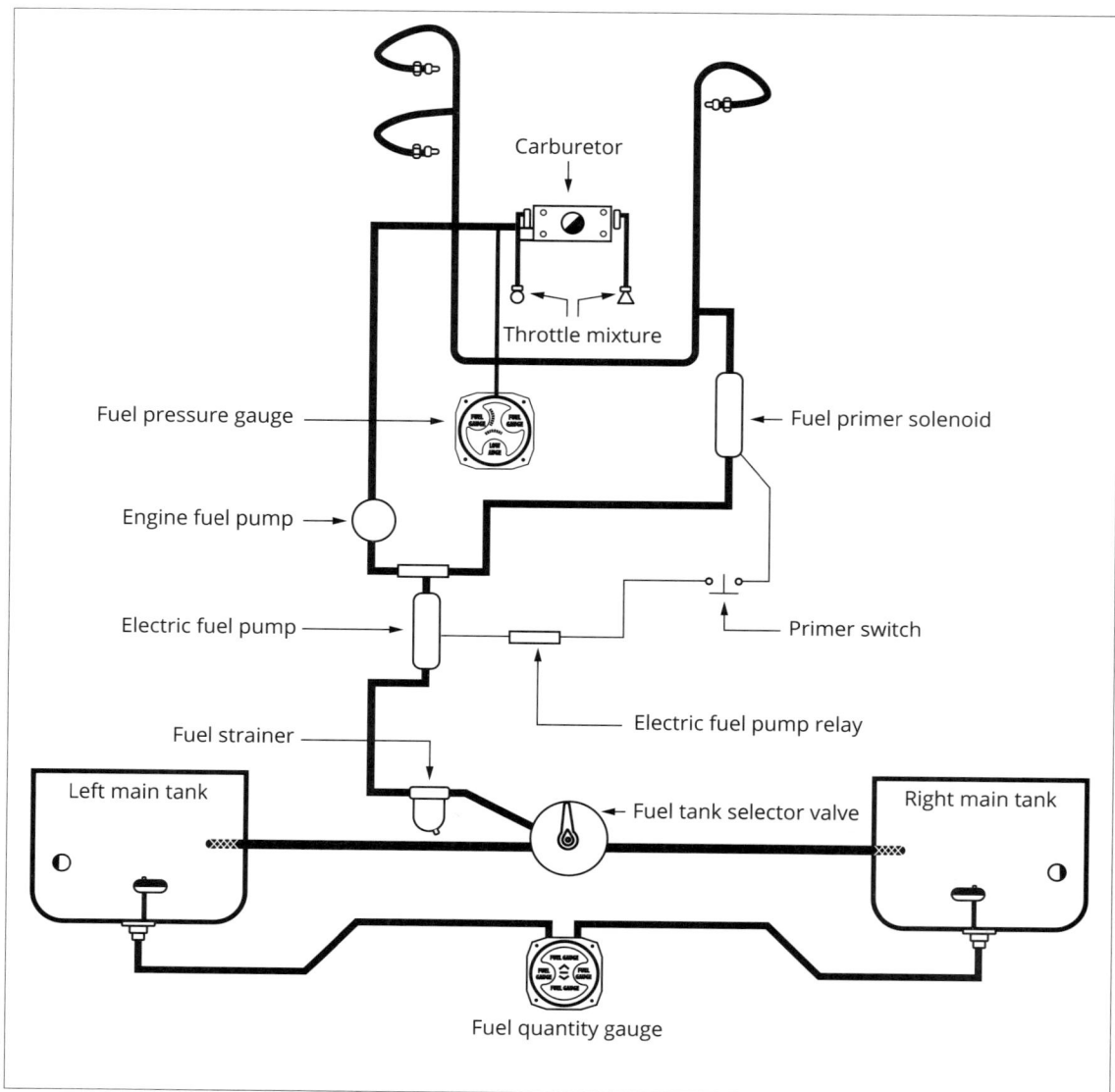

(Redrawn for clarity from the *Piper Archer III PA-28-181 POH*. For example only.)

Float-Type Carburetor

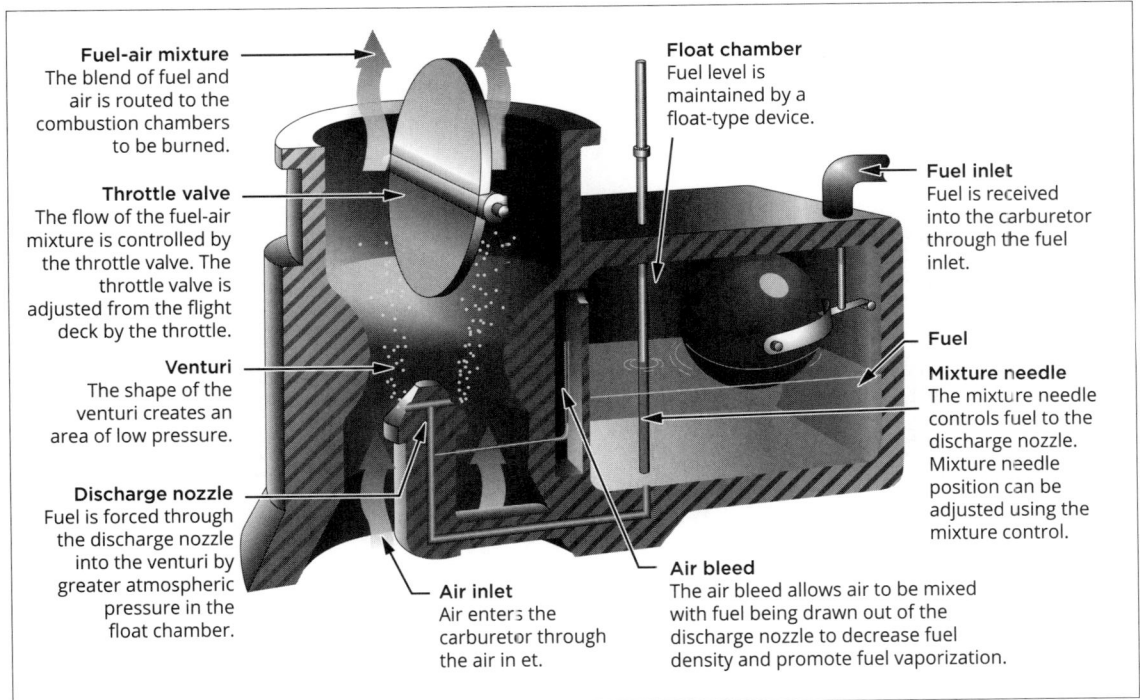

(FAA-H-8083-25B)

Airport Information for Denver Centennial (KAPA)

```
DENVER
  CENTENNIAL  (APA)( KAPA)   15 SE   UTC-7(-6DT)    N39°34.21´  W104°50.96´              DENVER
    5885   B   TPA—6885(1000)   NOTAM FILE APA                                        H-3F, 5A, L-10F, A
    RWY 17L-35R: H10000X100 (ASPH-GRVD)  S-56, D-75  2S-95   MIRL                          IAP, AD
      RWY 17L: PAPI(P4L)—GA 3.0° TCH 47´. 0.9% up.
      RWY 35R: MALSR. PAPI(P4L)—GA 3.0° TCH 45´. Rgt tfc. 0.9% down.
    RWY 17R-35L: H7001X75 (ASPH-GRVD)  S-30  MIRL   0.9% up S
      RWY 17R: REIL. PAPI(P4L)—GA 3.0° TCH 41´. Rgt tfc.
      RWY 35L: REIL. PAPI(P4R)—GA 3.0° TCH 37´. Fence.
    RWY 10-28: H4800X75 (ASPH-GRVD)  S-12.5  MIRL   0.6% up W
      RWY 10: PAPI(P2L)—GA 3.0° TCH 44´. Thld dsplcd 400´.
      RWY 28: REIL. PAPI(P2L)—GA 3.0° TCH 41´. Pole.
    SERVICE: S4  FUEL 100LL, JET A   OX 1, 2
    AIRPORT REMARKS: Attended continuously. Self serve 100LL fuel avbl.
      Waterfowl on and in vicinity of arpt. Numerous cranes nvof arpt.
      Advisory density altitude displays located at C-1, A-1, and A-18.
      +109´ twr located 1800´ east/northeast of Rwy 17L thld. Numerous
      flood lgts located 1/2 mile north of thld Rwy 17L SS-0700Z‡. Noise
      abatement procedures in effect, ctc noise office 303-790-0598. Rwy
      35R crosswind/base leg north of Lincoln Ave., Rwy 17L crosswind/base
      leg south of Arapahoe Rd. Rwy 17R-35L clsd tfc remain south of
      Arapahoe Rd and east of Interstate 25. Rwy 10-28 avoid noise
      sensitive areas 1 mile east and south of rwy. All acft blo 70,000 lbs
      maximum gross tkf weight and Stage III acft up to certificated 75,000 lbs maximum gross tkf weight may be operated,
      one-time exceptions may be authorized by Executive Director on a case-by-case basis. Twy S2 clsd indefly. Helicopter
      ops please ctc preferred FBO for ldg zone locations. Helicopter ops on front ramp not advised. U.S. Customs user fee arpt.
      Call U.S. Customs 303-768-0309. 24 hr user fee customs avbl. Ctc arpt for fee information. See Special Notices—USAF
      306 FTG Flight Training Areas, Vicinity of Colorado Springs and Pueblo Colorado.
    AIRPORT MANAGER: 303-790-0598
    WEATHER DATA SOURCES: ASOS 120.3 (720) 873-2799
```

(Chart Supplement U.S.)

CHAPTER 9   AIRCRAFT SYSTEMS

LESSON 4

FLIGHT INSTRUMENTS REVIEW

PURPOSE

The purpose of this lesson is to review and expand upon the knowledge of the flight instruments found on an aircraft.

ACCOMMODATIONS FOR LEARNING DIFFERENCES

It is important that lessons accommodate the needs of every learner. These lessons may be modified to accommodate your students with learning differences by referring to www.pacer.org/parent/php/PHP-c267.pdf.

PREPARATION

- Note cards
- Class copies of *Pilot's Handbook of Aeronautical Knowledge* (FAA-H-8083-25)
- Aircraft pilot's operating handbook (POH), Section 7, Piper Archer (PA-28-181)
- Gyroscope (optional)
- *Aeronautics for Introductory Physics* file (by NASA & American Association of Physics Teachers)[1] (optional)

DIRECTIONS

Introductory Activity: Ask students to remember the flight instruments introduced in Chapter 2, Aircraft Basics. Have students turn to Activity 1 (Flight Instrument Graphic Organizer) in their Student Notebooks. Have students draw the six instruments, one in each circle, and label as many as they can remember. (The six instruments include: airspeed indicator, attitude indicator, altimeter, turn coordinator, heading indicator, and vertical speed indicator.) Start a discussion to review what students drew and labeled on their graphic organizers.

Step 1: Review with students that the flight instruments are divided into two categories: pitot-static flight instruments and gyroscopic flight instruments.

- Pitot-static instruments: altimeter, airspeed indicator, and vertical speed indicator
- Gyroscopic instruments: attitude indicator, heading indicator, and turn coordinator

Step 2: Guide students through a discussion to define the components of the pitot-static system: ram or dynamic pressure, static pressure, static port, pitot tube, pitot-static mast (display a picture of a pitot-static mast and compare it to a pitot tube; show an aircraft with each, e.g., a Cessna 172 has a pitot tube and static port while a Piper Archer has a pitot-static mast), pitot heat, and alternate static port (see the *Pilot's Handbook of Aeronautical Knowledge* Chapter 8 for more information). Relate the terms to things students know or classes they may have taken, such as physics; for example. "Have you ever felt moving air?" (*Answer:* yes, when walking, running, sticking your hand outside the car window when driving. That is dynamic pressure.)

Display a picture of the pitot-static instruments, similar to the one shown below under Facilitator Information and in the Student Notebook.

Step 3: Lead a class discussion to help students learn more about the components of the pitot-static system and label them accordingly in Activity 2 (Pitot-Static Instruments Diagram) in their Student Notebooks. Students may also reference the *Pilot's Handbook of Aeronautical Knowledge*, Chapter 8, to complete the diagram. The PHAK will also help explain how each of the pitot-static flight instruments work.

Step 4: The facilitator will guide students through a brief discussion to define the components of the gyroscopic flight instruments. (Students will learn how these three flight instruments work in the next lesson.) The three gyroscopic flight instruments are the heading indicator, turn coordinator, and attitude indicator. Also, take time to define the following terminology while students record the definitions in Activity 3 (Gyroscopic Flight Instrument Definitions) in the Student Notebook: Gyroscope (find and show a video about gyroscopes and how they work), rigidity in space, and gyroscopic precession.

Note: If you have a toy gyroscope, you can show the students both rigidity in space and gyroscopic precession. They can be purchased online and in local retail hobby stores and are relatively inexpensive.

If a flight simulator is available, demonstrate the flight instruments reviewed in this lesson.

Extension activity: If time allows, consider reviewing the *Aeronautics for Introductory Physics* document for an experiment involving the pitot-static tube (Interactive Demonstration: Pitot-Static Tube, pages 59–64).[2]

Concluding Activity: On index cards, have students write questions about the flight instruments shared in this lesson. Consider giving students sentence stems to begin their questions. Students can then exchange cards and answer the question on the card given to them, sharing answers in small groups or with the whole class.

FACILITATOR INFORMATION

Pitot-static system and instruments

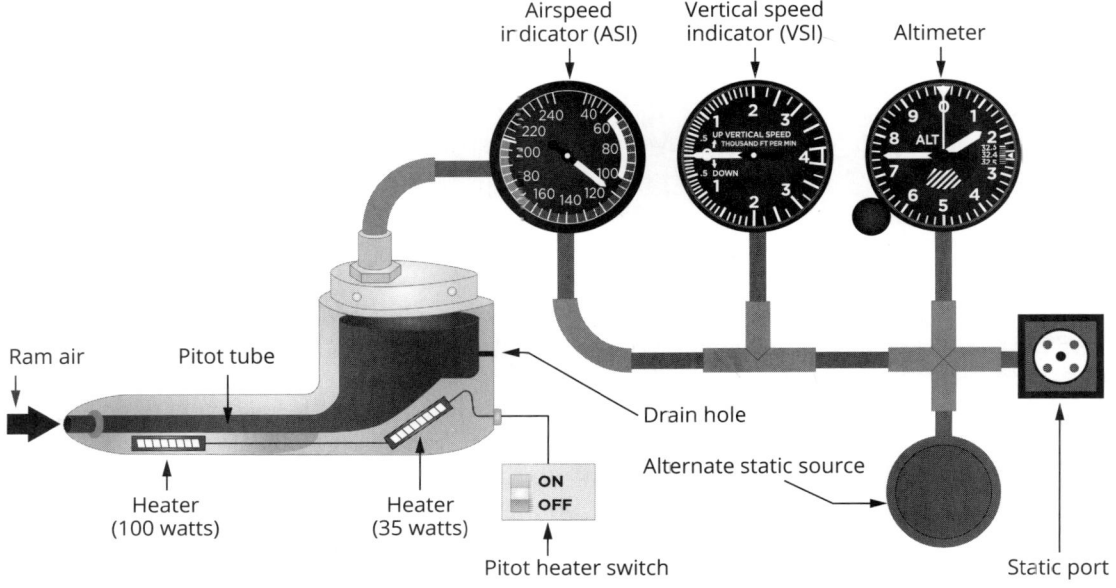

(FAA-H-8083-25)

CHAPTER 9   AIRCRAFT SYSTEMS

LESSON 5

VACUUM AND ELECTRICAL SYSTEMS

PURPOSE

The purpose of this lesson is to introduce students to the vacuum and electrical systems of an aircraft.

ACCOMMODATIONS FOR LEARNING DIFFERENCES

It is important that lessons accommodate the needs of every learner. These lessons may be modified to accommodate your students with learning differences by referring to **www.pacer.org/parent/php/PHP-c267.pdf.**

PREPARATION

- Printed pictures of vacuum system
- *Pilot's Handbook of Aeronautical Knowledge* (PHAK) (FAA-H-8083-25)
- Aircraft pilot's operating handbook (POH), Section 7, Piper Archer (PA 28-181)

DIRECTIONS

Introductory Activity: Ask students the following questions: "Think back to earlier when we discussed the flight instruments. What three flight instruments are the gyroscopic instruments?" (*Answer:* attitude indicator, heading indicator and turn coordinator.) "There are two systems that provide the power for those three instruments, the vacuum and electrical systems. Which instruments work off of what system?" (*Answer:* The heading and attitude indicators are typically vacuum driven and the turn coordinator is typically electrical in a round dial aircraft.) "Why?" (*Answer:* Redundancy, so if one system fails you will still have some information instead of none.)

Step 1: Create a presentation to discuss the vacuum system of an aircraft. Just as with the previous lessons, ask the students if they have heard of a vacuum system. Encourage them to share what they know about the systems and relate it to what a vacuum in their house does. Refer back to their responses throughout the lesson. Reference the *Pilot's Handbook of Aeronautical Knowledge*, Chapter 8, and the diagram provided under Facilitator Information at the end of this chapter to create the presentation.

   Major components of vacuum system: Engine vacuum pump, electrical vacuum pump, attitude indicator, heading indicator, suction gauge, regulator, and vacuum filter.

Step 2: Print pictures of each of the components of the vacuum system and give one to each student or pair of students. Allow students two minutes to research and learn more about their component. They can write notes on the back of their pictures. Research is important because students will be building a schematic, or complete picture, of the system in the next step.

Step 3: With the help of the facilitator, students will work together to build a schematic of the vacuum system. As the students build the schematic, they should be describing their component's function. The facilitator should add questions or bring up topics either during or after to see if the students fully understand what they are describing. Sample questions, and potential answers, are listed below:

- How would this schematic be different for an aircraft that had two vacuum pumps, and why would an aircraft have two pumps instead of one? (*Answer:* The schematic would have another line branching off to an electrical pump. Some aircraft will have both an engine-driven and electrical, backup pump.)
- How would we know if the vacuum pump has failed? (*Answer:* The suction gauge would indicate no pressure and the attitude indicator and heading indicator would not be working.)
- What can we do if we notice that the vacuum pump is not working? (*Answer:* Turn on the electrical [backup] vacuum pump.)
- If most aircraft have an attitude indicator and heading indicator, why would they not have a vacuum system? (*Answer:* Those two instruments could be electrically driven. This may be the case in an aircraft with a glass cockpit. The big screens are electrically powered, and the standby attitude indicator may be either electrically driven or vacuum driven.)

Once the students have an understanding of a basic vacuum system, refer to Chapter 8 in the *Pilot's Handbook of Aeronautical Knowledge* to explain how the attitude indicator and heading indicator work.

Step 4: Pose the following questions (also provided in the Student Notebook) to start a discussion: "What is an electrical system? What is its purpose?" Have students state an example (car, speakers, etc.). Display two cockpit pictures, one glass cockpit and the other round dial. Have students discuss the differences between these two aircraft as they relate to the electrical systems. For example, what components in the cockpit run off of electrical power? Have students write their thoughts n Activity 1 (Discussion Prompts) in their Student Notebooks.

Step 5: Cover the components of the electrical system by describing the components listed below or by showing a video covering the electrical system on a small aircraft such as a Cessna 172. An electrical system schematic is provided under Facilitator Information at the end of this lesson. Reference the *Pilot's Handbook of Aeronautical Knowledge*, Chapter 7 "Electrical System" section, for more information. Have students record this information in Activity 2 (Electrical Systems Graphic Organizer) in the Student Notebook.

- Major components of electrical system: alternator/generator, battery, bus bar, fuses, circuit breakers, voltage regulator, and ammeter/loadmeter.
  - What do each of these components do?
  - Discuss the importance of an electrical system to an aircraft.
    - If the alternator or generator were to fail, what happens to the aircraft? (*Answer:* The engine would still be running as that is a separate system; however, the battery would now be your sole source of electrical power.) How long will the battery last? (*Answer:* Depends on the load you are putting on the battery.) What could you do to prolong the battery power? (*Answer:* Turn off non-essential things.)

› It is what powers the turn coordinator. Refer to Chapter 8 in the *Pilot's Handbook of Aeronautical Knowledge*.

› Glass cockpit aircraft

- Have the student label the flight instruments on a glass cockpit (Student Notebook Activity 3: Glass Cockpit Flight Instruments).
  - Discuss with the students the definitions of air data computer (ADC) and attitude and heading reference system (AHRS).
  - Does a glass cockpit aircraft still have a pitot-static system? (*Answer:* Yes, the information just comes into a box called the ADC and then the information is displayed on the PFD.) (PFD should be a review from Chapter 2.)
  - The gyroscopic information is given to the PFD from the AHRS. Refer to a glass cockpit aircraft's POH to read about AHRS in Section 7.

- How would an electrical failure be different in an aircraft with a glass cockpit compared to an aircraft with a round dial cockpit?
  - Often, a glass cockpit aircraft will have a backup or emergency battery that will power the essential bus. This battery should provide enough power for the pilot to fly the aircraft to an airport.

Concluding Activity: Ask students to write four possible test questions related to vacuum and electrical systems (two questions per system). Questions must be in multiple choice or short answer format. Using index cards or half-pieces of paper, ask the students to write a question on one side and an acceptable, detailed answer on the other. These questions can be used to review for the exam or as a review during the next lesson.

FACILITATOR INFORMATION
Typical Vacuum System

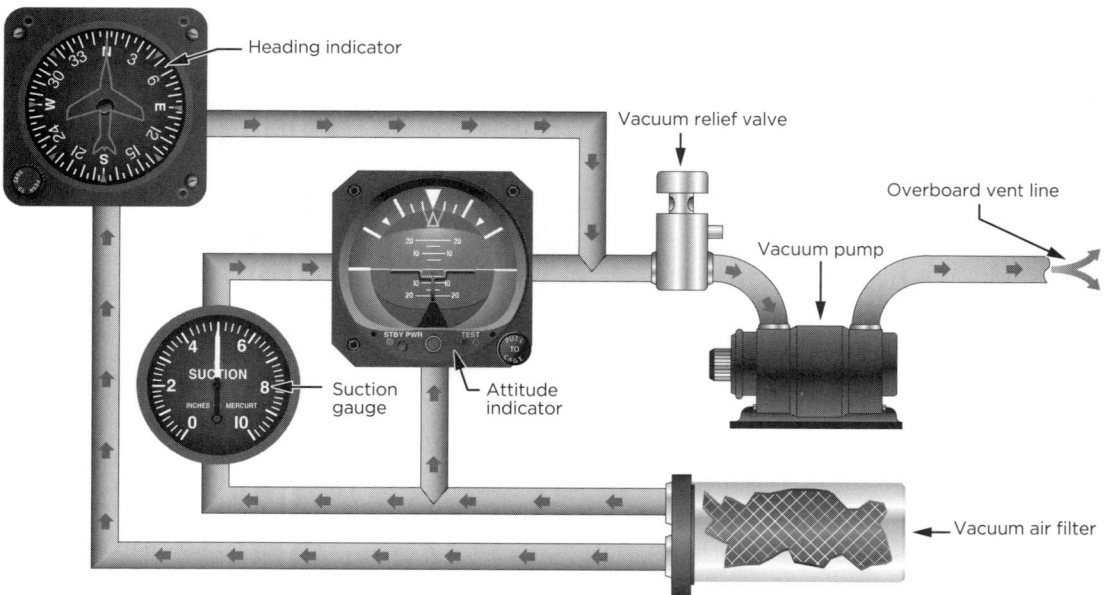

(FAA-H-8083-25)

Examples of Glass Cockpit and Round Dial Cockpit

▶ Example round dial cockpit.*

▶ Example glass cockpit.†

---

*   (Photo by Matti Blume, https://commons.wikimedia.org/wiki/File:Piper_Archer,_Treobin_(P1090112).jpg, Wikimedia Commons, CC BY-SA 4.0, https://creativecommons.org/licenses/by-sa/4.0/deed.en)

†   (Photo by H. Michael Miley, https://www.flickr.com/photos/44082489@N00/4850784801, CC BY-SA 2.0, https://creativecommons.org/licenses/by-sa/2.0/)

Electrical System Schematic

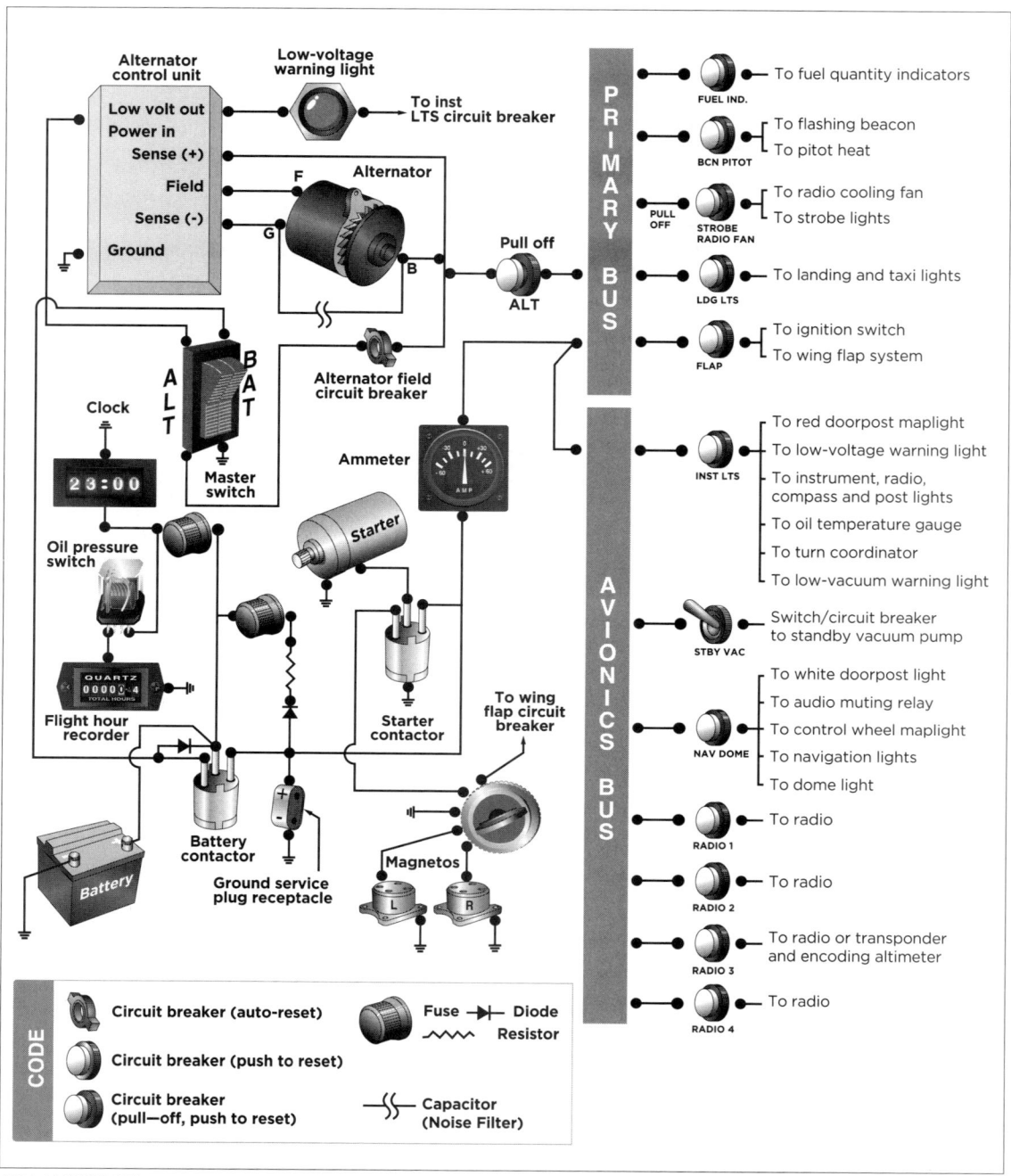

(FAA-H-8083-25)

CHAPTER 9   AIRCRAFT SYSTEMS

LESSON 6

REVIEW: AIRCRAFT SYSTEMS

PURPOSE

The purpose of this lesson is to review the main components of aircraft systems by conducting and sharing research on one particular aircraft.

ACCOMMODATIONS FOR LEARNING DIFFERENCES

It is important that lessons accommodate the needs of every learner. These lessons may be modified to accommodate your students with learning differences by referring to **www.pacer.org/parent/php/PHP-c267.pdf.**

PREPARATION

- Index cards listing different aircraft
- Computers with internet access to search for aircraft POH, or printed copies of aircraft POHs

DIRECTIONS

Introductory Activity: Prepare index cards before class, each listing one of the following aircrafts: Piper Archer, Piper Arrow, Piper Seminole, Cirrus SR22, Cessna 172, Cessna 182, Extra 300, Diamond DA40, Diamond DA42, and any other aircraft for which a Pilot's Operating Handbook (POH) can be located online. Prepare as many cards as you have students in the class. It would also be appropriate to pair up students if you have a larger number of students. Have each student (or pair of students) select a card with an aircraft listed. Explain that students will be doing aircraft systems research on their selected aircraft during today's lesson.

Step 1: Students can complete Activity 1 (Preview Questions) in their Student Notebooks to answer questions related to their assigned aircraft. These questions are also listed below for reference. Feel free to add or eliminate questions as necessary to prepare students for the exam on this chapter.

Fuel System:

1. What type of fuel system is it (pump type or gravity fed)?
2. How many gallons of fuel does the aircraft hold? How many gallons per tank? How much is usable fuel?
3. What type of fuel can the aircraft use?
4. How many fuel sumps does this aircraft have?
5. Does the aircraft have a primer?
6. Does the aircraft have an auxiliary fuel pump?
7. Does this aircraft have a carburetor or a fuel injection system?

Electrical System:
8. Does the aircraft have an alternator or generator? How many volts and amps is it?
9. Does the aircraft have a battery? How many volts and amps is it?
10. Does the aircraft have a back-up or standby battery?
11. If the alternator stops working in flight, how will you know? What equipment will be impacted? Will the engine stop running?
12. What is an electrical bus?
13. List one item that is on the main bus.
14. List one item on the essential/emergency bus.

Hydraulic System:
15. What on this aircraft is hydraulic?

Control Surfaces:
16. Are the primary flight controls controlled by cables and pulleys or are they electrical?
17. Are the flaps controlled by cables and pulleys or are they electrical?

Flight Instruments:
18. Does the aircraft have a pitot tube or a pitot static mast?
19. Where is the pitot tube or pitot static mast? Why?
20. Where are the static port(s)?
21. Is there a vacuum system? If so, what instruments does it power? Is there an auxiliary vacuum pump?

Engine:
22. How many cylinders does this engine have?
23. Is the engine horizontally opposed?
24. How many spark plugs does this aircraft have?
25. How much horsepower does the engine have?
26. What is the maximum RPM setting?
27. What is the maximum airspeed, V_{NE}?
28. Is there a prop control in this aircraft?

Step 2: The information required for this research can be found in sections 1 and 7 of the select aircraft's POH, which can be located online. Mention to students that some of the answers for the research questions may not be found in some POHs as the aircraft may not have every system or component.

Step 3: Students can use the remainder of class to answer the research questions. Either at the end of class or in the following class period, have students use a form of technology to share their findings. For example, one option would be to have them download the ChatterPix app on their smartphones. After locating a picture of their assigned aircraft, they can summarize what they learned in 60 seconds and record their statements using the picture within the app.

Step 4: As students are sharing their research findings, the rest of the students will be recording their findings in Activity 2 (Research Conclusions Graphic Organizer). Students will record answers to the following questions for *each* aircraft:

- How many gallons of fuel does it hold?
- Does it have a carburetor or fuel-injection system?
- How many batteries does it have?
- What components are hydraulic?
- Does it have a pitot tube or a pitot static mast?
- Does it have a vacuum system?
- What is the maximum horsepower?

Concluding Activity: Students complete Activity 3 (Two-Sentence Summary) in the Student Notebook to record two sentences that synthesize what all the aircraft have in common. To end class, ask several students to share one thing that most of the aircraft discussed have in common.

LESSON 7
CHAPTER 9 EXAM

PURPOSE
The purpose of this lesson is to evaluate students' learning on aircraft systems.

ACCOMMODATIONS FOR LEARNING DIFFERENCES
It is important that lessons accommodate the needs of every learner. These lessons may be modified to accommodate your students with learning differences by referring to www.pacer.org/parent/php/PHP-c267.pdf.

PREPARATION
- Prepared exam
- Computers and internet access for students or paper copies of article assigned to class

DIRECTIONS
Step 1: Administer an end-of-chapter exam to students. Sample test questions can be found below under Facilitator Information. (An answer key is provided at the end of the chapter.)

Step 2: When students have turned in the exam, make available to them the article, "Extreme Maneuvering: The performance maneuvers required for the commercial certificate are rarely used, but they can get you out of a situation," from *Aviation Safety* magazine.[3] Students will independently read the article and then under Activity 1 (Article Response and Rubric) in the Student Notebook, they will write a one-paragraph response that includes a summary and reflection on the prompts: (1) Explain why understanding/performing flight maneuvers makes you a safer, professional pilot, (2) Explain how these maneuvers help you understand the performance of your aircraft, (3) Explain how the turn coordinator and attitude indicators look differently in inverted flight? Responses will be graded using the rubric provided in the Student Notebook.

FACILITATOR INFORMATION
Chapter 9 Exam: Aircraft Systems

(This exam is available in the online Instructor Resources in a format ready for use in the classroom. An answer key is provided at the end of the chapter.)

1. Most low-wing aircraft have a gravity-feed fuel system.
   a. True
   b. False

2. If the alternator fails in flight, the aircraft's engine will quit.
   a. True
   b. False

3. A dual magneto system allows for redundancy in the system.
   a. True
   b. False

4. _____ is the angular difference between true north and magnetic north.
   a. Variation
   b. Oscillation
   c. Magnetic dip

5. 100LL (100 low lead) fuel is what color?
   a. Purple
   b. Blue
   c. Clear

6. What is the purpose of the battery?
   a. Primary source of electricity needed during flight
   b. Provide the electricity to start the aircraft
   c. A backup source of power in case the alternator fails
   d. A and B
   e. B and C

7. What is the purpose of the alternator?
   a. Primary source of electricity needed during flight
   b. Provide the electricity to start the aircraft
   c. Provide the electricity needed for the spark plugs
   d. A and B
   e. A and C

8. Which of the following instruments is electrically driven in a traditional round dial aircraft?
   a. Attitude indicator
   b. Heading indicator
   c. Turn coordinator

9. Which of following instruments would be affected if the pitot tube were to become blocked, not allowing any ram air or dynamic pressure into the system?
   a. Turn and slip indicator
   b. Airspeed indicator
   c. Altimeter

10. Which of the following is a gyroscopic principle?
    a. Oscillation
    b. Acceleration
    c. Precession

11. You have determined your carburetor has iced up in flight. How do you fix this problem?
    a. Declare an emergency and land at the nearest airport
    b. Turn the carburetor heat on
    c. Descend
    d. Both B and C

12. The Piper Archer has what anti-ice capabilities?
    a. Pitot heat
    b. Weeping wing
    c. Icing boots
    d. Prop heater

13. What is a benefit of a fuel-injection system over a carburetor system?
    a. Better cold weather starts
    b. Cheaper to install
    c. Do not have to deal with vapor lock
    d. Do not have to worry about plugged injectors

14. The correct order for the various stages in a reciprocating engine cycle is:
    a. Intake, power, compression, exhaust
    b. Power, intake, compression, exhaust
    c. Intake, compression, power, exhaust
    d. Compression, intake, power, exhaust

15. If the ADC or AHRS is not working, what information would you see on the flight instruments?

Questions 16–19: Label the parts of the vacuum system.
(Choices: vacuum pump, vacuum air filter, heading indicator, attitude indicator)

16. _____

17. _____

18. _____

19. _____

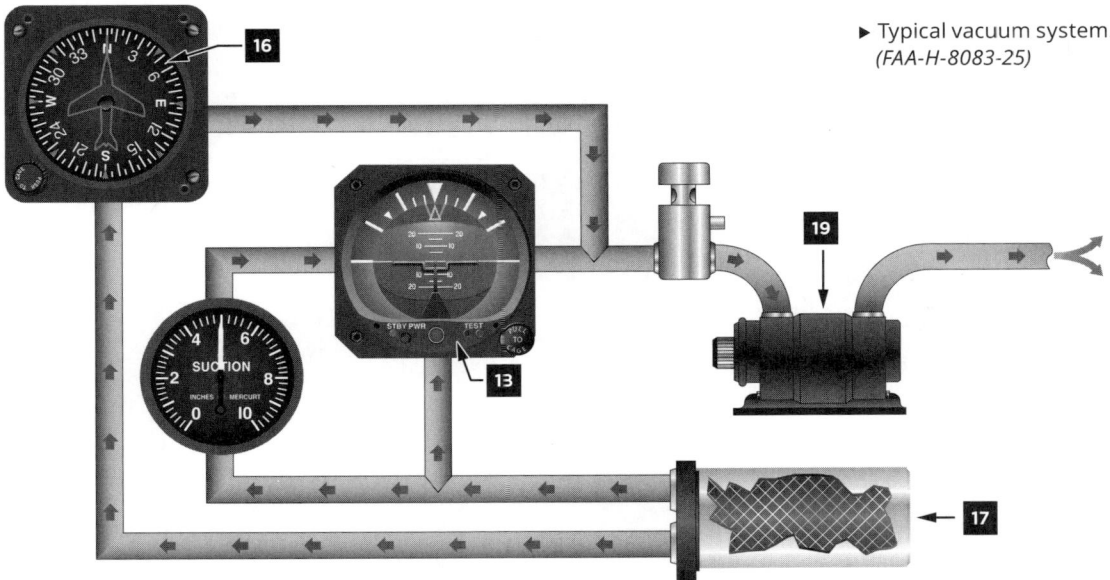

▶ Typical vacuum system. *(FAA-H-8083-25)*

Questions 20–22: Label the parts of the carburetor.
(Choices: fuel, mixture control, throttle valve)

20. _____

21. _____

22. _____

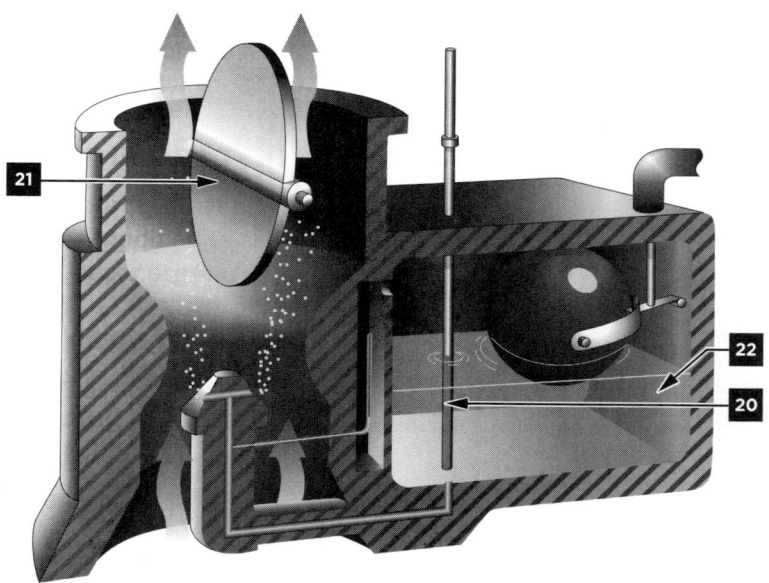

▶ Float-type carburetor.
(FAA-H-8083-25)

23. What would be an indication of possible carburetor icing?
    a. Better performance
    b. Rough-running engine
    c. Annunciator illumination

24. The Piper Archer that we have been discussing in class has
    a. 2 cylinders and 4 spark plugs
    b. 4 cylinders and 8 spark plugs
    c. 6 cylinders and 12 spark plugs

Questions 25–27: Label the parts of the fuel-injected system.
(Choices: engine-driven fuel pump, fuel-air control unit, fuel tank)

25. _____

26. _____

27. _____

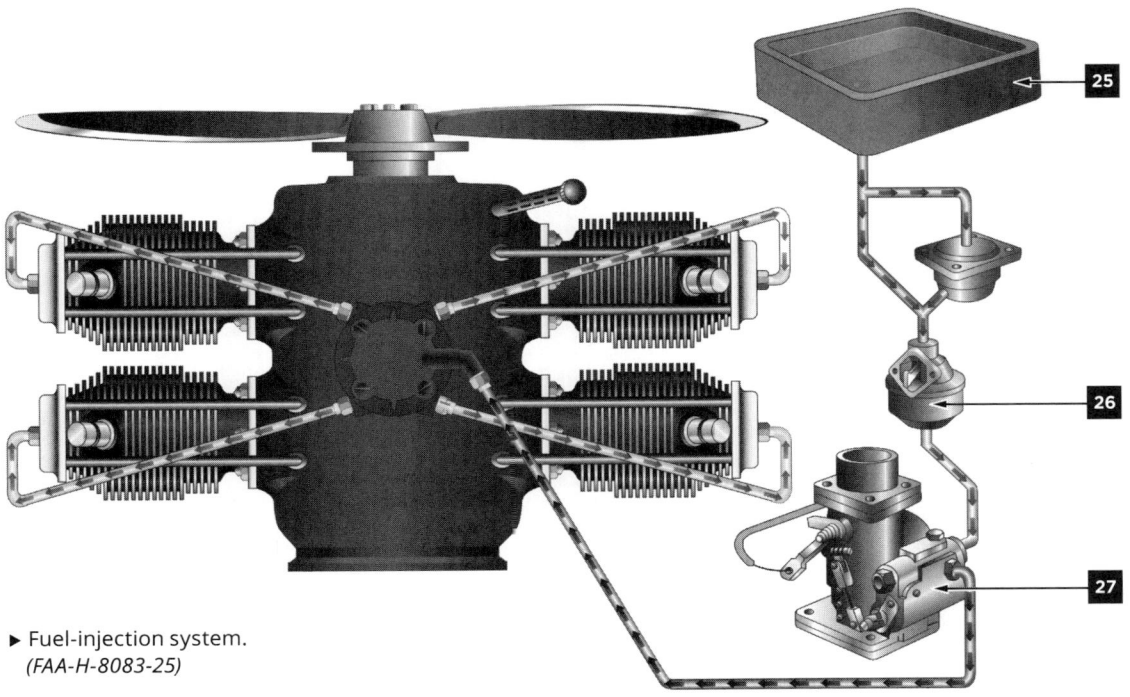

▶ Fuel-injection system.
(FAA-H-8083-25)

28. List one thing that oil does for the aircraft's engine.

29. Why might it be a bad thing if there was an increase in oil temperature?

30. Describe what happens in the four phases of combustion in reciprocating engines.

ANSWER KEYS

CHAPTER 9

LESSON 7

Chapter 9 Exam

1. (b) False
2. (b) False
3. (a) True
4. (a) Variation
5. (b) Blue
6. (e) B and C
7. (a) Primary source of electricity needed during flight
8. (c) Turn coordinator
9. (b) Airspeed indicator
10. (c) Precession
11. (b) Turn the carburetor heat on
12. (a) Pitot heat
13. (a) Better cold weather starts
14. (c) Intake, compression, power, exhaust
15. Red Xs on the airspeed indicator, attitude indicator, altimeter, VSI, heading indicator; depending on the system, you would also not have wind information, temperature information, or TAS.
16. Heading indicator
17. Vacuum air filter
18. Attitude indicator
19. Vacuum pump
20. Mixture control
21. Throttle valve
22. Fuel
23. (b) Rough-running engine
24. (b) 4 cylinders and 8 spark plugs
25. Fuel tank
26. Engine-driven fuel pump
27. fuel-air control unit

28. Cools, cleans, lubricates
29. An increase in oil temperature could indicate the existence of an oil leak, and if there is no oil the engine will cease and quit, there could be low oil pressure, and it could turn into an engine failure if it is not fixed.
30. In a four-stroke engine, the conversion of chemical energy into mechanical energy occurs over a four-stroke operating cycle. The intake, compression, power, and exhaust processes occur in four separate strokes of the piston in the following order.
    1. The intake stroke begins as the piston starts its downward travel. When this happens, the intake valve opens and the fuel-air mixture is drawn into the cylinder.
    2. The compression stroke begins when the intake valve closes, and the piston starts moving back to the top of the cylinder. This phase of the cycle is used to obtain a much greater power output from the fuel-air-mixture once it is ignited.
    3. The power stroke begins when the fuel-air-mixture is ignited. This causes a tremendous pressure increase in the cylinder and forces the piston downward away from the cylinder head, creating the power that turns the crankshaft.
    4. The exhaust stroke is used to purge the cylinder of burned gases. It begins when the exhaust valve opens, and the piston starts to move toward the cylinder head once again.

    (FAA-H-8083-25)

CHAPTER 10

FLIGHT MANEUVERS

Introduction

STANDARDS & OBJECTIVES

North Dakota Aviation Content Standards (Grades 10–12)

Demonstrate a variety of maneuvers using a flight simulator to include:

- A.1.2 and A.2.1.1—Straight-and-level flight.
- A.1.2 and A.2.1.1—Turns, climbs and descents.
- A.2.1.8—Power-on and power-off stalls.
- A.3.1.8—Various takeoffs and landings and related traffic pattern.
- A.2.1.1—Steep turns.
- A.1.2 and 2.1.1—Flight by reference to instruments.

Note: Standards beginning with "A" indicate the objectives align with but do not exactly match the identified ND Aviation Standards.

Science—Next Generation Science Standards (Grades 9–12)

- HS-PS2-2—Use mathematical representations to support the claim that the total momentum of a system of objects is conserved when there is no net force on the system.
- HS-ETS1-4—Use a computer simulation to model the impact of proposed solutions to a complex real-world problem with numerous criteria and constraints on interactions within and between systems relevant to the problem.

Language Arts—CCSS.ELA-LITERACY.CCRA

- L.1—Demonstrate command of the conventions of standard English grammar and usage when writing or speaking.
- L.2—Demonstrate command of the conventions of standard English capitalization, punctuation, and spelling when writing.

ESSENTIAL QUESTIONS

- Why is it important to be able to fly maneuvers within aviation standards on a consistent basis?
- How do the concepts about aircraft basics and aerodynamics assist in correctly demonstrating flight maneuvers?
- Why is it important for a pilot to know how to enter and recover from a stall and/or spin?

LESSONS

Lesson	Topic	Student Notebook Activities
Lesson 1	Fundamental Maneuvers: Straight-and-Level Flight, Climbs, Descents, Turns	1. Fundamental Maneuvers Worksheet
Lesson 2	Normal Takeoffs and Normal Landings	1. Normal Takeoff Thoughts 2. Normal Takeoff Completion 3. Normal Landing Thoughts 4. Normal Landing Completion
Lesson 3	Short-Field Takeoff and Landing	1. Short-Field Takeoff Thoughts 2. Short-Field Takeoff Completion 3. Short-Field Landing Thoughts 4. Short-Field Landing Completion
Lesson 4	Soft-Field Takeoff and Landing	1. Pre-Flight Preparation List 2. Soft-Field Takeoff Thoughts 3. Soft-Field Takeoff Completion 4. Soft-Field Landing Thoughts 5. Soft-Field Landing Completion
Lesson 5	Stalls: Power-On and Power-Off	1. Stalling Video Review 2. Power-Off and Power-On Stall Procedures 3. Conducting Power-Off and Power-On Stalls 4. Stall Summary Question
Lesson 6	Steep Turns	1. Steep Turn Procedures 2. Steep Turns Flight Simulation
Lesson 7	Flight by Reference to Instruments	1. Basic Flight by Instruments Outline 2. Flight by Reference to Instruments Simulation

CHAPTER 10 FLIGHT MANEUVERS

LESSON 1

FUNDAMENTAL MANEUVERS: STRAIGHT-AND-LEVEL FLIGHT, CLIMBS, DESCENTS, TURNS

PURPOSE

The purpose of this lesson is to have the students apply what they have learned in class to actually flying the maneuver using a flight simulator software.

ACCOMMODATIONS FOR LEARNING DIFFERENCES

It is important that lessons accommodate the needs of every learner. These lessons may be modified to accommodate your students with learning differences by referring to **www.pacer.org/parent/php/PHP-c267.pdf**.

PREPARATION

- Class copies of *Airplane Flying Handbook* (FAA-H-8083-3) or access to it on FAA's website
- Flight simulator equipment, preferably with joystick or yokes with rudder pedals

DIRECTIONS

This lesson requires a flight simulator. If flight simulation is unavailable, use maneuver videos, such as videos from the UND AeroCast YouTube Channel or ASA's Virtual Test Prep—Flight Maneuvers, to demonstrate the concepts. If you are using maneuver videos, adjust the Student Notebook activities and materials as appropriate.

Note: The facilitator may use these flight maneuver lessons as a complete chapter and/or interspersed after the related classroom discussions on the flight maneuvers have been introduced in Chapter 2 and Chapter 8.

Introductory Activity: Watch a short video of a small general aviation aircraft flying and have the students list which flight maneuvers they saw being performed. Watch a short video of a large commercial airline type aircraft flying and have the students list which flight maneuvers they saw being performed. Have a class discussion on how the flights were similar and different. Focus on the similarity that both aircraft are conducting fundamental flight maneuvers.

Step 1: Have the students find Activity 1 (Fundamental Maneuvers Worksheet) in the Student Notebook. If possible, each student should fly each of these maneuvers and then have the facilitator watch and verify that the student mastered the maneuvers. The facilitator will check off or initial in the Student Notebook when each flight maneuver has been flown successfully. (Successfully means that the student is able to maintain that attitude, airspeed, and heading for at least 5 seconds.) If students are not able to successfully complete a maneuver, they should write down what changes they need to make under that specific maneuver in their Student Notebooks. Once a maneuver is completed, students should answer the questions about the maneuver. (An answer key is provided at the end of the chapter.) If needed, the students can reference Chapter 3 in the *Airplane Flying Handbook*.

Step 2: Once the students have completed all the maneuvers, the facilitator will discuss the answers to the questions from the Student Notebook (also provided below under Facilitator Information for reference) about each maneuver.

Concluding Activity: Have the students think back to the introduction video of the large aircraft flight. You may want to pull up the video and replay it. Ask the students which flight instruments the pilot is referencing while conducting those maneuvers. (*Answer:* The pilot is referencing the same instruments as they would look at in a small aircraft.)

FACILITATOR INFORMATION
Fundamental Maneuvers

Fly the following maneuvers in the flight simulator and then answer the questions about which flight instruments you are looking at and why.

Straight-and-Level Flight

_____ 3,000 feet, 100 knots, 060° heading

1. What flight instruments are you looking at to verify that you are level at 3,000 feet, and are at 100 knots on a heading of 060°?

Level Turn

_____ 3,000 feet, 100 knots, turn from 090 to 270 degrees

_____ 3,000 feet, 100 knots, turn left from 270 to 090 degrees

2. What flight instruments are you looking at to verify the 3,000 feet and 100 knots and that you are in a turn?

Straight Climb

_____ Heading of 360 degrees, from 3,000 feet to 4,000 feet, 80 knots

3. What flight instruments are you looking at to verify the 80 knots on a heading of 360° and that you are in a climb?

Straight Climb

_____ Heading of 360 degrees, from 4,000 feet to 5,000 feet, 500 fpm

4. What flight instruments are you looking at to verify you are on a heading of 360° and in a climb at 500 fpm going to 5,000 feet?

Straight Descent

_____ Heading of 330 degrees, from 4,000 feet to 3,000 feet, 100 knots

5. What flight instruments are you looking at to verify the 100 knots on a heading of 330° and that you are in a descent?

Straight Descent

_____ Heading of 360 degrees, from 3,000 feet to 2,000 feet, 90 knots

6. What flight instruments are you looking at to verify the 90 knots on a heading of 360° and that you are in a descent?

Turning Climb

_____ Heading of 270 degrees to 090, from 3,500 feet to 4,500 feet, 80 knots

7. What flight instruments are you looking at to verify that you are at 80 knots in a turn and in a climb?

CHAPTER 10 FLIGHT MANEUVERS

LESSON 2

NORMAL TAKEOFFS AND NORMAL LANDINGS

PURPOSE

The purpose of this lesson is to have the students apply what they learned about normal takeoffs and landings by flying using a flight simulation software program.

ACCOMMODATIONS FOR LEARNING DIFFERENCES

It is important that lessons accommodate the needs of every learner. These lessons may be modified to accommodate your students with learning differences by referring to **www.pacer.org/parent/php/PHP-c267.pdf.**

PREPARATION

- Class copies of *Airplane Flying Handbook* (FAA-H-8083-3) or access to it on FAA's website
- Reference the students' normal landings and traffic pattern outlines in the Student Notebook, Chapter 2, Lessons 4 and 5
- Aircraft Pilot's Operating Handbook (POH)
- Flight simulator equipment, preferably with joystick or yokes with rudder pedals

DIRECTIONS

This lesson requires a flight simulator. If flight simulation is unavailable, use maneuver videos, such as videos from the UND AeroCast YouTube Channel or ASA's Virtual Test Prep—Flight Maneuvers, to demonstrate the concepts. If you are using maneuver videos, adjust the Student Notebook activities and materials as appropriate.

Introductory Activity: Have the students rewatch one of the normal takeoff videos referenced in Chapter 2. Have them talk with their tablemate or neighbor to describe how to conduct a normal takeoff in a Piper Archer, Cessna 172, or other general aviation aircraft found in your flight simulation program. Walk around the classroom and correct students if necessary.

Step 1: The facilitator should pick an aircraft that the students will be using for the flight simulation session and show the students where to find information about takeoffs for this specific aircraft and where to get the rotation and lift-off speeds in the aircraft POH (Chapters 4 and 5). The students can write the information down under Activity 1 (Normal Takeoff Thoughts) in their Student Notebooks.

Step 2: The students should use the flight simulation to fly a normal takeoff. After students perform three takeoffs, have them record two thoughts on their performance of a normal takeoff in their Student Notebooks. For example, a student might record, "The aircraft wanted to lift off at a lower takeoff speed than we discussed in class." Once the student is able to conduct a "good" takeoff (maintaining centerline, appropriate speeds, pitch attitude is normal), the student needs to show the facilitator. The facilitator can then initial or mark the takeoff as complete under Activity 2 (Normal Takeoff Completion) in the student's notebook. If the student is not able to show the facilitator a good takeoff, the facilitator will write comments in the Student Notebook about what the student needs to do to improve on it.

Step 3: Repeat Steps 1 and 2; however, instead of performing a takeoff, the students will be performing landings. The students can pre-position themselves on final approach or if the facilitator has already covered airport traffic patterns, the students can take off and fly the traffic pattern and then perform a normal landing. After students perform three landings, have them record two thoughts on their performance of a landing in their Student Notebooks under Activity 3 (Normal Landing Thoughts). The students must then demonstrate a normal landing for the facilitator, who will initial or mark the landing as complete under Activity 4 (Normal Landing Completion). If the student is not able to show the facilitator a satisfactory normal landing, comments should be recorded in the Student Notebook about what the student needs to do to improve on it.

Concluding Activity: Show the students a picture of a Boeing 737 or Airbus A320. Have them write down on an exit slip how they think a takeoff and landing will be different in that aircraft as compared to what they were using in the simulation.

LESSON 3

SHORT-FIELD TAKEOFF AND LANDING

PURPOSE

The purpose of this lesson is to have students apply what they learned about short-field takeoffs and landings by flying them in a simulation.

ACCOMMODATIONS FOR LEARNING DIFFERENCES

It is important that lessons accommodate the needs of every learner. These lessons may be modified to accommodate your students with learning differences by referring to **www.pacer.org/parent/php/PHP-c267.pdf**.

PREPARATION

- Class copies of the *Airplane Flying Handbook* (FAA-H-8083-3) or access to it on FAA's website
- Aircraft Pilot's Operating Handbook (POH)
- Flight simulator equipment, preferably with joystick or yokes with rudder pedals

DIRECTIONS

This lesson requires a flight simulator. If flight simulation is unavailable, use maneuver videos, such as videos from the UND AeroCast YouTube Channel or ASA's Virtual Test Prep—Flight Maneuvers, to demonstrate the concepts. If you are using maneuver videos, adjust the Student Notebook activities and materials as appropriate.

Introductory Activity: Bring up a picture of an airport with a really short runway, such as Ousel Falls Airport (MT94) in Billings, Montana. It is a private airport with a 900-foot-long turf runway. On the board, have the students list things to think about when preparing to either take off or land at this airport. (*Answers can include:* For takeoff, consider whether this is enough runway to take off on, density altitude since this airport is in the mountains, whether there are any obstacles at the end of the runway and are we going to clear them? For landing, consider whether we have enough runway to stop on, and can we clear the obstacles upon landing?) Ask students, "How will weight impact our takeoff?"

Step 1: The facilitator will walk through the short-field takeoff and landing procedures for the aircraft picked for use in today's flight simulator. The students are to reference the aircraft's POH to look up the aircraft's short-field takeoff and landing speeds and configuration. They should record their answers under Activity 1 (Short-Field Takeoff Thoughts) in the Student Notebook.

Step 2: The students should pick an airport with a short runway (between 2,000–3,000 feet long) and use that airport when flying short-field takeoffs and landings. Once the student has performed three "good"* takeoffs, they should call the facilitator to verify completion of that maneuver. The facilitator should initial the completion in the student's notebook under Activity 2 (Short-Field Takeoff Completion). If the student was not able to perform a good takeoff, the facilitator should list what they need to change to improve their performance of the short-field takeoff in the Student Notebook under comments.

*A good short-field takeoff is when the student performs the takeoff using the appropriate short field technique, maintains the climb out speed until 50 feet above field elevation, and maintains the extended centerline of the runway.

Step 3: Once students have shown a good takeoff, they can move on to short-field landings and repeat the procedures in step 2. Students should complete Activity 3 (Short-Field Landings Thoughts) in their Student Notebooks to record thoughts on their short-field landing performance and then complete Activity 4 (Short-Field Landings Completion) by demonstrating a short-field landing for the facilitator and obtaining initials verifying completion, adding any relevant comments on improvements needed.

Concluding Activity: Show a video of a large aircraft taking off on a short runway. Have the students write out on an exit slip how that takeoff is the same as the ones that they were conducting in class.

CHAPTER 10 FLIGHT MANEUVERS

LESSON 4

SOFT-FIELD TAKEOFF AND LANDING

PURPOSE

The purpose of this lesson is to apply what the students have already learned about takeoffs and landings to a soft-field takeoff and landing by flying the maneuvers in a flight simulation.

ACCOMMODATIONS FOR LEARNING DIFFERENCES

It is important that lessons accommodate the needs of every learner. These lessons may be modified to accommodate your students with learning differences by referring to **www.pacer.org/parent/php/PHP-c267.pdf.**

PREPARATION

- Class copies of *Airplane Flying Handbook* (FAA-H-8083-3) or access to it on FAA's website
- Aircraft Pilot's Operating Handbook (POH)
- Flight simulator equipment, preferably with joystick or yokes with rudder pedals

DIRECTIONS

This lesson requires a flight simulator. If flight simulation is unavailable, use maneuver videos, such as videos from the UND AeroCast YouTube Channel or ASA's Virtual Test Prep—Flight Maneuvers, to demonstrate the concepts. If you are using maneuver videos, adjust the Student Notebook activities and materials as appropriate.

Introductory Activity: Reference the short-field runway that was used for the short-field takeoff and landing lesson (Chapter 10, Lesson 3). That runway was short, but it was also a grass runway. In Activity 1 (Pre-Flight Preparation List) in the Student Notebook, have the students list the different preflight preparation or things they need to consider before taking off on a grass runway versus a paved runway. (*Answers include:* How wet is the grass runway? Are there any gravel or rough spots on the grass? Is the grass runway lighted for night operations?)

Step 1: The facilitator will walk through the soft-field takeoff and landing procedures for the aircraft selected for use in today's flight simulator. The students are to reference the aircraft POH to look up the aircraft's soft-field takeoff and landing speeds and configuration. They should record their answers under the Student Notebook activities for this lesson.

Step 2: The students should pick an airport with a soft or turf runway and use that airport when flying soft-field takeoffs and landings. Once the student has performed three "good"* soft-field takeoffs, they should record two thoughts about their performance in Activity 2 (Soft-Field Takeoff Thoughts). Students will then call the facilitator to verify completion of that maneuver and obtain the facilitator's initials in the Student Notebook under Activity 3 (Soft-Field Takeoff Completion). If the student was not able to perform a good takeoff, the facilitator should list what the student needs to change to improve performance of the soft-field takeoff under comments in the Student Notebook.

* A good soft-field takeoff is when the student performs the takeoff using the appropriate soft-field technique, maintains in ground effect until reaching V_Y, and maintains the extended centerline of the runway.

Step 3: Once students have shown a good takeoff, they can move on to soft-field landings and repeat the procedures in step 2. Students should complete Activity 4 (Soft-Field Landings Thoughts) in their Student Notebooks to record thoughts on their soft-field landing performance and then complete Activity 5 (Soft-Field Landings Completion) by demonstrating a soft-field landing for the facilitator and obtaining initials verifying completion, adding any relevant comments on improvements needed.

Concluding Activity: Ask the students to write their answer to the following question on an exit slip. "It just rained two inches yesterday. Why is it not a good idea to land on that grass or soft runway?" (*Answer:* You might create ruts in the runway, therefore causing damage to the runway. You might also sink into the runway and with all of the forward momentum, it could cause the nose gear to dig into the ground and the tail to rise, resulting in the prop striking the ground.)

LESSON 5

STALLS: POWER-ON AND POWER-OFF

PURPOSE

The purpose of this lesson is to apply what the students learned about stalls in Chapter 8, Lesson 5, to flying both power-off and power-on stalls in a simulation.

ACCOMMODATIONS FOR LEARNING DIFFERENCES

It is important that lessons accommodate the needs of every learner. These lessons may be modified to accommodate your students with learning differences by referring to **www.pacer.org/parent/php/PHP-c267.pdf.**

PREPARATION

- Class copies of *Airplane Flying Handbook* (FAA-H-8083-3), Chapter 4, or access to it on FAA's website
- Aircraft Pilot's Operating Handbook (POH)
- FAA stall training video, "Stalling for Safety"[1]
- Flight simulator equipment, preferably with joystick or yokes with rudder pedals

DIRECTIONS

This lesson requires a flight simulator. If flight simulation is unavailable, use maneuver videos, such as videos from the UND AeroCast YouTube Channel or ASA's Virtual Test Prep—Flight Maneuvers, to demonstrate the concepts. If you are using maneuver videos, adjust the Student Notebook activities and materials as appropriate.

Introductory Activity: Show a video of an aircraft stalling. Using the Student Notebook Activity 1 (Stalling Video Review), have the students write down what they think just happened to the aircraft shown in the video. (*Answer:* The aircraft did not lose power, it stalled; it did not have enough airflow over the wings to create lift for the weight of the aircraft.)

Step 1: Have the students reference the *Airplane Flying Handbook* and the aircraft POH to review the entry and recovery procedures for a power-off and power-on stall. They should record the procedures in Activity 2 (Power-Off and Power-On Stall Procedures) in their Student Notebooks. Review the power-off and power-on stall procedures with the class. (If more information on stalls is needed, reference the FAA stall training video, "Stalling for Safety."[2])

Step 2: The students will use the flight simulation to conduct both a power-on and power-off stall and record how the stalls went by answering the questions under Activity 3 (Conducting Power-Off and Power-On Stalls) in their Student Notebooks.

Step 3: Once the students have performed multiple power-on and power-off stalls, have them pick another aircraft. Without referencing the aircraft POH, have students take off and stall the aircraft. Note the similarities and differences in a class discussion; students can also record their observations in their Student Notebooks in Activity 3.

Concluding Activity: Upon completion of multiple stalls, have the students answer the following question in Student Notebook Activity 4 (Stall Summary Question) to show that they fully understand what is occurring when an aircraft stalls:

> "The angle of attack at which an airplane wing stalls will remain the same regardless of gross weight. Why?"

(*Answer:* When the angle of attack is increased to between 18° and 20° [critical angle of attack] on most airfoils, the airstream can no longer follow the upper curvature of the wing because of the excessive change in direction. The airplane will stall if the critical angle of attack is exceeded. The indicated airspeed at which a stall occurs will be determined by weight and load factor, but the stall angle of attack is the same.)

LESSON 6
STEEP TURN

PURPOSE
The purpose of this lesson is to apply what the students learned about aerodynamics in a turn to actually flying a steep turn in an aircraft through a simulation.

ACCOMMODATIONS FOR LEARNING DIFFERENCES
It is important that lessons accommodate the needs of every learner. These lessons may be modified to accommodate your students with learning differences by referring to www.pacer.org/parent/php/PHP-c267.pdf.

PREPARATION
- Class copies of *Airplane Flying Handbook* (FAA-H-8083-3), Chapter 9, or access to it on FAA's website
- UND AeroCast video, "Commercial Steep Turns"[3]
- UND Aerospace interactive demo: "Forces in a Turn"[4]
- Aircraft Pilot's Operating Handbook (POH)
- Flight simulator equipment, preferably with joystick or yokes with rudder pedals

DIRECTIONS
This lesson requires a flight simulator. If flight simulation is unavailable, use maneuver videos, such as videos from the UND AeroCast YouTube Channel or ASA's Virtual Test Prep—Flight Maneuvers, to demonstrate the concepts. If you are using maneuver videos, adjust the Student Notebook activities and materials as appropriate.

Introductory Activity: Earlier we discussed the fundamental flight maneuvers, and one of them was a turn. What makes a steep turn different than the turns we practiced during the fundamental lesson? (*Answer:* Those turns were not as steep. A steep turn is anything greater than 30 degrees.) For Private Pilot Certification, a steep turn is a 45-degree bank.

Step 1: Lead a discussion on what a steep turn is. Then have the students reference Chapter 9 in the *Airplane Flying Handbook* and the aircraft POH to answer the following questions in Activity 1 (Steep Turn Procedures) in the Student Notebook.

  Aircraft Type _____

  Maneuver Speed: _____

  Review: What flight instrument will tell the pilot what angle of bank the turn is at?

  Describe how to perform the steep turn.

  Why should the pilot use trim?

Step 2: Lead a discussion with the class on how to perform a steep turn. Then the students will be tasked to fly a steep turn with flight simulation. After they have completed a steep turn to the left and to the right, they should answer the following question in the Student Notebook under Activity 2 (Steep Turns Flight Simulation): "The *Airplane Flying Handbook* gives a list of common errors. During your first two steep turns, which of these common errors happened to you?"

Step 3: The students will fly steep turns until they are able to complete a turn to private pilot airman certification standards (ACS) (available on the FAA's website). These standards are ±100 feet of entry altitude, ±10 knots of entry airspeed, bank ±5 degrees, and roll out on the entry heading ±10 degrees. Once students can do this successfully, they need to have the facilitator check off that they are within standards by initialing their Student Notebooks.

Concluding Activity: Upon lesson completion, ask the following question of the students: "How would this maneuver differ if it were an 'instrument steep turn' (without referencing the outside of the cockpit)?"

LESSON 7

FLIGHT BY REFERENCE TO INSTRUMENTS

PURPOSE

The purpose of this lesson is to introduce students to what it is like flying only by reference to the flight instruments through an aircraft simulation.

ACCOMMODATIONS FOR LEARNING DIFFERENCES

It is important that lessons accommodate the needs of every learner. These lessons may be modified to accommodate your students with learning differences by referring to **www.pacer.org/parent/php/PHP-c267.pdf**.

PREPARATION

- Class copies of *Airplane Flying Handbook* (FAA-H-8083-3), Chapter 17, or access to it on FAA's website
- Video, "178 Seconds to Live," by Air Safety Institute[5]
- Private Pilot Airman Certification Standards (FAA-S-ACS-6)
- Flight simulator equipment, preferably with joystick or yokes with rudder pedals

DIRECTIONS

Introductory Activity: Show students the video, "178 Seconds to Live," by Air Safety Institute.[6] Have the students reflect on what they just watched/heard and discuss with their neighbor. Ask them to consider how they could have avoided that situation.

Step 1: Reference the section in Chapter 1 covering the requirements to become a private pilot. On a private pilot checkride, one needs to demonstrate basic instrument maneuvers. These maneuvers include straight-and-level flight, constant airspeed climbs and descents, turns to headings, and unusual attitudes. Lead a discussion and/or presentation on flight by reference to instruments, referencing Chapter 17 in the *Airplane Flying Handbook* for details on Inadvertent VFR Flight into IMC. Students should fill in information related to the maneuvers in Activity 1 (Basic Flight by Instruments Outline) in the Student Notebook.

Step 2: The student will now be asked to fly the fundamental maneuvers that they have already flown, only this time they are to take off in IMC (instrument meteorological conditions) and fly around without referencing anything outside of the cockpit. Similar to previous lessons in this chapter, students need to perform the maneuver and then have the facilitator sign off under Activity 2 (Flight by Reference to Instruments Simulation) that the student has satisfactorily completed the maneuver. The students should also add comments on any improvements needed. There are standards listed in the Private Pilot Airman Certification Standards (ACS) that the facilitator can reference for satisfactory completion of the maneuvers.

Step 3: The students will record how the flight by Instruments simulation went in the Student Notebook.

Concluding Activity: Have the students complete the following "I think" statement aloud: "I think instrument flying would be…" They must also include a reason for their statement.

ANSWER KEYS

CHAPTER 10

LESSON 1, Activity 1
Fundamental Maneuvers Worksheet (Student Notebook)

1. Altimeter, airspeed indicator, and heading indicator
2. Altimeter, airspeed indicator, and attitude indicator or turn coordinator
3. Airspeed indicator, heading indicator, and vertical speed indicator
4. Heading indicator and vertical speed indicator
5. Airspeed indicator, heading indicator, and vertical speed indicator
6. Airspeed indicator, heading indicator, and vertical speed indicator
7. Airspeed indicator, turn coordinator, and vertical speed indicator

CHAPTER 11

AIRSPACE

Introduction

STANDARDS & OBJECTIVES

North Dakota Aviation Content Standards (Grades 10–12)
- 3.2.1—Compare the classes of controlled and uncontrolled airspaces and airports.
- 3.2.2—Identify the airspace dimensions needed for each class of airspace.
- 3.2.3—Recognize various classes of airspace on sectional charts.
- 3.2.4—Identify the minimum weather requirements for each class of airspace.
- 3.2.5—Categorize the pilot qualifications needed for each class of airspace.
- 3.2.6—Explain the aircraft requirements for each class of airspace.
- 3.2.7—Determine when it would be necessary to request a special VFR clearance.
- A.3.2.8 and A.3.2.9—Use a sectional to identify airspace accurately.

Note: Standards beginning with "A" indicate the objectives align with but do not exactly match the identified ND Aviation Standards.

Language Arts—CCSS.ELA-LITERACY.CCRA
- L.1—Demonstrate command of the conventions of standard English grammar and usage when writing or speaking.
- L.2—Demonstrate command of the conventions of standard English capitalization, punctuation, and spelling when writing.
- R.1—Read closely to determine what the text says explicitly and to make logical inferences from it; cite specific textual evidence when writing or speaking to support conclusions drawn from the text.
- R.10—Read and comprehend complex literary and informational texts independently and proficiently.
- W.4—Produce clear and coherent writing in which the development, organization, and style are appropriate to task, purpose, and audience.

ESSENTIAL QUESTIONS
- Why is airspace divided into different classifications?
- Why is it important for pilots to know that they cannot fly in a certain area (e.g., the airspace above the White House, National Wildlife Preserve)?
- Why is it important for a pilot to know the cloud clearances for the different types of airspace?

LESSONS

Lesson	Topic	Student Notebook Activities
Lesson 1	Introduction to Airspace: Controlled vs. Uncontrolled	1. PHAK Chapter Outline 2. Class A and B Airspace Graphic Organizer
Lesson 2	Class C, D, and E Airspace	1. Class C, D, and E Airspace Graphic Organizer 2. Comprehension Questions
Lesson 3	Uncontrolled Airspace: Class G	1. Class G Airspace Graphic Organizer 2. Airspace Worksheet
Lesson 4	Special Use and Other Airspace	1. Notice to Airmen (NOTAM) Article 2. Airspace Quiz 3. Special Use and Other Airspace Graphic Organizer
Lesson 5	Review: Airspace	1. Review Study Guide
Lesson 6	Chapter 11 Exam	1. Article Response and Rubric

LESSON 1

INTRODUCTION TO AIRSPACE: CONTROLLED VS. UNCONTROLLED

PURPOSE

The purpose of this lesson is to establish the understanding of what airspace is and why there are different classifications.

ACCOMMODATIONS FOR LEARNING DIFFERENCES

It is important that lessons accommodate the needs of every learner. These lessons may be modified to accommodate your students with learning differences by referring to **www.pacer.org/parent/php/PHP-c267.pdf.**

PREPARATION

- Note cards
- Class copies of *Pilot's Handbook of Aeronautical Knowledge* (FAA-H-8083-25)
- Classroom copies of sectional charts
- Access to **www.skyvector.com** during lesson

DIRECTIONS

Introductory activity: Direct students to form pairs or triads. Pose the following questions for the groups to answer.

- What is airspace?
- Imagine if there were no signs on roads or in parking lots. Where would we park our cars when visiting the grocery store? How would we know where to go or what to do?
- What is the purpose of airspace?

Allow 3–5 minutes for student groups to generate responses. Ask groups to share out answers with the whole class and discuss responses. Display the parking lot photo on the next page to students and explain using an analogy of real-life experiences of a parking lot/car traffic to the profile and purpose of airspace classification.

Step 1: Students will complete Activity 1 (PHAK Chapter Outline) in the Student Notebook while referencing the *Pilot's Handbook of Aeronautical Knowledge* (PHAK), Chapter 15.

Step 2: Facilitate an interactive lecture using visual representations and pictures (consider using **www.skyvector.com** or sectionals) in the presentation that clarify and demonstrate key concepts (see list below) from Chapter 15 of the *Pilot's Handbook of Aeronautical Knowledge*. During the interactive lecture, students can complete the relevant portions of Activity 2 (Class A and B Airspace Graphic Organizer) in preparation for remaining airspace lessons. Students may also be directed to reference their sectionals to locate Class B airspace.

▶ Parking lot. *(iStock.com/Diy13)*

Ensure the following concepts are included in the interactive lecture:

- Difference between regulatory and non-regulatory airspace
- Types of airspace (controlled, uncontrolled, special use, other)
  › Class A
    - VFR weather minimums
      □ flight visibility
      □ distance from the clouds
    - Entry requirements
    - Minimum pilot certificate
    - Equipment requirements
    - What it looks like on a sectional
    - The altitudes included in Class A airspace
  › Class B
    - VFR weather minimums
      □ flight visibility
      □ distance from the clouds
    - Entry requirements
    - Minimum pilot certificate
    - Equipment requirements
    - What it looks like on a sectional
    - The altitudes included in Class B airspace

Concluding Activity: On a note card, have the students brainstorm cities or airports that have a Class B airport classification. The facilitator will collect the cards, review responses, and confirm answers using sectional or electronic resources such as **www.skyvector.com**.

LESSON 2

CLASS C, D, AND E AIRSPACE

PURPOSE

The purpose of this lesson is to build on the concepts of controlled airspace and associated requirements and regulations specifically for Class C, D, and E.

ACCOMMODATIONS FOR LEARNING DIFFERENCES

It is important that lessons accommodate the needs of every learner. These lessons may be modified to accommodate your students with learning differences by referring to **www.pacer.org/parent/php/PHP-c267.pdf**.

PREPARATION

- Class copies of *Pilot's Handbook of Aeronautical Knowledge* (FAA-H-8083-25)
- Classroom copies of sectional charts
- Access to **www.skyvector.com** during lesson

DIRECTIONS

Introductory activity: On the board, individual whiteboards, or pieces of paper at their desks, ask students to draw the profiles of Class A and B airspace classifications. Allow students to use their resources to add Class C, D, and E airspace to their drawings (see *Pilot's Handbook of Aeronautical Knowledge*, Figure 15-1). Correct any misconceptions and review key characteristics.

Step 1: Facilitate an interactive lecture about Class C, D, and E airspace using visual representations (using **www.skyvector.com** or have students reference sectionals) and pictures in the presentation that clarify and demonstrate key concepts from Chapter 15 of the *Pilot's Handbook of Aeronautical Knowledge* about Class C, D and E airspace. Students will complete Activity 1 (Class C, D, and E Airspace Graphic Organizer) in their Student Notebooks during the lesson.

Ensure the following concepts are included in the interactive lecture:

- Class C, Class D, and Class E airspaces
  › VFR weather minimums
    – flight visibility
    – distance from the clouds
  › Entry requirements
  › Minimum pilot certificate
  › Equipment requirements
  › What it looks like on a sectional
  › The altitudes included in each class of airspace

Step 2: To review how to identify different airspace on sectionals, complete the following steps:

1. Go to **www.skyvector.com**.
2. Type KGRB in the top left corner and click "Go" to display airports in Green Bay, WI.
3. Discuss with students: "What class airspace is KGRB?" (*Answer:* Class C)
4. Other Class C airports:
    a. KMDW, Chicago Midway International, IL
    b. KSNA, John Wayne, Orange County, CA
5. Class D airports:
    a. KGFK, Grand Forks, ND
    b. KFAR, Fargo, ND
    c. KFCM, Flying Cloud, Eden Prairie, MN
6. Class E airports:
    a. KJMS, Jamestown, ND (Class E, starting at the surface)
    b. KOBE, Okeechobee County, FL (Class E, starting at 700 feet)
    c. Airspace between KLCQ, Lake City Gateway, FL, and KVQQ, Cecil, FL (Class E floor 1,200 feet)
    d. L09, Stovepipe Wells, CA (Class E starting at 14,500 feet)
    e. Airspace north of KBTY, Beatty, NV—inside blue zipper on map (Class E, starting at 9,700 feet)

Concluding Activity: Pass out a sticky note or notecard to each student. Ask students to write down three important things to know regarding the differences in airspace classifications C, D, and E from the interactive lecture. Students will turn these into the facilitator.

Assign students Activity 2 (Comprehension Questions) in the Student Notebook to complete as homework. (An answer key is provided at the end of the chapter.)

FACILITATOR INFORMATION
Airspace Profile

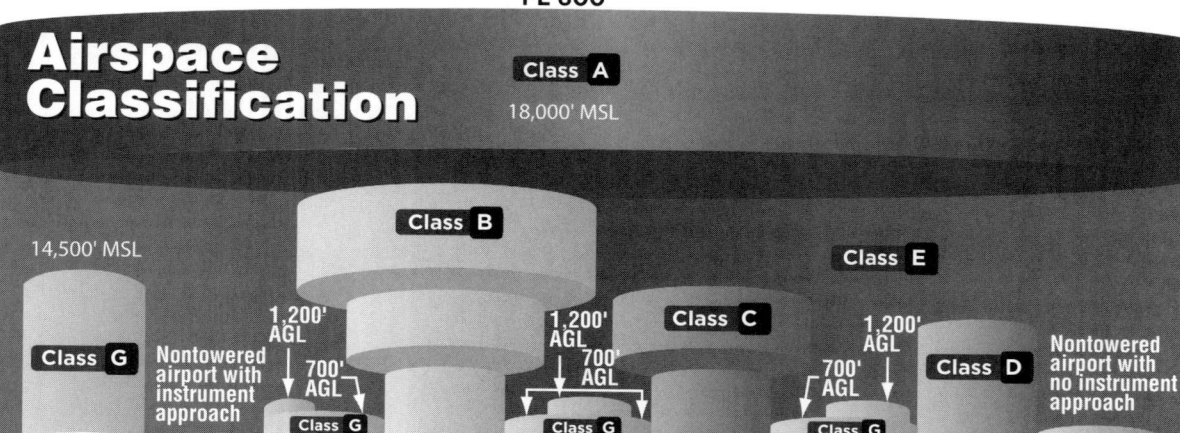

(FAA-H-8083-25)

CHAPTER 11   AIRSPACE

LESSON 3

UNCONTROLLED AIRSPACE: CLASS G

PURPOSE

The purpose of this lesson is to build on the concepts of airspace previously learned and apply them specifically to Class G, uncontrolled airspace.

ACCOMMODATIONS FOR LEARNING DIFFERENCES

It is important that lessons accommodate the needs of every learner. These lessons may be modified to accommodate your students with learning differences by referring to **www.pacer.org/parent/php/PHP-c267.pdf**.

PREPARATION

- Class copies of *Pilot's Handbook of Aeronautical Knowledge* (FAA-H-8083-25)
- Classroom copies of sectional charts
- Access to **www.skyvector.com** during lesson

DIRECTIONS

Introductory activity: Either on the board, on individual whiteboards, or on pieces of paper at their desks, ask students to draw the profiles of Class A, B, C, D, and E airspace (see *Pilot's Handbook of Aeronautical Knowledge*, Figure 15-1). Allow students to use their resources to add Class G to their drawings. Ask probing questions about entrance requirements, weather minimums, and equipment requirements. Correct any misconceptions and review key characteristics of Class G airspace.

Step 1: Direct students to form pairs or triads. Students will review the answers to the Comprehension Questions from the previous lesson with each other to reach consensus on an answer. Next, pairs will self-correct the questions as the facilitator reviews the correct answers. Correct any misconceptions from Lessons 1 and 2 and reteach concepts as needed.

Step 2: Facilitate an interactive lecture about Class G airspace using visual representations and pictures (using **www.skyvector.com** or have students reference sectionals) in the presentation that clarify and demonstrate key concepts from Chapter 15 of the *Pilot's Handbook of Aeronautical Knowledge*. Students will complete the Activity 1 (Class G Airspace Graphic Organizer) in their Student Notebooks during the lesson.

Ensure the following concepts are included in the interactive lecture:

- Class G Airspace:
    - VFR weather minimums
        - flight visibility
        - distance from the clouds
    - Entry requirements
    - Minimum pilot certificate
    - Equipment requirements
    - What it looks like on a sectional
    - The altitudes included in Class G airspace

Step 3: To review how to identify different airspace on sectionals, complete the following steps:

1. Go to **www.skyvector.com**.
2. Class E airports:
    a. KOBE, Okeechobee County, FL (Class G, starting at surface to 700 feet)
    b. Airspace between KLCQ, Lake City Gateway, FL, and KVQQ, Cecil, FL, (Class G starting at surface up to 1,200 feet)
    c. L09 Stovepipe Wells, CA (Class G starting at surface up to 14,500 feet)
    d. Airspace north of KBTY, Beatty, NV—inside blue zipper on map (Class G, starting at surface up to 9,700 feet)

Concluding Activity: Students will complete Activity 2 (Airspace Worksheet) in the Student Notebook in pairs; if not completed, assign as homework. (An answer key is provided at the end of the chapter.) Notify students that there will be a quiz on airspace in the next lesson.

Note: All questions for this homework assignment are based on using a Twin Cities sectional chart.

FACILITATOR INFORMATION
Airspace Profile

(FAA-H-8083-25)

LESSON 4

SPECIAL USE AND OTHER AIRSPACE

PURPOSE

The purpose of this lesson is to establish the understanding of controlled airspace and associated requirements and regulations.

ACCOMMODATIONS FOR LEARNING DIFFERENCES

It is important that lessons accommodate the needs of every learner. These lessons may be modified to accommodate your students with learning differences by referring to **www.pacer.org/parent/php/PHP-c267.pdf**.

PREPARATION

- Class copies of *Pilot's Handbook of Aeronautical Knowledge* (FAA-H-8083-25)
- Classroom copies of sectional charts
- Access to **www.skyvector.com** during lesson

DIRECTIONS

Introductory activity: Display the Notice to Airmen (NOTAM) published in Activity 1 (Notice to Airmen Article) in the Student Notebook. In either pairs or triads, have students explain the airspace classification and ask questions of one another related to what they have learned about airspace classifications. Students can reference their resources during this activity. Ask students to think of a situation or event that would warrant a change in airspace classification.

Step 1: Direct students to form pairs or triads. Students will self-correct the Lesson 3 Airspace Worksheet questions as the facilitator reviews the correct answers. Correct any misconceptions and reteach any concepts from Lessons 1, 2, and 3 as needed.

Step 2: Students will take the quiz in Activity 2 (Airspace Quiz). If students complete the quiz quickly, provide them a sectional on which to label airspace. Note: All questions for this quiz are based on using a Twin Cities sectional. (This quiz is also provided under Facilitator Information at the end of this lesson for reference, and an answer key is provided at the end of the chapter.)

Step 3: When all students have completed the quiz, facilitate an interactive lecture about special use and other airspace using visual representations and pictures (using **www.skyvector.com** or have students reference sectionals) in the presentation that clarify and demonstrate key concepts from Chapter 15 of the *Pilot's Handbook of Aeronautical Knowledge* about airspace. Students will complete Activity 3 (Special Use and Other Airspace Graphic Organizer) in the Student Notebook during the lesson. Ensure the following concepts are included in the interactive lecture for each type of airspace:

- Purpose
- Pilot responsibilities for entry
- (Note: Do not fill out the "Time of Use" or "Altitude" columns until the next step.)

Step 4: In either pairs or triads, have students locate each one of the special use and other airspaces on either their sectional or **www.skyvector.com**. Have students record findings in their Student Notebook under the "Time of Use" and "Altitude" columns of the graphic organizer. Time of use and altitude can be found on the sectional. Students can reference their resources during this activity. Guide discussions, correcting any misconceptions, and reteach any concepts that were inaccurate.

Concluding Activity: Students will share their findings of special use and other airspace locations with the class.

FACILITATOR INFORMATION
Airspace Quiz

(This quiz is available in the online Instructor Resources in a format ready for use in the classroom. An answer key is provided at the end of the chapter.)

Note: All questions for this quiz are based on using the Twin Cities sectional chart.

1. You are departing from St. Cloud Regional Airport, Minnesota (KSTC).
   a. What class airspace are you in at 700 feet?
   b. What altitude does that airspace start at?
   c. What altitude does that airspace end at?

2. You are flying to the west towards Sauk Centre (D39) and are halfway between St. Cloud (KSTC) and Sauk Centre at 2,500 feet.
   a. What class airspace are you in?
   b. What altitude does that airspace start at?
   c. What altitude does that airspace end at?

3. You descend into the traffic pattern and are now on final at Sauk Centre at 300 feet AGL.
   a. What class airspace are you in?
   b. What altitude does that airspace start at?
   c. What altitude does that airspace end at?

4. You take off and decide to land at Chandler Field Airport (KAXN) in Alexandria. You fly there and are on final at 300 feet.

    a. What class airspace are you in?

    b. What altitude does that airspace start at?

    c. What altitude does that airspace end at?

5. What is the VFR visibility minimum for Class B airspace?

    a. 1 SM visibility

    b. 3 SM visibility

    c. 5 SM visibility

6. What is the VFR cloud clearance for Class B airspace?

    a. Clear of clouds

    b. 500 feet below the clouds, 1,000 feet above the clouds, and 2,000 feet horizontal

    c. 1,000 feet below the clouds, 1,000 feet above the clouds, and 1 SM horizontal

7. What is the VFR visibility minimum for Class D airspace?

    a. 1 SM visibility

    b. 3 SM visibility

    c. 5 SM visibility

8. What is the VFR cloud clearance for Class D airspace?

    a. Clear of clouds

    b. 500 feet below the clouds, 1,000 feet above the clouds, and 2,000 feet horizontal

    c. 1,000 feet below the clouds, 1,000 feet above the clouds, and 1 SM horizontal

9. What is the VFR visibility minimum for Class E airspace above 10,000 feet?

    a. 1 SM visibility

    b. 3 SM visibility

    c. 5 SM visibility

10. What is the VFR cloud clearance for Class E airspace above 10,000 feet?

    a. Clear of clouds

    b. 500 feet below the clouds, 1,000 feet above the clouds, and 2,000 feet horizontal

    c. 1,000 feet below the clouds, 1,000 feet above the clouds, and 1 SM horizontal

LESSON 5

REVIEW: AIRSPACE

PURPOSE

The purpose of this lesson is to review the airspace requirements for safe flight.

ACCOMMODATIONS FOR LEARNING DIFFERENCES

It is important that lessons accommodate the needs of every learner. These lessons may be modified to accommodate your students with learning differences by referring to **www.pacer.org/parent/php/PHP-c267.pdf.**

PREPARATION

- Class copies of *Pilot's Handbook of Aeronautical Knowledge* (FAA-H-8083-25)
- Classroom copies of sectional charts
- Access to **www.skyvector.com** during lesson

DIRECTIONS

Introductory activity: Have students locate an airport of their choice and type it into **www.skyvector.com**. Have students work in pairs or triads to discuss differences among various airspace. Students should also note entrance and equipment requirements, VFR weather minimums, and altitudes.

Step 1: In pairs, have students complete the review in Activity 1 (Review Study Guide) in the Student Notebook. Students may use Chapter 15 in the *Pilot's Handbook of Aeronautical Knowledge* and class notes for reference. The facilitator will circulate through the room, answering questions and checking for understanding. Note: All questions for this study guide are based on using a Twin Cities sectional chart. (An answer key is provided at the end of the chapter.)

Step 2: Ask students to look through their course material and write down anything that they don't remember, missed, or are unclear on. Take turns answering their questions and clarifying; chances are that several students will have the same questions.

Step 3: Review the study guide questions with the students for accuracy. Correct any misconceptions or inaccuracies. Reteach as needed.

Concluding Activity: No formal concluding activity; students can continue to work on the study guide due for the next day prior to the exam.

LESSON 6
CHAPTER 11 EXAM

PURPOSE
The purpose of this lesson is to assess student knowledge of airspace.

ACCOMMODATIONS FOR LEARNING DIFFERENCES
It is important that lessons accommodate the needs of every learner. These lessons may be modified to accommodate your students with learning differences by referring to www.pacer.org/parent/php/PHP-c267.pcf.

PREPARATION
- Copies of exam
- Classroom copies of sectional charts
- Online access to display the article assigned to class or printouts of the article for students

DIRECTIONS

Introductory activity: Before beginning, provide instructions on what students are to do after they have completed their tests.

Step 1: Students will complete the airspace exam. The facilitator can create an exam using the question bank at the end of this lesson. Note: All questions for this exam are based on using a Twin Cities sectional chart. (An answer key s provided at the end of the chapter.)

Step 2: When students have turned in the exam, make available to them the article, "Pilot sets her sights on the eye of the storm," from *The Washington Post*.[1] Students will independently read the article and then under Activity 1 (Article Response and Rubric) in the Student Notebook, they will write a one-paragraph response that includes a summary and reflection on the prompts:

1. Besides being a pilot, what other background or schooling would be beneficial for a hurricane hunter pilot, and why?
2. Describe what a hurricane hunter aircraft and pilot do besides flying into a hurricane.
3. Describe some ways in which you think the hurricane hunter pilots can adjust to the job's demands, long hours, and odd start times, and why is it important that they do so?

Students should include at least two thoughtful, inquiry-related questions in the reflection. It will be graded using the rubric provided in the Student Notebook.

Concluding Activity: No formal summary activity. Students will work independently to finish the exam at different times and begin reading the article as an introductory activity to Chapter 12 on weather theory.

The facilitator may decide to review the correct exam answers to address incorrect responses and/or misconceptions prior to beginning Chapter 12.

FACILITATOR INFORMATION
Chapter 11 Exam: Airspace

(This exam is available in the online Instructor Resources in a format ready for use in the classroom. An answer key is provided at the end of the chapter.)

Note: All questions for this exam are based on using a Twin Cities sectional.

1. When in controlled airspace, you must always be in radio communication with ATC.
   a. True
   b. False

2. As a VFR pilot, I can enter an active MOA; however, I must look out for traffic.
   a. True
   b. False

3. Typically, Class D airspace's vertical distance is 2,500 feet MSL.
   a. True
   b. False

4. If you were to fly from Glencoe, Minnesota (KGYL) to Airlake, Minnesota (KLVN) at 2,000 feet MSL, you need to have a mode C transponder.
   a. True
   b. False

5. The primary airport located inside of the TRSA is Class _____ airspace.
   a. E
   b. D
   c. C
   d. B

6. Which airspace extends outward beginning at 3 NM from the coast of the United States and may contain activity that is hazardous to non-participating aircraft?
   a. ADIZ
   b. Warning
   c. Restricted
   d. National Security Areas

7. Typically, what is the vertical distance of Class C airspace?
   a. 2,500 feet AGL
   b. 2,500 feet MSL
   c. 4,000 feet AGL
   d. 4,000 feet MSL

8. Give one reason why a TFR would be issued.

9. What is the difference between controlled and uncontrolled airspace?

10. Why would airspace be designated as an alert area?

11. Give one example of why a prohibited airspace would exist.

12. You just took off from International Falls Airport in Minnesota (KINL). You are at 300 feet AGL. What airspace are you in?
    a. Class C
    b. Class D
    c. Class E
    d. Class G

13. What altitude does that airspace (from question 12) begin at?
    a. Surface
    b. 700 feet
    c. 1,200 feet
    d. 2,500 feet

14. What altitude does that airspace (from question 12) end at?
    a. 1,200 feet
    b. 10,000 feet
    c. 14,500 feet
    d. 17,999 feet

15. You decide to fly to from International Falls to Big Fork, Minnesota (KFOZ). You are currently halfway there at an altitude of 4,500 feet. What airspace are you in?
    a. Class C
    b. Class D
    c. Class E
    d. Class G

16. What altitude does that airspace (from question 15) begin at?
    a. Surface
    b. 700 feet
    c. 1,200 feet
    d. 2,500 feet

17. What altitude does that airspace (from question 15) end at?
    a. 1,200 feet
    b. 10,00 feet
    c. 14,500 feet
    d. 17,999 feet

18. You are now 5 miles north of Big Fork at 4,500 feet. What special use airspace are you in?

19. What altitude does that airspace (from question 18) begin at?
    a. Surface
    b. 300 feet
    c. 700 feet
    d. 1,200 feet

20. What altitude does that airspace (from question 18) end at?
    a. 700 feet
    b. 1,200 feet
    c. 14,500 feet
    d. 17,999 feet

21. What are the active times of that special use airspace from question 18?

22. You decide to overfly the field at Big Fork to check on the windsock at 1,000 feet AGL. What airspace are you in?
    a. Class C
    b. Class D
    c. Class E
    d. Class G

23. What altitude does that airspace (from question 22) start at?
    a. Surface
    b. 700 feet
    c. 1,200 feet
    d. 2,500 feet

24. What altitude does that airspace (from question 22) end at?

    a. 700 feet

    b. 1,200 feet

    c. 14,500 feet

    d. 17,999 feet

25. You are now descending into the traffic pattern at Big Fork and are preparing to land. You are at 500 feet AGL. What airspace are you in?

    a. Class C

    b. Class D

    c. Class E

    d. Class G

26. What altitude does that airspace (from question 25) begin at?

    a. Surface

    b. 700 feet

    c. 1,200 feet

    d. 2,500 feet

27. What altitude does that airspace (from question 25) end at?

    a. 700 feet

    b. 1,200 feet

    c. 14,500 feet

    d. 17,999 feet

28. You are planning a flight from Carrington, North Dakota (46D) to Bismarck, North Dakota (KBIS). When looking over the sectional, you notice that there is a gray line just a little way from Carrington labeled "IR644". What is this?

29. Should you plan your flight around the gray IR644 line? Why or why not?

30. You decide to go on the flight described in question 28. You are now en route and look at your sectional and notice that you are near your friend's private airport, Buchmiller (7ND5). You decide to fly close to it to check it out. You are currently at 4,500 feet MSL. What airspace are you in?

    a. Class C

    b. Class D

    c. Class E

    d. Class G

31. What altitude does that airspace begin at?
    a. Surface
    b. 700 feet
    c. 1,200 feet
    d. 14,500 feet

32. What altitude does that airspace end at?
    a. 1,200 feet
    b. 2,500 feet
    c. 14,500 feet
    d. 17,999 feet

33. You decide to do a landing at your friend's field (Buchmiller private strip) to see if he is around and because it's lunch time and you are hungry. You notice that there are some clouds moving in. In fact, the clouds are getting thicker and more widespread. You are now below 1,200 feet AGL. What are your VFR visibility and cloud clearance requirements?
    a. Visibility _____ SM
    b. Cloud clearance _____

34. What equipment and/or pilot requirements are needed to enter Class B airspace?
    a. _____
    b. _____
    c. _____
    d. _____

35. What are the VFR weather requirements to enter a Class B airspace?
    a. Visibility _____ SM
    b. Cloud clearance _____

36. What are the VFR weather requirements to enter a Class C airspace?
    a. Visibility _____ SM
    b. Cloud clearance _____

37. What equipment requirements are needed to enter a Class C airspace?
    a. _____
    b. _____

38. If you overfly the St. Paul Downtown Airport (KSTP) at 3,500 feet. What airspace are you in?
    a. Class B
    b. Class C
    c. Class D
    d. Class E

39. You are 10 miles north of Anoka (KANE) and you decide to call up the tower. You say, "Anoka Tower, Sioux 26 is 10 miles to the north inbound for full stop landing." Tower responds back with, "Aircraft calling standby." What are you allowed to do?

40. When entering the Anoka airspace, you notice that there are some clouds moving in. The clouds are reported to be at 3,000 feet MSL. How high can you fly and still meet your VFR cloud clearances?
    a. 1,000 feet
    b. 2,000 feet
    c. 2,500 feet
    d. None of the above

41. What does "ADIZ" stand for?

42. What is the difference between MSL and AGL?

ANSWER KEYS

CHAPTER 11

LESSON 2, Activity 2
Comprehension Questions (Student Notebook)

1. Class A airspace
2. 29.92 inHg
3. Controlled airspace
4. Up to and including 60,000 feet MSL
5. (a) True
6. (b) False. Each aircraft must establish two-way radio communications with the air traffic control (ATC) facility providing air traffic services prior to entering the airspace and thereafter must maintain those communications while within the airspace.
7. ATC clearance
8. Prohibited areas contain airspace of defined dimensions within which the flight of aircraft is prohibited. Such areas are established for security or other reasons associated with the national welfare. Restricted areas are areas where operations are hazardous to nonparticipating aircraft and contain airspace within which the flight of aircraft, while not wholly prohibited, is subject to restrictions.
9. Class D airspace
10. Yes, but it is advised to avoid these areas or contact the controlling agency when operating within an active MOA. MOAs consist of airspace with defined vertical and lateral limits established for the purpose of separating certain military training activities from IFR traffic.

LESSON 3, Activity 2
Airspace Worksheet (Student Notebook)

1. Class E
2. Class E starts at the surface and goes up to 18,000 feet MSL.
3. Class E
4. Class E starts at 700 feet AGL and goes up to but not including 18,000 feet MSL.
5. Class G
6. Class E
7. In between Aberdeen and Gettysburg, the Class E starts at 1,200 feet AGL and goes up to, but not including, 18,000 feet MSL.

8. (c) 3,000 feet MSL
9. (c) 8,500 feet MSL. (NOTE: You need to be 1,000 feet above the clouds; however, 7,000 feet is not a VFR cruising altitude. For that direction of flight, the aircraft needs to be at an even +500 foot altitude.)

LESSON 4, Activity 2
Airspace Quiz (Student Notebook)

1. a. Class D
   b. At the surface
   c. 3,500 feet MSL

2. a. Class E
   b. 1,200 feet AGL
   c. Up to, but not including, 18,000 feet MSL

3. a. Class G
   b. Surface
   c. Up to, but not including, 700 feet AGL.

4. a. Class E
   b. Surface
   c. Up to, but not including, 18,000 feet MSL

5. (b) 3 SM visibility
6. (a) Clear of clouds
7. (b) 3 SM visibility
8. (b) 500 feet below the clouds, 1,000 feet above the clouds, and 2,000 feet horizontal
9. (c) 5 SM visibility
10. (c) 1,000 feet below the clouds, 1,000 feet above the clouds, and 1 SM horizontal

LESSON 5, Activity 1
Study Guide Review (Student Notebook)

1. Pilots operating an aircraft in Class A airspace must conduct that operation under IFR and only under an ATC clearance received prior to entering the airspace.

2. All pilots operating an aircraft within a Class B airspace area must receive an ATC clearance from the ATC facility having jurisdiction for that area. The pilot-in-command (PIC) may not take off or land an aircraft at an airport within a Class B airspace unless he or she has met one of the following requirements:

   - A private pilot certificate
   - A recreational pilot certificate and all requirements contained within 14 CFR §61.101(d), or the requirements for a student pilot seeking a recreational pilot certificate in 14 CFR §61.94.

- A sport pilot certificate and all requirements contained within 14 CFR §61.325, or the requirements for a student pilot seeking a recreational pilot certificate in 14 CFR §61.94, or the aircraft is operated by a student pilot who has met the requirements of 14 CFR §§61.94 and 61.95, as applicable.

Unless otherwise authorized by ATC, all aircraft within Class B airspace must be equipped with the applicable operating transponder and automatic altitude reporting equipment specified in 14 CFR §91.215(a) and an operable two-way radio capable of communications with ATC on appropriate frequencies for that Class B airspace area. Additionally, beginning January 1, 2020, aircraft operating in the Class B airspace described in 14 CFR §91.225, must have ADS-B Out equipment installed, which meets the performance requirements of 14 CFR §91.227.

3. a. Class B: Nothing, you need clearance to enter.
   b. Class C: If your call sign was used, it is considered two-way communication. Continue but maintain two-way communication.
   c. Class D: If your call sign was used, it is considered two-way communication. Continue but maintain two-way communication.
4. (b) Uncontrolled
5. Mean sea level
6. Above ground level
7. (a) True. (While generally true, altitudes may vary. The height of Class D airspace will be depicted on the aeronautical chart in MSL.)
8. (b) False. (Not all controlled airspace requires two-way radio. Class D and C are controlled airspace that does require two-way communication.)
9. (b) 5 SM visibility; 1,000 feet below, 1,000 feet above, 1 SM horizontal distance from clouds
10. Not applicable—Unless otherwise authorized, all operation in Class A airspace is conducted under instrument flight rules (IFR).
11. 3 SM visibility; Clear of clouds
12. 3 SM visibility; 1,000 feet above, 500 feet below, 2,000 feet horizontal distance from clouds
13. 3 SM visibility; 1,000 feet above, 500 feet below, 2,000 feet horizontal distance from clouds
14. 3 SM visibility; 1,000 feet above, 500 feet below, 2,000 feet horizontal distance from clouds
15. 5 SM visibility; 1,000 feet above, 1,000 feet below, 1 statute mile horizontal distance from clouds
16. 1 SM visibility; Clear of clouds
17. 3 SM visibility; 1,000 feet above, 500 feet below, 2,000 feet horizontal distance from clouds
18. (c) 6,100 feet MSL
19. Temporary Flight Restriction

20. Some of the purposes for establishing a TFR are:
    - Protect persons and property in the air or on the surface from an existing or imminent hazard.
    - Provide a safe environment for the operation of disaster relief aircraft.
    - Prevent an unsafe congestion of sightseeing aircraft above an incident or event that may generate a high degree of public interest.
    - Protect declared national disasters for humanitarian reasons in the State of Hawaii.
    - Protect the President, Vice President, or other public figures.
    - Provide a safe environment for space agency operations.
21. Prohibited areas contain airspace of defined dimensions within which the flight of aircraft is prohibited. Such areas are established for security or other reasons associated with the national welfare. Restricted areas are areas where operations are hazardous to nonparticipating aircraft and contain airspace within which the flight of aircraft, while not wholly prohibited, is subject to restrictions.
22. The restricted area altitude is upward from 500 feet above ground level to, but not including 10,000 feet MSL.
23. The prohibited airspace is up to but not including 4,000 feet MSL.
24. Military Operation Area
25. Yes; use caution.
26. 4,000 feet up to but not including FL180
27. No; it is not an airspace designation but a services available designation.
28. Class D
29. Air Defense Identification Zone
30. Air Defense Identification Zones (ADIZs) are symbolized using the ADIZ symbol (::::::::::::::::), which is purple. As defined in the Code of Federal Regulations, 14 CFR Part 99, an ADIZ is an area in which the ready identification, location, and control of all aircraft is required in the interest of national security. ADIZ boundaries include Alaska, Hawaii, Guam, Canada, and the Contiguous U.S.
31. Class G unless the Class E extension is in effect. If within Class E extension effective hours, you will be in Class E airspace.
32. Class G airspace begins at the surface up to 700 feet AGL. If the Class E extension is in effect, Class E starts at the surface and goes up to 18,000 feet MSL.
33. Assuming you are entering from the south, you are in Class E airspace.
34. Up to, but not including, 18,000 feet MSL
35. 2,000 feet AGL
36. Class G
37. Surface up to, but not including, 700 feet AGL.

LESSON 6
Chapter 11 Exam

1. (b) False
2. (a) True
3. (b) False
4. (a) True
5. (b) Class D
6. (b) Warning
7. (b) 2,500 feet MSL
8. Some of the purposes for establishing a TFR are:
   - Protect persons and property in the air or on the surface from an existing or imminent hazard.
   - Provide a safe environment for the operation of disaster relief aircraft.
   - Prevent an unsafe congestion of sightseeing aircraft above an incident or event that may generate a high degree of public interest.
   - Protect declared national disasters for humanitarian reasons in the State of Hawaii.
   - Protect the President, Vice President, or other public figures.
   - Provide a safe environment for space agency operations.
9. Unlike Class G uncontrolled airspace, controlled airspace consists of those areas where some or all aircraft *may* be subject to air traffic control, such as: Class A, Class B, Class C, Class D, and Class E Airspace.
10. Alert areas are depicted on aeronautical charts with an "A" followed by a number (e.g., A-211) to inform nonparticipating pilots of areas that may contain a high volume of pilot training or an unusual type of aerial activity. Pilots should exercise caution in alert areas. All activity within an alert area shall be conducted in accordance with regulations, without waiver, and pilots of participating aircraft, as well as pilots transiting the area, shall be equally responsible for collision avoidance.
11. Prohibited areas contain airspace of defined dimensions within which the flight of aircraft is prohibited. Such areas are established for security or other reasons associated with the national welfare. These areas are published in the Federal Register and are depicted on aeronautical charts. The area is charted as a "P" followed by a number (e.g., P-40). Examples of prohibited areas include Camp David and the National Mall in Washington, D.C., where the White House and the Congressional buildings are located.
12. (c) Class E
13. (a) Surface
14. (d) 17,999 feet
15. (c) Class E
16. (c) 1,200 feet
17. (d) 17,999 feet
18. Beaver MOA
19. (b) 300 feet

20. (d) 17,999 feet
21. The MOA status will be given via a NOTAM and is scheduled for the following times: 0800–2200 Mon–Fri, 0800–1600 Sat–Sun. Other times may be indicated on the NOTAM.
22. (c) Class E
23. (b) 700 feet
24. (d) 17,999 feet
25. (d) Class G
26. (a) Surface
27. (a) 700 feet
28. It indicates a Military Training Route (MTR). MTRs are routes established for the conduct of low-altitude, high-speed military flight training (generally below 10,000 feet MSL at airspeeds in excess of 250 knots indicated airspeed [IAS]).
29. No, but be aware of it. MTRs with no segment above 1,500 feet AGL are identified by four number characters (e.g., IR1206, VR1207). MTRs that include one or more segments above 1,500 feet AGL are identified by three number characters (e.g., IR206, VR207).
30. (c) Class E
31. (c) 1,200 feet
32. (d) 17,999 feet
33. a. Visibility: 1 SM
    b. Cloud clearance: Clear of clouds
34. a. A Mode C transponder
    b. An operable two-way radio capable of communications with ATC on appropriate frequencies for that Class B airspace area.
    c. ADS-B Out equipment installed that meets the performance requirements of 14 CFR §91.227.
    d. The pilot must receive a clearance to enter the airspace, and must be a private pilot or student pilot with endorsement.
35. a. Visibility: 3 SM
    b. Cloud clearance: Clear of clouds
36. a. Visibility: 3 SM
    b. Cloud clearance: 1,000 feet above, 500 feet below, 2,000 feet horizontal
37. a. Two-way radio
    b. Transponder with altitude reporting capability
38. (a) Class B
39. Standby and do not enter airspace requiring two-way communication.
40. (c) 2,500 feet
41. Air Defense Identification Zone
42. MSL is above sea level and AGL is above ground level.

CHAPTER 12

WEATHER

Introduction

STANDARDS & OBJECTIVES

North Dakota Aviation Content Standards (Grades 10–12)
- **2.2.1**—Identify the gases within the atmosphere.
- **2.2.2**—Describe factors that affect atmospheric weather patterns.
- **2.2.4**—Explain the formation of clouds and the conditions necessary to form each type.
- **2.2.5**—Explain and compare the various types of precipitation.
- **2.2.6**—Explain the importance of atmospheric stability and cloud formation.
- **2.2.7**—Compare dew point and humidity.
- **2.2.8**—Identify the various stages of thunderstorms and the hazards to flight.
- **2.3.1**—Identify Terminal Aerodrome Forecast (TAF) codes (e.g., TEMPO, FM).
- **2.3.2**—Explain, analyze, and apply TAFs.
- **2.3.3**—Explain the importance of a winds aloft forecast.
- **2.3.4**—Identify abbreviations (e.g., RA, BR, and SN) used in METAR weather reports.
- **2.3.5**—Decode, analyze, and apply METARs.
- **2.3.7**—Determine weather products issuance and valid times.
- **2.3.8**—Describe how to obtain official weather briefings & FAA approved sources or products.
- **4.3.2**—Discuss the IMSAFE checklist.

Science—Next Generation Science Standards (Grades 9–12)
- **HS-ESS2-2**—Analyze geoscience data to make the claim that one change to Earth's surface can create feedbacks that cause changes to other Earth systems.
- **HS-ESS2-4**—Use a model to describe how variations in the flow of energy into and out of Earth's systems result in changes in climate.
- **HS-ESS3-5**—Analyze geoscience data and the results from global climate models to make an evidence-based forecast of the current rate of global or regional climate change and associated future impacts to Earth's systems.

Language Arts—CCSS.ELA-LITERACY.CCRA

- **L.1**—Demonstrate command of the conventions of standard English grammar and usage when writing or speaking.
- **L.2**—Demonstrate command of the conventions of standard English capitalization, punctuation, and spelling when writing.
- **R.1**—Read closely to determine what the text says explicitly and to make logical inferences from it; cite specific textual evidence when writing or speaking to support conclusions drawn from the text.
- **R.10**—Read and comprehend complex literary and informational texts independently and proficiently.
- **SL.1**—Prepare for and participate effectively in a range of conversations and collaborations with diverse partners, building on others' ideas and expressing their own clearly and persuasively.
- **SL.2**—Integrate and evaluate information presented in diverse media and formats, including visually, quantitatively, and orally.
- **W.2**—Write informative/explanatory texts to examine and convey complex ideas and information clearly and accurately through the effective selection, organization, and analysis of content.
- **W.4**—Produce clear and coherent writing in which the development, organization, and style are appropriate to task, purpose, and audience.
- **W.7**—Conduct short as well as more sustained research projects based on focused questions, demonstrating understanding of the subject under investigation.
- **W.8**—Gather relevant information from multiple print and digital sources, assess the credibility and accuracy of each source, and integrate the information while avoiding plagiarism.
- **W.9**—Draw evidence from literary or informational texts to support analysis, reflection, and research.

ESSENTIAL QUESTIONS

1. How does weather impact aircraft performance and flight safety?
2. Why must a pilot understand the theories behind weather?
3. How can technology be used to make decisions about weather conditions?

LESSONS

Lesson	Topic	Student Notebook Activities
Lesson 1	Weather Theory (Day 1)	1. Weather Theory Comprehension Questions
Lesson 2	Weather Theory (Day 2)	1. Weather Demonstration Notes 2. Reading Assignment Response Questions
Lesson 3	Weather Products: METAR	1. METAR Notes 2. Decoding METARs 3. METARs Worksheet
Lesson 4	Weather Products: TAF	1. TAF Notes 2. Decoding TAFs 3. TAF Homework
Lesson 5	Weather Products: AIRMETs and SIGMETs	1. AIRMET and SIGMET Notes 2. Prognostic Chart Summary Forecast
Lesson 6	Weather-Related Decision-Making	1. Go/No-Go Decision Scenarios
Lesson 7	Review: Weather	1. Review Questions Brainstorming
Lesson 8	Chapter 12 Exam	1. Article Response and Rubric

# LESSON 1

WEATHER THEORY (DAY 1)

PURPOSE

The purpose of this lesson is to examine important weather factors that influence aircraft performance and flight safety.

ACCOMMODATIONS FOR LEARNING DIFFERENCES

It is important that lessons accommodate the needs of every learner. These lessons may be modified to accommodate your students with learning differences by referring to **www.pacer.org/parent/php/PHP-c267.pdf.**

PREPARATION

- Class copies of *Pilot's Handbook of Aeronautical Knowledge* (FAA-H-8083-25)
- Student Notebook comprehension questions for interactive lecture
- One sticky note or note card per student
- Materials for making a barometer (introductory activity)
- Access to Aviation Weather Center's Aviation Digital Data Service (ADDS) (**www.aviationweather.gov/adds/**)

DIRECTIONS

Introductory Activity: Make a barometer in front of the class, and show the students a video explaining a barometer's design and function. Explain how the barometer works, and describe what would happen to the readings at low altitudes (sea level) and at high altitudes (mountains). In small groups, have students discuss the two application questions:

- How does barometric pressure impact an aircraft?
- What kind of weather-related decisions about flying can a pilot make by knowing barometric pressure?

Step 1: Display the current general weather information for your area using the National Weather Service (**weather.gov**) or The Weather Channel (**weather.com**), bringing attention to typical information students will encounter in aviation routine weather reports (i.e., precipitation, clouds with elevation, wind and wind direction). As students progress through this chapter, they will begin researching and obtaining weather using aviation-specific weather information obtained from The Aviation Weather Center (AWC) at **aviationweather.gov**. Ask the students to find a partner and provide three reasons why pilots need to know about the weather. Discuss responses with the whole class.

Step 2: Facilitate an interactive lecture using visual representations and pictures in the presentation that clarify and demonstrate key concepts about weather theory from Chapter 12 of the *Pilot's Handbook of Aeronautical Knowledge*. Ensure the following concepts are included in the interactive lecture:

- Composition of the atmosphere
- Atmospheric circulation
- Atmospheric pressure
- Coriolis force
- Altitude and atmospheric pressure
- Wind and currents
- Atmospheric stability
  › Inversion
  › Moisture and temperature
  › Relative humidity
  › Dew point
  › Saturation point
  › Dew and frost
  › Fog
  › Clouds
  › Ceiling
  › Visibility
  › Precipitation
- Air masses
- Fronts
- Hazards

Step 3: Students will complete the weather theory comprehension questions in the Student Notebook in Activity 1 (Weather Theory Comprehension Questions) during the interactive lecture for active processing. Pause and have students discuss and record answers as they are provided, ensuring frequent breaks for active processing.

Concluding Activity: Pass out a sticky note or note card to each student. Ask students to write down three weather factors from the interactive lecture and how they affect flight. Students will turn these into the facilitator.

LESSON 2

WEATHER THEORY (DAY 2)

PURPOSE

The purpose of this lesson is to examine important weather factors that influence aircraft performance and flight safety.

ACCOMMODATIONS FOR LEARNING DIFFERENCES

It is important that lessons accommodate the needs of every learner. These lessons may be modified to accommodate your students with learning differences by referring to **www.pacer.org/parent/php/PHP-c267.pdf.**

PREPARATION

- Class copies of *Pilot's Handbook of Aeronautical Knowledge* (FAA-H-8083-25)
- Lab materials: Cup, water, note card, balloon, two markers of different colors, jar, dish or light plastic tub that fits on top of jar, hot water, ice, hairspray, food coloring, plastic box with lid, match, ruler, desk lamp, paper towels, paper
- Access to Aviation Weather Center's Aviation Digital Data Service (ADDS) (**www.aviationweather.gov/adds/**)
- Access to AOPA article, "Current Altimeter Settings Really Matter,"[1] or printouts of article for students

DIRECTIONS

Introductory Activity: Display the current weather information for your location using the Aviation Weather Center (**www.aviationweather.gov**) bringing attention to typical information students will encounter in aviation routine weather reports (i.e., precipitation, clouds with elevation, wind and wind direction). Explain to the students why you would or would not fly that day based on weather theory to support your decision. Discuss responses with the whole class.

Step 1: Follow the instructions for "The Water Glass Trick" to demonstrate the concept of air pressure.

- Fill a cup one-third with water.
- Cover the entire mouth of the cup with an index card.
- Holding the card in place, take the cup to the sink and turn it upside down.
- Remove your hand from underneath. Because the water inside the cup is lighter than the air outside, the card is held in place by about 15 pounds of force from the air pushing up, while the force of the water pushing down is only about one pound of force.

Discuss how air pressure is being demonstrated in the example. Additionally discuss what density altitude is and how they both are related to aircraft performance. Have students take notes in Student Notebook Activity 1 (Weather Demonstration Notes) associated with the air pressure and density altitude demonstration, using the *Pilot's Handbook of Aeronautical Knowledge* for reference.

Step 2: Follow the instructions for modeling the Coriolis effect of atmospheric circulation.

- Grab a balloon and blow it all the way up.
- The balloon represents the Earth: the top of the balloon is the "North Pole" and the tie of the balloon is the "South Pole." Ask for a student volunteer. Ask them to draw the equator and label the poles.
- Have a student hold the balloon by the tie and bring it up to eye level. Now have the student simulate the rotation of the Earth by rotating the balloon from left to right.
- Have the class examine the movement of the Earth from the perspectives of both the North Pole and the South Pole while the student is continually rotating the balloon.
- Ask for two other student volunteers. While the balloon is continually rotated from left to right, have one student take a different colored marker and try to draw a line from the North Pole straight south to the equator. Ask the second student to try to draw a line from the South Pole north to the equator.

The lines should be curved or angled. The amount of curve may and should have changed as the students drew the line. Ask the students the following question: "If air is deflected to the right in the Northern Hemisphere, why can we not tell as we are walking around the Earth?" (*Answer:* We walk and travel relatively short distances as compared to the size and speed of rotation of the Earth.)

Discuss how wind, currents, and obstructions are being demonstrated in the example. Have students take notes on the demonstration and the Coriolis effect's impact on wind and currents under Activity 1 (Weather Demonstration Notes), using the *Pilot's Handbook of Aeronautical Knowledge* for reference.

Step 3: Follow the instructions for modeling atmospheric stability through cloud formation.

- Boil water. Add several drops of food coloring. Fill a jar with one third (between ½ to 1 cup) hot water. Note the water level.
- Spray a few full sprays of hairspray into the jar, and then put a cover on the jar. Have the students comment on what they see happening when the spray enters the jar. This is representing the dust in the air. Cloud droplets form around particles.
- Put a dish or plastic tub on top of the jar and put ice in it. This represents the cooling high up in the air.
- You will see some faint swirling of the steam inside the jar. (This may take a few minutes to occur). Have the students look closely at the clouds; they should be colored slightly if you used food coloring. Have the students comment on the water level inside the jar prior to opening it after the experiment. The water level should have gone down slightly due to the water being used for the cloud formation.
- Make several stations for the students to observe the clouds during different stages of the process. Refer to this experiment as "a cloud in a bottle."

Discuss how clouds and their relationship to weather are being demonstrated in the experiment. Have students take notes associated with the cloud formation demonstration in the Student Notebook under Activity 1 (Weather Demonstration Notes), using the *Pilot's Handbook of Aeronautical Knowledge* for reference.

Step 4: Follow the instructions for modeling how air masses influence weather and flight.

- Carefully pour 5 cm of water into the bottom of a box while keeping the sides of the box dry.
- While over the box, take a match and light the paper on fire. Blow out the flames on the match and paper and direct the smoke into the box so that the box fills with smoke.
- Take the cover off the box and place it upside down on the box.
- Put a handful (approximately 5–6) ice cubes inside one end of the lid.
- Place the lamp so the light is shining above the other (non-ice) side of the box.
- Have the students comment on what is happening to the:
  - ice on the end of the lid
  - middle of the lid
  - lamp end of the lid
  - inside of the box
- Move the lamp so that it shines over the middle of the box. Have the students comment on what is happening to the:
  - ice on the end of the lid
  - middle of the lid
  - lamp end of the lid
  - inside of the box

Discuss air masses and how their relationship to flight is being demonstrated in the example. Have students take notes associated with the air mass demonstration in the Student Notebook under Activity 1 (Weather Demonstration Notes), using the *Pilot's Handbook of Aeronautical Knowledge* for reference.

Concluding Activity: Have students read the short article, "Current Altimeter Settings Really Matter," from the Aircraft Owners and Pilots Association (AOPA) website.[2] The reading assignment will begin in the last five minutes of class and be assigned as homework for students to complete. The questions in Activity 2 (Reading Assignment Response Questions) in the Student Notebook will be answered together as a whole class in the introduction for Lesson 3.

CHAPTER 12 WEATHER

LESSON 3

WEATHER PRODUCTS: METAR

PURPOSE

The purpose of this lesson is to introduce students to weather products that are common for everyday flight, the METAR.

ACCOMMODATIONS FOR LEARNING DIFFERENCES

It is important that lessons accommodate the needs of every learner. These lessons may be modified to accommodate your students with learning differences by referring to **www.pacer.org/parent/php/PHP-c267.pdf.**

PREPARATION

- Class copies of *Pilot's Handbook of Aeronautical Knowledge* (FAA-H-8083-25)
- Student Notebook questions and outline
- Prepared interactive lecture on METARs
- Access to Aviation Weather Center's Aviation Digital Data Service (ADDS) (**www.aviationweather.gov/adds/**)

DIRECTIONS

Introductory Activity: Review the homework reading assignment questions from Lesson 2 (Activity 2) as a whole group. First have students share responses in pairs. Next, call on groups to share their answers. Clarify any misconceptions, and ensure the connection between weather theory and application to flight is made.

1. What factors influence atmospheric pressure?
2. Explain at least two ways the pilot could have prevented this accident. (Call on 2 groups.)
3. What weather principles affected the flight? (Call on multiple groups.)
4. Explain how one of the principles identified in question #3 works. (Facilitator should explain any impacting weather factors not brought up by students.)

Step 1: Re-engage the students on weather by pulling up current weather for your location at this exact time using the Aviation Weather Center (**www.aviationweather.gov**), bringing attention to typical information students will encounter in aviation routine weather reports (i.e., precipitation, clouds with elevation, wind and wind direction). In pairs or small groups, have students decode the weather, decide if they would fly today or not, and provide reasons for their decision supported by weather theory. Introduce the elements of the METAR from the current weather information.

CHAPTER 12 Lesson 3 / Facilitator Guide

Step 2: Conduct an interactive lecture using visual representations and pictures in the presentation that clarify and demonstrate key concepts of aviation weather services and aviation routine weather reports (METAR) from Chapter 13 of the *Pilot's Handbook of Aeronautical Knowledge*.

The interactive lecture will follow the "I do, we do, you do" model of direct instruction to ensure a gradual release of responsibility. When new material is being introduced, the facilitator has a prominent role in the delivery of the content. This is the "I do" phase. But as the student acquires the new information and skills, the responsibility of learning shifts from teacher-directed instruction to student processing activities. In the "We do" phase of learning, the teacher continues to model, question, prompt and cue students; but as students move into the "You do" phase, they rely more on themselves and less on the teacher to complete the learning task.

Use the following METAR example for the interactive lecture.

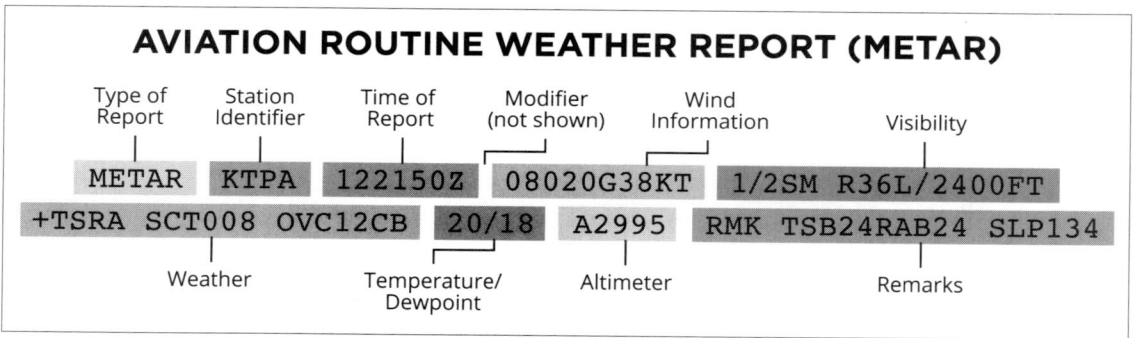

▶ Aviation Routine Weather Report (METAR) elements.

Ensure the following concepts are included in the interactive lecture:

- Definition of a METAR
- Frequency (if available)
- The following items are all elements that will be reported in order in a METAR. Present each, one at a time, referencing the example with the information being explained. Have students highlight and label the different elements in the example included in Activity 1 (METAR Notes) in the Student Notebook.

  › Type of report
  › Station identifier
  › Date and time (Zulu time) of report
  › Modifier (if included as AUTO, it is an automated station)
  › Wind
  › Visibility
  › Weather
  › Sky condition
  › Temperature and dew point
  › Altimeter setting
  › Remarks

- Common Abbreviations (refer to the table under Facilitator Information on the next page)
    - SN
    - TS
    - RA
    - FG
    - BR
    - SH
    - BKN
    - CLR
    - OVC
    - FEW
    - HZ
    - +
    - −

Students will complete the notes outline in Activity 1 (METAR Notes) in the Student Notebook for active processing during the interactive lecture. Pause and have students discuss and record answers as they are provided, ensuring frequent breaks for active processing.

Step 2: Demonstrate decoding METAR Example #2 and have students record notes in Activity 2 (Decoding METARs) in the Student Notebook:

```
KGFK 081253Z 28007KT 10SM CLR M01/M02 A3041 RMK AO2 SLP308
T10061022
```

Continue to model, question, prompt, and cue students as they fill in the answers in their Student Notebooks.

Step 3: Group students in pairs or triads, and have them work together to decode the next two METARs in their Student Notebooks:

METAR Example #3:

```
K40J 021835Z AUTO 29007KT 3SM +RA SCT008 BKN018 OVC046 24/23 A3008
RMK AO2 LTG DSNT E THRU SW P0031 T02350228
```

METAR Example #4:

```
K2J3 021835Z AUTO 09004KT 2 1/2SM -TSRA BR SCT031 SCT050 BKN090
24/24 A3006 RMK AO2 LTG DSNT NE E AND SW P0013 T02440239
```

Continue to question, prompt and cue students. Clarify any errors; if you notice a pattern of errors, address the issue with the whole class. Allow students to use the *Pilot's Handbook of Aeronautical Knowledge* for reference.

Step 4: Now working individually, have each student decode the next two METARs in the Student Notebook.

METAR Example #5:

```
KLAX 081253Z 11003KT 10SM FEW006 FEW200 14/12 A3005 RMK AO2 SLP174
T01440122 $
```

METAR Example #6:

```
KFMH 270535Z AUTO 03032G52KT 1/4SM SN OVC002 M01/M02 A2955 RMK AO2
```

Continue to question, prompt, and cue students. Clarify any errors; if you notice a pattern of errors, address the issue with the whole class. Allow students to use the *Pilot's Handbook of Aeronautical Knowledge* for reference.

Concluding Activity: Assign students Activity 3 (METARs Worksheet) as homework. If any class time remains, students can use this time to ask questions and complete the assignment. It will be due in class for Lesson 4. (An answer key is provided at the end of the chapter.)

FACILITATOR INFORMATION

Common Abbreviations Used in a Typical METAR

Qualifier		Weather Phenomena		
Intensity or Proximity 1	Descriptor 2	Precipitation 3	Obscuration 4	Other 5
– Light	**MI** Shallow	**DZ** Drizzle	**BR** Mist	**PO** Dust/sand whirls
Moderate (no qualifier)	**BC** Patches	**RA** Rain	**FG** Fog	**SQ** Squalls
+ Heavy	**DR** Low drifting	**SN** Snow	**FU** Smoke	**FC** Funnel cloud
VC in the vicinity	**BL** Blowing	**SG** Snow grains	**DU** Dust	**+FC** Tornado or waterspout
	SH Showers	**IC** Ice crystals (diamond dust)	**SA** Sand	**SS** Sandstorm
	TS Thunderstorms	**PL** Ice pellets	**HZ** Haze	**DS** Dust storm
	FZ Freezing	**GR** Hail	**PY** Spray	
	PR Partial	**GS** Small hail or snow pellets	**VA** Volcanic ash	
		UP *Unknown precipitation		

The weather groups are constructed by considering columns 1–5 in this table in sequence: intensity, followed by descriptor, followed by weather phenomena (e.g., heavy rain showers(s) is coded as +SHRA).
* Automated stations only

(FAA-H-8083-25)

METAR Resources

Additional METAR resources that can be helpful to students while completing independent work are listed in the online Instructor Resources.

LESSON 4

WEATHER PRODUCTS: TAF

PURPOSE

The purpose of this lesson is to introduce students to another very common weather product, Terminal Area Forecasts (TAFs).

ACCOMMODATIONS FOR LEARNING DIFFERENCES

It is important that lessons accommodate the needs of every learner. These lessons may be modified to accommodate your students with learning differences by referring to **www.pacer.org/parent/php/PHP-c267.pdf.**

PREPARATION

- Class copies of *Pilot's Handbook of Aeronautical Knowledge* (FAA-H-8083-25)
- Student Notebook questions and outline
- Interactive lecture on Terminal Area Forecasts (TAF)
- Access to Aviation Weather Center's Aviation Digital Data Service (ADDS) (**www.aviationweather.gov/adds/**)

DIRECTIONS

Introductory Activity: Re-engage the students on weather by pulling up current weather for your location at this exact time using the Aviation Weather Center (**www.aviationweather.gov**), bringing attention to typical information students will encounter in aviation routine weather reports (i.e., precipitation, clouds with elevation, wind and wind direction). In pairs or small groups, have students decode the weather, decide if they would fly today or not, and provide reasons for their decision supported by weather theory.

Ask the students if they think that the weather is likely to stay the same all day. Our weather normally changes throughout the day and therefore pilots need to have weather forecasts that can let them know what the weather may be like when they arrive at their destination (for example, after a four-hour flight). That is what a Terminal Area Forecast (TAF) is for.

Step 1: Review the METARs worksheet homework assignment from the previous lesson with the whole class. Call on groups to share their answers. Clarify any misconceptions or inaccuracies.

Step 2: Conduct an interactive lecture using visual representations and pictures in the presentation that clarify and demonstrate key concepts of aviation weather services and Terminal Area Forecasts (TAF) from Chapter 13 of the *Pilot's Handbook of Aeronautical Knowledge.*

Use the TAF Example #1 for the interactive lecture:

TAF Example #1:
```
MSP 241740Z 2418/2524 13013G21KT P6SM OVC018
   FM241930 13012G19KT 5SM -SHRA BR SCT008 OVC020
   TEMPO 2420/2422 1 1/2SM -SHRA BR OVC008
   FM250100 21010KT 5SM BR SCT020 OVC040
   FM250800 25012KT P6SM OVC015 PROB30 2510/2516 -SHSN
   FM251600 25015G23KT P6SM OVC035=
```

Ensure the following concepts are included in the interactive lecture:
- Definition
- Valid time frame
- The following are the elements in sequential order for a TAF. Present the elements one at a time, referencing the example with the information being explained:
    > Type of report
    > ICAO station identifier
    > Date and time of origin
    > Valid period dates and times
    > Forecast wind
    > Forecast visibility
    > Forecast significant weather
    > Forecast sky condition
    > Forecast change group
    > Probability group

Students will complete Activity 1 (TAF Notes) in the Student Notebook for active processing during the interactive lecture. Pause and have students discuss and record answers as they are provided, ensuring frequent breaks for active processing.

Step 2: Group students in pairs or triads and have them work together to decode TAF Example #2 in Activity 2 (Decoding TAFs) in their Student Notebooks.

```
KINL 201149Z 2012/2112 27012G20KT P6SM -SN BKN018 OVC025
   TEMPO 2012/2016 4SM -SN BR OVC012
   FM201900 28013G20KT P6SM VCSH BKN025 OVC040
   FM210100 28009KT P6SM SCT025 BKN050
   FM210600 29008KT P6SM VCSH OVC015
```

Continue to question, prompt, and cue students. Clarify any errors; if you notice a pattern of errors, address the issue with the whole class. Allow students to use the *Pilot's Handbook of Aeronautical Knowledge* for reference.

Step 3: Now working individually, have each student decode TAF Examples #3 and #4.

TAF Example #3:
```
KGFK 201120Z 2012/2112 27008KT P6SM SKC
   FM201700 30010KT P6SM SCTC30
   FM210000 27006KT P6SM SKC
```

TAF Example #4:
```
TAF AMD CYQM 201141Z 2012/2112 10005KT P6SM BKN020
   TEMPO 2012/2101 SCT020 OVC130
   BECMG 2014/2016 15015G25KT
   FM210100 14015G25KT P6SM -RA SCT008 OVC020
   FM210500 13012KT 5SM -RA ER OVC012
   PROB30 2105/2110 2SM RA BR OVC003
   FM211000 19010KT P6SM BKN040
   BECMG 2110/2112 29010KT
```

Continue to question, prompt, and cue students. Clarify any errors; if you notice a pattern of errors, address the issue with the whole class. Allow students to use the *Pilot's Handbook of Aeronautical Knowledge* for reference.

Concluding Activity: Assign students the worksheets on TAFs in Activity 3 in the Student Notebook as homework. If any class time remains, students can use this time to ask questions and complete the assignment. It will be due in class for Lesson 5.

CHAPTER 12   WEATHER

LESSON 5

WEATHER PRODUCTS: AIRMETS AND SIGMETS

PURPOSE

The purpose of this lesson is to explain the use of charts and other useful weather products to make aviation decisions.

ACCOMMODATIONS FOR LEARNING DIFFERENCES

It is important that lessons accommodate the needs of every learner. These lessons may be modified to accommodate your students with learning differences by referring to **www.pacer.org/parent/php/PHP-c267.pdf.**

PREPARATION

- Class copies of *Pilot's Handbook of Aeronautical Knowledge* (FAA-H-8083-25)
- Student Notebook questions and outline
- Prepared interactive lecture
- Access to Aviation Weather Center's Aviation Digital Data Service (ADDS) (**www.aviationweather.gov/adds/**)
- Devices for online access
- Note cards

DIRECTIONS

Introductory Activity: Re-engage the students on weather by pulling up current weather for your location at this exact time using the Aviation Weather Center (**www.aviationweather.gov**), bringing attention to typical information students will encounter in aviation routine weather reports (i.e., precipitation, clouds with elevation, wind and wind direction). In pairs or small groups, have students decode the weather, decide if they would fly today or not, and provide reasons for their decision supported by weather theory.

Step 1: Review the TAF worksheet homework assignment from Lesson 4 with the whole class. Call on groups to share their answers. Clarify any misconceptions or inaccuracies.

Ask the students if they were flying near an area of lower clouds if it would be useful to have a little more information about those clouds. That is just one of the reasons that AIRMETs were created.

Step 2: Conduct an interactive lecture using visual representations and pictures in the presentation that clarify and demonstrate key concepts of AIRMETs, SIGMETs and Convective SIGMETs, Winds & Temperature Aloft Forecasts, and Prognostic Charts from Chapter 13 of the *Pilot's Handbook of Aeronautical Knowledge*.

Use the AIRMET and SIGMET examples from the *Pilot's Handbook of Aeronautical Knowledge* for an interactive lecture. Ensure the following concepts are included in the interactive lecture:

- AIRMET
  - What AIRMET stands for
  - Valid time frame
  - Purpose
  - Three types
- SIGMET
  - What SIGMET stands for
  - Valid time frame
  - Purpose
- Convective SIGMET
  - What Convective SIGMET stands for
  - Valid time frame
  - Purpose
- Winds and Temperature Aloft forecasts
  - Definition
  - Valid time frame
  - Purpose
- Prognostic Charts
  - Definition
  - Valid time frame
  - Purpose

Students will complete the notes outline in Activity 1 (AIRMET & SIGMET Notes) in the Student Notebook for active processing during the interactive lecture. Pause and have students discuss and record answers as they are provided, ensuring frequent breaks for active processing.

Step 2: Demonstrate decoding AIRMET Example #1:

```
WAUS44 KKCI 021445
DFWZ WA 021445
AIRMET ZULU UPDT 3 FOR ICE AND FRZLVL VALID UNTIL 022100
AIRMET ICE...TN AL
FROM 40ESE BWG TO HMV TO GQO TO 50SW PZD TO 30W CEW TO 40ESE MEI
TO 40ESE BWG
MOD ICE BTN 140 AND FL300. CONDS CONTG BYD 21Z ENDG BY 03Z.
FRZLVL...RANGING FROM 130-170 ACRS AREA
    160 ALG 60W INK-80WSW INK-30NW MRF-20ESE MRF-30WSW PSX-70SSE
    PSX-110ENE BRO
```

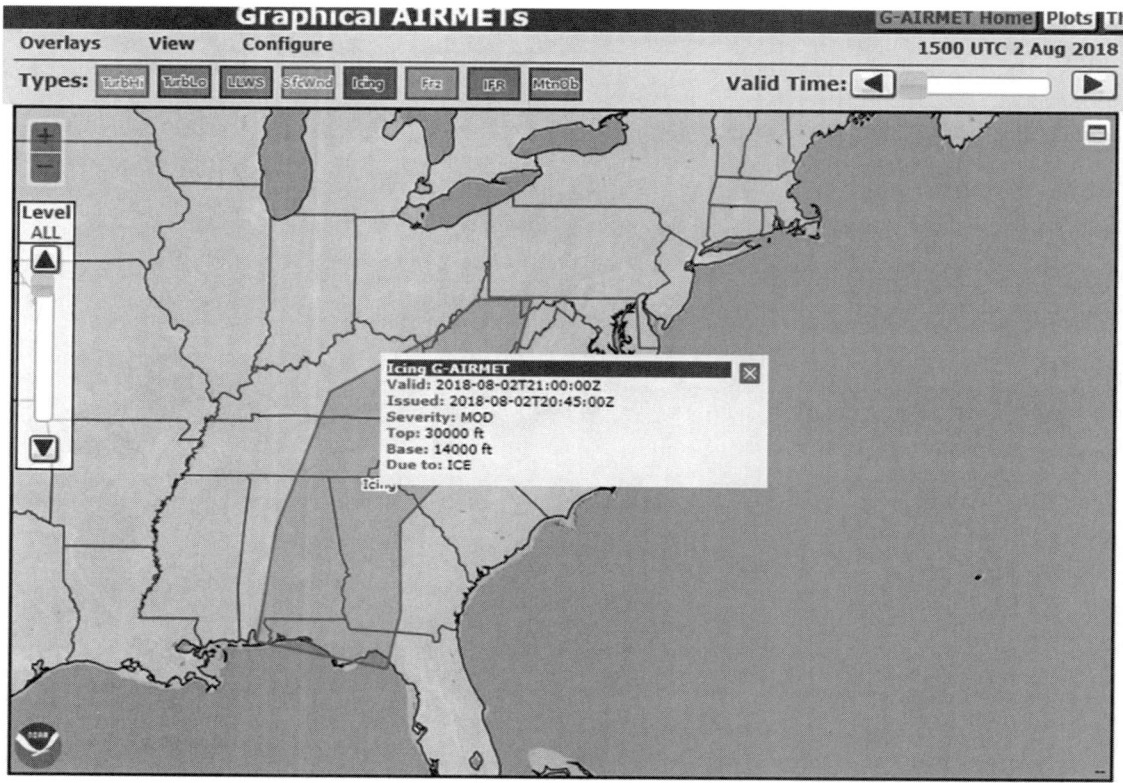

▶ Graphical AIRMET. *(NWS Aviation Weather Center)*

Step 3: Group students in pairs or triads, and have them work together to decode AIRMET Example #2 in their Student Notebooks. Continue to question, prompt and cue students. Clarify any errors; if you notice a pattern of errors, address the issue with the whole class. Allow students to use the *Pilot's Handbook of Aeronautical Knowledge* for reference.

Step 4: Demonstrate decoding SIGMET Example #1:

```
WSUS31 KKCI 022055
SIGE
CONVECTIVE SIGMET 06E
VALID UNTIL 2255Z
NC SC FL GA AND FL CSTL WTRS
FROM 40N SPA-30SE CAE-20SSE SRQ-40WSW CTY-30SE ATL-40N SPA
AREA SEV TS MOV FROM 20015KT. TOPS ABV FL450.
TORNADOES...HAIL TO 1 IN...WIND GUSTS TO 50KT POSS.

OUTLOOK VALID 022255-030255
AREA 1...FROM CON-50SSE ECG-50ENE CRG-PBI-70WSW EYW-100WSW
PIE-200SE LEV-SJI-BNA-30NNW EWC-CON
WST ISSUANCES EXPD. REFER TO MOST RECENT ACUS01 KWNS FROM STORM
PREDICTION CENTER FOR SYNOPSIS AND METEOROLOGICAL DETAILS.

AREA 2...FROM 40SSE SSM-30NE ECK-BVT-40NE ORD-40SSE SSM
WST ISSUANCES POSS. REFER TO MOST RECENT ACUS01 KWNS FROM STORM
PREDICTION CENTER FOR SYNOPSIS AND METEOROLOGICAL DETAILS.
```

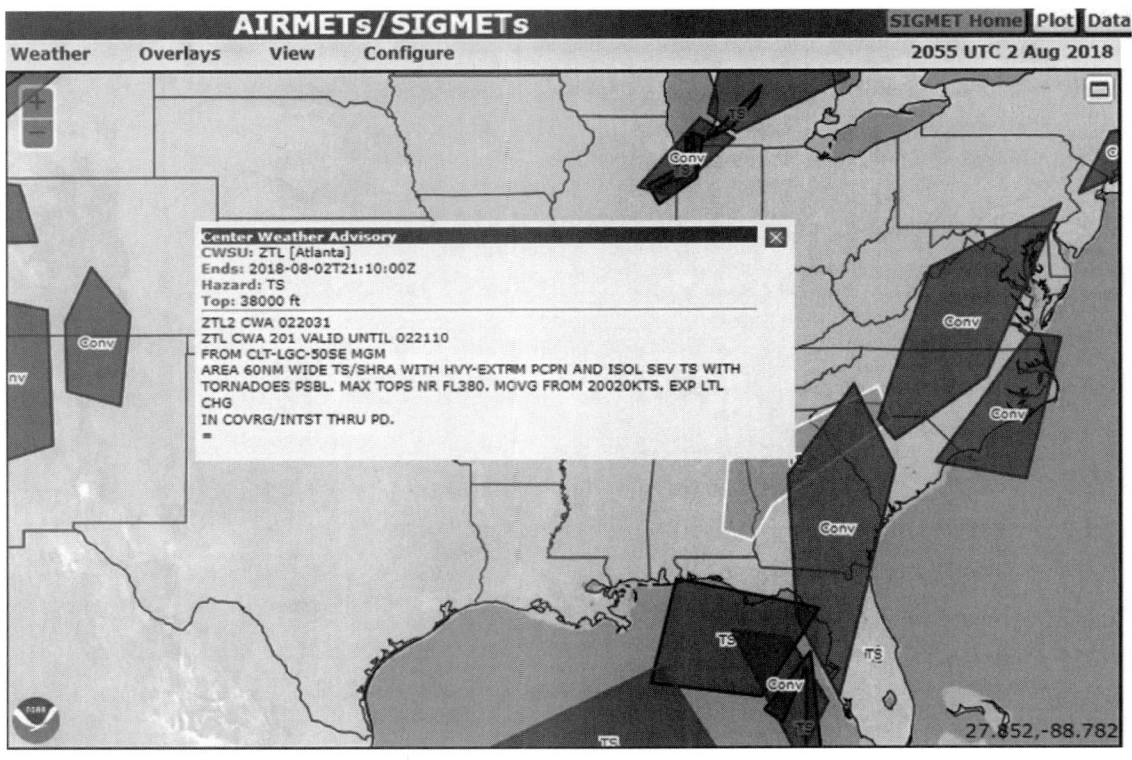

▶ SIGMET. *(NWS Aviation Weather Center)*

Step 5: Group students in pairs or triads, and have them work together to decode SIGMET Example #2 located in the Student Notebook. Clarify any errors; if you notice a pattern of errors, address the issue with the whole class. Allow students to use the *Pilot's Handbook of Aeronautical Knowledge* for reference.

Step 6: Complete the interactive lecture with an explanation of the winds and temperature aloft forecast and prognostic charts. Continue to question, prompt, and cue students. Clarify any errors; if you notice a pattern of errors, address the issue with the whole class. Allow students to use the *Pilot's Handbook of Aeronautical Knowledge* for reference.

Example of a Winds and Temperature Aloft Forecast:

```
DATA BASED ON 020000Z
VALID 020600Z    FOR USE 0200-0900Z. TEMPS NEG ABV 24000

FT   3000   6000     9000     12000    18000    24000    30000    34000    39000
BRL  2424   2721+14  2610+09  3017+01  2916-12  2815-24  331340   331150   262151
DBQ  2519   2523+13  2626+07  2724+01  2822-12  2818-23  281840   281650   272754
DSM  3509   2721+14  2924+09  3031+02  3122-12  3123-23  312340   312649   323352
MCW  3613   2815+10  2919+09  3021+03  3125-11  3027-23  312840   312350   322854
JOT  2420   2716+13  2611+07  2815+00  2716-12  2617-24  232540   223349   233852
SPI  2413   2914+14  3107+08  3410+01  2912-12  2513-24  232040   222448   232851
EVV  9900   9900+12  3405+07  9900+04  2309-10  2321-23  223539   215046   216552
FWA  2510   2506+12  2605+06  2809+01  2718-11  2522-22  233538   226046   228454
IND  2505   2905+12  9900+07  3006+02  2515-10  2318-23  233638   225046   216953
GCK         1914+18  0110+14  3318+08  3328-09  3337-19  325235   325546   325954
GLD         1818     2711+14  3111+07  3220-09  3331-20  334536   325646   325854
```

▶ Winds and Temperature Aloft Forecast. *(NWS Aviation Weather Center)*

Example of a Low-Level Significant Weather Prognostic Chart:

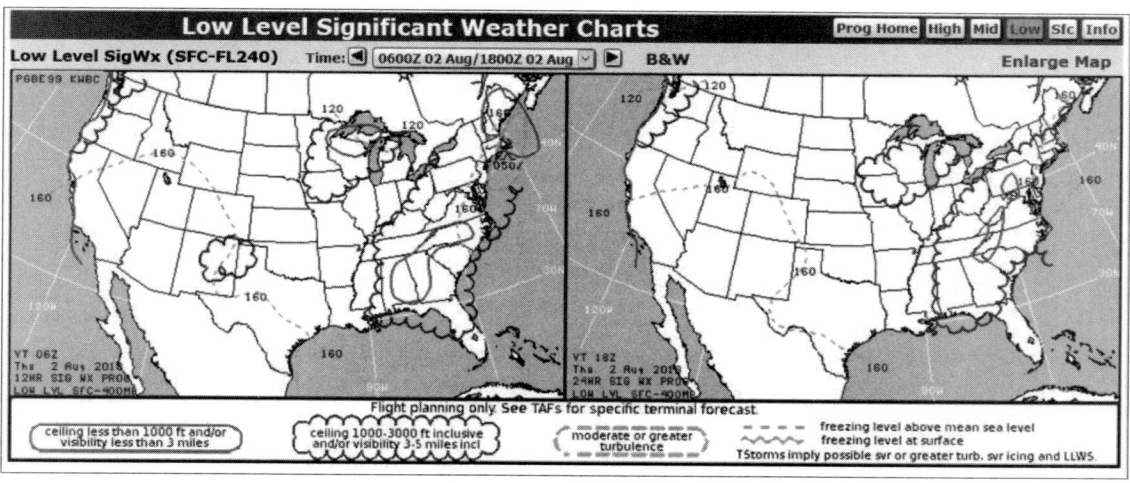

▶ Low-Level Significant Weather Prognostic Chart. *(NWS Aviation Weather Center)*

Concluding Activity: Have students decode the Prognostic Chart in Activity 2 (Prognostic Chart Summary Forecast) in their Student Notebooks. Have them decode it individually for review and turn it in on a note card to the facilitator as they exit the classroom.

LESSON 6

WEATHER-RELATED DECISION-MAKING

PURPOSE

Apply knowledge of weather to making aeronautical decisions in varied situations.

ACCOMMODATIONS FOR LEARNING DIFFERENCES

It is important that lessons accommodate the needs of every learner. These lessons may be modified to accommodate your students with learning differences by referring to www.pacer.org/parent/php/PHP-c267.pdf.

PREPARATION

- Class copies of *Pilot's Handbook of Aeronautical Knowledge* (FAA-H-8083-25)
- Student Notebook scenarios
- Article "Go or No-Go?" from *AeroSafety World*[3] for introductory activity
- Review Prep: Make a list of the four or five major concepts you want students to learn/know as a result of this study unit. Once you've made the list, create five or six questions that get at the most important points students should take away from the unit.
- Computers/devices and internet access for students

DIRECTIONS

Introductory Activity: Read the Flight Safety Foundation's *AeroSafety World* article, "Go or No-Go?" by Oddvard Johnsen, to the students.[4] Pose the question, "How did weather factor into the pilot's decision?" Solicit student responses and discuss the scenario.

Introduce the PAVE checklist from Chapter 2 in the *Pilot's Handbook of Aeronautical Knowledge*, calling attention to the V (Environment) component that is the topic of weather in this chapter. Using the scenario in the article, consider the weather-related prompts together as a whole class.

1. What is the current ceiling and visibility? In mountainous terrain, consider having higher minimums for ceiling and visibility, particularly if the terrain is unfamiliar.
2. Consider the possibility that the weather may be different than forecast. Have alternative plans and be ready and willing to divert, should an unexpected change occur.
3. Consider the winds at the airports being used and the strength of the crosswind component.
4. If flying in mountainous terrain, consider whether there are strong winds aloft. Strong winds in mountainous terrain can cause severe turbulence and downdrafts and be very hazardous for aircraft even when there is no other significant weather.
5. Are there any thunderstorms present or forecast?

6. If there are clouds, is there any icing, current or forecast? What is the temperature/dew point spread and the current temperature at altitude? Can descent be made safely all along the route?

7. If icing conditions are encountered, is the pilot experienced at operating the aircraft's deicing or anti-icing equipment? Is this equipment in good condition and functional? For what icing conditions is the aircraft rated, if any?

Step 1: Direct students to the worksheet of various go and no-go scenarios in Activity 1 (Go/Go-No Decision Scenarios) in the Student Notebook. Process through the decision for the first two scenario examples with students, demonstrating your thinking and providing supporting reasons from weather theory.

Step 2: Next, have students complete Go/No-Go Scenarios 3 and 4 in pairs.

Step 3: Finally, have students complete the last Go/No-Go scenario independently. Continue to question, prompt, and cue students. Clarify any errors; if you notice a pattern of errors, address the issue with the whole class. (An answer key is provided at the end of the chapter.)

Step 4: Students will share their independently completed scenario decision with a partner and compare responses and reasons.

Concluding Activity: Arrange students into groups of 4–5 students; mix student ability levels within each group. Assign each group one of the review questions you created that highlight the "essential learning" that students should carry away from the unit just completed. Students will write a "Study Guide" summarizing the most important information about the question/topic. Explain to students that you will present each group with a "big question" related to the topic of study. Their goal is to create a study guide of no more than a single page presenting everything their classmates "need to know" about that question. Students will share in their groups their "first response" ideas to their question. This activity is completed without referring to books. One student in each group will record the students' responses.

Homework: Students will work on their own to supplement the group's "first responses" to the question. They can refer to textbooks, class notes, or other key resources for more information.

LESSON 7

REVIEW: WEATHER

PURPOSE
The purpose of this lesson is to review and assess student knowledge and application of weather theory to flight and aeronautical decision-making.

ACCOMMODATIONS FOR LEARNING DIFFERENCES
It is important that lessons accommodate the needs of every learner. These lessons may be modified to accommodate your students with learning differences by referring to **www.pacer.org/parent/php/PHP-c267.pdf**.

PREPARATION
- Class copies of *Pilot's Handbook of Aeronautical Knowledge* (FAA-H-8083-25)
- Review Prep: make a list of the four or five major concepts you want students to learn/know as a result of this study unit. Once you've made the list, create five or six questions that get at the most important points students should take away from the unit.
- Access to Aviation Weather Center's Aviation Digital Data Service (ADDS) (**www.aviationweather.gov**)

DIRECTIONS

Introductory Activity: Pull up the current weather for your location at this exact time using the Aviation Weather Center (**www.aviationweather.gov/adds/**), or let students select airport locations around the country. Display relevant current weather information visually. In pairs or small groups, have students decode the weather, decide if they would fly today or not, and provide reasons for their decision supported by weather theory.

Step 1: Arrange students back into the groups set up at the end of Lesson 6. Students will share the results of their review question research conducted independently as homework.

Step 2: Students will determine the most common and accurate responses. As a group, they will agree on the responses and include them on the web graphic organizer in Activity 1 (Review Questions Brainstorming) in the Student Notebook. Each small group will share their questions and answers with the whole group and all students will record these questions and responses on the Review Questions Brainstorming graphic organizer. The facilitator will encourage students to list the final questions and beneath each question include three or four points to justify the answer.

Step 3: The facilitator can choose to share or post all student responses digitally via email or on a class website.

Concluding Activity: Students will ask each other the questions and practice providing responses to review for the exam in Lesson 8.

CHAPTER 12   WEATHER

LESSON 8
CHAPTER 12 EXAM

PURPOSE
The purpose of this lesson is to assess student knowledge and application of weather theory to flight and aeronautical decision-making.

ACCOMMODATIONS FOR LEARNING DIFFERENCES
It is important that lessons accommodate the needs of every learner. These lessons may be modified to accommodate your students with learning differences by referring to **www.pacer.org/parent/php/PHP-c267.pdf.**

PREPARATION
- Exam copies
- Newsela teacher account with access to article assigned to class
- Computer/device access per student or paper copies of the article and questions
- Response rubric
- Access to Aviation Weather Center's Aviation Digital Data Service (ADDS) (**www.aviationweather.gov**)

DIRECTIONS

Introductory Activity: Re-engage the students on weather theory by pulling up current weather for your location at this exact time using the Aviation Weather Center (**www.aviationweathercenter.gov**). Display relevant current weather information visually. In pairs or small groups, have students decode the weather, decide if they would fly today or not, and provide reasons for their decision supported by weather theory. Review all the elements of the METAR and TAF, questioning students to answer each. Before beginning the exam, provide instructions on what students are to do after they have completed their tests.

Step 1: Students will complete the Chapter 12 weather exam. Questions are available at the end of this lesson. (An answer key is provided at the end of the chapter.)

Step 2: When students have turned in the exam, have them independently read the article, "A few choose to climb world's tallest mountain without bottled oxygen" by *The Washington Post*, available on Newsela.[5] Students will complete the four-question automated quiz with the article on Newsela. Under Activity 1 (Article Response and Rubric) in the Student Notebook, have students write a two-paragraph response that includes a summary and reflection on the prompts: (1) How would the hypoxia experienced by the mountain climbers impact a pilot and flight safety? and (2) Explain the impact/importance of a pilot's health and understanding of physiological factors on flight performance. Responses will be graded using the rubric provided in the Student Notebook.

Concluding Activity: No formal summary activity. Students will work independently to finish the exam at different times and begin reading the article as an introductory activity to Chapter 13 on aeromedical factors.

The facilitator may decide to review the correct exam answers to address incorrect responses and/or misconceptions prior to beginning Chapter 13.

FACILITATOR INFORMATION

Chapter 12 Exam: Weather

(This exam is available in the online Instructor Resources in a format ready for use in the classroom. An answer key is provided at the end of the chapter.)

1. The Coriolis force deflects air to the right in the Northern Hemisphere.
    a. True
    b. False

2. The airflow surrounding a low-pressure system rotates clockwise.
    a. True
    b. False

3. The "E" in the PAVE model stands for environment.
    a. True
    b. False

4. What layer of the atmosphere has the greatest impact on weather?
    a. Troposphere
    b. Stratosphere
    c. Mesosphere
    d. Thermosphere

5. What is an indication that a front has passed through the area?
    a. Change in temperature
    b. Change in clouds/cloud cover
    c. Change in pressure
    d. All of the above could be an indication

6. What is the cloud ceiling height in the following METAR?
    ```
    KBAZ 111358Z AUTO 20004KT 5SM HZ SCT007 SCT018 BKN026 26/23 A3010
    RMK AO2 SLP186
    ```
    a. Scattered at 700 feet
    b. Scattered at 1800 feet
    c. Broken at 2600 feet

7. Is the cloud height value MSL or AGL in the following METAR?

    KBAZ 111358Z AUTO 20004KT 5SM HZ SCT007 SCT018 BKN026 26/23 A3010 RMK AO2 SLP186?

    a. MSL

    b. AGL

8. What does the abbreviation "HZ" mean in the following METAR?

    KBAZ 111358Z AUTO 20004KT 5SM HZ SCT007 SCT018 BKN026 26/23 A3010 RMK AO2 SLP186

    a. Hazardous weather

    b. Height above touchdown zone

    c. Haze

9. How would you decode the altimeter setting from the following METAR?

    KBAZ 111358Z AUTO 20004KT 5SM HZ SCT007 SCT018 BKN026 26/23 A3010 RMK AO2 SLP186

    a. 3.010

    b. 30.10

    c. 301.0

    d. 3010

10. What is the sea level pressure in the following METAR?

    KBAZ 111358Z AUTO 20004KT 5SM HZ SCT007 SCT018 BKN026 26/23 A3010 RMK AO2 SLP186

    a. 186

    b. 918.6

    c. 1018.6

11. You want to go fly at 10:00 a.m. local time. According to the TAF, what kind of visibility can you expect?

    TAF AMD KGLD 311316Z 3113/0112 VRB05KT P6SM BKN025 BKN100
       FM311500 17012KT P6SM VCTS FEW040CB BKN100
       FM312100 18015KT P6SM BKN250 TEMPO 3121/0101 5SM -TSRA BKN040CB
       FM010500 14010KT P6SM FEW040 BKN250=

    a. Less than 6 SM

    b. Greater than 6 SM

    c. 5 SM

12. What type of clouds is forecast for a flight at 1900 in reference to the TAF below?

    ```
    TAF AMD KGLD 311316Z 3113/0112 VRB05KT P6SM BKN025 BKN100
      FM311500 17012KT P6SM VCTS FEW040CB BKN100
      FM312100 18015KT P6SM BKN250 TEMPO 3121/0101 5SM -TSRA BKN040CB
      FM010500 14010KT P6SM FEWC40 BKN250=
    ```

    a. Cirrus

    b. Cumulonimbus

    c. Nimbostratus

For questions 13–15, refer to the following low-level significant weather prognostic chart.

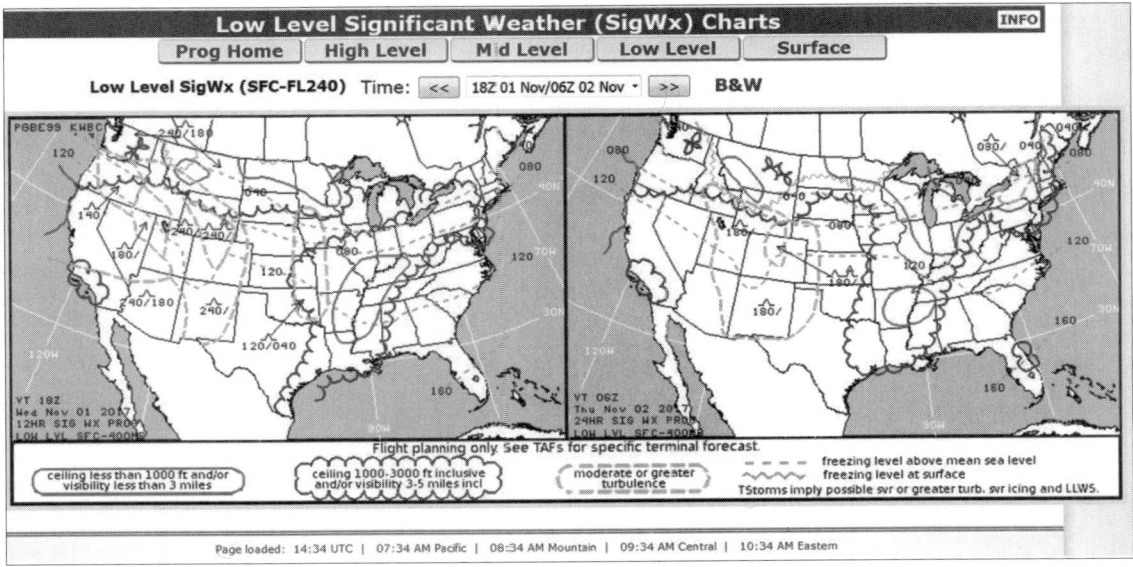

▶ Low-Level Significant Weather Prognostic Chart. *(NWS Aviation Weather Center)*

13. Referencing the 12 hr prog chart, what is the ceiling and visibility for the northern half of North Dakota?

    a. Better than 3000 feet ceiling and/or better than 5 SM visibility

    b. Ceiling 1,000–3,000 feet and/or 3–5 SM visibility

    c. Ceiling less than 1,000 feet and/or less than 3 SM visibility

14. Referencing the 12 hr prog chart, at what altitudes will you find turbulence in NE Oklahoma?

    a. Surface to 12,000 feet

    b. Surface to 4,000 feet

    c. 4,000 to 12,000 feet

    d. Above 12,000 feet

15. Referencing the 24 hr prog chart, what is the freezing level through central Iowa?
    a. Surface
    b. 4,000 feet
    c. 8,000 feet
    d. 12,000 feet

For questions 16–18, refer to the following winds and temperatures aloft forecast.

```
DATA BASED ON 110000Z
VALID 111200Z    FOR USE 0900-1800Z. TEMPS NEG ABV 24000
FT   3000   6000     9000     12000    18000    24000    30000    34000    39000
DIK         2920+12  3225+04  3237-03  3150-12  3161-23  317539   328550   811758
GFK  3317   3226+05  3231-01  3235-06  3145-19  3166-29  319342   318949   317050
MOT         3120+08  3134+01  3143-05  3152-16  3273-24  317740   317350   317056
```

16. What are the Winds and Temperatures aloft for MOT at 18,000 feet?
    a. 315 degrees at 2 knots, –16 degrees F
    b. 315 degrees at 2 knots, –16 degrees C
    c. 310 degrees at 52 knots, –16 degrees F
    d. 310 degrees at 52 knots, –16 degrees C

17. What are the winds aloft for DIK at 39,000 feet?
    a   310 degrees at 117 knots
    b. 810 degrees at 17 knots
    c. 031 degrees at 117 knots

18. Why are there no winds forecasted for MOT and DIK at 3,000 feet?
    a. No winds are forecast within 2,500 feet of the field elevation
    b. No winds are forecast within 1,500 feet of the field elevation

19. AIRMET Sierra is issued for:
    a. Icing
    b. IFR conditions and mountain obscurations
    c. Turbulence

20. What type of turbulence would an AIRMET be issued for?
    a. Severe
    b. Extreme
    c. Moderate

21. At what altitudes is the turbulence expected to be at for the AIRMET affecting LM, MI, LH?

    ```
    CHIT WA 110845
    AIRMET TANGO UPDT 1 FOR TURB VALID UNTIL 111500
    AIRMET TURB...LM MI LH
    FROM 20E SSM TO 20ESE SSM TO 30ESE GRR TO 30SW MKG TO 30NW MKG
    TO 30W TVC TO 40SW SSM TO 20E SSM MOD TURB BLW 030. CONDS ENDG
    11-13Z.-SKC
    ```

    a. Between 2,000 and 4,000 feet

    b. Between 2,000 and 3,000 feet

    c. Below 3,000 feet

    d. Above 3,000 feet

22. What is one reason a SIGMET would be issued?

    a. Tornado

    b. Embedded thunderstorms

    c. Volcanic ash

ANSWER KEYS
CHAPTER 12

LESSON 3, Activity 3
METAR Worksheet

1. −10°C
2. Coming from 140 degrees at 7 knots
3. 9 SM
4. Clear
5. −21°C
6. Overcast 2,800 feet
7. Snow
8. Light
9. Coming from 290 at 15 gusting to 18 knots
10. 30.17
11. Overcast at 2,200 feet
12. Calm
13. Rain and mist
14. Heavy rain and moderate mist
15. The 17th of the month at 1355 Zulu
16. It is an automated station
17. Vertical visibility of 500 feet
18. Freezing fog
19. Overcast at 100 feet
20. ¼ SM

LESSON 6, Activity 1
Go/No-Go Decision Scenarios

Scenario 1: The <u>Environment</u>: The winds are not that far off from the runway; however, they are 16 knots. Sixteen knots is a good amount of wind, so you need to ask yourself what kind of winds you have flown in before—that is the <u>Pilot</u> part of the PAVE model. The sky is clear and you have good visibility. It should be a good day to go fly. You have just conducted a preflight so hopefully the <u>Aircraft</u> is good to go. Are there any <u>External</u> pressures forcing you to go fly this day?

Scenario 2: The students' answers should reflect some of the following items using the PAVE Model:

Pilot: Are you comfortable flying today? How are you feeling?

Aircraft: Is everything working in the aircraft today? Are you comfortable with the cockpit configuration and radios? Are you within weight and balance limits for this cross-country flight?

Environment: Do you feel comfortable with the weather? Is it within your personal weather minimums? There are clear skies, good visibility, wind seems fairly light, but it is cold out. The TAF is calling for the clouds to become broken at 2,000 feet between 0700 and 1000 Zulu, and with it being cold there will be ice in the clouds.

External Pressures: Are there any external pressures forcing you to go fly this day?

Go/No-Go decision: depends on what time you will be in the air. If you are able to land before the ceiling comes down you could go.

Scenario 3: Pilot: With the low clouds and potential for snow showers, there will most likely be a reduction in flight visibility. Are you instrument rated? Have you flown in low visibility before?

Aircraft: Is your aircraft approved to fly into icing conditions?

Environment: The temperature is below freezing and there are clouds. There is potential for icing.

External Pressures: Are there any external pressures forcing you to go fly this day?

Go/No-Go Decision: Most likely not a good day to go fly.

Scenario 4: Pilot: Do you like getting bounced around continually throughout the flight? Most likely not.

Aircraft: Is your aircraft able to climb to a high altitude to distance yourself from the ground and convective turbulence?

Environment: We know that it is warm and the uneven heating of the Earth's surface creates the formation of convective turbulence.

External pressures: Are there any external pressures forcing you to go fly this day?

Go/No-Go Decision: The higher you are, the better to avoid this.

Scenario 5: Pilot: What is your experience flying around areas of precipitation? Are you current to fly that aircraft? How are you feeling today?

Aircraft: What kind of aircraft are you flying? Does it have weather radar?

Environment: Heavy rain could mean reduced visibility. If thunderstorms pop up, where will you divert? Thunderstorms have lots of hazards including hail, lightning, strong winds, heavy rain, tornadoes and turbulence. These things could cause damage to the aircraft and make it difficult to complete your flight.

External pressures: Are there any external pressures forcing you to go fly this day?

Go/No-Go Decision: It's not a good day to go fly.

LESSON 8
Chapter 12 Exam

1. (a) True
2. (b) False
3. (b) False
4. (a) Troposphere
5. (d) All of the above could be an indication
6. (c) Broken at 2600 feet
7. (b) AGL
8. (c) Haze
9. (b) 30.10
10. (c) 1018.6
11. (b) Greater than 6 SM
12. (b) Cumulonimbus
13. (c) Ceiling less than 1,000 feet and/or less than 3 SM visibility
14. (c) 4,000 to 12,000 feet
15. (c) 8,000 feet
16. (d) 310 degrees at 52 knots, −16 degrees C
17. (a) 310 degrees at 117 knots
18. (b) No winds are forecast within 1,500 feet of the field elevation
19. (b) IFR conditions and mountain obscurations
20. (c) Moderate
21. (c) Below 3,000 feet
22. (c) Volcanic ash

CHAPTER 13
AEROMEDICAL FACTORS

Introduction

STANDARDS & OBJECTIVES
North Dakota Aviation Content Standards (Grades 10–12)
- 4.3.2—Discuss the IMSAFE checklist.
- 4.3.3—Describe the medical qualifications requirements for pilots.
- 4.3.5—Identify each type of hypoxia and associated causes.
- 4.3.6—Describe symptoms of hypoxia.
- 4.3.7—Describe corrective actions for hypoxia.
- 4.3.8—Explain the development of night vision.
- 4.3.9—Discuss the importance of spatial awareness and disorientation.

Science—Next Generation Science Standards (Grades 9–12)
- HS-PS3-2—Develop and use models to illustrate that energy is associated with motion and relative position of particles (objects).
- HS-LS1-2—Develop and use a model to illustrate the hierarchical organization of interacting systems that provide specific functions within multicellular organisms.

Language Arts—CCSS.ELA-LITERACY.CCRA
- L.1—Demonstrate command of the conventions of standard English grammar and usage when writing or speaking.
- L.2—Demonstrate command of the conventions of standard English capitalization, punctuation, and spelling when writing.
- R.1—Read closely to determine what the text says explicitly and to make logical inferences from it; cite specific textual evidence when writing or speaking to support conclusions drawn from the text.
- R.10—Read and comprehend complex literary and informational texts independently and proficiently.
- W.2—Write informative/explanatory texts to examine and convey complex ideas and information clearly and accurately through the effective selection, organization, and analysis of content.
- W.4—Produce clear and coherent writing in which the development, organization, and style are appropriate to task, purpose and audience.
- W.9—Draw evidence from literary or informational texts to support analysis, reflection, and research.

ESSENTIAL QUESTIONS

- What are some examples of how poor health (mental or physical) relates to pilot performance?
- How might technology change how we monitor our health in the aircraft?
- Why must a pilot be aware of mental and physical standards for flight?
- What are the requirements of different medical certificates?
- How could medical conditions affect flying and decision-making?

LESSONS

Lesson	Topic	Student Notebook Activities
Lesson 1	IMSAFE Checklist	1. Before Graphic Organizer 2. IMSAFE Acronym
Lesson 2	Hypoxia and Hyperventilation	1. Guided Notes 2. Video Observations
Lesson 3	Other Aeromedical Factors	1. Illusion Training Graphic Organizer 2. Aeromedical Factors Outline

Lesson 4	Visual Illusions	1. Illusions Presentations
		  • *Presentation Checklist*
		  • *Illusions Presentations Graphic Organizer*

Lesson 5	Night Flight	1. Differences Between Flying During the Day and at Night 2. Night Flight Video Questions 3. Eyes and Night Vision Questions
Lesson 6	Review: Aeromedical Factors	1. Vocabulary BINGO 2. After Graphic Organizer
Lesson 7	Chapter 13 Exam	1. Article Response and Rubric

CHAPTER 13 AEROMEDICAL FACTORS

LESSON 1
IMSAFE CHECKLIST

PURPOSE
The purpose of this lesson is to provide the student with a self-awareness tool to assess if they are fit to fly an aircraft.

ACCOMMODATIONS FOR LEARNING DIFFERENCES
It is important that lessons accommodate the needs of every learner. These lessons may be modified to accommodate your students with learning differences by referring to www.pacer.org/parent/php/PHP-c267.pdf.

PREPARATION
- Class copies of *Aeronautical Information Manual*, Chapter 8: Medical Facts for Pilots, Section 1: Fitness for Flight (available on FAA's website)
- Blank note cards

DIRECTIONS
Introductory Activity: As a way to preview the information for aeromedical factors, have students complete the graphic organizer in Activity 1 (Before Graphic Organizer) in their Student Notebooks. Read through the statements aloud and have students indicate whether they agree or disagree by checking the appropriate column as you read each statement.

- If you want an aviation medical, go see a medical doctor.
- You should not fly if you are taking any medication.
- The Federal Aviation Regulations require 8 hours between drinking and flying.
- The effects of hypoxia can occur at low altitudes.
- Hyperventilation is when your body expels too much oxygen.
- Carbon monoxide poisoning is a real concern for pilots while flying.
- Ear blocks are more painful when climbing than descending.
- A somatogravic illusion is due to slow bank.
- The parts of your eyes that you use at night are called the cones.

Using the same graphic organizer, this exercise will be repeated in Lesson 6 of this chapter so students can compare their before and after responses. The correct answers to these statements can be found in the answer key at the end of the chapter.

Step 1: Write the acronym IMSAFE vertically on the board. As a review from Chapter 1, ask students to recall what each letter of the acronym stands for. Write the correct representation on the board (refer to the figure below). Students can record the IMSAFE acronym and what it stands for in Activity 2 (IMSAFE Acronym) in the Student Notebook.

I'M SAFE Checklist

Illness	Do I have any symptoms?
Medication	Have I been taking prescription or over-the-counter drugs?
Stress	Am I under psychological pressure from the job? Am I worried about financial matters, health problems, or family discord?
Alcohol	Have I been drinking within 8 hours?
Fatigue	Am I tired and not adequately rested?
Emotion	Am I emotionally upset?

Step 2: The facilitator will go through each of factors and describe in detail why each is important. The following questions could be used to facilitate a discussion:

- Illness:
  - "Can you sit in a car and read a book? Why or why not? How will that affect your ability to fly?" (*Answer:* The problem is motion sickness. This affects our ability to make decisions whether we are in a car or in an aircraft.) Follow-up question: "How can a person fix or overcome motion sickness?" (*Answer:* The solution is to focus on something not moving outside of the cockpit, drink water, open the air vents.)
  - "You have a stomach ache. Do you think it's a good idea to fly? Why or why not? How will that affect your ability to fly?" (*Answer:* On the ground, what is causing your stomach ache? Did you eat? If not, maybe you need to eat. If you did eat, what did you eat? If you are uncomfortable on the ground, do you really want to get into an aircraft that most likely doesn't have a bathroom? Inflight, it could be motion sickness again, or even worse, it might be the flu. This affects your ability to make decisions and fly because the thoughts are now focused on how to get better rather than on flying the aircraft.) Follow-up question: "How could you fix or overcome this?" (*Answer:* The solution should be to find a sick sac, and decisions should be considered for how to continue your flight or divert to another airport.)
  - "You have a severe head cold. Do you think it's a good idea to fly? Why or why not? How will that affect your ability to fly?" (*Answer:* You could have a sinus block. This can cause severe pain, especially on descent. Think back to what happens to pressure as you climb and descend.) Follow-up question: "Which is more painful, a climb or a descent?" (*Answer:* Have students think back to an airline flight they have been on— when were the toddlers crying? The pain will be worse during descent because the pressure is greater. If this occurs during flight, the solution is to climb back up to the altitude you were flying at and then shallow the descent. Next time, don't go fly with a head cold. Most who have done it once will not ever do it again.)

- Medication:
  - "You are sick and just prescribed antibiotics by a doctor. Can you fly while taking this medication?" (*Answer:* It depends on the medication; ask the doctor or pharmacist before taking the medication.)
  - "You are taking over-the-counter medication. Can you fly while taking this medication?" (*Answer:* It depends on the medication, ask the doctor or pharmacist before taking the medication, etc.)
- Stress:
  - "You have a job interview today and were up all night preparing for it and are really nervous. You have a flight scheduled right before the interview. Should you go fly today? If you decide to go fly, will you be focused on your flight or the interview?" (*Answer*: If you are stressed, your focus will not be on flying the aircraft. Most likely you will be thinking about what is causing you the stress.)
- Alcohol:
  - "You went to a party last night and had a few drinks but stopped drinking at 11:00 p.m. You have a flight scheduled for 9:00 a.m. tomorrow. Are you legally able to go on the flight?" (*Answer:* The FAA requires 8 hours bottle to throttle, 14 CFR §91.17.)
- Fatigue:
  - "You only got 5 hours of sleep last night and have a cross country (3-hour) flight scheduled for this afternoon. How will the lack of sleep impact your flight?" (*Answer:* If you are fatigued, you are not able to focus on flying the aircraft. You may actually doze off in flight. Get some rest and you will be much more alert and on the top of your game for flying the aircraft.)
- Emotion/Eating:
  - "A close family member or friend was in a car accident last night and is in the hospital. You have a flight scheduled later today. Should you go fly today? Why or why not?" (*Answer:* You are worried about your family member or friend and are not able to fully concentrate on the flight.)
  - "You skipped breakfast this morning and have a flight scheduled over lunch. How might the lack of food impact your flight?" (*Answer:* You need nourishment to stay focused.)

Step 3: Have students turn to a partner and discuss other factors that may impact flight (weather, aircraft technology, head colds, air sickness, etc.). Lead a discussion to help students come up with several other factors.

Step 4: Pose the question, "Why is studying aeromedical factors important?" (*Answer:* You need to know what you are up against, you are training to be a private pilot, or you will probably be flying with passengers and they might experience these things.) Next, pose the question, "How do you get an aviation medical?" (*Answer:* An aviation medical examiner.) More information about obtaining a medical certificate can be found in the *Pilot's Handbook of Aeronautical Knowledge*, Chapter 17.

Concluding Activity: Hand each student a blank note card. Ask them to list IMSAFE vertically on their note card and have them write down what each letter represents. Review the correct acronym representations.

LESSON 2

HYPOXIA AND HYPERVENTILATION

PURPOSE

The purpose of this lesson is to develop the students' understanding of common medical conditions that affect pilots.

ACCOMMODATIONS FOR LEARNING DIFFERENCES

It is important that lessons accommodate the needs of every learner. These lessons may be modified to accommodate your students with learning differences by referring to **www.pacer.org/parent/php/PHP-c267.pdf**.

PREPARATION

- Class copies of *Pilot's Handbook of Aeronautical Knowledge* (FAA-H-8083-25)
- Access to internet
- Video screen

DIRECTIONS

Introductory Activity: Write the words "Hypoxia" and "Hyperventilation" on the board. Ask students to share what they know about the two words, allowing time for students to share what they know. Then, divide the class into an even number of groups (e.g., 2 groups, 4 groups, 6 groups, etc.). Assign half of the groups the word "hypoxia" and the other half of the groups the word "hyperventilation." Have students research the meanings of hypoxia and hyperventilation using Chapter 17 of the *Pilot's Handbook of Aeronautical Knowledge*. Give students 5–10 minutes to write a song, rap, or poem to help them remember the meaning of each word. Students will share the songs, rap, and poems with the whole group.

Step 1: Prepare a presentation to share the following information about hypoxia and hyperventilation:

- Hypoxia
  - Definition
  - Causes
  - Types (hypoxic, hypemic, stagnant, histotoxic)
  - Symptoms
  - Corrective actions
- Hyperventilation
  - Definition
  - Causes
  - Symptoms
  - Corrective actions

As you review the presentation, students can complete the hypoxia and hyperventilation Activity 1 (Guided Notes) in the Student Notebook, and refer to Chapter 17 in the *Pilot's Handbook of Aeronautical Knowledge*.

Step 2: Students will watch several videos on hypoxia and hyperventilation, taking notes on each video using the guided notes in Activity 2 (Video Observations) in their Student Notebooks. Show students the Altitude Chamber Hypoxia Training video.[1] Have students record what they observe in the video each minute, and hold a discussion about how each participant changes over the course of the video. Ask students what causes these changes? Stop and discuss some of the highlights of the video as they relate to hypoxia.

Step 3: Next, show students a video of centrifuge G-force training (search online for videos or see the online Instructor Resources). Have students record what they observed (how do the participants look and what happens to their breathing) in the video and explain why they think the military requires this training (*Answer:* Pilots will pass out in flight without this training). Lead a discussion to decide what type of hypoxia is represented in the video. (*Answer:* stagnant hypoxia.)

Concluding Activity: Ask students to revisit their poems or songs, changing words or lines now that they have watched the videos. Students can once again share their poems/songs with the whole group as time allows.

LESSON 3

OTHER AEROMEDICAL FACTORS

PURPOSE

The purpose of this lesson is to develop the students' understanding of common medical conditions that affect pilots.

ACCOMMODATIONS FOR LEARNING DIFFERENCES

It is important that lessons accommodate the needs of every learner. These lessons may be modified to accommodate your students with learning differences by referring to www.pacer.org/parent/php/PHP-c267.pdf.

PREPARATION

- Access to internet
- Screen to show video
- *Aeronautical Information Manual* (AIM)
- *Pilot's Handbook of Aeronautical Knowledge* (FAA-H-8083-25)

DIRECTIONS

Introductory Activity: Show students the UND video on aerobatics: "UND Aerobatics: You're Next!".[2] Ask students to write down in Student Notebook Activity 1 (Illusion Training Graphic Organizer) how the pilots have trained their bodies to handle the illusions.

Step 1: Create a presentation with information on aeromedical factors, including the definitions, symptoms, and remedies/reactions:

- Decompression sickness
- Ear block
- Sinus block
- Toothaches
- Carbon monoxide poisoning
- Motion sickness
- Blood donation
- Dehydration
- Oxygen use

More information on these specific aeromedical factors can be found in Chapter 17 of the *Pilot's Handbook of Aeronautical Knowledge* and in Chapter 8 of the *Aeronautical Information Manual*.

Step 2: As students interact with the content through the presentation, they will be taking notes using Activity 2 (Aeromedical Factors Outline) found in their Student Notebooks.

Concluding Activity: Have students share one thing they learned about aeromedical factors that affect a pilot's performance. Have students share one question they still have about aeromedical factors. Answer students' questions as time allows.

CHAPTER 13 AEROMEDICAL FACTORS

LESSON 4
VISUAL ILLUSIONS

PURPOSE
The purpose of this lesson is to develop the students' understanding of the sensory illusions that commonly affect pilots.

ACCOMMODATIONS FOR LEARNING DIFFERENCES
It is important that lessons accommodate the needs of every learner. These lessons may be modified to accommodate your students with learning differences by referring to **www.pacer.org/parent/php/PHP-c267.pdf.**

PREPARATION
- *Pilot's Handbook of Aeronautical Knowledge* (FAA-H-8083-25)
- Access to internet
- Screen for video

DIRECTIONS

Introductory Activity: Define spatial orientation versus spatial disorientation (see *Pilot's Handbook of Aeronautical Knowledge*, Chapter 17, for more information on defining spatial orientation vs. spatial disorientation). Ask students to make note of the differences between spatial orientation and spatial disorientation as well as the illusions that spatial disorientation cause. Prompt students to recall the video "178 Seconds to Live" shown in Chapter 10, Lesson 7. Then show the Air Safety Institute video, "Accident Case Study: VFR into IMC."[3] Points of discussion to share with students related to factors that affect spatial orientation and can lead to spatial disorientation include: deteriorating weather (uneven cloud decks and reducing visibility), night time, broken flight instruments, distractions in the cockpit, etc.

Step 1: Split the students into groups of 3–4. Small groups will work together to create a multimedia presentation for an assigned topic related to spatial disorientation illusions. Topics to choose from include:

- **Vestibular Illusions:** The leans, Coriolis illusion, graveyard spiral, somatogravic illusion, inversion illusion, elevator illusion
- **Visual Illusions:** False horizon, Autokinesis
- **Optical Illusions:** runway width, slope, terrain, precipitation, and ground lighting illusions (information on these illusions can be found in Chapter 17 of the *Pilot's Handbook of Aeronautical Knowledge*).

Step 2: Presentations will include the following elements, as outlined in the Student Notebook under Activity 1 (Illusions Presentations):

- Name of Illusion
- Definition
- Why might a pilot experience this?
- How should a pilot learn to avoid this?
- Visual examples (pictures and/or videos)

Step 3: Students will create the presentations and share them in class. Each presentation will take approximately 3–5 minutes per illusion to complete. Refer to the Instructor Resources for videos to provide help for students who are looking for examples of each type of illusion.

Step 4: While small groups are presenting, the remaining students will complete the Illusions Presentations Graphic Organizer in their Student Notebooks to record the main points of each presentation. The facilitator can supplement the presentations by adding commentary relevant to the topic.

Concluding Activity: To conclude the lesson, show students the Smithsonian Channel video, "Does This Scenario Explain JFK Jr.'s Plane Crash," related to JFK Jr.'s death.[4] Have students identify which vestibular illusion lead to his death.

LESSON 5

NIGHT FLIGHT

PURPOSE

The purpose of the lesson is to develop the students' understanding of the effects of night operations on a pilot.

ACCOMMODATIONS FOR LEARNING DIFFERENCES

It is important that lessons accommodate the needs of every learner. These lessons may be modified to accommodate your students with learning differences by referring to **www.pacer.org/parent/php/PHP-c267.pdf**.

PREPARATION

- Access to internet
- Screen for video
- *Pilot's Handbook of Aeronautical Knowledge* (FAA-H-8083-25)

DIRECTIONS

Introductory Activity: Under Activity 1 in the Student Notebook, have the students write down what they think are the differences between flying during the day versus flying at night. Hint: Have them think of the visual illusions that were discussed during previous lessons in this chapter.

Step 1: As the facilitator, preview (prior to the lesson) the video showing a student pilot's first night flight and then show it to students.[5] This video is of a student pilot and his flight instructor on the student's first night flight. Stop the video at certain points to have the students write down their observations in Activity 2 (Night Flight Video Questions) in their Student Notebooks. An explanation of the answers will come in a later part of the lesson.

- 1:17—What color is the light on the flashlight? (*Answer:* Red)
- 2:02—Describe how easy or difficult it is to see the runway. (*Answer:* Find the white outline of the runway.)
- 2:10—What colors are the PAPIs (the four lights on the left side of the runway)? (*Answer:* All four lights were white; one eventually turns red.)
- 4:47—How does this touchdown compare to his first? (*Answer:* The touchdown was harder than the first.)
- 8:30—What did the student forget to turn on? How did this impact his landing? (*Answer:* He forgot to turn on the landing light; his landing was firmer/harder.)

Step 2: Create a presentation to discuss how the human eye works at night. Reference Chapter 17 in the *Pilot's Handbook of Aeronautical Knowledge* and the information below to create the presentation.

- Human eye:
  - Cones vs. rods
- Night vision:
  - Time it takes for your eyes to adapt to the darkness (approximately 30 minutes)
  - Techniques to save your night vision (close one eye, sunglasses, etc.)
- Lighting:
  - How to conduct a preflight at night. What color flashlight should be used. (White light, you need to be able to identify the color of the fuel.)
  - Inflight interior light
    - Flashlight (red flashlight; white will degrade your night vision)
    - Cockpit lighting (adjusting the setting to an appropriate level for night flight, similar to driving a car at night)
- Navigation, specifically pilotage
  - Day vs. night checkpoints (things need to be lit to be used at night)
  - Lack of visual cues (in dark, it's hard to make out horizon vs. sky)
- Landing
  - When to flare (lack of visual cues and change in depth perception)

Step 3: While the facilitator is presenting the material, students should follow along and record answers to the following questions in Activity 3 (Eyes and Night Vision Questions) in their Student Notebooks.

1. What do the cones do?
2. What do the rods do?
3. Where is your night blind spot?
4. How should your scan differ between a day flight and night flight?
5. How long does it take for your eyes to adjust to the dark?
6. How should you adjust your in-flight lighting at night?
7. What color flashlight should you use for exterior preflight? Why?
8. What color flashlight should you use while in flight? Why?
9. If, after preflight, you have to go back inside the FBO to go to the bathroom, how do you save your night vision?

Step 4: Now that the students have an understanding of night flight, have them go back to their answers from the night flight video shown at the onset of this lesson and the chart listing differences between day and night flying. Those answers can be found in Activities 1 and 2 in their Student Notebooks. Have students independently evaluate if the factors they listed are actually different when flying during the day compared to when flying at night. Have students circle the factors that are different during the day versus the night and explain their answers to their neighbor.

Concluding Activity: Pose the following question: "When navigating at night, what is a better checkpoint: a major road or a large body of water? Describe why?" (*Answer:* A major road where you know there would be traffic; bodies of water do not have lights on them.)

LESSON 6

REVIEW: AEROMEDICAL FACTORS

PURPOSE
The purpose of the lesson is to review important concepts related to aeromedical factors.

ACCOMMODATIONS FOR LEARNING DIFFERENCES
It is important that lessons accommodate the needs of every learner. These lessons may be modified to accommodate your students with learning differences by referring to **www.pacer.org/parent/php/PHP-c267.pdf**.

PREPARATION
- Markers for BINGO game
- *Pilot's Handbook of Aeronautical Knowledge* (FAA-H-8083-25)

DIRECTIONS

Introductory Activity: List the vocabulary words discussed throughout Chapter 13 on the board. Examples may include: hypoxia, hyperventilation, motion sickness, etc. Lead a discussion with students, highlighting the definitions of several key vocabulary terms.

Step 1: Using the vocabulary words you listed on the board from this chapter, instruct students to write the words randomly in the blank squares on the BINGO card in Activity 1 (Vocabulary BINGO) in their Student Notebooks. The class will play BINGO to practice the vocabulary learned in this chapter.

Step 2: Incorporate the aeromedical factors vocabulary words in the list you generated above by reading sentences from Chapter 17 in the *Pilot's Handbook of Aeronautical Knowledge*. As vocabulary terms are read, lead a discussion on the definition of these words by asking the students for the meaning of the vocabulary words in the sentences. After the words are called out and discussed, students will place a marker (coin, colored chips, etc.) over the correct vocabulary word.

When a student marks five places in a row (horizontal, vertical, or diagonal), that student calls out "BINGO." Check his or her card to make sure the student placed markers over the correct words. If the student marked the card correctly, that student wins a prize. You may choose to give extra credit points on the exam or hand out incentives (free flight simulator minutes, candy, UAV time, etc.).

Step 3: You may continue playing BINGO as many times as you choose. Allow five or ten minutes at the end of class to collect the markers (coins, colored chips, etc.) and to review the words one more time.

Concluding Activity: As a way to review what students have learned about aeromedical factors, have students complete the graphic organizer found in Activity 2 (After Graphic Organizer) in their Student Notebooks. Just as you did in Lesson 1, read through the statements aloud and have students indicate whether they agree or disagree by marking the appropriate column. The correct answers to these statements can be found in the answer key at the end of this chapter.

LESSON 7

CHAPTER 13 EXAM

PURPOSE

The purpose of this lesson is to assess the students' knowledge regarding aeromedical factors.

ACCOMMODATIONS FOR LEARNING DIFFERENCES

It is important that lessons accommodate the needs of every learner. These lessons may be modified to accommodate your students with learning differences by referring to **www.pacer.org/parent/php/PHP-c267.pdf.**

PREPARATION

- Copies of exam
- Computer/device access per student or paper copies of the article and questions

DIRECTIONS

Introductory Activity: Re-engage the students on aeromedical factors by sharing one of the most interesting and unusual pieces of information students learned in this chapter. Have students turn and talk with a partner about what impact these aeromedical factors have on the field of aviation. Provide instructions regarding what students are to do after the exam if they complete it early.

Step 1: Students will complete the Chapter 13 exam. The exam must include questions and prompts from the test bank provided under Facilitator Information below. (An answer key is provided at the end of the chapter.)

Step 2: When students have turned in the exam, have them independently read the article, "How coronavirus grounded the airline industry," from *The Washington Post*.[6] Students will write a one-paragraph response that includes a summary and reflection on the prompts:

1. Describe your thoughts on seeing how the air travel changed in China, the Middle East, and Europe prior to March 24.
2. When watching the animation of air travel over the United States, why does there appear to be a gap in the flights between Indianapolis and the District of Columbia?
3. Describe your thoughts on reading about the financial impact of COVID-19 on the airlines.
4. Describe your thoughts when seeing the pictures of the numerous airports where airplanes are parked across the world.

It will be graded using the rubric provided in the Student Notebook.

Concluding Activity: No formal summary activity. Students will work independently to finish the exam at different times and begin reading the article as an introductory activity to Chapter 14 on cross-country flight. The facilitator may decide to review the correct exam answers to address incorrect responses and/or misconceptions prior to beginning Chapter 14.

FACILITATOR INFORMATION

Chapter 13 Exam: Aeromedical Factors

(This exam is available in the online Instructor Resources in a format ready for use in the classroom. An answer key is provided at the end of the chapter.)

1. Over-the-counter medications are all OK to be taken before flight.
    a. True
    b. False

2. Spatial disorientation illusions typically occur in good weather.
    a. True
    b. False

3. Inversion illusion is caused by an abrupt change from a climb to straight-and-level flight.
    a. True
    b. False

4. The Federal Aviation Regulations require a minimum of 12 hours bottle to throttle.
    a. True
    b. False

5. Why is hypoxia particularly dangerous during flights with one pilot?

6. Which type of hypoxia is caused by being at a high altitude?

7. Which type of hypoxia is caused by you pulling excessive G forces?

8. What is hypemic hypoxia?

9. What are the common symptoms of hypoxia?

10. What happens to time of useful consciousness as you increase in altitude?

11. Hyperventilation is the lack of what?

12. Which procedure is recommended to prevent or overcome spatial disorientation?

13. A rapid acceleration during takeoff can create the illusion of a climb.
    a. True
    b. False

14. A sloping cloud formation, an obscured horizon, and a dark scene spread with ground lights and stars can create an illusion known as false horizons.

    a. True

    b. False

15. What are "the leans" caused by?

16. Which illusion is caused by an abrupt head movement?

17. Which illusion is caused by an abrupt vertical acceleration that results from up or down drafts?

18. A loss of altitude during a prolonged, coordinated, constant-rate turn creates the illusion of being in a descent with the wings level and causes the disoriented pilot to pull back on the controls, tightening the turn and increasing the loss of altitude. What illusion is this?

19. At night, which part of the eye do we rely on?

20. At night, if you choose to focus on an object for a prolonged period of time, that object may appear to move. This is an example of what illusion?

21. Due to the visual illusion when landing on a narrower-than-usual runway, the aircraft will appear to be lower than normal.

    a. True

    b. False

22. A downsloping runway gives the pilot the illusion that they are lower than normal.

    a. True

    b. False

23. Blocked ear and blocked sinus issues are typically problems that occur in climb.

    a. True

    b. False

24. You are flying with a non-pilot friend and you notice that your friend is looking kind of pale, is sweating, and is quieter than normal. What could the problem be?

25. If your passenger is getting motion sick and you tell him or her to look outside the window, what should the passenger look at?

26. How does stress impact your decision-making process?

27. If pilots are unsure if they can go fly while under a certain prescription medication, who can they ask to see if it is OK or not?

28. If a pilot goes scuba diving and does not have to control their ascent, how many hours does the pilot have to wait before they can go fly at less than 8,000 feet?

29. Define the elements of the IMSAFE checklist and describe what they mean to a pilot who is about to go fly.

ANSWER KEYS

CHAPTER 13

LESSON 1, Activity 1 (Before Graphic Organizer) & LESSON 6, Activity 2 (After Graphic Organizer)

Statement	Agree or Disagree
If you want an aviation medical, go see a medical doctor.	Disagree; you must visit an Aviation Medical Examiner (AME)
You should not fly if you are taking any medication.	It depends. You need to check with an AME or pharmacist to see how the medication impacts you.
The Federal Aviation Regulations require 8 hours between drinking and flying.	Agree, 14 CFR §91.17
The effects of hypoxia can occur at low altitudes.	Agree, hypoxic hypoxia is caused by high altitudes; hypemic, histotoxic, and stagnant hypoxia can occur at any altitude.
Hyperventilation is when your body expels too much oxygen.	Disagree, it occurs when your body has too much oxygen and is expelling too much carbon dioxide.
Carbon monoxide poisoning is a real concern for pilots while flying.	Agree; if you experience this, there is no way to fix it other than to get on the ground and wait for the side effects to subside.
Ear blocks are more painful when climbing than descending.	Disagree, it is more painful when descending, as the air pressure is greater at lower altitudes and there is more pressure pushing on your ear drums.
A somatogravic illusion is due to slow bank.	Disagree; it is due to a rapid acceleration.
The parts of your eyes that you use at night are called the cones.	Disagree; the rods are the part of the eye used for night vision.

LESSON 7
Chapter 13 Exam

1. (b) False
2. (b) False
3. (a) True
4. (b) False

5. A pilot may not recognize the symptoms, while another pilot on board may help to identify common symptoms. Single-pilot operations are more workload intensive. A single pilot may more quickly become overwhelmed when hypoxic.

6. Hypoxic

7. Stagnant

8. Hypemic hypoxia occurs when the blood is not able to take up and transport a sufficient amount of oxygen to the cells in the body. Hypemic means "not enough blood." This type of hypoxia is a result of oxygen deficiency in the blood, rather than a lack of inhaled oxygen, and can be caused by a variety of factors.

9. The symptoms of hypoxia vary with the individual, but common symptoms include cyanosis (blue fingernails and lips), headache, decreased response to stimuli and increased reaction time, impaired judgment, euphoria, visual impairment, drowsiness, lightheaded or dizzy sensation, tingling in fingers and toes, and numbness.

10. It decreases.

11. Hyperventilation is the excessive rate and depth of respiration leading to abnormal loss of carbon dioxide from the blood.

12. To prevent illusions and their potentially disastrous consequences, pilots can:
    - Understand the causes of these illusions and remain constantly alert for them. Take the opportunity to experience spatial disorientation illusions in a device, such as a Barany chair, a Vertigon, or a Virtual Reality Spatial Disorientation Demonstrator.
    - Always obtain and understand preflight weather briefings.
    - Before flying in marginal visibility (less than 3 miles) or where a visible horizon is not evident, such as flight over open water during the night, obtain training and maintain proficiency in aircraft control by reference to instruments.
    - Do not fly into adverse weather conditions or into dusk or darkness unless proficient in the use of flight instruments. If intending to fly at night, maintain night-flight currency and proficiency. Include cross-country and local operations at various airfields.
    - Ensure that when outside visual references are used, they are reliable, fixed points on the Earth's surface.
    - Avoid sudden head movement, particularly during takeoffs, turns, and approaches to landing.
    - Be physically tuned for flight into reduced visibility. Ensure proper rest, adequate diet, and, if flying at night, allow for night adaptation. Remember that illness, medication, alcohol, fatigue, sleep loss, and mild hypoxia are likely to increase susceptibility to spatial disorientation.
    - Most importantly, become proficient in the use of flight instruments and rely upon them. Trust the instruments and disregard your sensory perceptions.

13. (a) True

14. (a) True

15. A condition called "the leans" is the most common illusion during flight and is caused by a sudden return to level flight following a gradual and prolonged turn that went unnoticed by the pilot.

16. Coriolis illusion

17. Elevator illusion
18. Graveyard spiral
19. Rods
20. Autokinesis
21. (b) False
22. (a) True
23. (b) False
24. Motion sickness or airsickness
25. Focusing on objects outside the airplane that do not appear to be moving and avoiding unnecessary head movements may help alleviate some of the discomfort.
26. Chronic stress can be defined as a level of stress that presents an intolerable burden, exceeds the ability of an individual to cope, and causes individual performance to fall sharply. Unrelenting psychological pressures, such as loneliness, financial worries, and relationship or work problems can produce a cumulative level of stress that exceeds a person's ability to cope with the situation. When stress reaches these levels, performance falls off rapidly. Pilots experiencing this level of stress are not safe and should not exercise their airman privileges. Pilots who suspect they are suffering from chronic stress should consult a physician.
27. Aviation Medical Examiner
28. The recommended waiting time before going to flight altitudes of up to 8,000 feet is at least 12 hours after diving that does not require controlled ascent (nondecompression stop diving), and at least 24 hours after diving that does require controlled ascent (decompression stop diving). The waiting time before going to flight altitudes above 8,000 feet should be at least 24 hours after any scuba dive. These recommended altitudes are actual flight altitudes above mean sea level (MSL) and not pressurized cabin altitudes. This takes into consideration the risk of decompression of the aircraft during flight.
29. The IMSAFE Checklist:
    - Illness—Am I sick? Illness is an obvious pilot risk.
    - Medication—Am I taking any medicines that might affect my judgment or make me drowsy?
    - Stress—Am I under psychological pressure from the job? Do I have money, health, or family problems? Stress causes concentration and performance problems. While the regulations list medical conditions that require grounding, stress is not among them. The pilot should consider the effects of stress on performance.
    - Alcohol—Have I been drinking within 8 hours? Within 24 hours? As little as one ounce of liquor, one bottle of beer, or four ounces of wine can impair flying skills. Alcohol also renders a pilot more susceptible to disorientation and hypoxia.
    - Fatigue—Am I tired and not adequately rested? Fatigue continues to be one of the most insidious hazards to flight safety, as it may not be apparent to a pilot until serious errors are made.
    - Emotion—Am I emotionally upset?

CHAPTER 14

NAVIGATION AND CROSS-COUNTRY FLIGHT PLANNING

Introduction

STANDARDS & OBJECTIVES

North Dakota Aviation Content Standards (Grades 10–12)

- **2.5.1**—Calculate Time/Distance/Rate problems.
- **2.5.2**—Compute ground speed and wind correction angle.
- **3.4.1**—Identify pilotage and dead reckoning techniques.
- **3.4.2**—Explain when radio navigation would be beneficial.
- **3.4.3**—Plan a flight using VOR navigation techniques.
- **3.4.4**—Plan a flight using GPS navigation techniques.
- **3.4.5**—Demonstrate appropriate radio navigation techniques using VOR and GPS.
- **3.5.1**—Demonstrate use of flight planning tools (e.g., *Chart Supplement*, E6B, and plotter sectional charts).
- **3.5.2**—Plan a XC flight using multiple navigation techniques.
- **3.5.3**—Complete navigation log for preflight planning.
- **3.5.4**—Demonstrate a XC flight using a flight simulator.

Science—Next Generation Science Standards (Grades 9–12)

- **HS-PS4-1**—Use mathematical representations to support a claim regarding relationships among the frequency, wavelength, and speed of waves traveling in various media.
- **HS-ETS1-3**—Evaluate a solution to a complex real-world problem based on prioritized criteria and trade-offs that account for a range of constraints, including cost, safety, reliability, and aesthetics, as well as possible social, cultural, and environmental impacts.

Math—CCSS.MATH.CONTENT (Grades 10–12)

- **HS.N-Q.1**—Use units as a way to understand problems and to guide the solution of multi-step problems; choose and interpret units consistently in formulas; choose and interpret the scale and the origin in graphs and data displays.
- **HS.N-Q.3**—Choose a level of accuracy appropriate to limitations on measurement when reporting quantities.
- **HS.A-SSE.1**—Interpret expressions that represent a quantity in terms of its context.
- **HS.A-CED.1**—Create equations and inequalities in one variable and use them to solve problems.

- **HS.A-CED.4**—Rearrange formulas to highlight a quantity of interest, using the same reasoning as in solving equations.
- **MP.2**—Reason abstractly and quantitatively.
- **MP.4**—Model with mathematics.

Language Arts—CCSS.ELA-LITERACY.CCRA

- **L.1**—Demonstrate command of the conventions of standard English grammar and usage when writing or speaking.
- **L.2**—Demonstrate command of the conventions of standard English capitalization, punctuation, and spelling when writing.
- **R.1**—Read closely to determine what the text says explicitly and to make logical inferences from it; cite specific textual evidence when writing or speaking to support conclusions drawn from the text.
- **R.10**—Read and comprehend complex literary and informational texts independently and proficiently.
- **SL.1**—Prepare for and participate effectively in a range of conversations and collaborations with diverse partners, building on others' ideas and expressing their own clearly and persuasively.
- **SL.2**—Integrate and evaluate information presented in diverse media and formats, including visually, quantitatively, and orally.
- **SL.4**—Present information, findings, and supporting evidence such that listeners can follow the line of reasoning and the organization, development, and style are appropriate to task, purpose, and audience.
- **SL.5**—Make strategic use of digital media and visual displays of data to express information and enhance understanding of presentations.

ESSENTIAL QUESTIONS

- How does technology contribute to the safety of cross-country flight?
- How do the aeronautical knowledge areas of flight come together to plan a cross-country flight?
- In what ways is it important to follow a particular order when planning a cross-country flight?

LESSONS

Lesson	Topic	Student Notebook Activity
Lesson 1	E6B Introduction	1. Using an E6B Flight Computer
Lesson 2	Considerations for Planning a Cross-Country	1. Factors to Consider When Planning a Cross-Country • *Part A: Considerations* • *Part B: Additional Considerations* • *Part C: Two-Column Graphic Organizer* • *Part D: Making a Go/No-Go Decision*
Lesson 3	Introduction to Navigation and Using Pilotage	1. Navigation Log 2. Pilotage and Navigation Quiz
Lesson 4	Dead Reckoning	1. Navigation Logs 2. Definitions and Terms 3. Radio Navigation Practice
Lesson 5	Radio Navigation	1. VOR Practice Problems 2. Radio Navigation Homework Problems
Lesson 6	Cross-Country Planning	1. Weight and Balance Chart 2. Navigation Log 3. Takeoff and Landing Distances 4. Two-Column Graphic Organizer 5. Cross-Country Checklist
Lesson 7	Cross-Country Scenario	1. Filing a Flight Plan

CHAPTER 14 NAVIGATION AND CROSS-COUNTRY FLIGHT PLANNING

LESSON 1
E6B INTRODUCTION

PURPOSE

The purpose of this lesson is to use the E6B flight computer and sectional plotter to measure distance and solve calculations.

ACCOMMODATIONS FOR LEARNING DIFFERENCES

It is important that lessons accommodate the needs of every learner. These lessons may be modified to accommodate your students with learning differences by referring to **www.pacer.org/parent/php/PHP-c267.pdf**.

PREPARATION

- Class copies of *Pilot's Handbook of Aeronautical Knowledge* (FAA-H-8083-25)
- Classroom set of E6B flight computers
- E6B instructions
- Classroom set of sectional plotters
- Classroom copies of sectional charts

DIRECTIONS

Introductory Activity: Using the sectional chart, have students find the airport nearest to their school. Ask students to find the airport that represents the furthest location they have traveled from home. Have each student make note of the airport name and airport identifier.

Ask the students to share how long it took them to go to that location by car and discuss how much shorter it would be if they could have flown directly to that location.

Explain that if students were to use a sectional plotter they could accurately measure the distance "as the crow flies." They could use the E6B flight computer to make exact calculations regarding flight time and needed fuel.

Step 1: The facilitator will guide the class to use the sectional plotter to determine distance between two points/airports.

Things to point out and explain to students:
- Scale on the sectional
- Different scales on the sectional plotter
- Difference between statute miles (SM) and nautical miles (NM)

Step 2: Have the students measure the distance between the two airports they identified in the introductory activity. Students will write the distances on the board to determine who has visited the airport furthest away.

Step 3: Ask students to estimate (calculate) how long it would take to get to the airport if the airplane was traveling 108 nautical miles per hour (knots). Build upon what was stated in the introduction—that pilots use E6B flight computers or electronic flight computers to determine such things as flight time, wind correction angles, and fuel requirements.

Step 4: Create an interactive presentation by referencing both the *Pilot's Handbook of Aeronautical Knowledge*, Chapter 16, and the directions guide for the E6B. While you conduct the interactive lecture on how to use the E6B, the students will follow along using their E6B and fill in the answers using the worksheet in Activity 1 (Using an E6B Flight Computer) in the Student Notebook as you demonstrate. (Answers are provided in the answer key at the end of this chapter.) Include the following concepts in the interactive lecture:

- Time/speed/distance problems
- Fuel requirements
- Wind correction angles
- Ground speed
- Flight time
- Density altitude
- Conversions
- Usual mathematical calculations such as multiplication and division

Facilitators can download the ASA E6-B Flight Computer Instructions from ASA's website.

Concluding Activity: The students will complete the remaining problems on the worksheet in the Student Notebook. The facilitator will lead a discussion to review the students' responses and answer any remaining questions.

CHAPTER 14 NAVIGATION AND CROSS-COUNTRY FLIGHT PLANNING

LESSON 2

CONSIDERATIONS FOR PLANNING A CROSS-COUNTRY

PURPOSE

The purpose of this lesson is to use previous knowledge and resources to identify all the factors that must be considered in order to plan a cross-country flight.

ACCOMMODATIONS FOR LEARNING DIFFERENCES

It is important that lessons accommodate the needs of every learner. These lessons may be modified to accommodate your students with learning differences by referring to **www.pacer.org/parent/php/PHP-c267.pdf.**

PREPARATION

- FAR/AIM or **eCFR.gov**
- Class copies of *Pilot's Handbook of Aeronautical Knowledge* (FAA-H-8083-25)
- Classroom set of E6B flight computers and instructions
- Classroom set of sectional plotters
- Classroom copies of sectional charts

DIRECTIONS

Introductory Activity: Ask students how long a flight must be to be considered a cross-country flight to meet private pilot requirements? (*Answer:* Under 14 CFR §61.1 of the Federal Aviation Regulations, it must be 50 NM or more from your original departure location.) Have the students look up 14 CFR §61.1 and have the students write the requirements on the board.

Step 1: Have the students open up their sectional charts and decide on an interesting location on the map that the class would like to fly to. As the facilitator, lead an interactive discussion while having the students answer the following questions in teams or together as an entire class. ASA E6-B Flight Computer Instructions are available on ASA's website.

- How many nautical miles is it to the chosen destination?
- Using your E6B, how many statute miles is it to the destination?
- Using your E6B, with a 98-knot ground speed, how long will it take to get to your destination?
- Using the E6B, if our aircraft burns 7.5 gallons per hour, how many gallons will the aircraft burn if we are still traveling at 98 knots?
- Using your E6B, if the aircraft went 20 NM in 13 minutes, how fast is the aircraft moving?
- Using the E6B, if the aircraft traveled 140 NM in 60 minutes, how fast is the aircraft moving?

Step 2: As a class, have the students decide what time they are going to leave on the flight and have them compute what time they will arrive at their destination based on a ground speed of 100 knots. Make sure the students convert their times to Zulu so that they can properly identify forecasted weather for the route.

Step 3: Ask the students to use Part A of Activity 1 (Factors to Consider When Planning a Cross-Country) in their Student Notebooks to write down at least five considerations that should be thought of before flying to the destination. To assist the students in identifying five considerations, expand on the PAVE checklist model discussed in Chapter 12 and found in the *Pilot's Handbook of Aeronautical Knowledge*, Chapter 2. Have the students compare their results by writing all the different considerations on the board as well.

Student answers may include items related to:

- Weather forecasts and patterns
- Consider time of day for flight (currency requirements? Night with passengers.)
- Airport conditions and status
- Forms of navigation available
- Performance of aircraft
- Airworthiness of aircraft
- Items on PAVE Risk Assessment tool discussed in previous chapters

Step 4: Using Part B of Activity 1 in their Student Notebooks, have the students compare their results from Part A with those on the board. Have the students write down three additional considerations they did not think of but that they recognize as important.

Step 5: For your route of flight, assign students to groups to research the following weather and other key factors to initially consider for the departure and arrival time before flying. Tell each group they will be briefing the entire class on the weather they found.

1. METAR for along route, departure and arrival airports
2. TAF for along route, departure and arrival airports
3. Prognostic charts
4. Convective activity
5. Winds and temperature aloft forecast
6. NOTAMs for your departure and arrival airport
7. Are there hangars, parking, and lodging available at your destination airport?
8. Are there fuel services available at your destination airport?
9. Are there maintenance services available at your destination?

Direct the students to fill out the two-column graphic organizer in Part C of Activity 1 in their Student Notebooks as they listen to the presentations, writing down the weather and other important factors being briefed to them by the other students.

Concluding Activity: After looking at all the weather information researched and briefed by classmates, the students should be directed to Part D (Making a Go/No-Go Decision) of Activity 1 in their Student Notebooks to respond to the following: (1) "Based on the weather and other important factors discussed, I would GO or NO-GO (circle one) on this flight." and (2) "Explain your decision to Go or No-Go on this flight." The facilitator should use the weather and other airport information to help the group decide on a go/no-go decision for the chosen route of flight. Facilitate a discussion on alternate routes or different ways the students could get to their destination if conditions were less than ideal.

Answers may vary and could include:
1. Delay departure or leave earlier.
2. Plan a different route to go around the poor weather.
3. Go during daylight hours.
4. Go partway and wait until the next day to finish the flight.
5. Go to an airport nearby and rent a car.

CHAPTER 14 NAVIGATION AND CROSS-COUNTRY FLIGHT PLANNING

LESSON 3

INTRODUCTION TO NAVIGATION AND USING PILOTAGE

PURPOSE

The purpose of this lesson is to gain an understanding of the different methods of navigating and to define the term pilotage.

ACCOMMODATIONS FOR LEARNING DIFFERENCES

It is important that lessons accommodate the needs of every learner. These lessons may be modified to accommodate your students with learning differences by referring to **www.pacer.org/parent/php/PHP-c267.pdf.**

PREPARATION

- Class copies of *Pilot's Handbook of Aeronautical Knowledge* (FAA-H-8083-25)
- Classroom set of VFR aeronautical sectional charts
- Classroom set of sectional plotters

DIRECTIONS

Introductory Activity: Ask the students how they would be able to get to the destination covered in the previous lesson without getting lost. Ask, "How do you think a pilot is able to get to their destination and not get lost?" Explain that there are three forms of navigation that pilots use to arrive at their selected destination (pilotage, dead reckoning, and radio navigation).

Step 1: Ask students which tool they use to navigate while driving in their car. If they were going to the state capital, how would they get there? How would their GPS on the phone help them to get to a destination? The facilitator should explain that radio navigation for an aircraft is similar in its purpose and will be described more in Lesson 5. (Definition of Radio Navigation: any method where radio waves are used to follow a path over the ground. VOR and GPS use a combination of ground facilities and air systems. Ground facilities transmit signals to airborne instruments, and the pilot interprets the indications and then navigates by properly responding to the indications in the cockpit.)

Another form of navigation is called dead reckoning. Dead reckoning maintains a course by calculating heading based on wind direction and speed. This concept will be described in more detail in Lesson 4.

A third method of navigation is called pilotage. The facilitator will explain to the students that this form of navigation is accomplished by reference to landmarks or checkpoints. Further explain that good navigation involves using all methods—pilotage, radio navigation, and dead reckoning—together.

Step 2: Have the students take out their sectional charts. As a class, pick a new cross-country route. To plot the course, pick two airports at least 100 NM apart, and have students draw a straight line between the two airports on their sectional charts.

Referencing the charts, as a class discuss what would make good checkpoints (refer to *Pilot's Handbook of Aeronautical Knowledge*, Chapter 16). Discuss with the student, in contrast, what would make bad checkpoints.

	Good Checkpoints	Bad Checkpoints
Day	Identifiable things Large lake or group of lakes Large rivers Large towns Major road or highway	Small things on the map Small lakes or a group of lakes hard to distinguish Small river or creek Small towns Small road
Night	Identifiable lit things Towers with a light Major road or highway Large town	Unlit things Unlit towers Small road Rivers

As a class, mark at least three good checkpoints (on their sectionals) along their route. When deciding on good checkpoints, consider the following questions:

- How would the definition of a good checkpoint change if:
  - Flying very close to the ground, such as 500 feet or 1,000 feet above the surface?
  - Flying at night?
  - Flying 10,000 feet above the surface?
  - Visibility was less than 2 NM?
- How far apart should the checkpoints be?

Model for students how to write checkpoints into the navigation log. Show how to record your distance between each checkpoint. Note that adding up your distance between checkpoints should equal your total distance.

Step 3: Using the navigation log in Activity 1 in the Student Notebook, either independently or in a small group, the students can find another four "good" checkpoints and mark them on their sectional. Students can also record the distance between each checkpoint in the navigation log.

Concluding Activity: The students should complete Activity 2 (Pilotage and Navigation Quiz) in the Student Notebook. Discuss the answers to the quiz with students to ensure accurate understanding. (An answer key is provided at the end of the chapter.)

CHAPTER 14   NAVIGATION AND CROSS-COUNTRY FLIGHT PLANNING

LESSON 4
DEAD RECKONING

PURPOSE
The purpose of this lesson is to further expand on students' understanding of navigation by explaining the dead reckoning method.

ACCOMMODATIONS FOR LEARNING DIFFERENCES
It is important that lessons accommodate the needs of every learner. These lessons may be modified to accommodate your students with learning differences by referring to **www.pacer.org/parent/php/PHP-c267.pdf.**

PREPARATION
- Class copies of *Pilot's Handbook of Aeronautical Knowledge* (FAA-H-8083-25)
- Classroom set of E6B flight computers
- Classroom set of VFR aeronautical sectional charts
- Classroom set of sectional plotters
- Slips of paper

DIRECTIONS
Introductory Activity: Read the following visualization to students: "Imagine you are on a boat going across a lake. As you travel westward across the lake, you note the wind is from the north. You notice also as you travel west that even though your boat is heading west, you are getting pushed toward the south end of the lake! If you don't change your direction and go more to the north, you will never get to the west side!" Explain that this happens to an aircraft, so pilots must "crab" into the wind so they can stay on course between two points.

Step 1: Show students the example of a completed Navigation Log found in Activity 1 (Navigation Logs) in the Student Notebook. Ask students, "Why do we need to be precise when flying the airplane?" (*Answer:* If pilots are just a few degrees off, after 60 miles of flying they would be miles off course.)

Step 2: Lead an interactive lecture on the following definitions, having students record the definitions under Activity 2 (Definitions and Terms) in their Student Notebooks. Terms and explanations can be found in the *Pilot's Handbook of Aeronautical Knowledge*, Chapter 16.

- True course (TC)
- True heading (TH)
- Magnetic course (MC)
- Magnetic heading (MH)
- Wind correction
  > Wind side of E6B—wind triangle
- Compass deviation
- Compass heading (CH)
- Magnetic variation
- Isogonic lines
- Agonic lines

Step 3: Using the navigation log and route from Lesson 3, the facilitator will model how to obtain the following information by using the sectional plotter and sectional (referencing Chapter 16 of the *Pilot's Handbook of Aeronautical Knowledge*):

- True course
- Magnetic course
- Magnetic variation

The students should follow along, mirroring the steps of the facilitator with the navigation log in the Student Notebook from Lesson 3, sectional, and plotter.

Step 4: Have the students plot another route in a different direction and have them find and record the following information in their Student Notebooks under Activity 3 (Radio Navigation Practice):

- True course
- Magnetic course at the departure airport
- Magnetic course at the arrival airport

Concluding Activity: The facilitator will give the students a departure and arrival airport and then the students will determine the true course and write it out on a slip of paper and hand it to the facilitator at the end of class.

CHAPTER 14 NAVIGATION AND CROSS-COUNTRY FLIGHT PLANNING

LESSON 5
RADIO NAVIGATION

PURPOSE

The purpose of this lesson is to further develop the students' understanding of aircraft radio navigation.

ACCOMMODATIONS FOR LEARNING DIFFERENCES

It is important that lessons accommodate the needs of every learner. These lessons may be modified to accommodate your students with learning differences by referring to **www.pacer.org/parent/php/PHP-c267.pdf.**

PREPARATION

- Class copies of *Pilot's Handbook of Aeronautical Knowledge* (FAA-H-8083-25)
- FAR/AIM or **eCFR.gov**
- Make a course deviation indicator that can slide left and right to simulate a VOR or GPS instrument.
- Note cards

DIRECTIONS

Introductory Activity: As a visual aid, tie a string from one point (Point A) in the room to another point (Point B) on the opposite end of the room. Explain this is your "course" between two navigational aids, Point A and Point B. Remind students that this straight line is the most efficient and safe course to get to their destination. Using a small model plane, simulate flying along the course and ask your students how they would use pilotage to stay on the course (the students should indicate how they would see objects like desks, tables, and other animate objects on the ground that would help them stay on course).

Start over at the beginning of the string. Using a magnetic compass or a compass from an application on a smart phone, have the students determine the magnetic heading they would have to travel to stay on course. Ask the students to explain how the airplane would look while flying if there was a crosswind that they didn't correct for by doing wind calculations on an E6B (as a facilitator, help the students recognize how it would be easy to get "off" course using dead reckoning or pilotage, especially after long distances). The facilitator will explain that radio navigation instruments and navigational aids are used to keep pilots and aircraft on that specific course (the string).

Step 1: Present an interactive lecture using visual aids on the primary navigation instruments a pilot would use in a small aircraft—the VOR (VHF Omni Directional Range) and GPS (Global Positioning System). This should include the theory of operations of each, ground and airborne equipment needed, and the use of the navigational aids in flight.

Reference the *Aeronautical Information Manual* (AIM), Chapter 1, and the *Pilot's Handbook of Aeronautical Knowledge*, Chapter 16, to prepare for the interactive lecture. Consider referencing or showing videos that explain navigation using a VOR or GPS.

Note: This is to be a basic introduction to the navigation aids.

Step 2: Returning to the string that is tied from one side of the room to the other, fly the model airplane along the course (string), slowly beginning to go off course. Have the students demonstrate how the course deviation indicator made out of a paper plate (or whatever prop was used, reference the picture below) represents a VOR or GPS and how it would be deflected left or right if you went off course and would center as you went back on course. The students should complete the VOR practice problems in Activity 1 in the Student Notebook.

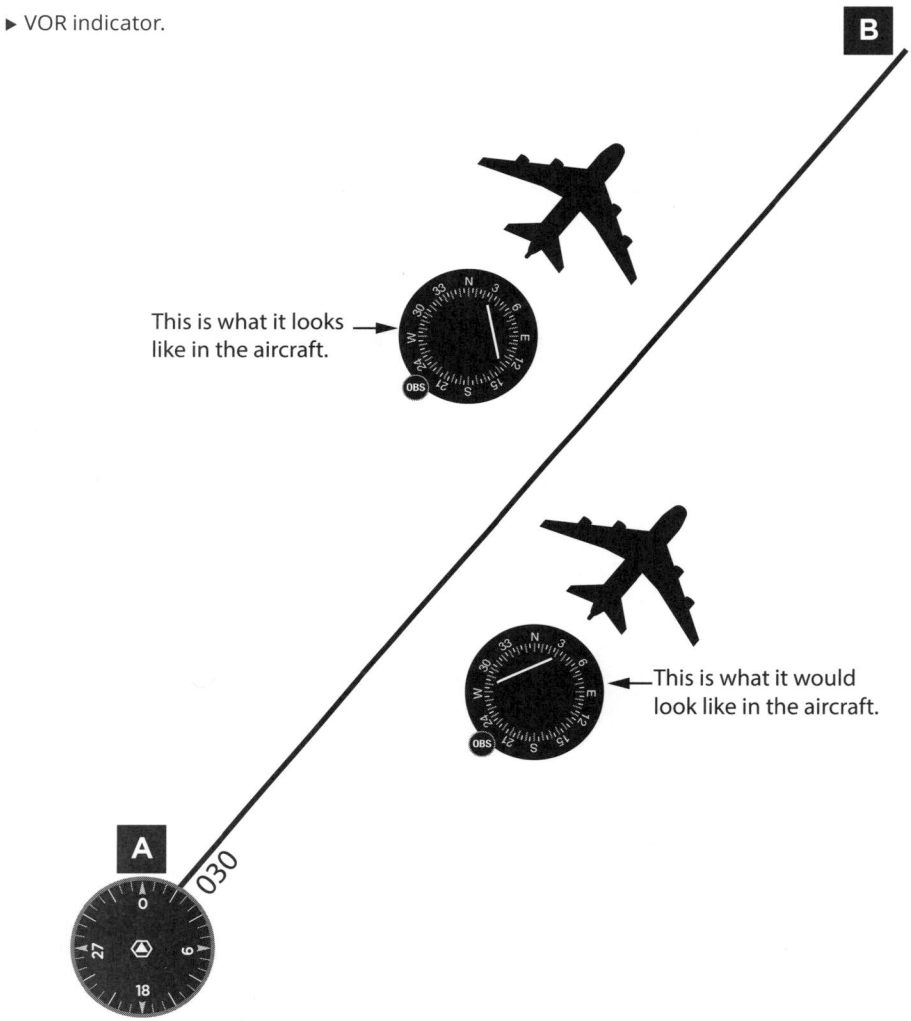

▶ VOR indicator.

Practice problems and answers

Use the pictures to determine the aircraft's location in relation to the VOR.

1. Where are you in relation to the VOR station? (*Answer:* Southeast)

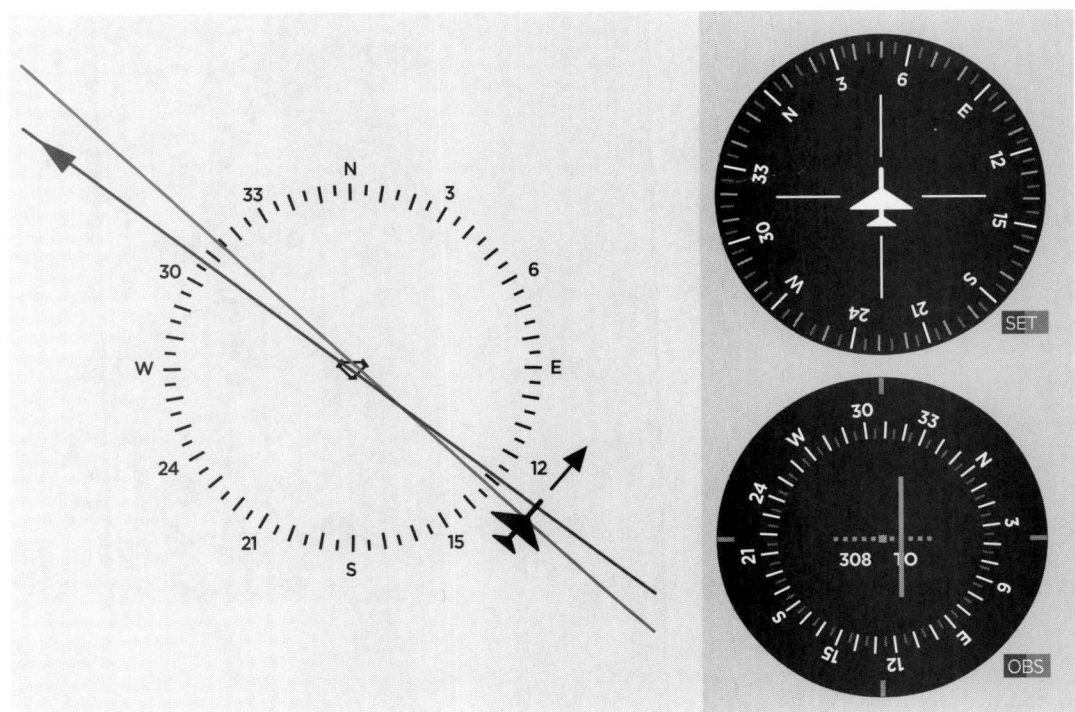

2. Where are you in relation to the VOR station? (*Answer:* Northeast)

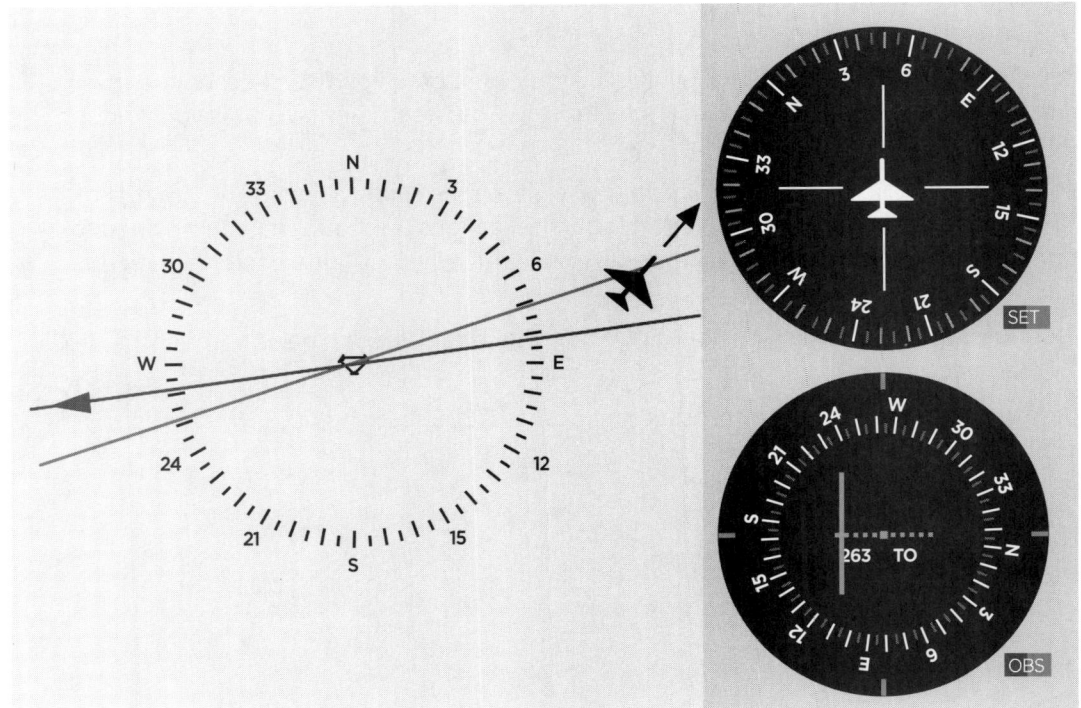

3. Where are you in relation to the VOR station? (*Answer:* Northwest)

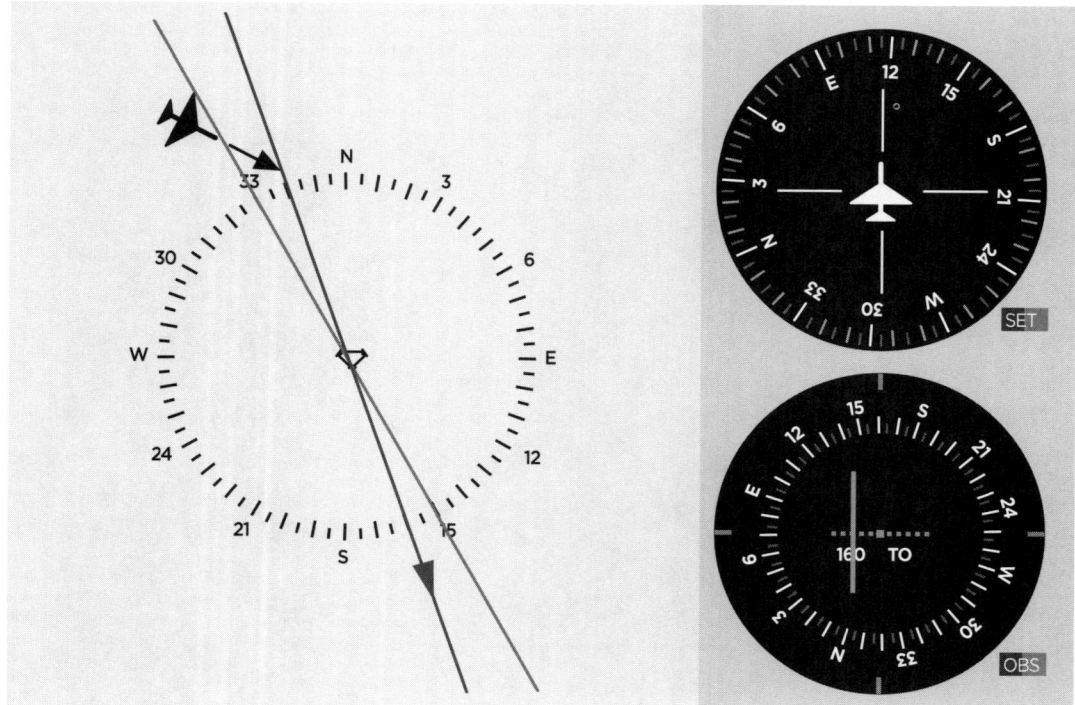

Concluding Activity: The facilitator will have the students write down on a note card what the "muddiest point" was from today's lesson. The facilitator should plan to take time to address the students' muddiest points at the end of class or at the beginning of the next class period.

In preparation for the full cross-country planning lessons, have students take home the Student Notebook assignment in Activity 2 (Radio Navigation Homework Problems). The questions and answers are below.

1. While en route on a cross country, you take your time between two checkpoints that were 15 NM apart. It took you 12 minutes to travel between them. What is your ground speed in nautical miles per hour? (*Answer*: 75 knots)

2. While planning for your cross-country, you want to see if you will have enough fuel to make it to your destination. Your aircraft burns 9 gallons per hour and you planned for your flight to take 3 hours and 20 minutes. How much fuel will it take to complete this flight? (*Answer:* 30 gallons)

3. If your aircraft burns 17 gallons per hour, how much fuel will you need to meet the VFR day reserves for the FARs? (*Answer:* 8.5 gallons)

4. You have calculated that your pressure altitude is 8,500 feet and 50°F. What is your density altitude? (*Answer:* 9,868 feet)

CHAPTER 14 NAVIGATION AND CROSS-COUNTRY FLIGHT PLANNING

LESSON 6
CROSS-COUNTRY PLANNING

PURPOSE
The purpose of this lesson is to use the skills previously learned to plan a cross-country flight.

ACCOMMODATIONS FOR LEARNING DIFFERENCES
It is important that lessons accommodate the needs of every learner. These lessons may be modified to accommodate your students with learning differences by referring to **www.pacer.org/parent/php/PHP-c267.pdf**.

PREPARATION
- Class copies of *Pilot's Handbook of Aeronautical Knowledge* (FAA-H-8083-25)
- FAR/AIM or **eCFR.gov**
- Classroom set of E6B flight computers
- Classroom set of VFR aeronautical sectional charts
- Sectional plotters
- *Chart Supplements*
- Navigation/flight planning logs
- Student calculators
- Piper Archer (PA-28-181) Pilot's Operating Handbook (POH), or POH from a different aircraft used in flight planning example.
- Computers/devices and internet access for students

Note: this lesson may require two class periods to accomplish.

DIRECTIONS
Introductory Activity: Have the students come up with a destination they would like to fly to as a class (the destination must be found on their sectional charts). Ask them to share with the class why they want to fly there. As a class, vote to select one destination.

Step 1: As a class, come up with a route. Have the students calculate the weight and balance in their Student Notebook using the worksheet in Activity 1 (Weight and Balance). Use 1,590 pounds as your basic empty weight (BEW) and a moment of 139,125 in-lbs. The pilot weighs 170 pounds and the one passenger weighs 185 pounds. Have the students answer the following questions:

1. Are you within limits?
2. How much gas are you able to carry?
3. Do you have enough gas to make it to your destination based on whatever performance you plan to use for the flight (for example, 75% Best Power)?
   a. Do you need to plan a fuel stop?

The students should draw the route line on their sectionals and highlight that route.

Step 2: As a class, pick good checkpoints along the route. The facilitator should explain that the first couple checkpoints should be no more than 10 NM apart so that the pilot can verify that the aircraft is on the right course. It is good practice for new students to make their checkpoints no more than 25 NM miles apart. Ask the students why this might be. (*Answer:* To help the pilot make sure he or she is on course and does not get lost.) The students should be entering the checkpoint information along with the distance between checkpoints and distances remaining on their navigation logs found in Activity 2 (Navigation Log) in their Student Notebooks.

Step 3: Have the students reference today's weather to compute the takeoff and landing distance. Students will then record these distances in Activity 3 (Takeoff and Landing Distances) in their Student Notebooks and compare them to the runway lengths for the departure and arrival airports found in the *Chart Supplement*. Have the students fill in the frequencies and navigational information from the *Chart Supplement* about the departure and arrival airports on the navigation log in the Student Notebook. Have the students read over the airport information and identify important information such as runway elevations, runway lengths, and general layout of the airports.

Step 4: The students should use their plotters to find the true course (TC), omni-bearing selector (OBS), and magnetic variation for the route. The facilitator will need to model how to obtain the OBS course using the sectional plotter and sectional, referencing Chapter 16 of the *Pilot's Handbook of Aeronautical Knowledge* for further directions. Students should enter that information on the navigation log in the Student Notebook.

Step 5: Have the students obtain current weather, to include forecast conditions along the route, winds aloft, Notices to Airmen (NOTAMs), and other applicable weather information. The students can fill out Activity 4 (Two-Column Graphic Organizer) in the Student Notebook to help organize their thoughts. Have the students transfer the applicable weather information (such as wind direction and speed and temperature) over to their navigation log in the Student Notebook.

Step 6: In referencing the weather, have the students determine the most appropriate altitude for flight. The facilitator should remind the students to think of the following information when making this decision:

- Check ceilings at departure, en route, and arrival.
- Check winds aloft to see which winds favor you most.
- Comply with 14 CFR §91.109 VFR cruising altitudes.
- Check terrain and obstructions.

Have the students talk to their neighbor about the altitude they picked and why, and then as a class determine which altitude to use for this scenario.

Step 7: Have the students decide what power setting they want to fly at—75%, 65%, or 55% (based on a Piper Archer). Have them determine the following information:

- True airspeed
- RPM setting
- Fuel burn

The students should record that information on the navigational log in their Student Notebook.

Step 8: The students can now use their E6B to determine wind correction angle and ground speed. Have students record ground speed and other appropriate information on the navigation log in the Student Notebook.

Step 9: With calculated ground speed, the students can now use the E6B to determine the time en route between each checkpoint and add up times to determine the total time for the flight. Have students enter the information on the navigation log in the Student Notebook.

Step 10: The students now will be able to complete the fuel section of the navigation log. Based on total time, the students will now determine the fuel required to arrive at the destination, including fuel reserve requirements (day vs. night). Remind the students to reference fuel available from weight and balance. (If students do not have enough fuel available for the route chosen, time permitting, the facilitator could discuss best economy and how to increase range and endurance.)

Concluding Activity: Using the Cross-Country Checklist in Activity 5 in the Student Notebook (also provided under Facilitator Information below), have students verify that all required areas of the navigation log are filled out. The students will show the facilitator the completed checklist and the facilitator will answer any remaining questions about the navigation log.

Note: Remind the students to keep their navigation logs, because they will be using this planning for Lesson 7 to learn how to file a VFR flight plan.

FACILITATOR INFORMATION
Cross-Country Checklist

Put a checkmark next to the following information verifying it is filled out on your navigation log.

Information	Completed
1. Frequencies	
2. Airport diagram	
3. Departure field elevation	
4. Checkpoints (all of them along your route of flight)	
5. Navigation aids, identification and frequency	
6. Course, OBS	
7. True course	
8. Magnetic variation	
9. Distance, total and between checkpoints	
10. Altitude	
11. Ground speed	
12. Wind correction angle	
13. Estimated time en route	

CHAPTER 14   NAVIGATION AND CROSS-COUNTRY FLIGHT PLANNING

LESSON 7
CROSS-COUNTRY SCENARIO

PURPOSE
The purpose of this lesson is to develop the student's understanding regarding how to file the cross-country flight plan and introduce students to standard enroute procedures.

ACCOMMODATIONS FOR LEARNING DIFFERENCES
It is important that lessons accommodate the needs of every learner. These lessons may be modified to accommodate your students with learning differences by referring to **www.pacer.org/parent/php/PHP-c267.pdf**.

PREPARATION
- Class copies of *Pilot's Handbook of Aeronautical Knowledge* (FAA-H-8083-25)
- Classroom set of VFR aeronautical sectional charts
- Navigation logs (use previously completed navigation log from Lesson 6)
- VFR plotters
- Classroom set of E6B flight computers
- Flight simulator (facilitator may elect to conduct this lesson on the simulator)

DIRECTIONS
Introductory Activity: This lesson is an opportunity to bring together the knowledge gained over all chapters. This lesson assumes the cross-country planning is complete and your students are preparing to take off on the flight. Once the planning has taken place, now they need to let people know where they are going in case there is an emergency. While not mandatory, filing a flight plan is a safe way of making sure someone starts looking for you if you are late to arrive.

This cross-country scenario is their final lesson in the course, so the scenario should encompass multiple other topics from the course.

If you have a flight simulator, students could use the navigation log to perform the cross-country as you conduct this lesson.

Step 1: Have the students use their navigation log from Lesson 6 to properly complete the flight plan filing form found in Activity 1 (Filing a Flight Plan) in their Student Notebooks.

An example of a properly filled out Flight Plan is shown under Facilitator Information at the end of this lesson. Detailed directions regarding how to fill out the flight plan are in Chapter 16 of the *Pilot's Handbook of Aeronautical Knowledge*.

Step 2: The facilitator could visit **1800wxbrief.com** and walk students through completing a flight plan filing online.

Step 3: Since filing a VFR flight plan is normally done right before takeoff, the students should reference the weather again. The facilitator should ask the students the following questions:
- Based on the weather, would you go on that flight today?
  › Why or why not?
- Would you need to make any changes to the route based on today's weather?
- Would you need to update anything on the planning based on today's weather?
  › Note that the weather may be completely different since this is the day after they have completed the planning, but it is still a good exercise for the students to think through.
- What reports, forecasts, text, or charts did you reference to make these decisions?

Step 4: Have the students write in their Student Notebooks three variables that could arise at the last minute that might change their planning, and then call students up to write their thoughts on the board. (*Some examples:* unforecasted weather, they are behind schedule and will arrive late or at night, they are tired or ill, temporary flight restrictions were issued due to forest fires, something on the aircraft is unairworthy.)

Step 5: The facilitator will lead a discussion with the class about how to open and close a flight plan in the airplane in flight. Reference the *Pilot's Handbook of Aeronautical Knowledge*, Chapter 16, to help create the discussion material. If possible, the facilitator should simulate what these conversations will sound like with the briefer or find an audio clip on LiveATC.net (liveatc.net).

> Note: If you do not have a flight simulator, go to step 9.
>
> Note: If you are using a flight simulator, this lesson may require more than one day to complete.

Step 6: Using the flight simulator, have the students prepare for the flight. They will need to set up the following information:
- Airport location
- Set radio frequencies
- Set navigation aids up appropriately
- Set the aircraft up on the appropriate runway for takeoff

Once all of that has been set, have the student take off on the cross-country route.

Step 7: The facilitator will act as air traffic control and flight service (FSS). Discuss how the student will open their flight plan: The FSS frequency will be on their *Chart Supplement* and on their aeronautical chart as well as on their navigation log from Lesson 6. Tell the students to let flight service know when they departed and their current location.

Step 8: The facilitator should walk around the room discussing with the students how they will determine if they are on course and if they are going faster or slower than planned. The students will need to take their time at one checkpoint and upon crossing the next to determine their ground speed using the E6B. Regardless of the route, the facilitator can have the student practice, and ask them questions such as, "You just arrived at your second checkpoint and it took you 3 minutes longer than you planned. What does this mean to you on this flight?" (Answers may vary, but it means they are going slower than expected.) Follow up questions are:

- What is the new ground speed?
- How long will it take you to get to your next checkpoint?

At various times throughout the flight simulation activity, have the students hit pause on the flight simulator to periodically answer the questions in Step 9.

Step 9: The facilitator should have a discussion with the students about things to think about while on a cross-country flight. These discussion items should include:

- How should you manage cockpit organization to ensure needed resources are available and to minimize disruptions while in flight?
- What if you can't make it to your destination as planned? What is your backup plan or plan B?
- What will you do if you encounter unexpected weather, or weather that is worse than forecasted?
- If you are tired and need to land sooner, where will you divert to in order to land?
- Conducting a cross-country flight is exciting, but it is also a lot of hard work that requires being alert at all times, keeping aware of your surroundings.
- Discuss how going slower or faster than planned will change their cross-country plans. Have the students use their E6B to help answer the following questions:
  › If you are going 15 knots slower than planned, how much longer will it take to get to your destination?
  › Will you have enough fuel to make it to your destination?
  › Discuss with the students what they would do if they were low on fuel.
    – If the students indicate they would stop earlier, ask, "Where do you plan to divert? Why did you pick that airport?"
- What would you do if you had a malfunction, such as if your alternator fails and your battery was almost dead? (*Answer:* Land as soon as practical. The airplane will still run with no battery or alternator, but you will lose electrical, including lights, communication, and navigation equipment. If you have remaining battery, you could also turn your battery off to save it until you approach an airport, then turn it back on so you can make a radio call before entering the pattern.)

Concluding Activity: Give students another cross-country route and have them complete a flight plan to the new destination using new weather.

FACILITATOR INFORMATION
Flight Plan Example

(See next page.)

International Flight Plan

U.S. Department of Transportation — Federal Aviation Administration

PRIORITY: `<=FF`
ADDRESSEE(S): `<=`

FILING TIME:
ORIGINATOR: `<=`

SPECIFIC IDENTIFICATION OF ADDRESSEE(S) AND / OR ORIGINATOR

- 3 MESSAGE TYPE: `<=(FPL`
- 7 AIRCRAFT IDENTIFICATION: N1963U
- 8 FLIGHT RULES: V
- TYPE OF FLIGHT: G `<=`
- 9 NUMBER:
- TYPE OF AIRCRAFT: C172
- WAKE TURBULENCE CAT.: /L
- 10 EQUIPMENT: S /C `<=`
- 13 DEPARTURE AERODROME: KMYF
- TIME: 400 `<=`
- 15 CRUISING SPEED: N0110
- LEVEL: A075
- ROUTE: DCT JLI KTRM KPSP

`<=`

- 16 DESTINATION AERODROME: KPSP
- TOTAL EET HR MIN: 0057
- ALTN AERODROME: KTRM
- 2ND ALTN AERODROME: `<=`
- 18 OTHER INFORMATION: —

`<=`

19 SUPPLEMENTARY INFORMATION (NOT TO BE TRANSMITTED IN FPL MESSAGES)

- ENDURANCE HR MIN: E/ 0800
- PERSONS ON BOARD: P/ 1
- EMERGENCY RADIO: R/ UHF [X] VHF [ ] ELBA [ ]
- SURVIVAL EQUIPMENT: POLAR [ ] / DESERT [X] MARITIME [X] JUNGLE [X]
- JACKETS: [X] / LIGHT [X] FLUORES [X] UHF [X] VHF [X]
- DINGHIES: D/ NUMBER [XX] CAPACITY [XXX] COVER [ ] COLOR: `<=`
- AIRCRAFT COLOR AND MARKINGS: A/ white, red stripe
- REMARKS: N/ `<=`
- PILOT-IN-COMMAND: C/ Joe Asa III)`<=`

FILED BY | ACCEPTED BY | ADDITIONAL INFORMATION

NOTE: File and close flight plans at www.1800wxbrief.com, www.duat.com, or www.duats.com, or call 1-800-WX-BRIEF. VFR pilots: remember to close your flight plan.

ANSWER KEYS
CHAPTER 14

LESSON 1, Activity 1
Using an E6B Flight Computer (Student Notebook)

Time, Speed, Distance Problems:
1. Time: 1 hour, 15 minutes
2. Time: 32 minutes
3. Distance: 20 SM
4. Distance: 97 NM
5. Rate: 150 knots
6. Rate: 103 knots

Fuel Consumption Problems:
7. Time: 36 minutes
8. Time: 21 minutes
9. Gallons: 12 gallons
10. Gallons: 14.5 gallons
11. Rate: 15 gph
12. Rate: 9.6 gph

Wind Correction Angle (WCA) and Ground Speed:
13. WCA: 13° Left; GS: 79 knots
14. WCA: 3° Left; GS: 70 knots
15. WCA: 5° Right; GS: 129 knots

Density Altitude (DA):
16. DA: Approximately 2,800 feet
17. DA: Approximately 600 feet
18. DA: Approximately 2,000 feet
19. DA: Approximately 9,200 feet

LESSON 3, Activity 2
Pilotage and Navigation Quiz (Student Notebook)

1. **Pilotage**—Pilotage is navigation by reference to landmarks or checkpoints. It is a method of navigation that can be used on any course that has adequate checkpoints, but it is more commonly used in conjunction with dead reckoning and VFR radio navigation.

   Dead Reckoning—Dead reckoning is navigation solely by means of computations based on time, airspeed, distance, and direction. The products derived from these variables, when adjusted by wind speed and velocity, are heading and GS. The predicted heading takes the aircraft along the intended path and the GS establishes the time to arrive at each checkpoint and the destination. Except for flights over water, dead reckoning is usually used with pilotage for cross-country flying. The heading and GS, as calculated, is constantly monitored and corrected by pilotage as observed from checkpoints.

   Ground-Based Navigation—Advances in navigational radio receivers installed in aircraft, the development of aeronautical charts that show the exact location of ground transmitting stations and their frequencies, along with refined flight deck instrumentation make it possible for pilots to navigate with precision to almost any point desired. Although precision in navigation is obtainable through the proper use of this equipment, beginning pilots should use this equipment to supplement navigation by visual reference to the ground (pilotage). This method provides the pilot with an effective safeguard against disorientation in the event of radio malfunction. There are three radio navigation systems available for use for VFR navigation. These are: (1) VHF Omnidirectional Range (VOR), (2) Nondirectional Radio Beacon (NDB), and (3) Global Positioning System (GPS). (Content from FAA-H-8083-25)

2. A good checkpoint is readily identified by other features or easy to spot—for example, major roads, lakes, rivers, power lines, and railroad tracks.

3. Things like major roads, lakes, rivers, and railroad tracks—checkpoints can be a little farther from your route line since you are at a higher altitude.

4. Since you are at a lower altitude, good checkpoints include power lines and things very close to your route line.

5. Checkpoints need to have a light on them for use at night; for example, towers with lights, or major roads like an interstate or major highway if lit up.

6. Major roads and lakes.

7. Things very close to your route line and things that would have lights.

LESSON 5, Activity 2
Radio Navigation Homework Problems (Student Notebook)

1. 75 knots
2. 30 gallons
3. 8.5 gallons
4. +9,868 feet

NOTES

To the Facilitator

1. Robert Keith, *Blue-Collar Wings: Remembering Thirty Years of Private Flying* (New York: iUniverse, 2007), 35.

Chapter 1

1. Charles A. Lindbergh, *The Spirit of St. Louis* (New York: Scribner, 2003), 261. First edition published 1953.
2. Dave English, *The Air Up There: More Great Quotations on Flight* (New York: McGraw-Hill, 2003).
3. Thrust Flight Academy, "Top 10 Flight School Scams," YouTube video, 6:26, April 20, 2017, https://youtu.be/9oY6VKyUzCM.
4. "Airman Medical Certification: Understanding Airman Medical Standards," Aircraft Owners and Pilots Association (AOPA), accessed November 30, 2020, www.aopa.org/go-fly/medical-resources/airman-medical-certification/.
5. Newsela, "The Once-Regal 747 Will Soon Be Reduced to Transporting Only Cargo," originally appearing in *Los Angeles Times*, March 27, 2017, https://newsela.com/read/replacing-boeing-747/id/28402.
6. Newsela, "The Once-Regal 747."

Chapter 3

1. *City in the Sky*, Episode 1, "Departure," Public Broadcasting Service (PBS), aired February 8, 2017, https://www.pbs.org/video/city-sky-ep-1-departure/.
2. *City in the Sky*, Episode 1, "Departure."
3. *Extreme Engineering*, Season 1, Episode 6, "Building Hong Kong's Airport," Discovery Channel, aired May 14, 2003, https://www.imdb.com/title/tt0364806/
4. NBR/CNBC, "Air Traffic Congestion Lengthens Flight Times," CNBC, March 24, 2017, http://nbr.com/2017/03/24/air-traffic-congestion-lengthens-flight-times/.
5. Caroline McGuire, "Should Passengers Pay Extra if They're Overweight?" news.com.au, November 24, 2017, https://www.news.com.au/travel/travel-advice/flights/should-passengers-pay-extra-if-theyre-overweight/news-story/634d89dd59efdb624453c7fd01868571.
6. McGuire, "Should Passengers Pay Extra."

Chapter 5

1. National Air Traffic Controllers Association, *NATCA: A History of Air Traffic Control*, accessed November 30, 2020, https://www.natca.org/wp-content/uploads/2019/12/NATCA_ATC_History.pdf.

2. "Air Traffic By The Numbers," Federal Aviation Administrations, last modified September 21, 2020, https://www.faa.gov/air_traffic/by_the_numbers/.

3. "A Flight Across America," Federal Aviation Administration, last modified November 27, 2020, https://www.faa.gov/air_traffic/flight_across_america/.

Chapter 6

1. "The Dream of Flight—Timeline of Flight," Library of Congress, accessed January 20, 2021, https://www.loc.gov/exhibits/dreamofflight/dream-timeline.html.

2. Dave English, *The Air Up There: More Great Quotations on Flight* (New York: McGraw-Hill, 2003).

3. "Analyze a Photograph," The U.S. National Archives and Records Administration, accessed April 25, 2020, https://www.archives.gov/education/lessons/worksheets/photo.html.

4. "Paper Hot Air Balloon," Space Foundation, accessed April 25, 2020, https://www.yumpu.com/en/document/view/12146386/paper-hot-air-balloon-space-foundation.

5. Newsela, "Is That Pilot in the Cockpit Human or Robot, and Does it Matter?" originally published by *Associated Press*, October 19, 2016, https://newsela.com/read/robo-pilot/id/23083/.

Chapter 7

1. *Career Interest Survey*, UCanGo2.org, accessed November 27, 2020, https://www.ucango2.org/publications/student/Career_Interest_Survey.pdf.

2. The UND AeroCast, "We'll See You Up Here!" YouTube video, 9:40, February 23, 2011, https://www.youtube.com/watch?v=tvqtfrJA7M4&t=5s.

Chapter 8

1. ERAU SpecialVFR, "Principles of Flight," YouTube video, 15:21, August 25, 2016, https://youtu.be/5O-j0w-h7v0.

2. NASA Aeronautics and American Association of Physics Teachers, "Terminal Velocity, Discovery Lab: Drag and Aircraft Design," *With You When You Fly: Aeronautics for Introductory Physics*, 99–106, accessed November 30, 2020, https://www.nasa.gov/sites/default/files/atoms/files/aero_introductory_physics.pdf.

3. NASA Aeronautics and American Association of Physics Teachers, "Discovery Lab: Drag and Aircraft Design," 99–106.

4. Ken Medley, "Teaching the Stall/Spin Safely: The Spin Training Story—and Why It's Still Important," Aircraft Owners and Pilots Association (AOPA), June 5, 2002, https://www.aopa.org/news-and-media/all-news/2002/june/flight-training-magazine/teaching-the-stallspin-safely.

5. D. Dumas, "July 19, 1989: Human Heroics Overcome Aircraft Failure in Sioux City," *Wired*, July 19, 2010, https://www.wired.com/2010/07/0719sioux-city-crash-184-survive/.

Chapter 9

1. NASA Aeronautics and American Association of Physics Teachers, "Interactive Demonstration: Pitot-Static Tube," *With You When You Fly: Aeronautics for Introductory Physics*, 59–64, accessed November 30, 2020, https://www.nasa.gov/sites/default/files/atoms/files/aero_introductory_physics.pdf.
2. NASA Aeronautics and American Association of Physics Teachers, "Interactive Demonstration: Pitot-Static Tube," 59–64.
3. Jeb Burnside, "Extreme Maneuvering: The Performance Maneuvers Required for the Commercial Certificate are Rarely Used, but They Can Get You Out of a Situation," *Aviation Safety*, November 25, 2014, www.aviationsafetymagazine.com/features/extreme-maneuvering/.

Chapter 10

1. Federal Aviation Administration, "Stalling for Safety—FAA video Private/Instrument/Commercial Pilot training 1976," YouTube video posted by Bad Gyro, 17:16, January 11, 2013, https://www.youtube.com/watch?v=0oms3r1q6Gs.
2. Federal Aviation Administration, "Stalling for Safety."
3. The UND AeroCast, "Commercial Steep Turns," YouTube video, 12:07, January 3, 2012, https://www.youtube.com/watch?v=24LySNN3SCE.
4. "Forces in a Turn" (web page), University of North Dakota Aerospace, accessed December 3, 2020, https://mediafiles.aero.und.edu/aero.und.edu/aviation/trainers/forces-in-a-turn/.
5. Air Safety Institute, "178 Seconds to Live," YouTube video, 2:06, September 3, 2014, https://www.youtube.com/watch?v=b7t4IR-3mSo.
6. Air Safety Institute, "178 Seconds to Live."

Chapter 11

1. Harrison Smith, "Pilot Sets Her Sights on the Eye of the Storm," *The Washington Post*, March 27, 2017, https://www.pilotonline.com/weather/article_ab7cbffd-e3fa-567c-a411-84717ac82357.html.

Chapter 12

1. "Current Altimeter Settings Really Matter: SEA03FA028," Aircraft Owners and Pilots Association (AOPA), accessed December 4, 2020, https://www.aopa.org/training-and-safety/air-safety-institute/accident-analysis/featured-accidents/epilot-asf-accident-reports-current-altimeter-settings-really-matter.
2. "Current Altimeter Settings Really Matter," Aircraft Owners and Pilots Association.
3. Oddvard Johnsen, "Go or No-Go?" *AeroSafety World*, Flight Safety Foundation, December 2007, 28–29, http://www.flightsafety.org/asw/dec07/asw_dec07_p28-29.pdf.
4. Johnsen, "Go or No-Go," 28–29.
5. Newsela, "A Few Choose to Climb World's Tallest Mountain Without Bottled Oxygen," adapted from original article in *The Washington Post*, May 26, 2016, https://newsela.com/read/everest-oxygen/id/18053/.

Chapter 13

1. Kevin Hayward, "Altitude Chamber Hypoxia Training Guy Passes Out," YouTube video, 6:50, March 31, 2010, https://www.youtube.com/watch?v=hSrGfElyfVE.

2. The UND AeroCast, "UND Aerobatics: You're Next!" YouTube video, 8:07, June 21, 2012, https://www.youtube.com/watch?v=bo9xI7lKg7A.

3. Air Safety Institute, "Accident Case Study: VFR into IMC," YouTube video, 16:01, June 8, 2016, https://youtu.be/bLmzy8ZPgtc.

4. Smithsonian Channel, "Does This Scenario Explain JFK Jr.'s Plane Crash?" YouTube video, 3:35, January 20, 2017, https://youtu.be/-P-3Kl1P0as.

5. Joe Andras, "Student Pilot—First Night Flight," YouTube video, 8:51, September 2, 2013, https://youtu.be/aU0ZzVfD_8w.

6. Andrew Freedman, John Muyskens, Chris Alcantara and Monica Ulmanu, "How Coronavirus Grounded the Airline Industry," *The Washington Post*, April 1, 2020, https://www.washingtonpost.com/graphics/2020/business/coronavirus-airline-industry-collapse/.